Aug 2018

Praise for *Forage, Harvest, Feast*

"Marie Viljoen is the real deal. In the heart of New York City, she takes her passion for food and the natural world and makes something extraordinary happen. In her hands a basket of weeds and berries becomes the centerpiece of a delicate, refined, and elegant lunch or a refreshing aperitif. Her curiosity about wild plants and foraging has taken her around the world, but in this book she proves that she—and her readers—can find both sustenance and delight just around the corner. *Forage, Harvest, Feast* is a joy to read, an inspiration, and a culinary adventure."

—**AMY STEWART**, author of *New York Times* bestsellers *Wicked Plants* and *The Drunken Botanist*

"Marie approaches her work with a rare combination of gifts   a deep knowledge of botany, the adventurous spirit of a forager, and most importantly for her readers, a keen appreciation of how to fill your life with good friends and delicious, locally sourced food."

—**STEPHEN ORR**, editor in chief of *Better Homes and Gardens*; author of *The New American Herbal*

"Marie has highlighted plants with unique and superb flavors, with straight-talk instructions for how to realize their culinary potential. For the widely occurring and well-known wild edibles, she has uncommonly good recipes. But Viljoen also digs up some more obscure foraged treasures, revealing gustatory possibilities that have remained underexplored and largely unappreciated. She does this with a vigilant eye for the common sense and sustainability that make foraged food a viable feature of the best kitchens."

SAMUEL THAYER, author of *The Forager's Harvest* and *Incredible Wild Edibles*

"*Forage, Harvest, Feast* takes wild edibles to their rightful place in the heart of every flavorful kitchen. Marie's passion for unlocking the deliciousness of nature and, at the same time, treading lightly on the earth fills every chapter of this lovely and timeless cookbook."

—**TAMA MATSUOKA WONG**, coauthor of *Foraged Flavor*

"Wild plants are one of the most natural things to eat. It's how we should live. Marie's book shows people how cooking plants from the wild is as easy and fundamental as learning your ABCs."

—**MADS REFSLUND**, cofounder of Noma; coauthor of *Scraps, Wilt and Weeds*

"This book represents by far the most impressive culinary exploration of wild edibles in the Northeast, though it is truly not limited to that region. The recipes can be easily adapted to similar plants in your area. The photos are beautiful, and most of the recipes are simple enough that you don't need a culinary degree to follow them, but at the same time they ooze creativity. Marie even invites you to create liqueurs, pickles, sauces, and countless condiments. It's not just a book of recipes, it's a celebration of local flavors. You can feel the love on every page. There are no other books like it—an amazing source of inspiration and a must have for anyone remotely interested in wild edibles."

—**PASCAL BAUDAR**, author of *The New Wildcrafted Cuisine* and *The Wildcrafting Brewer*

"I *love* this book! Marie Viljoen's passion for the last remnants of wild foods around us is a call to action. Reconsider the scraggly shrubs, weeds, and trash plants under threat from overzealous landscapers and urban planners. Foraging the wilds connects us to a forgotten and misunderstood piece of human history that's still here today, and it speaks to the resilience of ordinary folks who look around and see plenty when the dullards see weeds. We are weeds. Arise!"

—RICHARD MCCARTHY, executive director of Slow Food USA

"In her excellent cookbook—and 'this is a cookbook…not a field guide,' she implores—author Marie Viljoen reminds us that unless we live in a vacuum, we are all surrounded by wild food. Until now there has been a dearth of creative resources to help foragers cook what they find in the wild. Rich with both novel and traditional approaches to culinary recipes, Viljoen also takes us on an enlightening journey that includes cocktails, cordials, and other curiosities that strike me as, well, wildly creative. A well-researched and thoughtful book that conjures Thoreau and Gibbons but with a decisively urban spin. A wide-eyed joy to read."

—EVAN MALLETT, author of *The Black Trumpet*

"Whether you're a novice or experienced forager, gardener, or cook, this book will open your eyes—and taste buds—to the wonders of wild plants. With Marie Viljoen's masterful and friendly guidance, you'll not only make enticing, flavorful recipes, but you'll also cultivate a deeper relationship with the world around you. A truly lovely and substantial book."

—EMILY HAN, author of *Wild Drinks and Cocktails*

"A sensitive and delicious journey and a celebration of our lands."

—GILL MELLER, award-winning author of *Gather*, group head chef at River Cottage

"Marie Viljoen is one of the most beautiful humans I have met and a gifted immigrant who knows more about America's edible ecosystem than anyone I know. She has opened my eyes—and will open yours through this encyclopedic and intensely appealing collection of recipes, unprecedented in scope—to the delectable wild world surrounding us: common milkweed, day lilies, Japanese knotweed, pokeweed, spicebush, sweetfern, and so much more. After reading *Forage, Harvest, Feast* your walks in both city and country will never be the same. And neither will your cocktails or ice cream (spicebush and rhubarb, juniper and strawberry, pawpaw!). Marie's books have changed my life, and this cookbook will change yours. It is essential reading for anyone remotely interested in new ingredients or the flavors growing under their feet."

—GABRIELLE LANGHOLTZ, author of *America: The Cookbook*; culinary projects director at the Vilcek Foundation

"Humans are designed to eat a little of a lot, not a lot of a little; diet diversity is key to our health. Viljoen understands that, and her *Forage, Harvest, Feast* is a fantastic guide to 'wilding up' your meals—and doing it in style—whether you live in the countryside or the concrete jungle."

—HANK SHAW, winner of a James Beard Award; author of *Hunt, Gather, Cook*

"From simple snacks to exquisitely thought-out recipes, Marie Viljoen's gourmet cookbook helps readers grow familiar and comfortable using the wild abundance around their homes and neighborhoods. With obvious passion for the adventure of new and exciting culinary flavors, she offers wise advice on harvesting and preparing these glorious wild plants for food."

—KATRINA BLAIR, author of *The Wild Wisdom of Weeds*

Forage, Harvest, Feast

Forage, Harvest, Feast

A Wild-Inspired Cuisine

MARIE VILJOEN

Chelsea Green Publishing
White River Junction, Vermont
London, UK

Editor: Joni Praded
Project Manager: Patricia Stone
Copy Editor: Laura Jorstad
Proofreader: Eileen M. Clawson
Indexer: Linda Hallinger
Designer: Melissa Jacobson

Printed in the United States of America.
First printing July, 2018.
10 9 8 7 6 5 4 3 2 1   18 19 20 21 22

Our Commitment to Green Publishing

Library of Congress Cataloging-in-Publication Data

Names: Viljoen, Marie, author.
Title: Forage, harvest, feast : a wild-inspired cuisine / Marie Viljoen.
Description: White River Junction, Vermont : Chelsea Green Publishing, [2018] | Includes index.
Identifiers: LCCN 2018007866 | ISBN 9781603587501 (plc)
Subjects: LCSH: Cooking (Wild foods) | Wild plants, Edible. | LCGFT: Cookbooks.
Classification: LCC TX823 .V55 2018 | DDC 641.6—dc23
LC record available at https://lccn.loc.gov/2018007866

Chelsea Green Publishing
85 North Main Street, Suite 120
White River Junction, VT 05001
(802) 295-6300
www.chelseagreen.com

MIX
Paper from
responsible sources
FSC® C132124

To the Frenchman
for courage under botanical fire

Contents

Introduction

It is time to refresh our palates.

A cornucopia of edible wild plants is growing under our noses. Despite the appealing qualities of these feral foods, most of them have been forgotten, overlooked, or dismissed as useless. Some are simply invisible. They include uniquely American flavors, as well as international weeds of ill repute whose characters deserve reassessment.

Forage, Harvest, Feast is my culinary case for challenging perceptions of what is wild and what is domestic, what is desirable and what is unwanted. And what is food. And why.

My work with wild foods is born from an appetite for new flavors, and the thrill of discovery. It is dedicated to exploring—and normalizing—a collection of versatile plants that are seasonally exciting ingredients. I do not forage for survival. I forage because I love to cook and create. New flavors are thrilling. The plants featured in this cookbook are wild foods I use at home every day when they are in season. This is how I eat.

In the pages ahead I have chosen to focus on plants that have the potential to become familiar ingredients, to be used as herbs, spices, vegetables, and fruits in many kitchens. Some of these plants have the potential to be marketable crops—either foraged or sustainably or deliberately grown by enterprising kitchen gardeners and farmers. By providing a range of recipes for these plants, I am making what I hope is an irrefutable edible argument for bringing these ingredients from the enlightened foraging fringes to everyday cooking and horticultural consideration.

By illuminating the appealing edible qualities of indigenous American plants, I am hoping to draw attention to the enormous potential of largely forgotten native flavor growing at our feet. By propelling the farmer's and the gardener's weeds into the realm of the legitimate vegetable, I am reassuring the curious that there is food wherever they walk, and providing the cook and hungry forager with hundreds of recipes for the wild foods they love or are beginning to discover.

Some wild plants are starting to trickle into markets. Dandelions, lamb's quarters, nettles, and purslane appear sporadically. Garlic mustard is inching onto restaurant menus. Since I began evangelizing about noxiously invasive but delicious Japanese knotweed (*Edible Manhattan* magazine, 2010), I have seen it materialize at local farmers market stalls. Not always at quite the right stage of harvest. But five years ago it was absent, and there is a learning curve to negotiate.

Collecting and eating invasive edible weeds like these helps curb their spread without poisoning the environment. It also boosts income for farmers who are bringing produce to greenmarkets.

Other wild plants arrive at markets in a flood that requires stemming. Indigenous ramps and fiddleheads are now so recognizable that they and their habitats are abused. As pressure on these wild plant populations increases due to a burgeoning demand for a commercially foraged supply, it is time for overharvested species to be invited onto our land and into our gardens to relieve the pressure. I am suggesting, strongly, that we begin to treat some previously wild-only plants as kitchen-garden and small-farm crops. Growing indigenous plants at home preserves wild or urban populations and boosts local biodiversity.

Then there are the intensely interesting edibles that remain virtually unknown outside the creative niches of the foraging community: Bayberry, common milkweed, pokeweed, prickly ash, spicebush, and sweetfern are covered in these pages. These are a few of the forgotten flavors of North America. The more I reconnoiter the territory of the native American plant, the more thrilled I am to discover the range of flavors offered by plants that surround us in plain sight.

Most of us are used to eating passively. We eat what is put before us, neatly labeled and easily recognizable. We are not sure how it got there, how many people handled it, or what was required to grow it. But there it is. Foraging requires an interaction with and an awareness of our surroundings and our food in a way that mere consumption does not. You have agency.

The acts of foraging and of cultivating—literally—new flavors are pure pleasure. As much as it is a guide to eating, *Forage, Harvest, Feast* is also an act of remembering what has been lost, and a way of honoring a shared heritage. In an increasingly fractured society, we are connected by our appetites and the foods we have in common.

The Path to Wild Foods

As a plant-loving immigrant I straddle two worlds. One foot remains firmly on the African continent, my birthplace. I was born in the middle of South Africa, in a city called Bloemfontein. The dry, freezing winters saw frost on the ground; the summers were hot, with rain showers that made the *veld* smell rich. On the *koppie* across the road from our house, I nibbled the pale brown, sweet fruits of cross berry. My friend Anne-Lize and I collected spiny prickly pears and brought them home in my bicycle basket, learning how to peel them without being pricked. (I still bring edible things home in my bicycle basket, in Brooklyn.) My mother taught me the names of plants and to garden before I could read. I was happiest left to my own devices, growing radishes and flowers, roaming her vegetable garden and climbing trees to help myself to what was ripe. I haven't changed, much.

When I was twelve, my family moved to mountainous, coastal, and spectacularly beautiful Cape Town. The peninsular city is ground zero for the *fynbos* biome of the Cape Floristic Region—the smallest and also relatively the most diverse of the earth's six Floral Kingdoms.

The field guides that my mother bought to learn about fynbos taught me, too. In their pages I learned to identify the plants we saw on hikes up Table Mountain, or across a local common. We joined the Botanical Society of South Africa and went on walks where botanical Latin was commonplace and the average age over sixty. Equipped with backpacks and boots and walking sticks, the members bounded straight up mountains without breaking a sweat, stopping for hot tea and sandwiches at the top.

Closer to home my mother and I collected wild watercress from a nearby stream. We ate young shaggy ink caps on toast and went mushrooming in nearby pine plantations for milk caps in autumn. On solitary horseback one day, I discovered so many that I rode back with mushrooms stuffed down and bulging out of the front of my pink-stained shirt. In our garden I learned about edible weeds called *morogo* by Nomatiptip Titoti (known as Tipsi, even though she never is), who joined our family as a housekeeper when I was thirteen. In my mother's garden she pounced on tender young sow thistles or chickweed, adding these to her pot. We were opportunistic treasure hunters, finding what we loved when it was available.

By my midteens culinary and medicinal herbs drew my focus. After an inspiring trip to England, I designed a kitchen herb garden for my mother and immersed myself in the work of South African author Margaret Roberts, who often quoted traditional indigenous uses for plants.

The botanical world had become a passion, and I paid fascinated attention to whatever was growing at my feet, wherever I was.

My other foot is planted in North America, where I have made my home in Brooklyn with my French husband, Vincent. A brief career in opera diverted me from the plant path. But after a bout with whooping cough (I skipped the booster when I was a teenager), which left me literally breathless, I paid the rent by working at a garden center in the East Village. The interesting native and exotic plants I encountered there taught me about what grows in this climate. Soon I graduated to designing gardens and went to work at a garden design firm, creating green spaces for well-heeled New Yorkers. Wherever possible I included blueberries and serviceberries in my rooftop schemes.

I missed the singing, but I did not miss the world of opera.

In my downtime I reveled in growing edible and ornamental plants on my own tiny terrace and rooftop in Brooklyn, documenting it all in images and on my blog, *66 Square Feet*, and using the space as a lab for my first freelance writing projects.

I had already fallen in love with Euell Gibbons's *Stalking the Wild Asparagus*, but it was after a walk with forager Steve Brill that I began to focus on the local world of edible invasive plants. In the wake of the economic crash of 2008, I was laid off from my well-paid garden design job (suddenly $100,000 terrace gardens were not in high demand). I was despondent, to say the least. Steve's walk, on a chilly November day, meandered across Prospect Park, the huge group foraging as it went. As walkers bounded over fences and enthusiastically uprooted sassafras saplings, my husband looked down his long French nose. His memories of foraging were of gathering chanterelles in quiet pine forests in Provence.

It was the first time I had joined anything with the word *forage* in its name. It was also the first time I became aware of field garlic and garlic mustard, both denizens of spring that enjoy an autumnal resurgence. Both came home for dinner. I am indebted to Steve for the introduction.

I began to focus my plant-trained eyes on unusual edibles, and to read everything I could find about foraging. I cooked with new flavors and became fine-tuned to the seasonal availability of wild plants. My life began to revolve around a botanical world that remains largely invisible to most people. My first book, *66 Square Feet: A Delicious Life*, a twelve-month culinary and botanical exposition of New York City, was born from my intense interaction with the city's green offerings, at home or in the urban wilds.

In New York the people and the plants influence how I cook. In this megalopolis melting pot, my privilege has been to be exposed to wildly diverse cultures and culinary traditions. At the same time, a similarly cosmopolitan cross section of plants grows all over the city, where it is possible to immerse yourself in nature despite never leaving the five boroughs.

This diversity is also reflected in my current garden—a Brooklyn backyard with full shade from autumn through early spring, and full sun in the summer months. My foraging, gardening, and cooking lives have intermingled. I grow conventional food crops, hard-to-find ingredients, indigenous edibles that are unsustainable to harvest in the local wilds, and edibles viewed as weeds. My diverse collection includes Thai limes, a Meyer lemon, a finger lime, curry leaf trees, cardamom (these overwinter indoors), ginger, and curcumin. The subtropicals grow side by side with arugula, bayberry, chokeberry, common milkweed, daylilies, elderflower, fava beans, garlic, mâche, nettles, ostrich ferns (the source of fiddleheads), peas, potatoes, ramps, saffron, sheep sorrel, sunchokes, sweetfern, and wintercress. Foreigners and natives, all getting along and being eaten. In the concrete jungle.

I spend time in South Africa every year, exploring the flavors of home and making a ritual, local vermouth that is redolent of fynbos and local herbs. Back in New York I blend seasonal vermouths, too. These botanically eloquent fortified wines are symbols to me of how we can translate place to be understood by our palates.

Recognizing and exploring an environment through its plants is a vital way of orienting ourselves, of recognizing where we are, and of honoring it. For me, foraging is as much about learning from the plants around me as it is about promoting their best culinary qualities, and mitigating or transforming their worst. It is a rewarding, exciting, and never-ending mission.

It also means that I will never, ever be bored.

How to Use this Book

Forage, Harvest, Feast is written not just for my fellow foragers, but for curious cooks and enterprising growers. If you are new to the world of foraging and wild plants, my advice is simple: Read now, and you will know what to forage, or grow, later. Later might be tomorrow, no matter the season, and gradually you will build up the foundation of a wild pantry. Every season—every month—brings a new flavor into play. Be ready.

Being ready means learning more about the plants. This is a cookbook. It is not a field guide. Ten years ago writing a pure wild foods cookbook would not have been practical. But today good regional field and wild foods guides are available. Buy them if you don't already have them. Everything written by Samuel Thayer should be in your library, in addition to a regional guide for where you live.

Nothing beats in-the-field experience for pattern recognition, which is what plant identification is about. Sign up for walks with experienced local foragers. Take classes at botanical gardens. Join plant groups online (there are helpful ones on Facebook). Join wild foods communities and search the hashtag #wildfoodlove on Instagram, where you will connect with novices as well as very experienced foragers from across the planet, united by their common delight in wild foods.

The introductions to each plant chapter come with brief cultivation tips. Vulnerable native plants like ramps can be encouraged this way. Flavorful plants that usually only occur in the wild can be grown within reach—bayberry and sweetfern, for example. Annual, "weedy" plants like lamb's quarters also have huge potential as ordinary crops. For dangerously invasive plants like Japanese knotweed, I advise you strongly not to plant them—doing so would be highly irresponsible.

Suggested menus appear at the back of the book. So does a list of recipes by course. I am an omnivore, and the book reflects that, but there are ample options for pescatarians, vegetarians, and vegans, and the list of recipes is coded by diet type.

Why These Plants?

My mission here is to introduce the wild foods that I feel have wide appeal. Consequently, I have chosen to share a range of recipes for selected plants rather than to list every wild plant that can be eaten. The plants here are also those with which I have the most personal experience, so their choice is subjective. While I live in the Northeast, and love plants that define this region's flavor, some of them have close cousins farther afield, or have been domesticated and exported. The edible weeds tend to be widespread.

Interspersed among the heavy hitters like spicebush and mugwort are significantly appealing or "pop up" wild foods—evocative markers of the season—that are too delectable to omit. These include black locust flowers, fir needles, honeysuckle, and wisteria, all wonderful for making concentrated essences, infusions, or sugars, which have broad use.

What have I left out? A lot. I have chosen to omit many indigenous plants whose harvest cannot be sustainable. I was torn about including ramps; food writers have unwittingly signed the plant's death sentence by singing their praises. Commercial foragers have responded to the market's demand. But since ramps are irrevocably on the culinary radar, I feel it is better to be clear about the threat that they are facing, and to suggest ways to mitigate it, than to leave them out and remain silent.

Personal preference is a factor, too. There is no chapter on plantain. While I like baby plantain leaves (which taste just like raw button mushrooms) and young seeds, and grow a wild species, I mostly treat them as a salad green. This may change. The same goes for dock. Interesting, but not thrilling. Chickweed is an amazing spring green that I stuff into summer rolls, but that does not constitute enough for a chapter. Sow thistle? Wonderful plant, but it behaves like other wild greens in the pot (treat it like nettles when you find it). Acorns? They need a book of their own.

Where to Forage?

For urbanites, the local farmers market is becoming an exciting place to find and sell wild foods. I am enchanted to see edible invasives in neat bundles on market tables. But it is all about context. If paying $5 for a bunch of field garlic or $25 for ¼ pound of mugwort that you could forage for free is unappealing (or wildly funny when you see it growing 10 feet away along a chain-link fence), begin scouring your neighborhood. As you learn a new plant, you will begin to notice where it grows. Even in cities there are places where you can gather lamb's quarters and amaranth in abundance, or pick pounds of ripe serviceberries and black cherries. Make friends with local community gardens, and with your neighbors.

Liaise with the stewards of your local parks and advocate for removing invasive edible species for them. Sometimes you can join a volunteer day of weeding and take home the spoils. And if diplomacy fails, I certainly admit to furtive invasive weed foraging where I know the plant is simply a pest.

Increasingly, landscape architects and city planners are deploying more edibles in their projects. If that is not already happening in your area, encourage it. I am very lucky to have a spectacular local classroom, the Brooklyn Bridge Park. Its creators and designers included a significant list of edible American plants. While foraging is not allowed, it is an ideal setting to learn and teach about plants with native edible potential in order to encourage their use in home gardens, large or small. Down the road the Gowanus Nursery sells many of these plants. This kind of natural partnership (which happens to be fortuitously accidental, in this case) should be more common.

If you have access to bona fide nature, you are privileged. Be respectful. Forage for the future, in moderation, and without stomping native ephemerals. If you are city-bound but would like a wild foraging spot, connect with local land trusts and preserves and make friends with landowners who might allow you to forage on their land. They do exist. If *you* are a landowner, consider the wild edible potential of your land and how best to curate and conserve it.

Some of my best forages have come from farm meadows and fencerows, with the farmer's permission. Again, it is about approaching the

Don't Kill Yourself

I mean, it's obvious. Foraging is an act of independence. It carries with it the grave responsibility of informing yourself. Treat all information, including mine, with some circumspection and an open mind. Cross-reference, double-check, and remember that anyone can say anything on the internet with a voice of digital authority. Even published authors get it wrong, sometimes.

Be 100 percent sure of the identification of your plant or mushroom before you swallow it. Eat only the prescribed part of a plant, at the right stage of growth. If a recipe says cook the plant, cook the plant.

If you are eating a new food, there is always a rare possibility of an allergic reaction. Eat a small amount and wait twenty-four hours to see if you puff up or lose your lunch.

Foraging can be an individual act or a communal one—just like eating. Incorporating wild foods into your everyday cooking means finding them, and finding them often leads to meeting others with similar passions. As much as I hope this book leads to the rediscovery of lost tastes and a renewed appreciation for the plants that provide them, I hope it leads to feasts with family and newfound friends.

Or if you are a misanthropic loner like so many of us foragers are, a feast at a table for one.

people in charge and asking, nicely. Usually, the answer is an amused affirmative. Weeds in crop rows can be good to gather *if* they have not been subjected to herbicides or high fertilizer application rates. (In relevant chapters I elaborate on safety concerns for specific foraged foods.)

Gardeners and growers are also lucky. You have a lot to draw on in terms of wild flavor. Depending on your microclimate and USDA hardiness zone, many edible wild plants can be cultivated. Bring the forages to your own backyard.

Amaranth

OTHER COMMON NAMES: Pigweed, callaloo, Chinese spinach

BOTANICAL NAMES: *Amaranthus hybridus*, *A. retroflexus*, *A. palmeri*, *A. viridis*, and other species

STATUS: Widespread annual weeds, some species are ubiquitous exotics, some are indigenous, some are grown as crops

WHERE: Gardens, open ground, fields, farmers markets, ethnic markets

SEASON: Midsummer to late summer

USE: Vegetable, pseudograin

PARTS USED: Tender stems, leaves, flowers, and seeds

GROW? Yes

TASTES LIKE: Earthy chard

There are more than sixty species of amaranth (forty-seven in the United States), not counting the hybrids, and all are edible.

But amaranths elicit conflicting reactions from humans: love, loathing, and—mostly in the United States—complete indifference. Boxed as pseudocereals, they are revered. Those with pretty leaves (*Amaranthus tricolor*—a popular crop in China and Southeast Asia) are increasingly grown for food. The genus's most glamorous members—the statuesque red-tressed supermodels collectively known as red amaranth (*A. hybridus*)—were domesticated centuries ago. Their seeds were a labor-intensive staple of the Aztec diet. Yet few twenty-first-century shoppers who buy the trendy, gluten-friendly seeds recognize their

cousins—the despised plants sprawling in their gardens and yards, or the ignored weeds flourishing along sidewalks in city tree pits. Fewer would consider growing or collecting them for food.

These are the lowly pigweeds. They appear uninvited in gardens and in rows of cultivated crops, where they are met with a deluge of increasingly ineffective and virulent poisons. Pigweeds are often considered toxic to livestock because they absorb so much of the nitrogen from synthetic fertilizer application—converting it to nitrates—that it becomes a reflection of our agricultural malpractices. The plant turns on us, giving as good as it gets. But pigweed is ubiquitous, which means there are plenty of spots away from conventional agriculture sites where you can collect the plants unscathed—delicious and ripe for the picking.

There are cultures that recognize the value of these amaranths. They are important leafy crops in regions as diverse as East Africa, India, and China. In Cape Town, Tipsi Titoti, who is amaXhosa, taught me to make a traditional rural stew based on edible wild greens, known collectively (in the same way as the Greek *horta*) as morogo. Foraged amaranth (*imbuya*) is a prized ingredient. Cooked in a little water until tender, with some potato or *mealie meal* (cornmeal or grits, Stateside), and with nothing more than salt as seasoning, it makes a comforting and nutritious stew. It has fed families when the larder was bare. And if you have to eat a food because you are poor, you can learn to despise it when times are better. I have South African friends who are loathe to eat amaranth, because it reminds them of the past.

In Jamaica sonorous *callaloo* refers both to a stew and to the two edible greens on which it relies: amaranth and taro, which form its soulful and leafy base. When I lived in Harlem, I was able to buy lush greenmarket bunches of amaranth from a Caribbean-born farmer who grows them in upstate New York. A local food store sold them on 125th Street. Ethnic markets and groceries are often the only commercial source for wild greens.

Amaranths are generous summer plants, growing in the hot months when good old spinach and chard and even lamb's quarters have given up the ghost. Their slightly rough raw texture begs for cooking, and I find them frankly more appealing than cooked spinach. Cooked, both young and mature greens are soft and mild in flavor. Include them in dishes where Swiss chard, spinach, or beetroot leaves feature.

CULTIVATION TIPS

USDA Hardiness Zones:
All, as it is an annual

Amaranth is an annual, meaning that it completes its life cycle in one growing season. This is beneficial for growers in a wide range of USDA hardiness zones and climates, as they can adjust the sowing time to their region. Before planting, test your soil's pH and also test for heavy metals. Lead is one heavy metal whose absorption *can* be controlled by soil remediation. The more acidic the soil, the more lead will be absorbed (most plants will absorb very little, if any, regardless, but amaranth is an exception). If your soil is acidic, raise the pH to neutral or slightly alkaline by adding egg- or oyster shells, ground to a powder. Test the soil annually.

If the heavy metals in your soil include cadmium or arsenic, you are out of luck and should build raised beds with fresh soil.

Broadcast amaranth seed in late spring for summer harvest. If you do not want it to spread, harvest before it sets seeds.

The late-summer flowers and seeds have a different, grainier texture, which is very appealing (as well as nutritious, containing many minerals, as well as protein).

How to Collect and Prepare

Amaranths are one of the few plants that accumulate heavy metals to high levels. Boiling does not affect heavy-metal levels. Avoid collecting amaranths from highway edges or old industrial sites. Also avoid cropland subjected to high doses of synthetic fertilizers.

Pick the tender stems, leaves, flower, and seed heads. At home, refresh wilted amaranth by submerging it in a bowl of cool water. Discard tough stalks, which will not break down in cooking. If you are deeply patient, collect the seeds by shaking mature heads into a paper bag.

Potentially high levels of nitrates, as well as oxalic acid (as in spinach), are reduced by boiling. Boil amaranth greens for a couple of minutes, drain, refresh under cold water, and squeeze dry.

Caution

Do not feed amaranths to babies: Infants under the age of six months have digestive bacteria that convert nitrates to nitrites, which are potentially carcinogenic and can also cause oxygen starvation in the blood. By the time babies are six months old, the acid levels in their digestive systems rise and kill these bacteria. Exercise caution if you are breastfeeding. High and frequent consumption of amaranth can be anti-nutritional in adults, as it might prevent the absorption of some nutrients.

Fried Green Tomato and Amaranth Salad

Serves 4 as a side, 2 as an entrée

Amaranth begins to set seed in late summer, around the time that green tomatoes arrive at market alongside their ripe brothers and sisters. This composite salad is almost a meal in its own right. To make it one, all you need is some crunchy bread on the side.

4 ounces (113 g) amaranth seed heads
    and leaves
3 tablespoons extra-virgin olive oil, divided
1 pound (453 g) green (unripe)
    tomatoes, sliced
¼ teaspoon salt
¼ teaspoon lemon zest
8 ounces (227 g) ripe tomatoes, cubed
1 tablespoon pomegranate molasses
    (or good balsamic vinegar)
Black pepper
8 ounces (227 g) buffalo mozzarella

Bring a pot of water to a boil. Drop in the amaranth and blanch for 1 minute at a boil (if it rises above the water, dunk it back in). Remove, drain, refresh in cold water, and squeeze dry (much easier than squeezing spinach). Set aside.

Heat 1 tablespoon of the oil in a skillet over medium-high heat. Add the green tomato slices, season with some salt, and sauté until one side is beginning to brown, about 3 to 4 minutes. Turn the slices, season the other side, and sauté for about another 3 to 4 minutes. Remove the slices and arrange on a serving dish.

Place the blanched amaranth in the skillet with the rest of the olive oil and toss until it heats through. Season with salt, add the lemon zest, and toss again.

When the seasoned greens are hot, drape them across the sliced green tomatoes on the serving plate. Add the cubed ripe tomatoes on top, drizzle the pomegranate molasses over them, sprinkle with some salt, and add lots of cracked black pepper. Finally, pinch equal-sized segments off the mozzarella and scatter those across the top. Finish with an extra lashing of extra-virgin olive oil.

Amaranth Breakfast Tacos

Serves 4

Eggs and amaranth are a superb combination, with a just-toasted flour tortilla as a luxurious little blanket for them. Hot sauce is essential.

2 tablespoons olive oil
4 cloves garlic, sliced thinly
1 pound (453 g) blanched, squeezed,
    and chopped amaranth leaves and
    tender stems
1 tablespoon lime juice
Salt
Black pepper
8 flour tortillas
1 tablespoon unsalted butter
4 eggs, boiled for 8 minutes, peeled,
    and halved (or chopped)
Sriracha, or Wintercress Green Chile Sauce

Warm the olive oil in a pan over medium heat and add the garlic. Cook for about 5 minutes until it is turning translucent. Add the amaranth and stir well. Add the lime juice, and salt and pepper to taste.

Meanwhile, in a hot skillet, toast each tortilla on both sides until it begins to puff up. Keep them warm inside a folded napkin.

To serve, scatter the warm greens over the tortillas, dot with small pieces of butter, top with the halved eggs, and finish with a flourish of hot sauce. Fold, eat.

Amaranth Greens with Sumac Schwarma Spice

Serves 4 as a side

These schwarma-inspired greens are such an unexpected hit at home that I make this dish with every green as it comes into season. It is excellent cool, eaten with a dollop of plain yogurt. Bottle the extra spice mixture in an airtight jar. It lasts many months and is divine with slow-roasted lamb or chicken, or stirred into yogurt for dips.

WILD SCHWARMA SPICE MIX

1 tablespoon Ground Sumac
2 teaspoons ground cumin
2 teaspoons ground spicebush
1 teaspoon black peppercorns
¼ teaspoon ground cloves
3 cardamom pods' seeds

AMARANTH GREENS

12 ounces (340 g) amaranth leaves, tender
    stalks, or flower heads
3 tablespoons olive oil
3 cloves garlic, crushed and chopped
2 tablespoons lemon juice
1 tablespoon Wild Schwarma Spice Mix
¼ teaspoon salt

TOPPING

⅓ cup (80 ml) yogurt
3 tablespoons water
⅛ teaspoon Ramp Leaf Salt

Combine the spices in a small bowl and stir very well.

Bring a medium pot of water to a boil and drop in the amaranth for 1 minute. Remove, drain, and refresh in cold water. Squeeze dry. In a large pan over medium heat, warm the oil and add the garlic. Sauté until translucent, then add the amaranth. Add the lemon juice, 1 tablespoon of the spice mix, and the salt, stirring. Cook for 5 minutes.

In a small bowl, thin the yogurt with the water and stir until smooth. Season with the Ramp Leaf Salt. Pour over the amaranth before serving.

Preserved Lemon and Pigweed Pesto

Serves 4

When in doubt, make pesto. I like saying *pigweed pesto*. This was one of the first ways I ate the wild amaranth that volunteered in the pots on our little roof farm in Cobble Hill, Brooklyn. I keep a stash of salted lemons in my preserve cupboard. Meyer lemons are wonderful for this preservation technique, because their very aromatic skins are so thin. If you have a large haul of amaranth, double the recipe and freeze some. And substitute pecans for pine nuts, if you like. Stir it into hot egg yolk pasta, smear it on bread, stuff it under the skin of a roasting chicken . . .

4 ounces (113 g) amaranth leaves or flowers

4 tablespoons butter, divided

2 tablespoon lemon juice

⅓ cup (40 g) salt-preserved lemon skin, chopped finely

3 cups (180 g) finely grated Parmigiano-Reggiano

2 cloves garlic, peeled and sliced

⅓ cup (40 g) pine nuts

Salt

Black pepper

Bring a small pot of water to a boil and drop in the amaranth. Blanch for a minute (dunk it under if it floats), then fish it out, drain, refresh, and squeeze the water out. Melt 2 tablespoons of the butter over medium-high heat in a pan and add the leaves when it is foaming. Add the lemon juice. Sauté for a couple of minutes, then turn off the heat. Allow the leaves to cool a little. In a food processor combine the remaining butter, lemon skin, cheese, garlic, pine nuts, and amaranth and press Destruct. When you have a coarse paste, it is ready. Taste. Add salt and pepper if necessary—it may not require any. It is ready to eat.

Amaranth and Caramelized Onions on Toast

Serves 2 as an entrée, 4 as an appetizer

Hearty amaranth makes a filling lunch or snack, sweetened by slow-cooked onions. A dense brown bread works very well with the iron-rich greens.

¼ teaspoon salt

1 cup (150 g) finely sliced onions

3 tablespoons extra-virgin olive oil

1 pound (453 g) amaranth leaves, washed, stripped from tough stems

6 cloves garlic, finely chopped

2 teaspoons lemon juice

4 slices brown seed bread

1 clove garlic, for rubbing

Salt the onions. In a medium pan over medium-low heat, sauté the onions in the oil until darkly golden—about 15 to 20 minutes. While they are cooking, bring a pot of water to a boil and drop in the amaranth for 1 minute. Remove and squeeze dry. Add the chopped garlic to the caramelized onions and stir well. Add the blanched amaranth and increase the heat to medium. Stir well. Add the lemon juice and cook for a few minutes until the leaves are bite-tender. Taste for seasoning and add some more salt and lemon if you like. Toast some very good seedy bread, rub it with garlic, and top it with the greens.

Amaranth Callaloo

Serves 4

Callaloo is a traditional chicken stew made in the Caribbean with bunches of lush giant-leafed amaranth or taro (both known as callaloo). When we lived in Harlem, I shopped at the local farmers market where a Caribbean-born farmer, who farms outside Albany, sold luxuriant bunches of callaloo. I could never resist. Any green amaranth can be used for this richly flavored and economical stew. Because common milkweed produces pods around the time amaranths are ready, I like to add some to the stew (in the spirit of okra). But it is perfectly good without them.

2 tablespoons unscented oil

1 large onion, finely chopped

2 tablespoons hot curry powder

8 chicken drumsticks

2 pieces of ginger, each thumb-sized, peeled and sliced finely

2 tablespoons Sumac Essence

1 tablespoon sugar

2 cups (500 ml) coconut milk

¼ teaspoon salt

2 cups (500 ml) chicken broth

1 pound (453 g) amaranth, washed and picked from tough stems

OPTIONAL*

4 ounces (113 g) small, tender common milkweed pods

In a large pot warm the oil over medium heat. Add the onion and cook until golden, about 15 minutes. Add the curry powder and stir well. Add the chicken, ginger, Sumac Essence, sugar, coconut milk, and salt and stir well. Increase the heat to high and add the chicken broth. Bring the liquid to a boil, cover the pot, and reduce the heat to keep the liquid at a gentle simmer. Cook for 30 minutes. Add the amaranth to the pot and push some of it down into the hot liquid with a spoon. Increase the heat until the liquid returns to a steady simmer, cover, and cook for another 30 minutes, occasionally pushing more of the wilting amaranth down into the liquid. Remove the lid, increase the heat till the liquid bubbles, and cook to reduce and concentrate the sauce for a final 30 minutes. Taste for seasoning and add a little salt, if necessary. The chicken should be fall-apart tender. Serve in shallow bowls with spoons for sauce scooping.

* If you are using the milkweed pods, blanch them in boiling water for a couple of minutes (to dispel latex) before adding them to the stew after 1 hour.

Amaranth and Sheep Sorrel Chicken Bredie

Serves 4

Bredie is an Afrikaans word for a stew featuring a seasonal vegetable (there is another recipe in the purslane chapter—see *Porseleinbredie*). Interestingly, amaranth may be at the word's root: *Bredos* was apparently an Indian Ocean Creole term for wild greens, which is derived from the same Portuguese word, which in turn refers to amaranth. The word probably arrived in South Africa in the eighteenth century, with Southeast Asian or Indian Ocean–rim slaves who were able to bring nothing from home but their traditions.

12 ounces (340 g) fresh amaranth leaves

2 tablespoons unscented oil

8 chicken thighs

¼ teaspoon salt

2 shallots, sliced

5 cloves garlic, peeled and sliced

½ teaspoon Field Garlic Salt

3 cups (750 ml) chicken broth

1 cup (30 g) sheep sorrel

4 medium potatoes, quartered

1 teaspoon Ground Sumac

Blanch the amaranth for a minute in boiling water, then drain, refresh, and squeeze out. Heat the oil in a large skillet over medium-high heat. Season the chicken with salt and brown the pieces in batches, about 3 minutes per side. Add the shallots and garlic to the pan. Season everything with the Field Garlic Salt. Pour the chicken broth over the meat. Add the sheep sorrel. Cover the skillet and bring the liquid to a boil, then reduce to a steady simmer over medium to medium-low heat. Cook for 1 hour and add the potatoes. Cook another hour until the chicken is very tender. For the last 10 minutes, increase the heat to high and reduce the liquid *if* it is still very soupy—you want a loose but well-flavored sauce. Check for seasoning and add more salt if necessary. Before serving, sprinkle with sumac.

Amaranth and Spiced Lamb Stew

Serves 4

Salted amaranth greens cooked slowly are exceptional sponges for fragrant meat juices.

2 pounds (907 g) stewing lamb (cut into 2-inch/5 cm pieces) or 3 pounds (1⅓ kg) shoulder chops

3 tablespoons unscented oil

1 tablespoon coriander seeds

1 tablespoon Ground Sumac

2 teaspoons cumin

1 teaspoon black pepper

1 teaspoon cinnamon

6 cardamom pods

6 allspice berries

3 cups water

1½ pounds (680 g) amaranth (leaves and tender stems only)

¼ cup salt

In a large pot over medium-high heat, brown the lamb in the oil, in batches, removing the browned pieces to a shallow bowl to catch the juices. When all the lamb has browned, add the coriander to the pot for a minute, stirring as it toasts. When it smells good, return the lamb to the pot with all the other spices and stir well. Add the water and bring to a boil. Cover the pot and reduce the heat to keep the liquid at a simmer. Cook for 1 hour.

While the lamb is stewing, place the amaranth in a large bowl and sprinkle with the salt. Massage the salt in well, bruising the leaves and stems as you work. Let the amaranth sit for an hour as some juices are drawn out. Bring a pot of water to a boil and blanch the already wilted amaranth for 30 seconds. Strain, refresh in cold water, and squeeze out. Add the amaranth to the lamb pot, cover, and return to a simmer. After 30 minutes lift the lid and stir the amaranth well into the cooking juices. Taste the juices. If necessary, add a little salt (it may be quite salty enough). Increase the heat and continue to cook uncovered, to reduce and concentrate the liquid, for another 30 minutes. Serve in bowls with spoons for scooping.

American Burnweed

OTHER COMMON NAMES: Fireweed, pilewort

BOTANICAL NAME: *Erechtites hieraciifolius* and subspecies

STATUS: Indigenous North American annual, viewed as a weed

WHERE: Disturbed ground, postburn areas, light woodland, meadows in eastern North America and West Coast

SEASON: Early to midsummer

USE: Aromatic, vegetable

PARTS USED: Tender stems and leaves

GROW? Yes, experimentally

TASTES LIKE: Cilantro meets culantro by way of shiso and lime (well, you asked)

On a walk through Central Park's North Woods one sticky summer, a 4-foot-tall, unfamiliar plant stood in front of me. Its leaves, stalk, and stature reminded me of a wild lettuce, but as soon as I rubbed those leaves an intense scent was released. My cooking instincts began to ping wildly. This was new. What *was* it? The smell was as pungent as cilantro's, but more perfumed, like shiso. Also reminiscent of culantro (*Eryngium foetidum*) with some Thai lime (*Citrus hystrix*) skin thrown in. Its presence was as unique and associative as basil's, or mint's. Southeast Asian curries flashed before my eyes.

I took pictures, picked some leaves, and went back home to dive into the deep end of plant identification.

That is how I met American burnweed, an indigenous member of the Asteraceae family, also known commonly as fireweed (not to be confused with another fireweed, the pink-flowered species of *Epilobium*, also edible). My initial searches for the American culinary uses I expected to find for the American plant came up close to empty. Hearsay. Speculation. Very little personal experience. There were dismissive comments about its "rank odor," followed by downright rudeness like: "Very unattractive in appearance, and ill-scented besides." That was R. M. Harper, writing in 1944 in a report on weeds in Alabama. Native Americans used the plant medicinally, treating poison ivy rash, among other ailments. It is an ingredient in modern homeopathic treatment for poison ivy, too.

And then I reached, at long last, the digital shores of Indonesia and Malaysia, where this American weed, along with its local tropical counterpart *Erechtites valerianifolius*, has enjoyed a solid culinary tradition as well as some serious study, which reveals high vitamin A, protein, and zinc levels.

I was no longer alone in wanting to eat this plant.

There are also warnings of alkaloids, which burnweed contains. Eaten in sufficient quantity (but no one can tell us what that is), the plant could potentially cause harm—a warning never to ignore. But as Sam Thayer, the renowned wild foods author, wrote in an emailed conversation about burnweed's use in other cultures, "People spent a few million years or whatever figuring this stuff out, and science keeps verifying that these traditions

are pretty darn precise (despite the fearmongering that masquerades as science often enough about wild food)." Perhaps consuming a large amount, as a grazing herbivore might (often studies involving wild plants are conducted within the context of their effect on livestock—no one has the money to fund studies for foragers!), would result in trouble. But in the context of dinner and using the plant as an herb, an overdose is unlikely.

Our first meal with burnweed has become a rite of summer: soy-and-mugwort-marinated short ribs, coal-cooked and sliced, each bite wrapped in an aromatic young leaf.

American burnweed's immature leaves are good to eat raw or cooked. The juicy stems are tender enough to steam or blanch before dressing as you like. Later, when the plant grows tall and sturdy, the leaves are useful as wraps, if you like their taste. Once the flower buds form, you might like to ferment them, pickle them, and turn them into capers. The herb's pungency and slight bitterness suits strong flavors: Japanese-style braises with miso. Peanuts. Soy. Chiles and lime. Mexico beckons, with smoky chiles and orange and tomato. Slow adobos, Filipino-style, with coconut milk. The leaves are also a perfumed counterpart to delicate sushi, or sour ceviches. And they hold their own in bold salads, with herbs like shiso, Thai and purple basil, nasturtium, cilantro, and mint.

American burnweed's common names are a clue for where to find it. It has a reputation for popping up after burns have swept through an area. It occurs through the North American continent (and in those countries it has invaded successfully). I find it mostly in woodland clearings where some sun reaches to the ground, near paths or rough roads, as well as in local gardens and parks, where it favors disturbed earth.

Burnweed is virtually unknown in the American eating world. It is waiting for you to discover it. Expect bold flavor, as with love-it-or-loathe-it cilantro.

How to Collect and Prepare

Young American burnweed plants appear in early summer around the time that common milkweed blooms.

Burnweed wilts rapidly, once gathered. At home, snip the cut end, plunge the leaves and stems into a large bowl or basin of cool water, and wait until it has revived. This may take a few hours. Once it has perked up and looks fresh again, *dry it very well*, wrap, and keep in the fridge. I wrap mine in paper towels and then in a container. If left in water on the counter, the stems turn slimy, and leaves that are stored wet will darken and turn slimy, too, almost overnight. Clipping off the large leaves and stacking them separately from the stem is also a good way to keep them fresh longer.

CULTIVATION TIPS

USDA Hardiness Zones:
All, as it is an annual

Growing American burnweed is uncharted territory, and I have not yet grown it myself. The plant is an annual and occurs on both coasts, skipping only the bumpy line of the Rockies, from north to south. My guess is that seed should be sown once your region's first frost date has passed. To my knowledge the seed is not commercially available and ought to be wild-collected when it turns to fluff on tall plants in late summer.

American Burnweed and Lime Butter

Makes about 7 tablespoons

This tangy butter is good on anything. Need pointers? Hot griddlecakes and muffins, baked potatoes, Lamb's Quarter and Sheep Sorrel Greenballs, or meat just off the barbecue.

6 tablespoons butter

2 tablespoons (about 10 medium leaves) finely chopped American burnweed

2 teaspoons lime juice

½ teaspoon chile flakes

¼ teaspoon Ramp Leaf Salt

You could mash all the ingredients together on a chopping board with the back of a chef's knife, mix them in a bowl, or whiz them in a food processor. I find the board-mashing to be the quickest way, and easiest to clean up.

Once the ingredients are thoroughly mixed together, spoon the butter mixture onto the near side of a piece of parchment paper. Starting at your end, fold the paper over the butter, pressing down gently to shape it into a log. Roll away from you, exerting downward pressure with the covering parchment to coax it into an even shape. Once it is in the shape you want, twist the paper ends tightly like a candy wrapper. Chill until needed. Use within a week, or freeze.

American Burnweed Green Sauce

Makes 1 cup (250 ml)

Burnweed's midsummer appearance coincides conveniently with barbecue season. This bright herb sauce is all a coal-cooked steak (like the Spicebush Tequila Skirt Steak) or a short rib needs. It is also a bright and aromatic companion for grilled chicken, dark-fleshed fish (like mackerel and bluefish), and humble cheese sandwiches.

2 cups (120 g) roughly chopped cilantro

1 cup (30 g) young American burnweed leaves

½ cup (32 g) scallion greens

⅓ cup (10 g) sheep sorrel leaves

2 tablespoons lime juice

2 teaspoons sugar

½ teaspoon salt

Chop all the leaves very finely and transfer to a bowl. Add the lime juice, sugar, and salt and stir well. Alternatively, combine all the ingredients in a food processor and pulse until smooth.

That's it. Done.

Mango, Avocado, and American Burnweed Salad

Serves 4 as a side

Judiciously seasoned with herbs and spices, simple fruit salads become savory side dishes. Deeply perfumed burnweed leaves are a stimulating foil for sweet mango. I like to serve this salad with spicy curries or barbecued meats.

4 very ripe mangoes (or substitute peaches, in season), sliced

2 ripe avocados, cubed

1 cup (30 g) tender, immature American burnweed leaves

¼ cup (about 8 g) mint leaves

1 tablespoon fresh lime juice

¼ teaspoon salt

Black pepper

½ teaspoon toasted sesame oil

½ teaspoon Prickly Ash Paste

1 jicama, thinly sliced

3 radishes, thinly sliced

Place the fruit from one mango and half an avocado in the bowl of a food processor. Add the American burnweed and mint leaves, lime juice, salt, pepper to taste, sesame oil, and Prickly Ash Paste. Pulse until you have a very smooth sauce. Taste. It should be perfectly balanced between sweet and sour. Place the rest of the fruit and vegetables in a bowl, pour on about ⅓ cup of sauce, and toss well with your hands (do not squash the avocado). Pile in a bowl. Serve immediately.

(If you are making this in advance, dress the salad just before serving, and stir the sauce well before pouring it over, as it may separate.)

Leftover sauce is delicious as a side for spicy grilled steak, chicken, or fish.

Scallop Ceviche with Ginger, Sumac, and American Burnweed

Serves 4 as an appetizer

I grow a small annual crop of ginger in containers, which has taught me how delicate young ginger rhizomes can be. Fresh, young ginger is also available in summer at the local greenmarket, just when burnweed is about 2 feet tall. And when the greenmarket fish stall has plump scallops, I buy a few to make this fragrant and delicate summer ceviche. Adding the burnweed just before serving preserves its unique perfume and prevents it from bruising.

8 large scallops

¼ cup (60 ml) fresh lime juice

1 tablespoon grated fresh ginger

2 teaspoons Sumac Essence

2 teaspoons sugar

½ teaspoon salt

6 prickly ash leaflets, very finely chiffonaded

4 shiso leaves, finely chiffonaded

Slice or dice the scallops, not too thinly. Lay them in a bowl. Add the other ingredients, swirling the bowl to distribute the liquid. Cover and chill in the fridge for a minimum of 2 hours and up to 12.

To serve, lift the scallop slices or pieces and their herbs from their marinade and arrange in a bowl, or in individual cocktail glasses.

Fast Mango and American Burnweed Salad

Serves 4 as a side

I can't get enough of burnweed's perfume paired with mangoes. No less satisfying than the previous salad, this one is simply faster, for when you have just three minutes before dinner has to be on the table. Peel, slice, shake, serve. This recipe works well with very ripe, or completely unripe, mangoes. It is excellent barbecue fare.

2 mangoes, sliced thinly
1 tablespoon fish sauce
2 tablespoons lime juice
½ cup (15 g) American burnweed leaves
¼ teaspoon red chile flakes

Toss the mango with the fish sauce and lime juice in a bowl. Transfer to a serving plate. Top with American burnweed leaves and sprinkle with the chile.

Chargrilled Chicken Stew with Coconut and American Burnweed

Serves 4

Inspired by a Kenyan chicken stew featuring cilantro (perversely a European herb but so little part of that culinary landscape), this dish features piquant burnweed instead—creating a sweetly aromatic, slow sauce. Peanut butter adds to the velvety texture. The stew's tartness pierces the creaminess of the coconut, and wiry field garlic flowers provide an onion backbone. Charring the chicken before it becomes a stew is more work, yes, but you will be won over by the depth of flavor it brings to the dish. Burnweed's brilliant green darkens once cooked, but do not be sad; it will be present in terms of flavor.

¼ cup peanut butter

2 tablespoons lime juice

2 tablespoons soy sauce

4-inch (10 cm) piece of ginger, grated

1 tablespoon ground spicebush

8 chicken thighs

1 can (13.5 fluid ounces/400 ml) coconut milk

1 tablespoon cumin

2 tablespoons tamarind paste

1 tablespoon Sumac Essence (or pomegranate molasses)

1 tablespoon palm or unrefined sugar

10 field garlic flowers

2 cups (about 60 g) young American burnweed leaves

Place the peanut butter in a small bowl and thin it with the lime juice and soy. Add the grated ginger and spicebush. Slash each chicken thigh across the top with a very sharp knife and place the pieces in a dish. Pour the peanut butter marinade over them and massage well into the meat, turning the pieces to coat. Marinate for as long as possible—up to 24 hours, but an hour will do.

Grill the chicken above ashed-over coals until one side is brown and sizzling, then turn to brown the other side. The chicken should not cook through—you're looking for delicious smokiness—15 minutes, tops. Remove and reserve in a bowl to catch the juices.

Pour the coconut milk into a large pot and bring to a brief boil over high heat. Add the cumin, tamarind paste, Sumac Essence (or pomegranate molasses), and sugar, and stir well. Place the chicken in the sauce and add enough water to reach the top of the meat. Break up the field garlic flowers and add them to the pot. Reduce the heat to keep the liquid at a gentle simmer, and cook for 1½ hours, covered. Now add the burnweed leaves, dunking them below the surface. Cook for another 30 minutes, uncovered, with the heat high enough to keep the gravy at a brisk simmer. Serve in bowls.

Banh Mi Burgers with Prickly Ash and American Burnweed

Makes 8 burgers

The time to make these vibrant burgers is a week or two beyond midsummer, when young burnweed plants are rising and prickly ash fruit is fat but still green. Combining two stages of fruit—green and the previous season's red—intensifies the prickly ash experience in the meat (it is not hot, but very aromatic). The highly perfumed burnweed leaves seem designed for this treatment. (If you prefer to skip the buns, use large lettuce leaves instead, wrapping pieces of the cooked burgers inside them.)

BURGERS AND SCALLIONS

2 teaspoons dried red prickly ash fruit

1 teaspoon green prickly ash husks

2 pounds (907 g) ground beef (or pork)

2 tablespoons fish sauce

1 tablespoon Soy-Pickled Oyster Mushroom brine (or 1½ teaspoons soy and 1½ teaspoons vinegar)

1 tablespoon palm or unrefined sugar

8 brioche buns (or 32 large lettuce leaves)

16 scallions, trimmed

PICKLED VEGETABLES

2 tablespoons sea salt

⅓ cup (67 g) sugar

½ cup (125 ml) white wine vinegar

1 cup (250 ml) water

2 cups (180 g) julienned carrots

2 cups (180 g) thinly sliced radishes

1 teaspoon crushed green prickly ash husks

HERBS

2 cups (60 g) American burnweed leaves

1 cup (30 g) cilantro

1 cup (30 g) Thai basil (or mint)

SAUCE

⅓ cup (80 ml) soy sauce

1 tablespoon sugar

2 tablespoons lime juice

2 teaspoons red chile flakes

FOR THE BURGERS: Mix the burgers at least an hour before you want to cook them. Crush the red and green prickly ash fruit in a pestle and mortar (or use a coffee grinder). Place the meat in a bowl with the prickly ash, fish sauce, Soy-Pickled Oyster Mushroom brine (or vinegar/soy substitute), and sugar. Mix very well with your hands (then rub them with a cut lime and wash very well to destink from the fish sauce!). Form the mixture into eight patties. Cover and keep in the fridge for up to 24 hours.

FOR THE PICKLES: Make these 45 minutes before you need them. Combine the salt, sugar, vinegar, and water in a bowl and stir until the granules have dissolved. Add the carrots, radishes, and crushed prickly ash husks. The liquid should cover the vegetables (add more vinegar and water if it does not). Just before serving, strain them. (You can keep the pickling liquor for salad dressings or braising.)

FOR THE HERBS: Wash and dry all the herbs and arrange them in separate heaps on a large plate, so that everyone can choose their own combinations.

FOR THE SAUCE: In a small bowl combine all the sauce ingredients and stir well. Have a small spoon handy for drizzling sauce over the burgers.

COOKING THE BURGERS AND SCALLIONS: I prefer to cook these burgers over coals, but pan-frying in a heavy skillet works very well. Cook each side until it is brown and firm, 5 to 8 minutes per side, depending on your heat source. Cook the scallions at the same time, turning them when one side begins to char and they become limp. Toast the buns over the heat for the last few minutes of cooking time.

ASSEMBLING: Arrange the burgers, buns (or lettuce leaves), and scallions on a large platter, each in their own spot. To assemble, place some herbs on a bun bottom, top with a burger, a scallion or two folded in half, and some pickled vegetables; drizzle with sauce, add more herbs, and slap on the top of the burger. Take a bite. The scallion may offer some resistance but you will win. If you are using lettuce leaves instead of buns, break the burgers into bite-sized pieces before wrapping.

Happy summer!

Spicy Beef with American Burnweed Leaf Wraps

Serves 4

Similar in inflection to the Banh Mi Burgers but with some vegetable and spice variations, here spicy meat is spooned onto a large perfumed burnweed leaf, topped with crisp relishes, and wrapped, to be bitten as juices run down your fingers. Thai basil, mint, cilantro, and maybe shiso are the traditional accompaniments to these Southeast Asian wraps, but your local burnweed patch will complement them perfectly. Despite its simplicity at table, this dish takes some time to prepare. Set aside an hour for all the peeling, chopping, and marinating.

SPICY BEEF

1½ pounds (680 g) ground beef

2 tablespoons unscented oil

1 cup (150 g) finely chopped shallots

⅓ cup (50 g) peanuts

3 tablespoons grated ginger

1 tablespoon Sumac Essence

1 tablespoon spicebush

1 tablespoon fresh green prickly ash
    fruit, crushed

2 teaspoons red chile flakes

1 teaspoon black pepper

3 tablespoons fish sauce

PICKLED VEGETABLES

2 cups (180 g) julienned carrots

⅓ cup (67 g) plus 2 teaspoons sugar, divided

2 tablespoons plus 2 teaspoons salt, divided

½ cup (125 ml) white wine vinegar

1 cup (250 ml) water

1 teaspoon green prickly ash fruit, crushed

12 whole baby Japanese turnips (or radishes)

4 Persian cucumbers, sliced lengthwise

SAUCE

⅓ cup (80 ml) fish sauce

2 tablespoons sugar

2 tablespoons lime juice

2 teaspoons exceptionally finely chopped
    lemongrass heart

2 teaspoons red chile flakes

HERBS

32 large American burnweed leaves
    (6–8 per person), well washed

1 cup (30 g) Thai basil

1 cup (30 g) mint leaves

1 bunch cilantro leaves and stems

FOR THE BEEF: Heat a large dry skillet over high heat and add the beef to it. Brown the meat, breaking it up as it cooks until it is evenly sized, finely textured, and browning at the edges, about 12 minutes. Add all the other ingredients and stir very well to combine. Add 2 cups (500 ml) water. Bring the mixture to a gentle boil before reducing the heat to cook at a steady simmer for 1 hour. Stir every 10 minutes as it reduces and sticks and leaves a brown crust around the edges of the pan. If the moisture evaporates altogether, add a little more water. The mixture will become steadily browner. Taste. You want a balance of hot, sour, salty, and sweet (like that exceptional book by Naomi Duguid). When almost all the moisture has evaporated and the meat is glossy and rich tasting, transfer the beef to a serving bowl. It is best served at room temperature, so cool it down in the fridge.

FOR THE VEGETABLES: While the beef cooks, make the vegetable toppings. Place the julienned carrots in a bowl and cover with ⅓ cup of the sugar, 1 teaspoon of the salt, and all of the vinegar, water, and prickly ash. Muddle to dissolve the sugar. Trim the baby turnips' tails but leave about an inch of tender stems—wash very well to dislodge any grit trapped where the stem meets the bulbs. Place them in a bowl and douse in 2 tablespoons of the salt. Massage it in. Lay the sliced cucumbers in a bowl and sprinkle them with the remaining 1 teaspoon of salt and 2 teaspoons of sugar.

Before serving, lift the carrots from their pickling brine and rinse the turnips off quickly.

FOR THE SAUCE: Combine all the ingredients in a small bowl and stir well to dissolve the sugar.

TO SERVE: Place all the bowls within reaching distance on the table, with some spoons for the beef and a small spoon for the sauce. Place a spoonful of beef along the midrib of a burnweed leaf. Top with the vegetables you prefer, some herbs, and a drizzle of sauce, and roll into a package.

Finger bowls are a really good idea . . .

Bayberry

OTHER COMMON NAMES: Northern bayberry, southern bayberry, wax myrtle, California wax myrtle

BOTANICAL NAMES: *Myrica pensylvanica*, *Morella cerifera*, *Myrica gale*, *Morella californica*

STATUS: Shrubs indigenous to northeastern, southeastern, and western US

WHERE: Shorelines and scrub

SEASON: Spring to late fall

USE: Aromatic, fresh herb

PARTS USED: Leaves

GROW? Yes

TASTES LIKE: Bay leaf meets juniper

It was chance that led me to crush the leaves of northern bayberry (*Myrica pensylvanica*), a hardy shrub that occurs up and down the northeastern coast of the United States. It was 2011, and I was on a barrier island in Brooklyn, heading to the beach. The anonymous shrubs were an even green velvet over the dunes, stretching to the west. As I opened my hand, the scent of aromatic summer foliage whispered, "Cook me!" In my garden-designing life I overlooked this native denizen of our dunelands, until I learned its value as a tough rooftop plant, withstanding winds and dry conditions. And then that aroma changed everything. I brought home some leaves.

I had been aware of bayberry fruit's old-timey application in candle making. They are hard little blue nuggets coated in wax; boil them long enough and the wax floats free. You would need tons of fruit. And while most foraging resources I consulted back then listed the dried leaf as the edible part, no one spoke about using it as a fresh herb. That scent was

used the hard, powdery blue fruits only to flavor bitters. The leaves are the real prize.

Morella cerifera is known as southern bay, and as its name suggests, its native range is southern, extending to Florida and west through Texas. Its flavor is very similar to northern bay's, and I use it in the same way (I grow a shrub in a pot). On the West Coast, bayberry's cousins include sweet gale (*Myrica gale*) and California wax myrtle (*Morella californica*).

How to Collect and Prepare

From early spring, when tender new buds and then leaflets appear, to late fall, when the leaves are tough and bronzed by cold, simply pick the buds or leaves from the plant and store in a paper bag until you are home. Whole branches can be picked if you need a large quantity. Make sure to cut them cleanly, just above a leaf and at a slight angle, using sharp pruning shears or a knife. This effectively prunes the plant. At home store cut branches in water for several days to preserve freshness. Leaves can be kept covered in the fridge until you need them.

calling out to be used in quantity. I obeyed. Bayberry is now a staple in my kitchen.

In every stage from delicate spring shoots and flowers to tender leaves, through midsummer toughening and fall intensity, bayberry is useful.

Spring bayberry leaves are soft enough to chop finely and to use as prolifically as you would parsley or cilantro (although their flavors have nothing in common). Later, when the leaves are too fibrous to chew, they can be used whole to perfume roasts, braises, pies, sauces, infusions, and fruit.

While bayberry has a flavor profile reminiscent of Mediterranean bay leaf (*Laurus nobilis*), it is less pronounced, and I use more of it. The leaves do dry well, but I find them very bland and dusty. Bayberry sings when it is fresh.

The leaves are very successful in infusions. Gin with bayberry takes on a delicately green herbal note, which works well with the spirit's juniper kick (an indigenous juniper often grows side by side with bayberry). My vermouths often feature bayberry. I have fermented the unripe green fruit—the resulting juice makes a powerful condiment used in moderation (the seeds remain uncrackably hard)—and I have

CULTIVATION TIPS
USDA Hardiness Zones 3–7

Northern bayberry thrives in full sun but will grow in high shade and semi-shade. Shaded plants will be less strongly flavored. At home on shorelines, it is extremely adaptable and drought-tolerant but will tolerate moist, well-drained soils, as well as alkaline or acidic conditions. It grows well in pots and in ground. If you want fruit—mainly for ornamental purposes, or to provide food for birds—you need a male and a female plant.

Bayberry Oil

Makes about ¾ cup (190 ml)

I use spring bayberry leaf tips preserved as a fragrant oil in dozens of ways: in green salad vinaigrettes, warm potato salads, painted onto roasting meats or vegetables, or drizzled onto feta that is roasting inside a foil package in a hot oven, waiting to be slathered onto bread. Never store oils with fresh herbs on the counter (hello, botulism); keep this herb oil in the fridge, or freeze. Use within 2 months or the flavor turns stale (stir before using, as the solids will settle).

2 cups (60 g) packed tender bayberry leaf tips	Blend the tender tips of bayberry with the oil until the mixture is very finely smooth. Transfer to a clean jar and keep in the fridge.
½ cup (125 ml) extra-virgin olive oil	

Bayberry Feta Packages

Serves 2

Salty feta with fresh, herbal bay makes a quick and satisfying meal, the oven's heat mellowing the harsh edge of the cheese. Serve with dense, seedy brown bread or crackers.

4 ounces (113 g) feta, in a slice	Preheat the oven to 400°F (200°C).
1 tablespoon Bayberry Oil	Place the feta on a square of foil. Drizzle the bayberry oil over it, and sprinkle the chile flakes across the cheese. Wrap the package up and transfer it to the oven for 10 minutes. Unwrap, and spread on good bread.
½ teaspoon red chile flakes	

Bayberry Rub

Makes about ⅓ cup (80 ml)

This bright fresh herb rub is a spring staple before the bayberry leaves become too tough to chew. Use it as an alternative marinade for a Roadkill Chicken, for a pork loin (before wrapping in prosciutto and roasting), for barbecued baby back ribs, for Hangar Steak with Bayberry Rub, and for mushrooms.

2 cups (60 g) young bayberry leaves
½ teaspoon salt
1 teaspoon black pepper
1 tablespoon lemon juice
3 tablespoons extra-virgin olive oil

Place the ingredients in a food processor and pulse until the leaves are very fine. Or just chop the bayberry leaves exceptionally finely and mix with the other ingredients in a bowl.

Bayberry Gin

Makes 1 cup (250 ml)

Barely a recipe, but oh so worthwhile, with a taste of the northeastern shoreline. Make any quantity—just fill a jar with leaves and cover them with gin. This is best with early-summer bayberry and a juniper-forward (increasingly, many of them are not) gin.

1 cup (250 ml) gin
1 cup (60 g) bayberry leaves

Fill a clean glass jar with the bayberry leaves. Cover with gin. Strain off after 4 days (left longer, it becomes too harsh for my taste).

The Bay Rose

Makes 1 drink

This is an autumn cocktail made with mature bayberry leaves and rose hip jam, a staple in my cupboard. It is a killer drink, and one of my favorites.

ROSE HIP SYRUP

2 tablespoons rose hip lekvar or jam
3 tablespoons water
6 bayberry leaves

COCKTAIL

2 fluid ounces (4 tablespoons) Rose Hip Syrup
3 fluid ounces (6 tablespoons) Bayberry Gin
1 fluid ounce (2 tablespoons) Northeast
    No. 1 Bitters

FOR THE SYRUP: Thin the jam with the water in a small bowl. Pour this mixture into a small saucepan, add the bayberry leaves, and heat gently, whisking with a fork. As soon as the mixture simmers, turn off the heat and let it cool.

FOR THE COCKTAIL: Combine all the ingredients in a shaker with ice. Shake, strain, and pour.

Baybreaker

Makes 1 drink

I shook up this wild Gibson when Hurricane Irene was rattling our Brooklyn roof and threatening the barrier islands edging Jamaica Bay. "The Ocean Will Meet the Bay," said the headlines.

3 fluid ounces (6 tablespoons) Bayberry Gin	Shake the ingredients with ice, strain, and pour. Garnish with a couple of Pickled Field Garlics.
1½ fluid ounces (3 tablespoons) dry vermouth	
Splash of Pickled Field Garlic juice	

Bayberry Beach Plum Gin

Makes about 5 cups (1¼ liters)

Beach plums (*Prunus maritima*) are bayberry's dune country neighbors. The fruit and the herb complement each other beautifully. In late summer I am sometimes lucky enough to find enough beach plums to make this gin. Cooking them lightly adds a deeper note to their otherwise recognizably plummy flavor. Combining the cooked fruit with bayberry and gin for a couple of weeks creates something memorable—a North American version of sloe gin. You can use any domestic or wild plum for this recipe.

1 pound (453 g) beach plums	Place the beach plums in a saucepan with the water, sugar, and bayberry leaves. Heat gently over medium heat until the liquid begins to boil. Turn off the heat and allow the fruit to cool. Place the plums and their cooking liquid in a jar and cover with the gin. Macerate for 1 week. Strain through a fine-mesh sieve and again through double cheesecloth before bottling in a clean bottle. (The leftover strained plums make an outstanding ice cream or compote).
½ cup (125 ml) water	
¼ cup (50 g) sugar	
40 bayberry leaves	
3 cups (750 ml) gin	

Bayberry Beach Plum and Red Wine Syrup

Makes about 2 cups (500 ml)

After tasting the juices from poaching plums in red wine with bayberry, I realized that the resulting syrup was too good to treat as an afterthought. Add it to cocktails or to chilled red wine with ice; use it as an aperitif; drizzle it warm over ice cream (it is especially good with Serviceberry Ice Cream), or add it to savory sauces and pan juices. (Use the leftover plum pulp in ice cream or as a condiment for pork, duck, or charcuterie.)

1 pound (453 g) beach plums
1 cup (250 ml) red wine
¼ cup (60 ml) water
¼ cup (50 g) sugar
20 bayberry leaves

Combine the ingredients in a saucepan and heat over medium heat. Cook until the plums are beginning to break up, about 15 minutes. Cool, strain through a double-mesh sieve, and then again through cheesecloth. Bottle and keep in the fridge. It keeps well for 2 weeks.

Lady Sailor

Makes 1 drink

A voluptuous drink, just in time for the start of hurricane season. Purchase flood insurance, and batten down the hatches. Chin up.

3 fluid ounces (6 tablespoons) silver tequila
1½ fluid ounces (3 tablespoons) Bayberry
  Beach Plum and Red Wine Syrup
½ fluid ounce (1 tablespoon) lime juice

Shake these all up with ice, strain, and pour.

Bayberry Cheesebread

Makes 1 loaf

An instant crowd pleaser, to be torn apart while the rest of dinner cooks on the fire. It is also a delicious meal in its own right, washed down with some red wine or crisp beer.

4 ounces (113 g) butter
1 cup (30 g) tender spring bayberry leaves
⅓ cup (16 g) finely snipped field
  garlic leaves
¼ teaspoon Field Garlic Salt
1 small sourdough boule
1–2 balls fresh mozzarella, cut into slices

Preheat the oven to 375°F (190°C).
  On a chopping board, using the flat of a chef's knife, mash together the butter, bayberry leaves, field garlic leaves, and salt. Cut even slices into the sourdough boule, stopping short of severing its base. Smear the butter between the slices. Tuck a slice of cheese between every two slices (if you prefer it cheesier, fill every space with mozzarella). Wrap the boule in foil and place it in the hot oven for about 20 minutes, until it has heated all the way through and the cheese is melting. Unwrap, and dig in.

Bayberry and Spicebush Pickled Shrimp

Serves 12 as an appetizer

Pickled shrimp are party food, to me. I made these first for a *Tweede Nuwe Jaar* (second New Year, a traditional holiday in Cape Town) lunch under the huge London plane tree in my parents' garden, using bay leaves picked from a 20-foot bay growing nearby. The recipe adapted very well to milder bayberry. The acid in the vinegar cooks these shrimp thoroughly. Serve with good bread and better butter. (Save and freeze the shrimp shells for Wild Roast Salmon with Spring Forages.)

1¼ cups (310 ml) cider vinegar

½ cup (100 g) sugar

30 fresh bayberry leaves

1 tablespoon ground spicebush

1 tablespoon plus 1 teaspoon salt

3 pounds (1⅓ kg) raw shrimp, shells
    removed and cleaned

1 large red onion, thinly sliced

2 teaspoons black pepper

1 tablespoon chile flakes (optional)

Combine all the pickling ingredients except the pepper, onion, shrimp, and chile flakes in a pot; stir until the sugar and salt have dissolved. Heat over medium-high heat for 10 minutes or until tiny bubbles rise, then turn off the heat. Let the liquid cool completely to room temperature (you can skip this step, but it allows the bayberry flavor to bloom). Place the shrimp and onions in a mason jar or food-safe container that has a sealable lid. Pour the pickling liquid over them, add the black pepper and chile if using, cover, and chill for 12 hours. Turn the jar or container upside down a few times while chilling. To serve, strain the shrimp and onions and serve in a bowl.

Bayberry Ratatouille

Serves 4 as a side

Late-summer bayberry leaves are tough but flavorful, and good for adding entire to the produce that now pours from gardens and gluts greenmarkets. My recipe benefits from the startling combination of coffee and red wine. Try it. You'll see. I use leftover coffee from my breakfast stovetop espresso. Serve the ratatouille as a side dish or as a meal with good bread or with a poached egg poised on top of individual portions.

3 tablespoons olive oil

1 pound (453 g) tomatoes, quartered

1 large onion, cut into eighths

8 ounces (227 g) eggplant, cut in half
    (if small), or into chunks

2 medium leeks, slit lengthwise and
    cut in half

1 head garlic, loose skin trimmed off

1½ cups (375 ml) red wine

3 tablespoons coffee, preferably espresso

10 bayberry leaves

2 teaspoons sugar

½ teaspoon salt

In a pot heat the oil over medium-high heat. Add all the vegetables (and fruits, really). Stir. Cover with a lid and cook for 5 minutes, shaking the pot every now and then to turn the vegetables. Remove the lid and add the red wine, allowing it to bubble for a few seconds. Add the coffee, bayberry leaves, sugar, and salt. Stir, reduce the heat, cover, and cook very gently for 40 minutes. Remove the lid and taste. Adjust the seasoning if necessary. Cook uncovered for another 25 minutes at a simmer. Serve hot or at room temperature.

Bayberry Paprika Pulpo

Serves 4

This Galicia-inspired stew is given exceptional dimension by adding octopuses after charring over hardwood charcoal. You can also grill them over gas, of course, or under the broiler, before stewing. Serve this bold springtime dish with Ramp Aioli.

MARINADE FOR GRILLING

2 pounds (907 g) baby octopuses, cleaned
1 tablespoon lemon juice
¼ teaspoon salt
2 teaspoons smoked paprika
1 teaspoon chile flakes
1 tablespoon tomato paste
½ cup (15 g) tender bayberry leaves, finely chopped
¼ cup (60 ml) extra-virgin olive oil
8 ramps

STEW

2 tablespoons extra-virgin olive oil
⅓ cup (50 g) finely chopped shallots
3 cloves garlic, thinly sliced
2 tablespoons smoked paprika
3 tablespoons tomato paste
2 cups (500 ml) white wine
1 teaspoon sugar
¼ teaspoon salt
10 bayberry leaves
Black pepper

POTATOES

16 baby potatoes
2 tablespoons extra-virgin olive oil
Salt
Lemon juice
⅓ cup (10 g) finely chopped tender bayberry leaves

TO CLEAN: If the octopuses have not been cleaned, make a lengthwise slit in their head sacs, turn the sac inside out, and scrape out the innards. Rinse well. To remove the beak, use the point of a knife to make a small slit next to the opening where the tentacles attach. Pry out the hard beak. If the octopuses are quite large, cut them in half. Otherwise, leave entire. Place the octopuses in a large bowl.

TO MARINATE: Add to the bowl all the marinade ingredients except the ramps. Mix well with your hands. Cover and refrigerate. Allow the octopuses to marinate for at least 1 hour, and up to 12.

TO GRILL: Place the octopuses with the ramps on a grill over a charcoal fire once the coals have ashed over. Allow the ramps to brown slightly before returning them to the bowl. Cook the octopods until one side begins to color deeply—about 5 minutes. Turn and cook for a few more minutes (you are adding flavor, not cooking through). Some blackened edges are fine. Return the charred octopuses to their marinade bowl and toss.

TO STEW: In a large pot heat the olive oil over medium heat and add the shallots and garlic. Cook for 5 minutes, then add the paprika and tomato paste, cooking for another minute to caramelize and deepen the flavor. Add the octopuses, ramps, and their marinade liquid, and increase the heat. Pour in the wine and add the sugar, salt, and bayberry leaves. Stir well. Allow the liquid to bubble for a few seconds, then turn the heat to low and cook, covered, for 1½ hours.

FOR THE POTATOES: Cook the potatoes in boiling water until just tender. Remove them and drain well, then break in half with the tip of a knife. Reserve. Ten minutes before you are ready to serve the stew, heat the olive oil in a pot over medium heat and add the potatoes. Shake well to prevent them from sticking. Cook until one side begins to crisp up—about 8 minutes—then flip them. Season them with salt and a squeeze of lemon juice, using a spatula to scrape up any crisp brown residue on the bottom of the pan. When the potatoes are brown, pile them into the middle of the octopus stew (or serve them on the side if you want to show off all those tentacles), and finish with a scattering of chopped bayberry and black pepper.

Bayberry Bone Broth

Makes about 8 cups (2 liters)

My bone broth is really beef broth, the classical backbone of French cooking. It is full-bodied, comforting, and nourishing, especially when life has thrown you a curveball. It reaches a pinnacle of culinary satisfaction when it has been reduced to concentrate flavor. Serve the reduction with crunchy toast spread with ramp butter or Smooth Field Garlic Butter. (Save the succulent meat after straining: Shred it for Bayberry Meat Pies, a ragu, or a good sandwich, with Garlic Mustard Root Relish and peppery wintercress leaves.)

3 pounds (1⅓ kg) beef short ribs,
    cut into small sections
1 teaspoon salt
3 tablespoons tomato paste
3 stalks celery, chopped
2 medium carrots, chopped
2 medium leeks, cleaned very well
    and chopped
1 medium onion, chopped
10 field garlic bulbs, trimmed (or 4–5
    cloves garlic)
2 teaspoons sugar
3 tablespoons soy sauce
3 tablespoons balsamic vinegar
Black pepper
30 bayberry leaves
5 stalks thyme

Preheat the oven to 400°F (200°C).

Sprinkle the short ribs liberally with the salt. Place them in a large skillet and slide into the oven. Roast for 1 hour. Remove from the oven and transfer the beef to a large pot. Add the tomato paste, celery, carrots, leeks, onions, and field garlic to the fat and juices in the original skillet and cook over medium heat for 5 minutes. Add the sugar, soy, balsamic vinegar, and a generous amount of fresh black pepper; stir well. Pour in ½ cup (125 ml) of water, increase the heat to high, and stir very well. Pour everything into the pot with the beef. Add 10 cups (2½ liters) of water and the herbs.

Bring the liquid to a boil over high heat. Reduce the heat to medium-low and keep the broth at a simmer for 3 hours, uncovered.

Strain the broth through a fine-mesh strainer into a smaller pot. It is ready as a regular broth to be added to other dishes. Or reduce it by half at a steady simmer to concentrate the flavor (highly recommended). Taste when it is done and season if necessary. Whether reduced or at regular strength, chill in the fridge before skimming off the hardened fat.

Bayberry Meat Pies

Makes 1 pie or 4 individual pies

These unassuming pies hit the hungry spot. If you have no beef leftovers, use raw ground chuck. No duck fat lurking in the freezer? Substitute lard or butter.

Making a hot-water crust involves everything you were told not to do with pastry. There is no cold butter, no handling it as little as possible, no chilling, no resting. The pastry is hot, you work it, it can be rolled out at once, it is sturdy, and it has great bite. Liberating.

Serve with BC Ketchup.

BEEF FILLING

2 tablespoons butter

1 medium onion, finely chopped

1 pound (453 g) cooked, shredded beef
    short rib, or raw ground chuck

12 ounces (340 g) cooked potatoes,
    peeled and roughly chopped

1 teaspoon salt

¼ teaspoon black pepper

10 juniper berries

20 bayberry leaves

HOT-WATER PASTRY

15 ounces (425 g) all-purpose flour

½ teaspoon salt

3½ ounces (99 g) duck fat, melted and hot

7½ fluid ounces (225 ml) just-boiled water

EGG WASH

1 large egg yolk

1 tablespoon water

FOR THE FILLING: Heat the butter over medium heat in a pan, and add the onion. Sauté gently for 10 minutes. In a bowl combine the cooked onion with the beef, potatoes, salt, pepper, and juniper. Mix well.

FOR THE PASTRY: Place the flour and salt in a bowl. Make a well. Pour in the *hot* duck fat and the very hot water. Mix well, then knead in the bowl for a minute until smooth. If you're making a large pie, cut two-thirds off the dough for the base and one-third for the lid. If you're making four pies, cut eight pieces, larger for the base, smaller for the lids.

Preheat the oven to 375°F (190°C). Lightly butter a 8-inch (20 cm) springform pan or four 5-inch (15 cm) pans.

Roll the pastry out at once on a lightly floured board. It may adhere to the pin, but it peels off easily. Roll out to fit the pans with a 1-inch (2½ cm) overlap. Transfer the pastry to the pan or pans. Pack the meat filling into the pastry and place the bayberry leaves on top of the meat. Roll out the pastry lids. (Placing the baking pan on the rolled-out pastry and cutting around the edge will give you a perfect fit.) Lay the lid on top of the filling, gather the hanging edges of the pastry base up and over the lid, and crimp all the way around. Pierce a steam vent.

Whisk the egg wash in a bowl and paint it over the pastry. Slide the pie or pies into the hot oven and bake until deeply golden and crisp—about 1 hour.

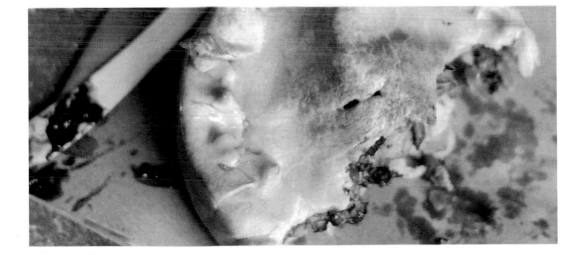

Bayberry Porchetta

Serves 8–10

Bayberries leaf out just when the first soft fennel fronds and early garlic are ready in my late-spring garden. It is also the tail end of ramp season. In this forager's rendition of a Roman classic, traditional fennel and lemon are joined by the wilder flavors. For simplicity and succulence I use pork belly, but pork shoulder works very well, if you are prepared for the extra work of deboning, flattening, trimming, and shaping. A sizable porchetta is a party piece, easy to start early and slice just before serving. Use a smaller piece of belly if you are not feeding a crowd, in which case cut back on the stuffing and trim the cooking time to 3 hours.

1 pork belly, 16 inches (41 cm) long,
    or 1 deboned shoulder (8–10 pounds/
    3½–4½ kg)

3 tablespoons lemon juice, divided

2½ teaspoons Ramp Leaf Salt, divided

2 tablespoons finely chopped
    preserved lemon rind

2 teaspoons grated fresh lemon zest

3 ounces (85 g) chopped fennel fronds

1 ounce (28 g) tender bayberry leaves

2 ounces (57 g) chopped ramp leaves

2 ounces (57 g) chopped green garlic

2 teaspoons hot chile flakes (optional)

1 lemon, sliced, seeds removed

12 whole fennel fronds

2 ounces (57 g) whole bayberry leaves

1 cup (250 ml) verjuice (substitute
    white wine)

FOR THE PORK BELLY: Cut the skin from the pork belly, leaving a thin layer of fat over the meat. Cut the extra fat off the skin and discard (or save for roast potatoes), leaving a thin layer. Reserve the skin in the fridge.

FOR THE SHOULDER: Remove the skin. Cut the deep fat from the skin, leaving a thin layer of fat all over the meat. Remove the bone by slitting the meat along the length of the bone, cutting down, and severing all the meat around it. Once the bone is free, butterfly the shoulder by cutting deeply down into the muscles and opening it out. You are looking for an even shape, very roughly rectangular. There will be some obvious uneven edges, especially at the hock end. Trim them off, as they will make the later rolling and shaping difficult (save them for a Forager's Spring Curry).

Turn your pork meat-side up on a large chopping board. Sprinkle it with 1 tablespoon of the lemon juice and 1 teaspoon of the Ramp Leaf Salt. Add the chopped preserved lemon rind and the fresh lemon zest. Add the herbs, ramp leaves, and garlic, spreading them all evenly across the meat. Finish with the chile flakes, if using, or a generous grinding of black pepper.

FORM THE PORK INTO A ROLL: Using the long side nearest yourself, turn the meat over on itself and roll away from you. You won't be able to do this all at once, so work in sections. Once the whole piece is rolled as snugly as possible, rest it seam-side down. Using kitchen twine, tie the entire length of pork tightly, using loops. Leave about a 2½-inch (6 cm) space between ties. Transfer the pork to a large dish (if it does not fit lengthwise, you can curl it loosely in a large bowl). Cover, and let it rest in the fridge for 6 to 24 hours. Remove the porchetta and the skin 30 minutes before cooking.

Preheat the oven to 500°F (260°C).

Lay the lemon slices in a row on the bottom of a large roasting pan. Top them with the fennel fronds and the bayberry leaves. Place the porchetta on this fragrant nest. Pour the remaining lemon juice over the meat. Season the top of the meat with ½ teaspoon of Ramp Leaf Salt. Use another ½ teaspoon to season the underside of the pork *skin*. Drape the skin across the top of the porchetta, like a blanket.

Transfer the pan to the oven and roast the porchetta for 40 minutes. Reduce the heat to 300°F (150°C), and add ½ cup of the verjuice (or white wine) to the pan (do not pour it over the skin). Cook for another 4 hours.

As it cooks, add more verjuice and occasional splashes of water to the pan to make sure it does not dry out. Remove the pan a couple of times and pour off the copious fat. With 45 minutes left on the cooking time, check on the crackling: It should be crisp and hard by now. Remove it, uncovering the pork so that the top of the meat browns a little. Break the crackling into shards, season with the remaining ½ teaspoon of Ramp Leaf Salt (it sticks better to the fatty side), and pass around as snacks with cocktails.

Cut the string from the porchetta. Cover the meat and allow it to rest on a large platter or a board with runnels for 30 minutes. While it rests, transfer the roasting pan to the stovetop. Pour off the excess fat. Pour some water into the pan and deglaze it over medium-high heat, scraping up all the brown pieces. Taste for seasoning and adjust. Strain the juices into a jug.

Once it has rested carve the porchetta into slices, pour the pan juices over the top, and serve.

Bayberry and Lemon Roast Chicken

Serves 4

Roast chicken is the cook's blank canvas, ready to take on whatever aromas and flavors are applied. After early summer, when bayberry leaves are too tough to chop, I slide whole leaves under the skin. Sliced lemons inside and under the chicken add a citrus complexity. I like to serve this chicken with a strong green salad of dandelion greens and nasturtium leaves dressed with a garlicky vinaigrette.

1 roasting chicken, 3½ 4 pounds (1½–2 kg)
8 slices lemon
40 whole bayberry leaves
1 teaspoon salt
1 tablespoon cold butter, cut into 4 slices
3 tablespoons lemon juice
1¼ pounds (567 g) fingerling potatoes
  (or your favorite)

Preheat the oven to 450°F (230°C).

Rinse the chicken and pat dry. Place 5 lemon slices on the bottom of a skillet and top with 20 bayberry leaves. Place the chicken on top. Put 3 lemon slices inside the bird with 10 bayberry leaves and a pinch of salt. Separate the skin over the chicken's breast from the meat and slide 2 butter slices down over each breast. Push 5 bayberry leaves in to cover each breast. Pour the lemon juice over the top of the bird and sprinkle with ¼ teaspoon of the salt.

Cut the unpeeled potatoes into narrow wedges and arrange them around, but not under, the chicken. Sprinkle them with more salt. Add ½ cup (125 ml) of water to the pan.

Transfer the skillet to the oven and roast for 1¼ hours. Check the pan juices a couple of times and add a little water if the juices turn to caramel. When the chicken's skin is very brown and crisp and a skewer inserted into the thick part of the thigh releases clear juice, remove from the oven. Transfer the bird to a platter to rest for 10 to 15 minutes. Place the skillet over medium-high heat, add a little water or white wine, and stir up the good brown bits (the potatoes can stay in the pan). Taste for seasoning. When you have a sticky sauce, it is ready. Carve the bird into joints, and slice the breasts, placing the meat back in the skillet, on top of the potatoes.

Hangar Steak with Bayberry Rub

Serves 4

This simple and fresh herb rub is a spring staple in my house, before the bayberry leaves become too tough to chew. Use it on, well, just about anything—from grilled mushrooms to gamy fish to beef. It is exceptional with this quick-seared hangar steak, inspired by a perennial dinner dish at Al di La, an Italian restaurant in Park Slope, Brooklyn. Tip: The better the balsamic, the more delicious this will be.

1 oz (28 g) young, tender bayberry leaves, chopped very finely
¼ teaspoon salt
1 teaspoon black pepper
2 hangar steaks (each about 1 pound/453 g)
6 tablespoons balsamic vinegar, divided
2 tablespoons unscented oil
½ teaspoon Ramp Leaf Salt (optional)

In a small bowl mix the chopped bayberry leaves with the salt and pepper. Lay the steaks in a flat dish and rub the bayberry mixture all over them, top and bottom. Add 4 tablespoons of the balsamic vinegar. Marinate for at least 1 hour or up to 24 hours (covered and chilled). Remove the meat from the fridge 30 minutes before you want to cook it.

Open the windows. There will be smoke. In a skillet (or skillets, if the steaks cannot fit into one) over high heat, warm the oil. When it is hot, add the steaks. Sear one side for about 3 minutes, then turn. Sear for another 3 to 4 minutes—the exterior will be dark with some charred edges. Remove the steaks from the pan or pans and transfer to a large platter. Cover the meat and let it rest for 10 minutes. Carve it on the diagonal into thin slices. Drizzle another tablespoon of balsamic over each sliced steak. Dust with some Ramp Leaf Salt before serving, if you like.

Bayberry Meatballs with Field Garlic Salt and Sumac

Serves 4

Serve these aromatic meatballs with a side of thick yogurt flavored with Field Garlic Salt.

1½ pounds (680 g) ground beef
½ cup (30 g) panko (or coarse) bread crumbs
¼ cup (60 ml) milk
½ teaspoon Field Garlic Salt
1 ounce (28 g) tender bayberry leaves, finely chopped
1 anchovy, finely chopped
1 large egg
1 tablespoon lemon juice
1–2 tablespoons olive oil, for frying
1 teaspoon Ground Sumac

In a large mixing bowl combine all the ingredients except the oil and the sumac. Mix thoroughly. Form each meatball, about golf-ball-sized.

PAN-FRY: Heat a heavy skillet over high heat, and add 1 tablespoon of oil. Fry each meatball until brown, about 4 minutes. Reduce the heat to medium-high, flip the meatballs, and cook until brown all over, about another 8 minutes. Use more oil if needed.

OVEN-ROAST: Preheat the oven to 450°F (230°C). Oil a roasting tray or baking sheet. Place the meatballs on the tray and slide into the oven. Cook for 8 minutes. Remove the tray and turn the meatballs over. Cook another 8 minutes.

Just before serving, sprinkle the meatballs with the sumac.

Bayberry Back Ribs

Serves 4

Succulent back ribs invite many variations. When spring and early-summer bayberry leaves are tender and choppable, this simple marinade delivers tons of wild flavor.

6 pounds (2¾ kg) sliced pork riblets

3 ounces (85 g) tender bayberry leaves

1 cup (250 ml) buttermilk

¼ cup (60 ml) lemon juice

Zest of 2 lemons

¼ cup (60 ml) extra-virgin olive oil

1 tablespoon black pepper

1 teaspoon salt

If the ribs are attached in a rack, slice between each bone to separate them. Place all the ribs in a large bowl. Place all the other ingredients in a blender and blend until smooth. Pour over the ribs. Toss well and cover. Marinate at least 1 hour or up to 24 in the fridge.

For barbecuing, grill the ribs above ashed-over coals, and cook until they are brown on one side—about 10 minutes. Flip. (If they burn, just turn them more often.) Cook the other side, about another 10 minutes.

For broiling, place the ribs on a baking sheet and broil until dark brown on one side, 10 to 15 minutes. Turn and repeat.

Once the ribs are cooked, cover them and let them rest for 10 minutes— yes, even little ribs benefit from resting—before serving stacked on a platter.

Lamb Shoulder with Bayberry

Serves 4–6

Mature autumn bayberry infuses this slow-cooked lamb shoulder with its fresh resin scent. The sharp flavors of verjuice and vinegar balance the fatty succulence of the melting meat. Use your favorite vinegar.

1 lamb shoulder (about 4 pounds/1¾ kg)

60 mature bayberry leaves, divided

¼ cup (60 ml) sherry vinegar

1 teaspoon salt

1 teaspoon black pepper

2 cups (500 ml) verjuice (substitute white wine), divided

Preheat the oven to 450°F (230°C).

Place the lamb in a large roasting tray on top of 40 of the bayberry leaves. Pour the sherry vinegar over the meat. Season with the salt and the pepper. Cover the pan with foil or a large lid and roast in the hot oven for 40 minutes. Remove the covering, reduce the heat to 300°F (150°C), and add 1 cup of the verjuice. Cook for another 2½ hours. Remove the pan from the oven. Add the other cup of verjuice and use a wooden spoon to wash and scrape the crusting sides of the pan with the liquid. Add the last 20 bayberry leaves to the pan juices. Return to the oven to cook for 1 more hour. Serve with spoonfuls of the juice poured over each portion of meat.

Bayberry Plums

Serves 4

Late-summer beach plums and mature bayberry leaves create an aromatic dessert.

1 pound (453 g) beach plums
   (or 4 regular plums)
1 cup (250 ml) red wine
10 bayberry leaves
⅓ cup (67 g) sugar

Place all the ingredients in a pot over medium heat and cover. Bring the wine to a gentle simmer and cook the plums for 30 minutes (if the liquid boils, they will fall apart). Remove the fruit to a serving plate and reduce the wine over high heat until it is syrupy, about 5 minutes. Pour the strained poaching syrup over the fruit and serve at room temperature.

Black Cherry

OTHER COMMON NAMES: Wild black cherry, rum cherry

BOTANICAL NAME: *Prunus serotina*

STATUS: Indigenous but weedily prolific North American tree, mostly east of the Rockies

WHERE: Disturbed ground, forests, parks

SEASON: Late summer

USE: Fruit, spice

PARTS USED: Fruit

GROW? Yes

TASTES LIKE: Plums meet grapefruit; baked kernels taste like marzipan

Some of the professional gardeners I know describe black cherry trees as a woody and weedy nuisance. Their seedlings appear in formal rose gardens and in containerized rooftops, in manicured cemeteries and in Central Park's perennial beds. Birds love the fruit and carry it with them, and urban raccoons and possums spread the love on the ground.

The tall trees are adaptable, favoring disturbed ground and tolerating poor soil. They grow in parks and empty lots, and in sunlit patches of forest. Unlike many successful weeds, *Prunus serotina* is not an import but native to the eastern part of this continent, occurring from Nova Scotia to Texas and Florida, and spreading as far as northern South America. It has even invaded South Africa. The New York Metropolitan Flora Project, initiated by the Brooklyn Botanic Garden in 1990 to document all flora found within 50 miles of New York City, established that black cherries dominate the urban woody landscape.

This makes my foraging heart glad.

The trees become briefly conspicuous in spring, when their graceful white flowers are borne in fragrant racemes that appear once the leaves have formed (unlike their ornamental cherry cousins, whose blossoms appear before foliage emerges). The fruit occurs in pearl-sized drupes, hanging from pendulous strings. In late summer they turn a matte crimson before softening and ripening to glossy black.

Black cherries do not taste or look like domesticated cherries. Unripe and red, they are horrible. But when they are plump and black, their flavor is like a cooked plum meeting the aroma of grapefruit peel. The pit is large relative to the amount of edible flesh, so eating and preparing black cherries in quantity requires a certain resolve. You will need a lot of fruit to earn your smooth pulp and juice reward. The flavor is worth it for me. The raw, fresh juice is tartly sweet with a tannic element, and I like to shake it up immediately in cocktails or mocktails. The raw juice can also be added to sauces and stews, or sweetened and cooked into a syrup.

Common names are notoriously confusing, and my black cherry might be your chokecherry, but that common name refers to a different species—*Prunus virginiana* (and its subspecies), a smaller tree that is even more widespread. Its fruit, identical in appearance, can be used interchangeably in any of the recipes here.

Interestingly, *Prunus mahaleb*, the tree that produces the cherries whose pits yield *mahlab*, the Mediterranean spice, is used widely as a rootstock for cultivated cherries in the United States, thanks to its disease resistance. It has escaped and naturalized in many parts of the country. Its small black fruit—borne singly, or in upright, splayed clusters, not in vertical racemes—tastes similar to wild black cherries and can be used in the same way.

How to Collect and Prepare

Early in their season each raceme has just a few ripe, perfectly black cherries on it, accompanied by inedibly tannic unripe red drupes. At this stage I pick the ripe fruit off one by one. Later you will find entire racemes ripe and glossy black. Now it is easy to run your dominant hand down the stalk to funnel all the ripe fruit into the paper bag your other hand is holding.

At home, unless you are using the cherries whole, you will need to pit them. The best way to deal with the seeds is by using a food mill. Mine is the kind you balance over a bowl.

Whether you are processing the fruit raw or cooked, a fair amount of pulp is left behind in a food mill with the pits. I hate to waste that flavor. The pulp with the intact pits (see Caution) is an excellent foundation for infusions and ferments, which take on a marzipan warmth. And after you strain the liquid, the seeds remain useful: If you have the patience to crack the shells and extract the kernels, the soaked, dried, and baked kernels make an American mahlab, the bitter almond spice used in the eastern Mediterranean to flavor pastries.

Caution

If you are using the pulp with pits for infusions, discard any that have been cracked, exposing the kernel. The raw kernels are toxic. In our gut the substances they contain (like amygdalin) are converted to hydrogen cyanide; they may reach toxic levels in an infusion (this is a guess—it has never been measured, to my knowledge). Do not eat the kernels raw: For mahlab, they must be soaked and baked.

CULTIVATION TIPS
USDA Hardiness Zones 3–9

Despite its weedy reputation, black cherry is very beneficial to insects and birds (as well as humans who like its fruit, of course!). Plant black cherries in full sun for optimal fruit production and in soil that is slightly acidic. While they are tolerant of some drought, well-watered trees will deliver more fruit. *P. serotina* is large at maturity, reaching up to 80 feet. If you have a smaller garden, choose chokecherry, *P. virginiana*, which matures at less than half the size.

Black Cherry Juice

Fresh black cherry juice is startling. There is some tongue-whipping tannin there, but also black plum and grapefruit. It is a great foundation for cocktails, punches, marinades, braises, and sauces. I cannot imagine making the juice without a food mill, and even then it requires some dedication: Small fruit, big pits, lots of grinding, and some splashing. The stains are indelible. Dress wisely. The reward is the unique flavor. This is not a recipe, but an accounting of the yields you can expect. Make the largest batch you can stand, and freeze the extra in ice cube trays, storing the cubes in small bags or containers when they are ready.

1 cup black cherries weighs about 5½ ounces (156 g) and yields around ¼ cup (60 ml) juice

4 cups (620 g) fruit = 1 cup (250 ml) juice

Place the ripe fruit in the food mill's bowl. Using a coarse strainer, work it through, reversing the handle often to dislodge the pits. Scrape off any collected pulp clinging to the underside of the mill. The juice lasts in the fridge for 1 week. Freeze any excess.

August

Makes 1 drink

The first really ripe black cherries of late summer are so tempting that I always juice them. It's a lot of effort for a drink or two, but this bittersweet freshness is compelling.

3 fluid ounces (6 tablespoons) white rum

1½ fluid ounces (3 tablespoons) Black Cherry Juice

½ fluid ounce (1 tablespoon) Fermented Serviceberry Syrup

Combine all the ingredients in a shaker with ice. Shake, strain, and pour.

Sweetened Black Cherry Pulp

Makes about 1 cup (250 ml) black cherry pulp with juice

Cooked black cherry pulp has a plummy flavor with a noonday shadow of grapefruit. It is a versatile ingredient: Fold it into a whipped cream fool for dessert, add it to panna cottas and cakes, or stir it into savory braises and pan juices. If you do not own a food mill, black cherries (and elderberries) will change your mind about buying one. Seeds. So many. You *can* use a medium, single-mesh sieve, pushing the fruit through it with a large wooden spoon, but it will require a lot of elbow grease.

3 cups (465 g) black cherries
1 cup (250 ml) water
¾ cup (150 g) sugar

Place the cherries in a pot with the water and the sugar. Stir. Bring to a boil over medium-high heat. Reduce the heat to keep the liquid at a healthy simmer and cook for another 5 minutes. Turn off the heat and let the mixture cool until tepid. Place a food mill over a bowl. Pour the cherries and their juices into the food mill and push through a coarse sieve to catch the juice and pulp below. Reverse the food mill's handle often to unstick packed cherries.

If you need less than 1 cup for a recipe, store the extra pulp in bags in the freezer after freezing it into cubes.

Black Cherry Mahlab

Mahlab is a Mediterranean spice made from the kernels of *Prunus mahaleb*. It is used in small amounts, and traditionally around Easter. I first tasted it in sweet breakfast rolls bought at Sahadi's, a Middle Eastern grocery in my neighborhood. I was hooked. When they no longer stocked them, I decided to make my own from our native cherries. It is a labor-intensive process, and if you are not sure about it, order some mahlab online, or look for it in a Middle Eastern emporium—it will give you a good sense of the flavor to expect.

2 ounces (57 g) whole pits yields 1 tablespoon powdered mahlab

When you have made black cherry juice, or sweetened pulp, or a ferment, save the pits. Spread the pulp on a tray or trays and allow it to dry—this may take up to a week, depending on your conditions. Pick the pits from the pulp. With a hammer and a very hard surface, get to work to extract the kernels. Place the kernels in a bowl of water overnight or for 12 hours. Pat them dry and spread them out on a tray to air-dry for 24 hours. Now you bake them.

The baking is important for flavor but also because heat destroys substances (like amygdalin) that are converted to hydrogen cyanide in our guts. *Do not consume raw kernels.*

Preheat the oven to 300°F (150°C).

Transfer the tray to the oven for 25 minutes, shaking it several times to turn the kernels.

Remove the tray and let it cool. Once cool, the kernels can be frozen for later use or ground in a spice grinder and stored in a small jar. The flavor stays fresh if frozen.

Black Cherry Soda Pop

Makes 6 cups (1½ liters)

Black cherries make a fantastic soda. Serve with a splash of cold seltzer, or blend it with more bitter botanical libations, like Northeast No. 1 Bitters. It makes a very good long drink, with white rum and lime. Aged longer, it turns into excellent vinegar (on page 98).

3 cups (465 g) very ripe black cherries
¾ cup (150 g) sugar
6 cups (1½ liters) water

Combine the ingredients in a large glass jar and stir well. Cover the mouth of the jar with cheesecloth secured with string or a rubber band. Leave at room temperature and stir once a day. Once there is a lot of fizzing, perhaps on Day 4 or 5, strain the pop twice through a fine-mesh sieve and then through cheesecloth. Bottle and keep in the fridge. This one is volatile, and warm weather with additional fermentation in the bottle can cause an explosion.

To make vinegar, simply return the strained pop to its jar, cover with cheesecloth, and allow to sit at room temperature for 3 to 6 weeks. Gradually it will turn to vinegar as naturally occurring acetobacter get to work. A vinegar mother may or may not form, but when it tastes and smells like vinegar, it is vinegar. Strain and bottle in clean, narrow necked bottles.

Noons of Dryness

Makes 1 tall drink

A long drink at the end of the day in hot August, stirred up. Summer's black cherry cordial (fizzy, with a hint of bitterness), botanically alive vermouth, and a dash of Elderberry Gin.

4 fluid ounces (8 tablespoons) Black Cherry
   Soda Pop
3 fluid ounces (6 tablespoons) Northeast
   No. 1 Vermouth
1 fluid ounce (2 tablespoons) Elderberry Gin
1 sprig Thai basil

Fill a tall glass with ice. Pour in the ingredients and stir. Add the basil. Let it sweat for 3 minutes before sipping.

Black Cherry Rum

Makes about 4 cups (1 liter)

One of black cherry's common names is rum cherry. I make this two-step infusion with pits and the pulp left over after processing cherries for juice or pulp. *Do not use crushed pits or exposed kernels from raw cherries* (see Caution, page 44). You can also use whole fruit, if you have not done any processing. The rum is a luxurious last-minute flavor swirled into pans after cooking pork chops or pork belly, or in punches, panna cotta, and other puddings.

2 cups (500 ml) leftover whole black cherry pits and pulp
1 cup (200 g) sugar
4 cups (1 liter) rum

In a glass jar cover the pits and pulp with the sugar. Shake or stir well. Cover the mouth of the jar with cheesecloth secured with string or a rubber band. Let the jar sit at room temperature for a week, shaking every day. After a week pour the rum into the mixture and stir. Infuse for 24 hours. Strain through a fine-mesh sieve, again through cheesecloth, and decant into a glass bottle. It will keep indefinitely.

(You can use the pits one more time, for drying, roasting, and turning into Black Cherry Mahlab.)

Summer Thunder

Makes 1 drink

Black cherries are ripe in late summer when stately cumulonimbus clouds roll in. Picking the fruit after rain is a pleasure. Black Cherry Rum is sweet, so it needs some dryness, which is where the sherry helps. Sumac Vodka's sour edge keeps things fresh.

2 fluid ounces (4 tablespoons) Black Cherry Rum
2 fluid ounces (4 tablespoons) dry sherry
1 fluid ounce (2 tablespoons) Sumac Vodka

Combine in a shaker with ice. Shake, strain, and pour.

The General

Makes 1 drink

I think George Washington might have drunk something like this. Martha was all over the rum cherries. But did she know about mugwort (it appears to have arrived the previous century)?

2 fluid ounces (4 tablespoons) Black Cherry Rum
2 fluid ounces (4 tablespoons) Mugwort Raspberry Liqueur
1 fluid ounce (2 tablespoons) dry sherry

Shake them up with ice, strain, and pour.

Chopped Duck Liver with Black Cherry Rum

Makes toast for 2

This is the substantial snack you make while your spring or late-fall Spicebush Roast Duck is cooking. Of course, you can go out and buy duck livers—in which case I suggest doubling the recipe.

2 tablespoons butter, divided
2 tablespoons finely chopped shallot
4 ounces (113 g) duck liver
Large pinch salt
1 tablespoon Black Cherry Rum
2 slices sourdough boule, toasted
2 teaspoons chopped field garlic leaves

Heat 1 tablespoon of the butter over medium heat in a small skillet. Add the shallot. Cook for about 8 minutes, or until translucent with brown bits. Stir a few times. Season the duck livers with salt. Increase the heat under the skillet to medium-high. Add the duck livers and sear for 3 to 4 minutes, then turn and cook the other side. Remove the livers from the pan and rest on a plate. Add the second tablespoon of butter to the pan with the Black Cherry Rum and stir well. Chop the livers, and divide between the two pieces of toast. Top with the juices and shallot from the pan. Scatter the field garlic greens over the top.

BC Ketchup

Makes about 2 cups (500 ml)

Dark, sharp, sweet, and spicy, this black cherry concentrate is a precious condiment in our house, wonderful spread on cheese sandwiches (grilled or uncooked), sausages bursting out of their skins, cold meats that need enlivening, or just spooned into porky tacos.

4 cups (620 g) black cherries
4 cups (1 liter) water
2 tablespoons unscented oil
11 ounces (312 g) finely chopped onion
3 tablespoons tomato paste
¾ cup (150 g) sugar
¾ teaspoon salt
¼ cup plus 2 tablespoons (90 ml)
    Elderflower Vinegar
10 bayberry leaves
3 chipotle chiles
20 spicebush fruit
4 cloves
1 teaspoon black peppercorns

Combine the cherries and the water in a pot and place over medium heat. Bring to a brief boil and turn off the heat. Cool completely. Strain off the liquid and reserve. Process the fruit through a food mill into a bowl set below. Combine the reserved cooking liquid and strained juice and pulp in one bowl.

Warm the oil over medium heat in the pot. Add the onion and sauté for 10 minutes, stirring occasionally. Add the tomato paste and cook for 2 minutes to allow it to caramelize. Pour in the reserved cherry juices, and add the sugar, salt, Elderflower Vinegar, bayberry, and chipotle. Tie the spicebush, cloves, and peppercorns into a piece of cheesecloth and add those to the liquid. Bring to a simmer and cook gently for 30 minutes. Turn off the heat. Fish out the bayberry leaves, the chipotles, and the cheesecloth bag (squeeze to extract trapped flavor). Chop up the softened chipotles (if you do not want all their heat, scrape out the seeds). Return them to the pot. Transfer the liquid in a couple of batches to a blender and process until smooth. Strain back into the wiped pot through a medium-mesh sieve. Place the pot over medium heat and bring to a gentle boil. Cook until the liquid has reduced by about half and is quite thick (but just pourable), stirring occasionally—this will take about an hour. Pour into clean jars *and keep in the fridge.* It lasts well for months. But you will eat it before then.

Spiced Cornish Hens with Black Cherry and Bayberry Leaves

Serves 4

The combination of wild summer fruit juices and red wine with bayberry and bacon turns these little chickens almost gamy. The recipe works for quail, too. White sweet clover (*Melilotus albus*) is an opportunistic weed that blooms from midsummer, and its flowers are powerfully fragrant and honey-like when introduced to heat. About 20 flower stalks yield 1 tablespoon of stripped flowers.

¾ cup (190 ml) Black Cherry Juice

2 tablespoons Elderberry Juice

⅓ cup (80 ml) red wine

½ teaspoon black pepper

32 bayberry leaves

4 Cornish hens

20 white sweet clover flowers, on the stalk

½ teaspoon salt

3 slices bacon

2 tablespoons butter

3 ounces (85 g) very finely chopped shallots

1 tablespoon stripped white sweet clover flowers

4 slices sourdough toast

Preheat the oven to 400°F (200°C).

Combine the juices, red wine, and pepper in a jug.

Place 8 bayberry leaves inside each bird's cavity, along with 5 white sweet clover sprigs and a pinch of salt. Tie the legs together. Cover the hens' breasts with half a slice of bacon each. Place the birds in a skillet or low-sided dish that accommodates them. Dice the third slice of bacon. Add the butter, the diced bacon, and the shallots to the skillet, and pour half the juice blend over the birds. Transfer to the oven and roast for 45 minutes.

Remove the birds from the oven and transfer to a platter to rest for 10 minutes, covered.

Place the skillet over medium-high heat. Add the rest of the juice blend with ¼ cup (60 ml) of water. Bring the liquid to a boil, stirring well to dislodge the good brown bits. Tilt each bird over the pan and pour its accumulated cavity juices into the pan. Add the tablespoon of white sweet clover flowers to the pan and cook at a simmer for 2 more minutes. Taste the pan juices and season, if necessary.

Serve with the toast to accompany the crispy bacon, for sopping up the sauce (and for wiping fingers).

Mugwort and Black Cherry Roasted Pork Loin

Serves 4

Lean pork is infused with mugwort and black cherries and wrapped in a cloak of fatty bacon. After roasting, a slosh of Black Cherry Rum ignites and deglazes the pan. Serve with Sweetfern Polenta.

1½ pounds (680 g) pork loin
   (1 large or 2 small)
1 teaspoon Mugwort Salt
6 mugwort sprigs
3 tablespoons Sweetened Black Cherry Pulp
Black pepper
6 slices bacon, cut thickly
2 tablespoons butter
¼ cup (60 ml) Black Cherry Rum

Preheat the oven to 500°F (260°C).

Season the pork loins with the Mugwort Salt. Arrange mugwort leaves from the sprigs along the top of the pork. Drizzle the Sweetened Black Cherry Pulp over them. Season liberally with black pepper. Wrap the bacon pieces around the pork.

Heat the butter in a skillet over medium-high heat. Lay the wrapped pork in the skillet. Sear for a couple of minutes and turn. Transfer at once to the hot oven for 12 to 15 minutes. Remove from the oven and place the skillet on the stove over medium-high heat. Keeping your face away from the skillet, pour in the rum. If it does not ignite at once, light it with a match. Allow the flames to die down, and taste the pan juices. They should be about perfect, but add a little salt if necessary. Turn off the heat and cover the skillet, allowing the pork to rest for 15 minutes. Carve it into medium slices, spoon over some juices, and serve.

Black Cherry Granita

Serves 6 in liqueur glasses

This intense summer granita is made from lightly cooked cherries scented with mint and white rum. A food mill is indispensable.

4 cups (620 g) ripe black cherries
2 cups (500 ml) water
½ cup (100 g) sugar
¼ cup (60 ml) Black Cherry Rum
¼ cup (60 ml) lime juice
8 sprigs mint (the tips of each stem)

In a pot over high heat, bring the cherries and water to a simmer. Cook for 10 minutes. Turn off the heat. Strain off the juice and reserve. Work the still-warm cherries through a food mill set on coarse grind. Add the saved cooked juice to the freshly milled juice and the sugar. Stir to dissolve and then taste, adding some more sugar if you like. Stir in the rum, the lime juice, and the mint. Let sit for an hour.

Remove the mint and pour the juice into a shallow dish where it does not reach more than 2 inches (5 cm) deep (to make a smooth sorbet, use an ice cream maker instead). Cover the dish, and place it in the freezer. After 2 hours use a fork to scratch up the crystals that are forming on the edges and pull them to the middle. Cover and return to the freezer. Scratch every hour or so until the granita is fluffily granular. Just before serving give it one last scratch.

Mahlab Clafoutis

Makes 1 clafoutis

This simple dessert is a beautiful way to enjoy perfectly fresh in-season *domestic* cherries (even I can't eat a wild black cherry clafoutis—too many pits) without changing their character. The mahlab from their wild cherry cousins adds a note of marzipan. (I like to keep cherry pits in the bigger fruit as they add even more flavor, but pit them if you are worried about tooth lawsuits.)

2½ cups (388 g) ripe domestic cherries
2 large eggs plus 1 egg yolk
4 tablespoons sugar
4 tablespoons flour
½ teaspoon Black Cherry Mahlab
⅛ teaspoon salt
1½ cups (375 ml) whole milk

Preheat the oven to 350°F (180°F). Butter a 10-inch (25 cm) tart dish.

Scatter the cherries across the bottom of the dish.

In a mixing bowl whisk the eggs, egg yolk, and sugar. Add the flour gradually. The mixture must be very smooth. Whisk in the mahlab and salt. Slowly pour and stir in the milk, switching from a whisk to a wooden spoon.

Pour the batter gently over the cherries and slide into the oven. Bake until the center of the clafoutis is just set (it should barely wobble when shoved), about 35 minutes.

Mahlab and Plum Cake

Makes 1 cake

The first fresh batch of mahlab can be made in time for plum season. Best served warm from the oven, with ice cream or whipped cream.

3 medium plums (about 4 ounces/113 g
   each), pits removed, quartered
4 ounces (113 g) unsalted butter,
   plus extra for buttering
½ cup (100 g) sugar
2 large eggs
1 cup (120 g) all-purpose flour
1½ teaspoons baking powder
1 teaspoon Black Cherry Mahlab
⅛ teaspoon salt
¼ cup (60 ml) buttermilk

Heat the oven to 325°F (170°C).

Place the plums on a lightly oiled baking sheet and roast in the oven for 40 minutes. When you remove them turn the heat up to 350°F (180°F).

Butter an 8-inch (20 cm) springform pan. Line the bottom of the dish with a circle of parchment paper.

In a bowl beat the butter and sugar until pale and fluffy. Add the eggs with a dusting of flour and mix well. Add the rest of the flour, baking powder, mahlab, salt, and buttermilk, stirring well.

Spread a thin layer of the batter in the bottom of the pan. Arrange the roasted plum quarters in circles around the pie dish, skin-sides down. Add the rest of the batter and smooth into all the spaces between the plums.

Slide into the oven and bake until risen and pale golden, with juices oozing, 45 to 50 minutes.

Remove from the oven and let cool for a few minutes. Release the spring. Place a serving plate on top of the cake and invert the cake swiftly. Peel the parchment off. Eat warm.

Black Locust

OTHER COMMON NAMES: Acacia, false acacia

BOTANICAL NAME: *Robinia pseudoacacia*

STATUS: Southeastern and northeastern native trees, but widespread

WHERE: Street trees, gardens, forests, parks

SEASON: Late spring

USE: Aromatic, fresh ingredient

PARTS USED: Flowers

GROW? Maybe

TASTES LIKE: The sweet taste and scent are unique

One of the many excitements on a forager's calendar in late spring is the ephemeral and much-anticipated appearance of black locust blossoms, festooning trees just when roses and clematis and peonies are peaking in gardens. You have to pounce the second you see them in bloom, while the flowers are fresh. Luckily for me, a city the size of New York has diverse micro climates, allowing for a succession of bloom and giving me a few extra days to make my way around the boroughs as sightings are called in.

Clusters of white flowers drip from these tall native trees, perfuming the air for miles. Planted as street trees in Brooklyn, they improve the smell of the urban grid immeasurably for a delicious week (later, the lindens take over). While they hail from the southeast United States, they occur widely in North America, thanks to civic planting.

Black locusts are also an integral part of the European landscape. These American natives made such an impression that they were introduced there in the early seventeenth century and were happy enough to naturalize. Their ability to fix nitrogen meant that they could colonize poor soils, while their high seed production rate as well as ability to reproduce by suckering ensured that they became what is now considered a highly invasive species. The trees' hard and rot-resistant wood ensured that they were planted as timber centuries ago on that continent, where they are often viewed as locally indigenous, especially in central Europe (Hungarians claim the tree as their own). The imported and expensive "acacia honey" sold in the States is in fact black locust honey, sent back over the Atlantic.

Acacia honey is rather mild for my taste. Unlike chestnut honey, which conveys the essence of that flower, black locust's best attribute is muted somehow by bee digestion.

As with other scented edible flowers, I find the best way of capturing their unique scent, by far, is in either a cold-infused syrup (heat kills delicate flavors) or a fermented cordial (and I call it a

cordial because it is meant to be drunk diluted). These then form the base of recipes whose limit is only the scope of your imagination.

The flowers themselves have a luscious presence in terms of texture—not all edible flowers do. The pea-like blossoms offer a silky crunch and yield a delectable sweetness. I like them best raw and can't bring myself to cook them with pleasure. An exception is the traditional European acacia beignet. Like Elderflower Fritters, these are a rare treat. The first time I made them (from blooms collected on Staten Island), my French husband's face lit up. They disappeared rapidly. I drizzle them with a double-infused honey—that pale acacia honey infused with the fresh flowers overnight. Frying flowers is inherently silly; all you are really tasting is good, crisp batter (though that in itself is a reward). But the whimsy of catching the fragile season in a mouthful carries a nostalgic weight that overrides the scrutiny of cold, calorie-counting logic.

How to Collect and Prepare

Harvesting the flowers is simple. Pick open clusters and collect them in a basket or paper bags (plastic makes them sweat, which is not good for perfume retention). Make sure to select perfectly fresh flowers, ignoring bunches with withered blooms. The closed white buds are also good to eat but have not yet developed the aroma, if a cordial or syrup is your goal.

At home, use them as soon as possible, to make the most of their delicious scent. Process flowers for infusions quickly, or the scent will dissipate. If you must, keep the fresh flowers in a paper bag overnight, folded tightly closed, but do not refrigerate. Washing them will dilute the perfume, too, so just give them a shake to discourage any small critters.

If you are saving flowers for fritters or salads, the clusters will keep fresh for several days in a covered bowl or wrapped in a plastic bag in the fridge. You will lose scent but not texture.

Caution

Another tree, Kentucky yellowwood (*Cladrastis kentukea*), has very similar—*and* fragrant— flowers, as well as compound leaves, like black locust. It is far less widely spread than black locust but blooms at the same time. I strongly suspect that it has been collected by foragers who have mistaken it for black locust. A quick "tell" is to look at each leaflet. On Kentucky yellowwood the leaflets are distinctly pointed at the tips. On black locust the more numerous leaflets are rounder; the two sides of each meet at the tip like lips ready for a kiss (that is my scientific description, yes). The flower clusters of Kentucky yellowwood are looser and skinnier looking and less plush than black locust's. Finally, there is a bright yellow center spot on the upper hood of Kentucky yellowwood's flowers, whereas the spot on black locust is lime or pale green. Having said all that, I do not know if the yellowwood flowers will hurt you.

CULTIVATION TIPS
USDA Hardiness Zones 3–8

Despite its native American status, and because it can grow in a wide variety of sites, including in barren soil (it is a nitrogen fixer), black locust, like black cherry, is sometimes viewed as invasive. It also grows very large, so plant only if you have a lot of room. Grow black locust in full sun for best flower production. Prune off any suckers that occur near its base or away from the tree.

May Wine with Black Locust Flowers

Makes 7 cups (1¾ liters)

In this fortified and floral wine infusion, American black locust blossoms replace the traditional sweet woodruff used in European recipes. It is very easy quaffing on a balmy late-spring evening. It also keeps well, bottled and chilled, like a pared-down vermouth.

2 bottles dry, fruity unwooded white wine

¾ cup (190 ml) vodka

4 cups (80 g) black locust blossoms, stripped from stalks

¼ cup Concentrated Wisteria Syrup (or substitute sugar)

2 pieces lemon zest, each 2 inches (5 cm) long

Combine all the ingredients in a large carafe and mix well. Infuse overnight. Strain and chill before serving as an aperitif.

Black Locust Flower Cordial

Makes 6 cups (1½ liters)

Boiling flowers in syrups kills the flavor you are trying to preserve. Making a fermented cordial, however, allows you to catch and keep black locust's ephemeral late-spring scent. The cordial—like elderflower in method, but with its own distinctive flavor—can then be used diluted in drinks or stirred into desserts like panna cottas and ice creams. When I do not have enough flowers in one harvest, I begin the cordial with the first day's catch and add to it over the next couple of days. This is better than keeping the flowers I do have in the fridge, where they lose their vitality. The ferment simply grows in strength.

5½ cups (110 g) flowers, stripped from stalks

1 pound (453 g) sugar

6 cups (1½ liters) water

Peel of 1 lemon

1 teaspoon lemon salt (citric acid)

Pack the flowers into a clean glass jar. Add the sugar, water, and lemon peel and stir well with a long, clean spoon. Cover loosely with cheesecloth secured with string or a rubber band. Keep at room temperature and stir daily until it begins to fizz (usually on Day 3, but it may take 2 to 5 days), then give it another day. Strain. Stir in the lemon salt. Bottle in clean bottles and keep in the fridge. (Even with the lemon salt, fermentation can continue. Accumulated gases in a room-temperature bottle can cause it to explode.)

Santa Robinia (Black Locust Liqueur)

Makes 4 cups (1 liter)

The sweetness of black locust flowers is remarkably translated into high-proof alcohol, as I discovered happily one spring with this creation. Sipped on its own, poured over ice with lemon zest, or shaken up and strained into a coupe frosted with a rim of Sumac Sugar, it is unique.

6 cups (120 g) black locust flowers,
   stripped from stalks
4 cups (1 liter) good vodka
⅓ cup sugar (67 g)

Combine all the ingredients in a large, clean jar. Swirl it to dissolve the sugar. Close the jar and let it sit at a cool room temperature for 10 weeks. The liquid will slowly turn sepia.

Strain it through a fine-mesh sieve. Squeeze out the flowers by hand to make sure you capture as much liquid as possible. Strain again through muslin. Bottle in clean jars.

Steamy Shore

Makes 1 drink

Floral black locust is given a light whipping by sour Sumac Vodka. Herbal vermouth mediates and smooths. The intensely sweet-and-sour sugar rim tempts you to lick it all off before you've reached the drink.

FOR THE RIM

1 tablespoon lime juice

2 teaspoons Sumac Sugar

DRINK

2 fluid ounces (4 tablespoons) Santa Robinia

2 fluid ounces (4 tablespoons) Sumac Vodka

1 fluid ounce (2 tablespoons) Northeast
  No. 1 Vermouth

Place the lime juice in one saucer. Sprinkle the Sumac Sugar in another. Dip the glass's edges gently in the lime juice, then in the sugar. Set aside for a minute to dry.

Combine the liquors in a shaker with ice. Shake, strain, and pour.

Black Locust and Pickled Field Garlic Flower Couscous

Serves 4 as a side

Unlike many edible flowers, black locust blossoms and wisteria (which you can substitute in this salad) have a really good crunchy texture. I love their snap-pea-like sweetness in a salad of mellow couscous. If you do not have tender greenbrier (*Smilax* species) tendrils, you can use young grape tendrils or sheep sorrel leaves. This dish is shown on the cover.

2 cups (500 ml) water

1 tablespoon extra-virgin olive oil

10 ounces (283 g) quick-cooking couscous

½ teaspoon Ground Elder Salt

1½ cups (30 g) fresh black locust flowers,
  picked off the stalks

2 ounces (57 g) tender greenbrier tips

6 Pickled Field Garlic Flowers
  (or pickled chive flowers)

Bring the water to a boil in a pot. Add the olive oil and the couscous. Turn off the heat, add the salt, and cover. Let the couscous steam for about 5 minutes as it absorbs the water. Lift the lid and gently scratch the entire surface of the couscous with a fork, gradually working deeper as you loosen up the grains. When all the couscous has been fluffed up, transfer it to a bowl to cool. When it is close to room temperature, add the black locust flowers and greenbrier tips. Toss. Tear up the Pickled Field Garlic Flowers or chive flowers and add them. Toss again. Serve at once, or chill until you are ready to eat.

Black Locust Fritters

Serves 4

A traditional dish in Europe (where the trees, known as acacia, have been growing since the seventeenth century), these fritters are often made with a beer batter. I prefer the crisp sweetness of hard apple cider, which supports the perfume of the blossoms. I think fritters are too rich to eat after a meal. I would serve them midmorning or midafternoon to hungry people.

3 ounces (85 g) all-purpose flour
⅛ teaspoon salt
1 tablespoon sugar
5½ fluid ounces (160 ml) hard apple cider
5 fluid ounces (150 ml) unscented oil
20 black locust flower clusters
1 tablespoon powdered sugar
¼ cup (60 ml) acacia honey (optional)

In a bowl combine the dry ingredients. Whisk in the cold apple cider. Let the mixture rest in the fridge for 30 minutes. Heat the oil over medium-high heat in a skillet (test with a drop of the batter—if it floats and sizzles at once, the oil is hot enough).

Dip each cluster of flowers delicately into the batter. Do not drown it. Shake off the excess batter; you don't want to end up with a doughy lump of gloop (technical culinary term). Lay each cluster in the hot oil, frying about 5 or 6 at a time. Turn after about 1 minute—each side should be dark gold. Lay on paper towels to absorb the extra oil. When they are all done, pile the clusters onto a serving plate, dust with the powdered sugar, and serve immediately. If you are using acacia honey, drizzle it over them now.

Burdock

OTHER COMMON NAME: Gobo

BOTANICAL NAMES: *Arctium minus, A. lappa*

STATUS: Invasive biennial weed, widespread in western and eastern US and Canada

WHERE: Open ground, gardens, occasional supermarkets, Chinatowns

SEASON: Spring, late fall

USE: Vegetable

PARTS USED: Taproot and immature stem

GROW? If you have the room and the soft soil

TASTES LIKE: Globe artichoke heart meets Jerusalem artichoke

Most people know burdock as a weed that generates a flurry of tenaciously lockjawed and persistent seed capsules (their hook-and-loop design inspired the invention, famously, of Velcro, in 1950s England).

In culinary terms, burdock is better known as gobo (*Arctium lappa*), cultivated for millennia in Japan for its impressively long, starchy taproot, whose earthiness lends itself to cold-weather comfort cooking, providing a backdrop of gently sweet carbohydrate satisfaction for sauces and stews. In wild plants the root is good to eat late in the first year, or in its second spring, becoming more fibrous late in its last season. But unearthing a 2- to 3-foot taproot whose last desire is to remain in the earth requires exceptional determination and good digging skills. If you have the time, the spade, and the patience, go for it. And if you have seen sturdy cultivated gobo sold at market, wild-dug specimens, usually the smaller *A. minus*, will seem rather thin. I admit that after an annual exertion at digging them, I find myself heading to Manhattan's Chinatown, where their fatter, 4-foot-long domesticated cousins are sold in stores where nothing is labeled in English. A different sort of foraging.

The roots contain indigestible inulin. Not a fact I had managed to glean in any foraging guides. So it took a couple of uncomfortable post-burdock-dinner evenings to recognize the symptoms: Jerusalem artichoke syndrome—gas attack. I grow those for the table and learned to disarm them by parboiling or soaking (if I am using them raw). Inulin is water-soluble. Pour off the water, pour off the problem.

I assuage my lazy root-digging conscience by telling myself that uprooting that first-year plant also means depriving myself of burdock's second edible stage: the luscious immature flowering stems. Appearing in late spring, they are a delicious and very easily foraged wild food. Cooked, they are a semantic and gustatory marriage of globe and Jerusalem artichokes. Prime harvest height is between 1 and 3 feet, although the actual measurement is meaningless, rather an indication of what to look for. The stem should

CULTIVATION TIPS
USDA Hardiness Zones 3–7

Often described as a biennial, burdock in fact lives two or three seasons, producing flowers and seed in its second or third year. Because it is invasively abundant where I live and because my garden is small—each plant has a spread of about 3 feet—this is not a crop I grow; it is a vegetable for large spaces or cultivated farm fields. Burdock can be grown in virtually any soil, but harvesting is much easier if your soil is light and a little sandy. (If you have ever dug wild burdock you will know that removing the taproot intact from compacted soil is a huge, calorie-shedding mission.) The plants will grow in full sun to dappled, high shade. Sow seeds in fall or in early spring. Once a first-year rosette has filled out nicely, with large leaves, the taproot can be harvested in the plant's first late fall. The flowering stem generally appears in the plant's second full growing season, in midspring. Collect any unharvested stems before they set seed, to prevent invasion.

still be immature and actively growing—in the meristem stage—or it will be wildly fibrous. By the time it has begun to produce laterals, on its way to making flowers, it is too late. The best stalks remain hidden within the green depths of the wide leaves. And the stouter, the better.

Raw, the peeled stem is succulent and crisp. When cooked, it absorbs the flavors to which you introduce it and caramelizes beautifully when sautéed with oil or butter. I prepare the stems, cut into inch-long pieces, à la grecque, adding white wine, lemon juice, fennel fronds, coriander seeds, and extra-virgin olive oil at the last minute, to turn the cooking liquid into a glossy emulsion. To stretch a precious supply of burdock, I may add whole garlic cloves or disks of sweet carrot. To trick and entertain a dinner guest, sliver the stems lengthwise and blanch before sautéing and adding to identical linguine, finishing them in the bowl with a cloud of microplaned bottarga (or Mugwort-Cured Egg Yolks). Miso and soy are natural partners for the stems, cooked whole and served like pale, supple asparagus on a warm platter.

The peeled midribs of the large leaves are a crisp and worthwhile vegetable in their own right, chopped and raw in any sort of salad, or pickled.

By collecting burdock you are disarming this invasive plant of its reproductive arsenal and saving civic employees and landowners the time and trouble of rooting them up or spraying them down with herbicides.

Very, very gradually, I see the roots appearing at greenmarkets, foraged by curious and enterprising farmers. I look forward to knowing that every year bunches of burdock stems will also be considered standard late-spring fare.

How to Collect and Prepare

To collect the stems, begin by lopping off the leaves that radiate from them. Cut the stem as low as possible to the ground, and discard the very skinny top. You can keep some of the leaves' midribs, filleting them on the spot—just strip the leaf from each midrib.

Peeling is key. If you happen to lick your fingers after working with any aboveground parts of burdock, you will recoil. Horribly bitter. Some foragers collect and eat the young leaves, but you have to boil them to death to get rid of the bitterness, and I hardly see the point.

If you have ever groomed a globe artichoke for the table, you have what it takes to prepare a burdock stem. You have passed through the valley of the shadow of peeling. Every bit of green must be stripped and trimmed from the stem to reveal the core, or pith, which is pale cream and tender. With fat stalks this is easy, the fibrous parts pulling off like celery strings. You do lose a lot of volume. To give you a sense: 8 ounces (227 g) of prepared burdock stems is the yield from 1½ pounds (680 g)

unpeeled. So do not leave any stalks behind in your burdock patch. You will need them all. Like globe artichokes, the peeled parts will discolor. If this bothers you, drop them into a bowl of acidulated water as you work. Unlike the roots, the stems do not need to be soaked or parboiled.

Digging the roots is easiest in early winter or early spring when the ground is workable but before the new leaves have appeared. Dig deeply, straight down, all around the burdock crown. It is unavoidable sometimes to sever the root. Once you have dug as deep as you can, angle your shovel under, tilt, and lift. At home, scrub the roots well and trim off any whiskery side roots, but do not remove the flavorful skin. If you are making pickles, soak the shredded or cut root in water for at least an hour before rinsing and pickling. If you are cooking, cut the roots into sections 2 inches (5 cm) long or less and parboil for 45 minutes, discarding the water.

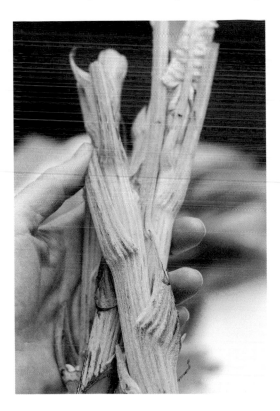

Burdock Root Pickles

Makes about 2½ cups (625 ml)

I first made these pickles as part of a pickle smorgasbord for a Lunar New Year party. They were surprisingly popular. No foragers were present, but the pickles disappeared in a flash. Soak the burdock root to avoid later tummy troubles, from inulin-induced distress.

8 ounces (227 g) burdock root, scrubbed

1 cup (250 ml) soy sauce

½ cup (125 ml) sherry vinegar

1 cup (250 ml) water

3 tablespoons sugar

1 teaspoon salt

1 teaspoon crushed prickly ash husks

Cut the burdock root into thin slices, lengthwise. Stack the slices on top of one another and cut again into matchstick thicknesses (they should be as long as your chosen pickling jar is tall). Rinse in a bowl of water. Empty the bowl and fill with fresh water. Soak for 1 hour. Drain, and pack the burdock upright into a jar or jars. In a jug combine the soy sauce, vinegar, water, sugar, and salt. Stir until the granules have dissolved. Pour the brine into the jar to reach the top. Add the prickly ash. Screw the lid on and marinate for a minimum of 2 hours. Simply drain to serve.

Beef and Burdock Root Osso Buco

Serves 4

A homely stew, this is very welcome in chilly weather. Instead of veal, use budget-friendly and underrated beef shins. It is delicious on Day 1 but tastes even better on Day 2, after cooling its heels (shins!) in the fridge overnight. Serve sprinkled with Ground Elder Gremolata in season—it will be less pale.

4 pieces beef shin (about 4 pounds/
    1.75 kg—1 piece per person)

2 tablespoons flour

½ teaspoon salt

Black pepper

8 bayberry leaves (or 1 regular bay leaf)

8 ounces (227 g) peeled burdock root,
    cut into 1-inch (2½ cm) pieces

2 heads fennel, finely chopped

2 medium carrots, finely chopped

2 cups (500 ml) white wine

6 sprigs mugwort leaves or seedheads

Preheat the oven to 350°F (180°C).

Place the beef shins in a large Dutch oven. Dust them with the flour and season with salt and pepper. Add the bayberry leaves. Cover and cook in the oven for 1½ hours. While the meat is cooking, bring a pot of water to a boil and cook the burdock in it for 45 minutes. Drain, and reserve.

Remove the beef from the oven. Add the burdock, fennel, carrots, white wine, and mugwort to the pot. Cover and return to the oven for another 2½ hours. Taste for seasoning after an hour and adjust, if necessary. Serve in wide bowls, with spoons.

Beef Cheeks with Burdock Root, Cocoa, and Ramps

Serves 4

Lowly and often underpriced beef cheeks are succulent when braised slowly in moist heat. Hearty burdock root and spring ramps make this a rewarding stew for a chilly spring night. Goes well with Garlic Mustard Root Relish or Lacto-Fermented Garlic Mustard.

6 ounces (170 g) burdock root, scrubbed and cut into 2-inch (5 cm) lengths

4 beef cheeks (about 2½ pounds/1.1 kg)

¼ teaspoon salt

12 ramps

½ cup (125 ml) dry sherry

2 tablespoons sherry vinegar

⅓ cup (80 ml) water

1½ teaspoons sugar

2 teaspoons cocoa powder

Place the burdock pieces into a pot of cold water, cover, and bring to a boil before reducing the heat to a simmer for 45 minutes. Drain the roots and reserve.

Preheat the oven to 400°F (200°C).

Trim the beef cheeks of any loose connective tissue, loose fat, or veins. Season with the salt. Place the beef in a Dutch oven with the ramps and drained burdock root. In a bowl whisk together the sherry, sherry vinegar, water, sugar, and cocoa powder. Pour over the meat. Cover the pot and place in the oven. Cook for 40 minutes, then reduce the heat to 300°F (150°C). Cook another 2 hours. When it is ready the meat should be sticky and tender, easily broken apart with a fork. Taste the juices for seasoning and add a little more salt if necessary.

Burdock Root and Beef Short Rib Hotpot with Mugwort

Serves 4

Burdock and beef are two strong ingredients presenting endless possibilities. The soy-turmeric-ginger triumvirate never gets old for me, and here the addition of galangal and miso send this simple hotpot into the realm of super umami.

6 ounces (170 g) burdock root, scrubbed and cut into 2-inch (5 cm) pieces

2 boneless beef short ribs (about 1 pound/ 453 g each), each cut into 3–4 pieces

3 tablespoons white miso

2 cups (500 ml) red wine

2 tablespoons soy sauce

1 thumb-length piece of turmeric, peeled and chopped

1 tablespoon grated galangal

2 teaspoons grated ginger

2 teaspoons sugar

2 tablespoons dried mugwort leaves

Place the burdock pieces into a pot of cold water, cover, and bring to a boil before reducing the heat to a simmer for 45 minutes. Drain the roots and reserve.

Place a Dutch oven over medium-high heat. When it is hot add the pieces of beef in batches and sear till the meat is brown on two sides, about 1 minute per side. In a small bowl thin the miso to a slurry with a little of the red wine. Add the miso, wine, soy sauce, turmeric, galangal, ginger, sugar, and mugwort to the saucepan with the beef and stir well. Add the burdock. Bring the liquid to a simmer and reduce the heat. Cover and cook over low heat at a simmer for 3 hours.

Burdock and Turkey Meatball Curry

Serves 4

These tender meatballs in a richly aromatic curry marry Southeast Asian influences with foraged botanicals. Earthy and slightly sweet burdock root absorbs the flavors beautifully.

SAUCE

1 pound (453 g) burdock root, scrubbed and cut into 2-inch (5 cm) pieces

2 tablespoons unscented oil

3 shallots, halved

6 field garlic bulbs

1 ounce (28 g) chopped cilantro stems

2 tablespoons grated ginger

1 lemongrass heart, halved

1 teaspoon ground green prickly ash

⅓ cup (80 ml) Sumac Essence

2 tablespoons fish sauce

TURKEY MEATBALLS

2 pounds (907 g) ground turkey

½ cup (30 g) panko bread crumbs

2 lemongrass hearts, exceptionally finely chopped

1 ounce (28 g) finely snipped field garlic greens

6 field garlic bulbs, very finely chopped

2 tablespoons fish sauce

2 tablespoons lime juice

½ teaspoon sugar

1 large egg

3 tablespoons unscented oil

FOR THE SAUCE: Place the burdock pieces into a pot of cold water, cover, and bring to a boil before reducing the heat to a simmer for 45 minutes. Drain the roots and reserve.

Heat the oil over medium-high heat. Add the shallots and field garlic and sauté, reducing the heat to medium for 10 minutes. Add the cooked burdock, cilantro, grated ginger, lemongrass, and prickly ash. Stir and cook for another 2 minutes. Add 5 cups (1.3 liters) of water, the Sumac Essence, and the fish sauce. Stir well. Increase the heat and bring to a boil. Simmer for 30 minutes. Taste and adjust the seasoning if necessary.

FOR THE MEATBALLS: Combine all the ingredients (except the oil) in a large bowl and mix very well. I like large meatballs for this curry, about 2 inches (5 cm) in diameter. Form the meatballs, place them on a plate, cover, and refrigerate from 1 to 12 hours.

Remove the meatballs from the fridge 30 minutes before cooking them.

Heat the oil in a skillet over high heat and add the meatballs in batches, cooking just long enough to brown them—about 5 minutes. When they are all brown add them (with any accumulated juices) to the simmering sauce. Increase the heat to maintain a healthy simmer, and cook for 8 to 10 minutes, until cooked through.

Serve in bowls, with a side of steamed rice.

Burdock Stem, Pokeweed, Asparagus, and Pea Stew

Serves 4 as an appetizer

I fell in love with berbere when I waitressed at an Eritrean restaurant in New Haven. This East African riff on a midspring vegetable stew can be further improvised with ramps, fava beans, artichoke hearts—or even a morel or two, if you have been lucky! Preparing each vegetable takes a little planning, but the integrity of their flavor at the end is worth the finessing.

If you cannot find berbere (which is a blend of spices), substitute paprika or píment d'espelette with a pinch of cinnamon.

4 burdock stems, peeled and cut into
  3-inch (7½ cm) pieces
8 asparagus spears, cut into thirds
2 teaspoons plus 1 tablespoon olive oil,
  divided
4 pokeweed shoots
1 cup (150 g) peas
1 tablespoon berbere pepper
1 tablespoon lemon juice
½ teaspoon Ramp Leaf Salt

Preheat the oven to 450°F (230°C).

Bring a pot of water to a boil and cook the burdock pieces until barely tender, about 6 minutes, depending on the thickness of the stems. Drain and reserve.

Roast the asparagus in a skillet in the hot oven with 2 teaspoons of the olive oil for 12 to 15 minutes, shaking the skillet once to turn them. Add the burdock to the roasting asparagus for the last 5 minutes.

Prepare the pokeweed shoots by peeling any red membranes from them and slicing the shoots into 4-inch (10 cm) pieces. Keep the tips with young leaves intact. Bring a pot of water to a boil over high heat. Drop in the pokeweed pieces and cook for 3 minutes. Remove the poke, refresh under cold water, pat dry, and reserve.

Cook the peas in boiling water until barely tender, about 5 minutes. Drain and reserve.

In a large skillet heat the remaining 1 tablespoon of olive oil over medium-high heat. Add all the vegetables, cook for a minute, and toss. Sprinkle the berbere over them and toss again. Add the lemon juice, and Ramp Leaf Salt to taste. Give one more toss to coat everything evenly. Serve alone or with crunchy bread.

Burdock Stem and Preserved Lemon Sauce

Serves 2

Peeling burdock stems is time consuming, but transforming the tough-looking stalks into this succulent topping for tender egg yolk pasta is very rewarding.

8 ounces (227 g) prepared burdock stems
   (about 1½ pounds/680 g unpeeled)
½ preserved lemon, rind only
2 tablespoons butter
1 tablespoon fresh lemon juice
½ cup (125 ml) water
Salt
Black pepper
9 ounces (255 g) egg yolk linguine
½ cup (30 g) microplaned
   Parmigiano-Reggiano

Cut the burdock stems into thin rounds. Dice the preserved lemon very finely. Melt the butter in a saucepan over medium heat; when it foams, add the burdock. Sauté until the burdock rounds begin to take some color. Add the lemon juice and the preserved lemon and stir well. Add the water and continue to cook until the water has evaporated, 10 to 12 minutes. Taste a piece of burdock. Season with salt if needed (the preserved lemon is very salty). Add fresh-cracked black pepper. Keep warm.

Meanwhile, bring a pot of salted water to a boil over high heat. Add the fresh pasta and cook at a boil until just tender, about 10 minutes. Drain the pasta. Either add the pasta to the pan with the burdock and toss well, or mound the pasta onto individual (warm) plates before topping it with the burdock. Finish with the microplaned Parmigiano-Reggiano.

Burdock Stems in Soy

Serves 4 as a side, 2 as an entrée

Crisp burdock stems caramelize tenderly with soy sauce in this plate-licking relish for steamed sticky rice or barley.

1 pound (453 g) prepared burdock stems
   (approximately 12 stems, or 3 pounds/
   1.3 kg, before peeling)
2½ cups (625 ml) water
⅓ cup (80 ml) soy sauce
2 ancho chiles
2 tablespoons lime juice
2 tablespoons sugar

Slice the peeled burdock stems into 2-inch (5 cm) pieces. In a saucepan over medium heat, combine all the ingredients and simmer until the sauce is syrupy, about 1 hour. Check occasionally to make sure that the syrup has not dried up and started scorching—add a little water if necessary. Serve warm or cool with sticky rice.

Braised Artichokes Stuffed with Burdock

Serves 2 as an entrée, 4 as an appetizer

A couple of times a season I torture myself with globe artichokes (and then remember, with massive nostalgia, the streets of Istanbul where vendors clean them right in front of you, handing you a bag of peeled, naked artichoke hearts—a gesture of exquisite civility). Stuffing a plucked artichoke heart with peeled burdock is something of a culinary pun, since their textures, flavors, and preparation have a few things in common. Peas and garlic scapes are added for sweetness, and it is all finished with carroty ground elder flowers.

3 tablespoons extra-virgin olive oil, divided

4 cloves garlic, cut into matchsticks

4 large artichokes, leaves broken off, cut above the heart, hairs scraped out

¼ teaspoon salt

2 teaspoons sugar

1 tablespoon lemon juice

1–2 cups (250–500 ml) water or chicken broth

6 ounces (170 g) burdock stem, peeled and cut into 1-inch (2½ cm) pieces

1 cup (150 g) green peas

Black pepper

8 garlic scapes

2 tablespoons ground elder flowers

Heat 2 tablespoons of the oil in a skillet over medium-high heat. Add the garlic and then the artichoke hearts, bottoms down, and season the hearts with salt and sugar. Pour the lemon juice over them. Allow the pan to sizzle for a few seconds and then add the water or broth. Pack the burdock pieces lightly into the hearts. Drizzle the rest of the oil over them. Add the peas to the skillet. Bring the liquid to a boil, then cover and reduce the heat to keep it at a simmer. Cook gently for 35 minutes, then add the garlic scapes and ground elder flowers. Spoon some of the hot cooking liquid into the artichoke hearts. After another 40 minutes remove the lid and increase the heat to high. Boil the liquid until it has reduced to a syrupy consistency, constantly basting the hearts with it. Taste for seasoning and add black pepper to taste. Serve hot or at room temperature, with toasted sourdough.

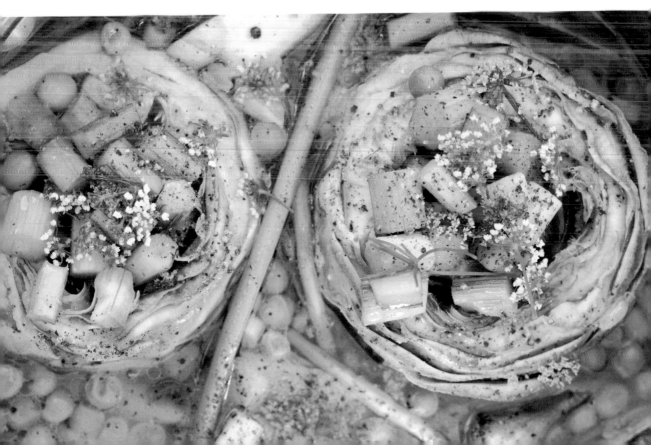

Pork Belly, Burdock, and Pickled Field Garlic Curry

Serves 4–6

I first made this curry when we lived high in Manhattan, in Harlem, close to some of my favorite parks. It was a bumper season for invasive field garlic. So I had a lot of pickles to spare. I borrowed heavily from the flavor profile of a superb curry served at Pok Pok, Andy Ricker's Thai restaurant in Red Hook, Brooklyn.

Serve this with steamed sticky rice. And spoons.

2 tablespoons unscented oil

2 pounds (907 g) skinless pork belly, cut into
  2-inch-by-1-inch (5 × 2½ cm) pieces

½ cup finely chopped field garlic bulbs

1 fat thumb-sized piece of fresh galangal,
  sliced thinly

2 thumb-sized pieces of peeled ginger,
  cut into matchsticks

2 tablespoons peeled, grated fresh turmeric

2 lemongrass hearts, cut in half

2 tablespoons soy sauce

1 tablespoon curry powder

1 tablespoon shrimp paste, thinned in a
  little water

3 tablespoons fish sauce

3 tablespoons Pickled Field Garlic brine

2 tablespoons palm or unrefined sugar

3 tablespoons Sumac Essence

6 hot red chiles

6 ounces (170 g) burdock stem, peeled
  and cut into 2-inch (5 cm) pieces

⅓ cup (50 g) Pickled Field Garlic

2 cups (500 ml) water

Heat the oil in a pot over medium-high heat. Add the pork and sauté for 1 to 2 minutes until one side takes on some brown color, then turn. Sauté another couple of minutes and add the chopped field garlic. Stir well and cook for a minute before adding the galangal, ginger, turmeric, lemongrass, and soy sauce. Stir well, cooking for another minute. Add the rest of the ingredients and stir very well. Bring the liquid to a boil, then reduce the heat to maintain a gentle simmer. Cook for a gentle 2 hours, uncovered. You should be left with a very soupy, strong-flavored sauce. (If the liquid reduces too much and the sauce becomes sticky, add extra water.)

Cattail

OTHER COMMON NAMES: Narrow-leaf cattail, broad-leaf, bulrush

BOTANICAL NAMES: *Typha angustifolia, T. latifolia, T. domingensis, T. × glauca, T. × provincialis*

STATUS: Perennial native to and widespread in North America

WHERE: Damp, wet, and marshy ground

SEASON: Spring, summer, fall

USE: Vegetable, flour, aromatic

PARTS USED: Rhizomes, buds, laterals, hearts, flowers, pollen

GROW? If you have a wetland or pond

TASTES LIKE: Buds and hearts like heart of palm, flowers and pollen like roasted corn

Widely distributed across North America and many other parts of the globe, all species of *Typha* are edible from nose to (cat)tail. In early summer I have spent happy hours in Cape Town foraging for the flowers of the local bulrush, *T. capensis,* watched by two long-suffering corgis (my parents' dogs) who could not imagine why a human would spend so long in a patch of boring reeds. They sighed, audibly. In Brooklyn I have collected cattail hearts and pollen, watched with mild interest by tourists and completely ignored by New Yorkers, who are so tolerant of unusual behavior that they will only pay attention if there is blood on someone's hands.

Beginning at the nose then, which is in the mud, you will find cattail rhizomes. Growing in a fibrous network within the colony, they store an edible starch that has been collected by humans for millennia, for processing into a flour. Read Sam Thayer's absorbing cattail chapter in *Forager's Harvest* if you would like to follow suit. I satisfy myself with less labor-intensive parts of the plant, of which there are many.

Self-contained pale buds form on the tips of mature rhizomes and at the base of the stem. Appearing from late summer through late spring (when they evolve into new leaves and stalks), the buds are rounded at the base and taper to point upward. Also growing from the rhizome, as well as from the base of the mature stalks, are tender white laterals—these are immature shoots of new rhizomes. Sam Thayer (again) made this helpful distinction (there is a *lot* of nebulous language when it comes to what cattails are doing at mud level). Look for them after the flowers have appeared.

Going up. Hidden within cattails' green leaf clusters are their soft hearts. Trimmed of all their tough surrounding leaves (the farther from the base, the tougher they will be), these hearts look a little like leeks and are the Cossack asparagus of wild food legend. Raw, the shoots have the crunch of heart of palm, or (cooked) bamboo shoots. Some authors report a scratchy throat when eating them raw, but we do not know the cause, and this has not happened to me. Maybe I have not eaten enough in one sitting. Erring on the side of

caution, I soak and then pickle most of them. Cooked, they are soft and very mild.

At last, the flowers. Cattail flowers are the green spike that appears in late spring, still gift-wrapped in a sheath of leaves, resembling a very slender ear of corn. I think they are the best part of the plant: They are easy to gather, taste wonderful, and yield a lot of food. As the spike matures the leaves split to reveal a top section of male flowers, and a female section below. The flowers look like green velvet, with a visible separation between the male and female. Each section contains thousands of tiny flowers, the male producing pollen, the female, seed. The male flowers are softer than the more compact female flowers. Part the male flowers with your fingers and their brilliant yellow bases are revealed. This is the pollen.

When immature (before pollen is being shed from the drying male flowers) both male and female sections can be eaten. The thinner female part is tenderized—eventually—by cooking, but compared with the heartier and flavorful pollen-laden section it seems pasty and disappointing, to me. Renowned California forager Pascal Baudar disagrees; he loves the lady cattails. At this young stage I either simmer the male flowers whole on the stem (like corn on the cob), or strip them loose. The stripped immature flowers have a rich, toasted-corn flavor once cooked—it is phenomenally good. I also find that pastries containing cattail flowers or pollen keep remarkably well. The male flowers can be dried for use in later months. When dry they eventually shed their pollen, which will settle in the jar they are stored in, but they retain their characteristic toasty-corn flavor.

And finally, if you have left some flowers behind to mature in the cattail patch, another week will deliver electrically yellow pollen into your hands. This silky and magical ingredient is flavorful and easy to collect. I use it in pastries and to color and coat delicate ingredients, like plump, seared scallops.

How to Collect and Prepare

Buds: Once you are in the mud, they are fairly easy to snap or cut off. Wash very well.

Laterals: In strong contrast with the tough rhizomes, the young laterals are tender enough to slice or simply break off.

Hearts: In spring through early summer, cattail hearts can be collected by either slicing the leaf cluster at its base, peeling off the green leaves and revealing the delicate and tender shoots, or pulling on the middle leaves of a whole cluster (the way you might pull grass or phragmites stems to reveal their tender hearts). Pull firmly and steadily enough and the whole heart will pop out. Yank too hard and the base may break off.

Male flowers: To collect, simply slice the still-green flower spike with a sharp knife. To prepare the pollen-rich and flavorful immature male cattail flowers for use in recipes, peel off the leafy sheath if it is still in place. Use your fingers to strip or flake the tiny, immature yellow-and-green flowers from the upper part (male) of the flower. They come off very easily. These flowers can be dried for later use—spread them thinly on trays and air-dry for a couple of days. Make sure they are 100 percent dry before bottling them, or they can turn moldy. With time their pollen will separate in the jar, in which case simply sift it out as you need it.

Pollen: Bend the mature flower stalks into a paper bag (or narrow-necked container) and shake like mad, whacking the sides of the bag or container. The fine pollen is released easily. If you have a good cattail colony, you can collect about 4 cups in an hour (you need twelve to sixteen mature male cattail flowers to collect ¼ cup of pollen). At home sift the pollen to separate any fluff and insects you may have collected. Spread the pollen out to dry on parchment, then bottle in small jars. Freeze till needed for optimum freshness.

Caution

Choose your waterway or wetland with care.

The most worrying issue is the potential presence of sewage or animal waste. Harmful microbes and liver flukes might be lurking in that tasty-looking patch. If in doubt, avoid all parts at or below water and mud level, although thorough cooking will kill critters.

Cattails are bioremediators, cleaning waterways by sucking up heavy metals and other pollutants, like herbicide or pesticide residue. If your cattails are growing in a polluted site (and the pollution could be historic in former industrial areas, or downstream from them) the chances are they are filled with whatever is in the water. The parts most affected will be the rhizomes. Boiling does not affect heavy-metal levels. The leaves contain significantly lower levels of heavy metals, and I have not to date found data on the flowers. Personally, I would harvest the pollen.

Be aware, know your habitat, and do your own research. Information evolves.

CULTIVATION TIPS
USDA Hardiness Zones 3–10

I would love my own cattail patch. If you have a pond or boggy area, cattails will soon colonize it. Once established, their spread is hard to control, so be prepared for a complete takeover (despite this, cattails are losing native ground to *Phragmites australis*). Choose *Typha latifolia* plants or a cattail native to your region from reputable sources. Avoid *T. angustifolia*, as it hybridizes easily with natives. Cattails will not grow in fast running water.

Cattail Bud Pickles

Makes 2 small jars

Once trimmed the buds are good to eat raw, but their novelty factor is sufficient—and collecting them takes so long and is so messy—that I like to preserve them as pickles, serving them on cheese platters or sliced into a flaky smoked fish topping for chewy brown bread. The buds have a tough outer covering that should be peeled off.

20–30 small cattail buds, peeled
1 cup (250 ml) rice wine vinegar
1 cup (250 ml) water
1 tablespoon plus 1 teaspoon salt
4 tablespoons sugar
1 teaspoon prickly ash fruit

Place the clean and peeled cattail buds into clean jars. In a bowl, combine all the other ingredients and mix well to dissolve the salt and sugar. Pour the pickling solution into the jars. Screw the lids on. The pickles can be eaten within hours, but last very well for months. Refrigerate once opened.

Cattail Shoot Pickles

Makes 2 cups (500 ml)

Cattail shoots are delicious raw, sliced thinly into salads *if* they are growing in a clean place. I like to preserve them by pickling, which retains their crunch. This is a very simple pickle, relying only on elder for flavoring.

8 ounces (227 g) cattail shoots, all tough
    parts peeled away
1 cup (250 ml) Elderflower Vinegar
1 cup (250 ml) water
1 tablespoon salt
2 tablespoons sugar

Trim the shoots to fit your clean jars. Place them inside. In a large jug stir together the vinegar and water and the salt and sugar. Pour over the cattails and place the lids. Refrigerate once opened.

Cattail Blinis

Makes 10 blinis, 2 inches (5 cm) each

These corn-rich and versatile blinis (really just griddle cakes) are ready for savory toppings. I like to serve them with American Burnweed Green Sauce and a hit of chile. They also lend themselves well to Southeast Asian–style dipping sauces, as well as shavings of ham with mustard, smoked salmon and salmon roe for a weekend smørrebrød, or dollops of cucumber raita. The recipe doubles very well.

1 cup (70 g) unripe male cattail flowers, stripped from the stalk
1 cup (175 g) blanched corn kernels
¼ cup (30 g) flour
½ teaspoon baking powder
⅛ teaspoon salt
¼ teaspoon chile flakes (optional)
¼ cup (60 ml) plain yogurt
1 large egg, beaten
2 tablespoons butter

Place the cattails, corn kernels, flour, baking powder, salt, and chile (if using) in a mixing bowl. Make a well in the center and add the yogurt and beaten egg. Stir well. If the mixture is too dry, add a little more yogurt.

Heat a skillet over medium-high heat and melt some of the butter to coat the bottom. Scoop a spoonful of the thick batter into the pan. Repeat, making sure not to crowd the pan. When some bubbles in the surface of the blinis pop, flip them over and cook the other side until they are golden and their insides are cooked, about 4 minutes. Keep warm in a napkin, or reheat under a broiler or toaster oven.

Cattail Quiskets

Makes 12

They are not biscuits, and they are quick. They are quiskets. The kind of thing to make when you have picked immature cattail flowers while camping. Great for Dutch oven baking over and under glowing embers. Toasting freshly shucked male flowers (before they have released their pollen) in a hot pan brings out the characteristic cornsilk notes of the cattail pollen.

1 cup (70 g) fresh, unripe male cattail flowers, stripped from the stalk
1 cup (120 g) all-purpose flour
⅓ cup (40 g) corn flour
1½ teaspoons baking powder
½ teaspoon salt
⅓ cup (80 ml) whey, buttermilk, or watered-down yogurt
⅓ cup (80 ml) milk
3 tablespoons butter, melted and lightly browned

Preheat the oven to 400°F (200°C). Butter a baking sheet.

Heat a dry pan over medium heat. Toss the male flowers into the pan. Toast them, shaking and tossing every minute, until they smell like fresh corn, about 5 minutes.

Place the flour, corn flour, toasted cattail flowers, baking powder, and salt in a bowl. Stir well to combine. Add the whey (or buttermilk or yogurt) and the milk. Stir briefly until a sticky dough begins to form, then add the melted butter. Stir until it is incorporated.

You will need two spoons for this next step. With one, scoop a generous tablespoonful from the sticky dough. Drop it onto the baking sheet, and use the other spoon to dislodge it. Repeat until you have twelve quiskets.

Slide into the oven and bake for 30 minutes, until the edges are golden brown. Remove from the baking tray and keep covered in a napkin. Serve warm.

Cattail Flower Muffins

Makes 10

These deliciously aromatic muffins still taste freakily fresh one week later (if you can eke them out that slowly). Somehow, the pollen works as a preservative. I like to eat them with homemade apricot jam.

1½ cups (180 g) all-purpose flour
1 cup (70 g) freshly shucked, unripe male
  cattail flowers
1 tablespoon dry mustard
1 tablespoon plus 1 teaspoon baking powder
2 teaspoons sugar
¼ teaspoon salt
4½ ounces (128 g) cold butter
2½ ounces (70 g) grated cheddar
⅓ cup (80 ml) beer
⅓ cup (80 ml) milk

Preheat the oven to 400°F (200°C). Lightly oil or butter a muffin tray.

Combine all the dry ingredients in a mixing bowl and stir. Grate or cut the cold butter onto the mixture and rub it in with your fingers until it resembles evenly coarse crumbs. Add the grated cheese and then the beer and the milk, stirring gently. Drop a large spoonful of the dough into each muffin slot. Slide into the oven and bake for 15 to 20 minutes, until an inserted skewer is drawn out clean.

Cattail Pollen Biscuits

Makes about 12

The fresh-shucked corn flavor of cattail pollen is amplified by baking. Serve with butter and maple syrup, thinly sliced ham, or shredded, quick-pickled vegetables.

3¾ cups (450 g) all-purpose flour
4 tablespoons cattail pollen
1 tablespoon plus 2 teaspoons
  baking powder
1 teaspoon salt
2 tablespoons sugar
6 ounces (170 g) cold unsalted butter,
  cut into pieces
1½ cups (375 ml) buttermilk

Preheat the oven to 375°F (190°C). Butter a cookie sheet.

Combine all the dry ingredients in a mixing bowl and stir to combine. Drop the cut-up butter into the ingredients and work it in with your fingers, lifting your hands high to get some air, and rubbing the mixture together to form evenly sized crumbs. Pour in the buttermilk and give the mixture as few swipes with a wooden spoon as possible, before bringing the biscuit dough together with your hands.

Lift the dough onto a lightly floured work surface and press lightly into an even shape 1½ inches (4 cm) thick. Gently press out as many biscuits as possible. Collect the leftover dough pieces and press them together quickly, then cut out a few more biscuits. Place the biscuits gently on the baking sheet and slide into the oven.

The biscuits are done when risen and golden brown, about 20 to 23 minutes. Delicious eaten at once, they freeze very well, too.

Cattail on the Cob

Serves 4 as a snack

Cooking and serving immature cattail flowers with a quick sprinkle of hot butter, a cloud of cheese, and a puff of fiery chiles is a lot of fun. If you can find some pungent Canadian fleabane (*Erigeron canadensis*) to chop and scatter across the top, all the better.

Leftover cattail on the cob can be stripped and used in muffins and biscuits.

12 immature male cattail flower heads
3 tablespoons butter
⅓ cup (20 g) microplaned
    Parmigiano-Reggiano
1 teaspoon Aleppo pepper or chile flakes
2 teaspoons Canadian fleabane,
    chopped finely
Salt
Pepper
1 lemon, cut into eighths

Bring a pot of salted water to a boil. Drop in the male cattails and cook until tender, 8 to 10 minutes. While they are cooking, melt the butter over medium-high heat in a saucepan. Drain the cattails. (If you have a fire going with glowing embers, now give them just 2 minutes above the coals for added flavor—they dry out fast.) Place them on a serving board or plate. Pour the hot butter over them, and scatter with the cheese, chile, and fleabane, if using. Season with a little salt and pepper, and serve with lemon to squeeze on the side.

Cattail and Sweetfern Crusted Hake

Serves 4

Pollen-rich cattail flower fibers turn toasty with that characteristic fresh cornsilk aroma. I like mild, flaky, sustainable hake for this delicate crust. Whiting, catfish, and trout would work well, too.

4 hake fillets, about 6 ounces (170 g) each
4 tablespoons Dried Male Cattail Flowers
½–1 teaspoon Sweetfern Salt
4 tablespoons Sweetfern Butter,
    with extra on standby
½ cup (30 g) panko bread crumbs
Lemon wedges, for serving
½ cup (125 ml) Ramp Aioli, for serving

Season one side of all the fish with half the cattail flowers and the salt.

Use two skillets if one is not large enough to accommodate all the fish. Over medium heat melt 2 tablespoons of Sweetfern Butter in each pan. When it is foaming sprinkle ¼ cup of the crumbs evenly across each pan. Wait for the butter to be absorbed by the crumbs and then lay the fillets, seasoned side down, across the crumbs. Increase the heat to medium high. While the fillets are cooking dust the upper sides with the rest of the cattail flowers and the salt. When the edges of the fish are turning opaque (about 6 minutes), carefully slide a spatula under the fillets and flip them over. If the pans need a little more butter, add some. Cook until the fish is just cooked through, about another 5 minutes. Serve hot, straight out of the pan, with lemon wedges and the aioli on the side for dipping.

Pan-Fried Scallops with Cattail Pollen and White Sweet Clover

Serves 4 as an appetizer

The sweetness of plump sea scallops is a delicious contrast with cattail's toasty-corn character, offset by the smokiness of good bacon. Adding white sweet clover (invasive *Melilotus albus*) adds an additional layer of honey-like complexity to a quick dish that you will not forget in a hurry.

4 ounces (113 g) bacon

3 tablespoons Dried Male Cattail Flowers

8 sea scallops

½ teaspoon Sweetfern Salt

4 tablespoons white sweet clover stripped from the stalk (80 flower stalks)

2 tablespoons butter

Chop the bacon very finely and add it to a skillet over medium-high heat. Cook until the fat begins to run and the bacon to brown. While it is cooking, scatter the cattail evenly on a clean work surface and roll the scallops gently over it to coat them. Sprinkle one side of the scallops with some Sweetfern Salt. Reduce the skillet heat to medium. Place the scallops salted-side down in the pan and cook for 4 to 5 minutes with the bacon. Just before turning them over, sprinkle half of the white sweet clover flowers across the scallops. Add the butter to the pan and as it begins to melt, flip the scallops gently over. Tilt the pan occasionally to catch the fat and baste the cooking scallops with it. Sprinkle the rest of the white sweet clover flowers across the scallops. Continue to cook for a total of about 4 minutes, until the scallops offer a small amount of resistance when pressed. It is fine for their middles to be slightly uncooked. Serve hot, with the pan scratchings piled on top of the scallops.

DRIED MALE CATTAIL FLOWERS

In early summer I strip immature, green male cattail flowers—before they have opened enough to shed their pollen—to dry and use later in the year. Simply spread them out in a very thin layer on parchment and allow them to air-dry, turning a couple of times a day. If the flowers are not dry when you seal them in jars or bags, they can become mildewy (although if this happens, toasting them for 10 minutes in a 300°F/150°C oven does wonders). Dipping into that jar months later, you may find that the pollen has become separated from the fibers—it is bright yellow, feeling as silky as cornstarch on your fingers. Just shake the jar up and measure what you need.

Cattail Clam Chowder

Serves 4

This chowder is creamy, briny, and sweet with cattail, carrot, and corn rising through the smoky bacon. The helpful fishmongers at Fish Tails in Brooklyn or Lobster Tails in Manhattan shuck clams, which is a big help. (Remember to ask for the juice.) If you are buying whole shellfish, just steam them open.

2 tablespoons butter

½ cup (70 g) diced carrots

½ cup (70 g) very finely chopped onion

3 strips bacon, cut into ½-inch (1 cm) pieces

1 tablespoon cattail pollen

2 tablespoons all-purpose flour

Clam juices, reserved (about 1½ cups/ 375 ml)

2½ cups (625 ml) milk

1 cup (225 g) cubed potato

2 cups (350 g) sweet corn kernels, about 2 ears

1 tablespoon white sweet clover flowers

36 steamer clams, shucked (about 1½ cups/ 375 ml out of shell) *or* 24 steamer clams plus ¾ cup (190 ml) water

½ lemon

Melt the butter in a pot over medium heat. Cook the carrots and onion until they caramelize a little, about 10 gentle minutes. Add the pieces of bacon and turn up the heat. Cook until its fat runs—about 5 minutes. Sprinkle the cattail pollen and flour evenly over the bacon and vegetables and stir well. Cook for a minute.

IF YOU ARE USING SHUCKED CLAMS: Gradually add the clam juice, stirring all the time as the mixture thickens. Add the milk next, stirring continuously. Bring the liquid to a boil, and then reduce the heat to keep it at a simmer. Add the cubed potatoes. Cook until they are tender, about 10 minutes. Stir occasionally to discourage sticking. Taste: The clam juices can be extremely salty. If the soup is too salty, add a little more milk. Add the corn and the white sweet clover and cook for 5 minutes. Last, add the clams and turn up the heat. The instant they become firm—about 1 minute—be ready to serve the chowder. Taste one last time, and add a conservative squeeze of lemon juice.

IF YOU ARE USING IN-SHELL CLAMS: Scrub the clams very well. Bring water to a boil in a large pot with a lid. Add the clams, cover the pot with a lid, and steam until they open—remove each clam *as it opens*, or they will overcook and become tough. Once they have all been removed, collect the clam juice by straining it through cheesecloth. Proceed with the recipe above—adding the clam juice after you have made the roux. Add the cooked clams at the last minute, and allow them to heat through for a few seconds before serving.

Cattail Pollen and Honey Madeleines

Makes 24 3-inch (8 cm) madeleines

Madeleines are very easy to make, as long as you have the proper pan (or two). The secret to this recipe belongs to the browned butter: Together with the toasty-corn aroma of cattail pollen and dark chestnut honey, it makes an unforgettable three mouthfuls of each madeleine. Do not overbake the madeleines—focus on that oven for the final 5 minutes. I use 2 madeleine trays. (For a variation, see Elderflower Madeleines.)

3 ounces (85 g) butter
1 tablespoon chestnut honey
2 large eggs
3 ounces (85 g) sugar
3 ounces (85 g) all-purpose flour
1 tablespoon cattail pollen, sifted
¼ teaspoon salt
1 teaspoon baking powder
2 tablespoons melted butter, for brushing

Melt the butter in a small saucepan over medium heat. Cook it until the milk solids sink and begin to turn golden brown. Pour at once into a jug or it will burn in the hot pan. You want toasty, not scorchy. Add the honey to the warm butter and stir well.

In a mixing bowl beat the eggs with the sugar until pale and very fluffy about 2 minutes. In another bowl combine the flour, cattail pollen, salt, and baking powder. Gradually fold this mixture into the beaten eggs. Add the tepid brown butter and honey, and stir well. Cover and place the batter in the fridge for 10 minutes.

Paint melted butter evenly into madeleine molds and their edges (if overfilled, the madeleines will spread). Transfer the buttered tray or trays to the freezer to chill.

Preheat the oven to 425°F (220°C).

When the batter has chilled, spoon it conservatively into the madeleine molds. Bake for 3 to 5 minutes. Reduce the heat to 400°F (200°C), *and* open the oven for 15 seconds to dispel some extra hot air. Close the door and bake about another 5 minutes. Toward the end the madeleines bake fast and must be removed as soon as the very middle of the madeleine springs back after it has been touched. Have a wire rack waiting. Flip the tray upside down and shake the madeleines out. If they stick, loosen their edges gently with a knife. Serve them warm, or wait until they have cooled completely before storing them in an airtight container. They are still very good the following day.

Common Milkweed

OTHER COMMON NAMES: Butterfly flower, silkweed, cotton weed

BOTANICAL NAME: *Asclepias syriaca*

STATUS: Indigenous perennial, mostly east of the Rockies

WHERE: Open ground, farmlands, highway shoulders, gardens

SEASON: Early spring to late summer

USE: Vegetable, aromatic

PARTS USED: Shoots, tender stems, buds, flowers, and young pods

GROW? Yes, if you do not mind unruliness

TASTES LIKE: Fava bean meets asparagus (but not really)

In North America we have a largesse of indigenous edible plants that heralds the edible year. Common milkweed is the most generous. Every stage of the plant's aboveground growth is edible, from its downy spring shoots, through early-summer stems and buds, mid-summer flowers, and late-summer seedpods.

But for most people common milkweed is just that, common, and a weed. Its colonies, spreading via determined stolons underground, often interfere with the orderly plans of gardeners, farmers, landowners, and highway managers, who view it as a nuisance plant and kill or mow it. It usually falls victim to herbicides, since digging it out is relatively ineffective.

Fortunately, foragers have an unusual ally (and the converse is true, too): the monarch butterfly. Increasingly, interested citizens of the twenty-first century are becoming aware of the association between the beleaguered butterflies and milkweed. Monarch butterfly larvae (caterpillars) *only* feed on milkweed. This has led to a growing advocacy for the planting and preserving of milkweed populations.

Dozens of species of milkweed are indigenous to North America. While some are reputedly toxic, ethnobotanical records show that many Native Americans used several species for food, including *Asclepias syriaca* (our common milkweed), *A. speciosa*, *A. incarnata*, *A. viridiflora*, and *A. verticillata*. Most modern foragers are acquainted with the first. I would happily eat the others, if I could find them readily.

Common milkweed's earliest stage of eating is the young shoot whose leaves have not yet infurled. They appear in early spring and closely resemble a toxic plant called dogbane (*Apocynum cannabinum*). The shoots of dogbane and common milkweed look so similar (and both bleed latex) that this confusion may have led to the myth promulgated by Euell Gibbons, who popularized American foraging in 1962 in his seminal book *Stalking the Wild Asparagus*. His advice to boil the milkweed three times to dispel "the extremely bitter principle" has been repeated by countless subsequent writers and obeyed by legions of obedient foragers. I did it, too, the first time I ate the vegetable.

But common milkweed is not bitter, not even when raw. Dogbane is. Sam Thayer's seminal book *The Forager's Harvest* contains six pages of enlightening and entertaining reading

on this subject. He deserves an award for dissolving this widespread untruism that common milkweed itself is toxic unless boiled to death.

Driving in the Catskills one spring day, my husband stepped on the brakes as I waved wildly at a green field (this happens quite often). The field was filled with cows, green grass, and young common milkweed, already in leaf. The farmer was nearby (castrating some very unhappy pigs) and managed to keep a reasonably straight face when this city person asked him if she could collect the milkweed in his field. "Take it all," he said, and went back to the vocal pigs. In a borrowed pair of rubber boots I waded through a quagmire of cowpats to emerge in the milkweed patch. I picked a huge bundleful, and we drove home to the city, thinking quite unhappily about pork chops. These young stalks may be my favorite part of the plant. They can be eaten in any way that you would prepare asparagus (though common milkweed's flavor is essentially its own). I remove and reserve their tender leaves, serving the supple and elegant stems alone. After blanching the young leaves, I purée them and freeze to keep for green tarts, pizzas, and dumplings. Their texture is similar to fava beans.

In early summer, when local strawberries are ripe, milkweed buds form, looking a little like fuzzy broccolini. Their stems are still very tender, and the uppermost leaves are still good to eat, once cooked. Again, all they need is a quick blanch before cooking them any way you like. They are memorably delicious.

A few weeks later the heavy umbels of powerfully aromatic flowers open. Their perfume, caught in a fermented cordial or syrup (cold-infused or you lose most of the fragrance), makes a drink that tells of a summer field under a blue June sky. It mixes beautifully with gin and lime juice, or Prosecco, or sparkling water, and can be the inspiration for summer popsicles, sorbets, and syllabubs. Fermented flowers create a unique and gorgeously lilac vinegar.

In late summer the young, prehistoric-looking seedpods are an exceptional vegetable, blanched for a few seconds and then pan-roasted or sautéed until tender. They are reminiscent of okra but not as mucilaginous. You can also slit the larger pods to remove the immature white silk inside, eating only this morsel, briefly cooked—it is soft and startlingly sweet, with a flavor like the flowers' scent. The leftover skins can be deep-fried to make a crisp botanical *chicharrón*.

Common milkweed's usefulness in so many stages suggests that it could be grown as a bona fide crop. It is a plant we should be nurturing for a host of reasons, not least of which is its cash potential to open-minded growers. And my personal feeling is that everything above can be applied not just to the commonly foraged *Asclepias syriaca* but also to the other milkweed species used by Native Americans. I have not personally eaten them, but others have, and the ethnobotanical record is significant.

Because I live in New York City, where common milkweed colonies compete with and always lose to development, I now grow my own (along with a few other species for pollinators). Some of my plants were ordered online; others came from a feral milkweed colony around the corner on a construction site. The home's new owner allowed me to dig them up in springtime. And yes, the Brooklyn monarchs have found them. Ideally, it is better to grow and buy plants from local stock, and I have no doubt that more nurseries will be stocking this milkweed. The edible word continues to spread, in tandem with the burgeoning awareness that growing indigenous plants helps boost and support local biodiversity. What we plant matters.

How to Collect and Prepare

When foraging for wild common milkweed, do be respectful. Don't be a glutton. Forage only in healthy populations. Never take it all.

The plant is a haven for insects. You will often see ladybug larvae on the leaves, as well as distinctive red-and-black milkweed bugs and beetles, and, of course, if you are lucky, a striped monarch caterpillar munching away. Be very careful and considerate when collecting. Check for critters, and shake them off if you have picked any accidentally. Check the back of milkweed leaves for monarch eggs before picking, and stems and leaves for chrysalides. Leave them alone if you find them. Only remove one

or two flower umbels from a plant, leaving the rest to feed the tiniest foragers.

Take some time to collect your shoots, stems, or buds in a neat bunch, stems pointing down, instead of tumbling them together in a bag. This will help prevent the sticky latex from coating every piece you harvest.

As with other greens, submerge any green parts of common milkweed in a bowl of water if they have wilted in transit. Once they have plumped up, they last well for several days, stems submerged. When you are ready to eat them, treat them to a dunk in boiling water to dispel the congealed latex from the cut end. Then proceed as you might with asparagus or broccolini.

To prepare the flowers for a cordial, snip each blossom from its thread-like stalk—the less stalk you get, the more flower flavor you retain. You can also fritter the flowers, elderflower- and black-locust-style, in which case keep the umbels intact.

Caution

In its shoot stage common milkweed has a poisonous lookalike: dogbane (*Apocynum canabinum*). How to tell them apart? Milkweed shoots and leaf undersides are slightly furry; dogbane's are smooth. Milkweed stalks are often hollow (but not always, when young); dogbane stems are solid. Milkweed's sap is mild to sweet; dogbane's is bitter (a tiny taste won't hurt).

CULTIVATION TIPS
USDA Hardiness Zones 4–9

Common milkweed seeds are increasingly available. Before being sown, they need to be cold-stratified to spur germination.

Planting young plants from nurseries or transplanting mature plants is a quicker and easier option. Common milkweed resents being transplanted midseason. The aboveground parts will go into shock and drop their leaves, but the roots and runners will remain busy underground. Very, very busy. The following spring shoots will pop up where you least expect them. This plant will never grow in a neat vegetable row, which may present a challenge to growing it as a crop, as it would have to be managed very differently from well-behaved corn. In a garden, grow this lovely plant where it has room to move. And it will.

Tolerant of various soils, as long as they are well drained, common milkweed does require sun in its growing season, six hours or more being ideal. My own colony manages with much less (well, none) in the months from late fall through spring, but in summer it gets its full dose, and it grows prolifically, topping out at 6 feet tall.

Milkweed Shoots with Pancetta

Serves 2

Your harvest, your hunger, and how many friends you may be feeding will determine how many bundles you make. But this makes a beautiful brunch dish for two, with two bundles each.

12 common milkweed shoots

3 tablespoons olive oil

4 slices pancetta

4 large eggs

Black pepper

Preheat the broiler.

PREPARE THE MILKWEED SHOOTS: Snap off all but the topmost leaves (save the tender leaves for a purée). Trim the stalk end where old latex may have congealed. The latex will run again but the boiling will clean it up.

FOR THE SHOOTS: Bring a pot of water to boil over high heat. Drop the milkweed shoots into the water. Cook at a boil for 4 minutes, or until just tender. The shoots should still be bright green. Remove to a strainer and refresh under cold water, then pat dry.

TO ASSEMBLE: Use a little of the olive oil to grease a baking sheet. Gather 3 milkweed shoots and wrap a piece of pancetta around the center of the bundle. Place on the baking sheet. Repeat until all the shoots have been wrapped. Drizzle the rest of the olive oil over the bundles. Slide the tray under the broiler and cook until the pancetta begins to sizzle and turn dark, about 6 minutes.

FOR THE EGGS: While the bundles are broiling, bring another pot of water to a boil. Crack the eggs into the boiling water one by one. As soon as they turn opaque, flip them very gently in the water with a wooden spoon. Cook until the white is just set, about 1 minute. Scoop them out with a perforated spoon and place on a clean dish towel.

Place the milkweed bundles on two warmed plates and top each bundle with a just-cooked egg. Season with pepper to taste, eat at once!

Young Common Milkweed Stems with Miso Mayonnaise

Serves 4

This exquisitely simple dish is made with the young milkweed stems that are between shoot and bud-forming stage. I pick off all the leaves (and save them for making Milkweed and Fava Bean Pâté), and blanch just the tender stems, like asparagus.

32 tender common milkweed stems,
    leaves removed except for the tips

1 tablespoon yellow miso

⅓ cup (80 ml) mayonnaise

Bring a large pot of salted water to a boil. Drop the milkweed in and cook until just tender, about 5 minutes. Remove, and drain. Pat well dry.

In a small bowl mix the miso with a little mayonnaise until it has thinned, then add the rest of the mayonnaise. Serve the milkweed shoots alongside the mayo for dipping.

Common Milkweed Vignole with Fava and Artichoke

Serves 4

Vignole is an Italian vegetable stew, an edible celebration of spring. I love combining all-American milkweed with the classic Mediterranean pairing of fava beans and artichoke hearts. Serve as a side dish, on bruschetta, or as a sauce for fresh pasta.

4 ounces (113 g) common milkweed shoots or buds with tender stems (15–20 shoots)

3 tablespoons extra-virgin olive oil, divided

4 raw, fresh artichoke hearts, chokes removed, quartered

1 cup (250 ml) water, divided

2 cups (about 300 g) shelled fava beans

12 field garlic bulbs (substitute 6 garlic cloves)

3 tablespoons lemon juice

Salt

Black pepper

6 dill branches

⅓ cup (about 10 g) roughly chopped mint leaves

OPTIONAL MARINADE (FOR A REFRIGERATED VARIATION)

⅓ cup (80 ml) fresh lemon juice

¼ teaspoon salt

1 teaspoon sugar

¼ teaspoon black peppercorns

⅓ cup (80 ml) extra-virgin olive oil

Blanch the milkweed by immersing in boiling water for 1 minute or less. This dispels the latex. Remove and refresh under cold water. Pat dry.

Heat 1 tablespoon of the olive oil in a saucepan over medium-high heat. Add the artichoke hearts. Sauté for 4 minutes, turning once. Add ½ cup of the water to the saucepan and cover. Cook for 8 minutes at a high simmer. Remove the lid and add the second tablespoon of olive oil along with the milkweed, fava beans, field garlic, lemon juice, and remaining ½ cup of water. Season with salt and pepper. Replace the lid and stew over medium heat for 15 minutes. Remove the lid, add the dill and mint, and stir. Cook for another 10 minutes, then add the last tablespoon of olive oil.

FOR THE OPTIONAL MARINADE: To make a refrigerated variation, double the vegetable quantities above. When cooked, allow the vignole to cool and transfer it to a clean glass jar. Whisk together all the marinade ingredients and pour over. Marinate for 12 hours in the fridge and serve at room temperature.

Milkweed and Fava Bean Pâté

Makes 1 cup (250 ml)

For this mild green paste, I use the tender, immature leaves that I have pulled from young milkweed shoots used for other dishes. It is an excellent snack, schmeared on crackers or dense seed bread.

6 ounces (170 g) fresh young common
    milkweed leaves (yield, about
    1 cup cooked)
1 cup (150 g) shelled fava beans
1 tablespoon extra-virgin olive oil
Squeeze of lemon juice
Salt
Black pepper

Bring water to a boil in a pot over high heat. Drop the milkweed leaves into the pot. Cook until the leaves are tender, about 3 minutes. Remove the leaves and refresh under cold water. Squeeze the leaves out well (they retain a lot of moisture).

Meanwhile bring another pot of salted water to a boil and cook the fava beans until just tender, about 8 minutes. Refresh under cold water. Pop them out of their skins.

Place the cooked milkweed leaves with the beans in a food processor with the tablespoon of olive oil and pulse until blended. Add the squeeze of lemon juice. Taste, and season with salt and pepper. Taste again. Add more lemon, if you like. Pulse again till very smooth. Transfer to a bowl and serve right away with crackers and bread, or store in the fridge for up to 4 days.

Fried Milkweed Buds

Serves 2 as an appetizer

Italians have fried artichokes. Americans (should) have fried milkweed buds. These crisp morsels melt in the mouth.

6 ounces (170 g) common milkweed buds
    with tender stems attached
Unscented oil
1 teaspoon fresh lemon juice
¼ cup (60 ml) Ramp Aioli
½ teaspoon Ramp Leaf Salt

Pick any mature leaves from the milkweed stems. Smaller leaves at the tips can remain. Trim the ends off the stems. Bring a pot of water to a boil and blanch the milkweed for 1 minute. Drain, refresh, and roll up in a kitchen towel to dry.

Pour the oil 1 inch (2½ cm) deep into a pot or frying pan. Heat over high heat, and add about half the milkweed. Reduce the heat a smidge so that the milkweed does not scorch. Fry for about 6 minutes—the buds will lose quite a lot of volume and turn a very dark green. When done, the remaining leaves will be very crisp at the tips. Scoop them out and lay on paper towels to absorb excess oil.

While the milkweed is frying, mix the fresh lemon juice into the Ramp Aioli and transfer to a small dish, for dipping.

When all the stems are cooked, sprinkle with Ramp Leaf Salt and serve at once.

Pan Sauté of Common Milkweed Buds with Daylily Buds and Legumes

Serves 4 as an appetizer

Elderflower brightens early summer's milkweed buds and complements the sweetness of garden peas. A gentle slick of buttery lemon brings balance. This recipe multiplies successfully.

12 ounces (340 g) common milkweed buds
    with tender stems attached
2 cups (about 300 g) fava beans
    or peas, shelled
3 tablespoons butter
3 tablespoons pine nuts
2 tablespoons Fermented Elderflower Cordial
½ teaspoon green ground elder seed
2 ounces (57 g) daylily buds
1 tablespoon fresh lemon juice
½ teaspoon Ground Elder Salt

Bring a pot of water to a boil and blanch the milkweed for 1 minute. Drain, refresh, and roll up in a kitchen towel to dry. Bring fresh water to a boil and drop the fava beans in for 2 minutes. (If you're using peas, add them for 1 minute.) Drain, refresh, and dry.

In a skillet over medium-low heat, melt the butter. Add the pine nuts and cook gently for a few minutes until they think about turning brown. Add the Fermented Elderflower Cordial and cook for a minute. Increase the heat to medium. Add the fava beans or peas and ground elder seed; toss well. Add the daylily buds and toss again to coat with butter. Cook for a minute (they cook fast). Now add the lemon juice and give the pan another toss. Finally, add the blanched milkweed buds and toss just long enough to heat through. Season with the Ground Elder Salt, and eat immediately.

Common Milkweed and Garlic Scape Soup

Serves 2 as an entrée

A simple broth from the border regions between late spring and early summer amplifies the clear green flavors of garlic scapes and common milkweed. The bright mint complements the creaminess of the two vegetables.

12 ounces (340 g) common milkweed buds
    and tender stems
4 ounces (113 g) garlic scapes
3 cups (750 ml) vegetable broth
½ teaspoon Field Garlic Salt
1 cup (about 30 g) mint leaves
¾ cup (75 g) grated Parmigiano-Reggiano
1 tablespoon lemon juice
Black pepper

Bring a pot of water to a boil and cook the milkweed for 1 minute. Drain, refresh, and roll up in a kitchen towel to dry. Keep the common milkweed buds intact but slice their tender stems into ¼-inch (½ cm) pieces.

Cut the tough ends off the garlic scapes. Slice the scape stems into ¼-inch (½ cm) pieces but keep the flower bud attached to the stem. Heat the broth over high heat. Add the garlic scapes and cook at a simmer till just tender, about 10 minutes. Add two-thirds of the blanched milkweed and cook until barely tender, about 2 minutes. Add the Field Garlic Salt to taste.

Meanwhile, in a food processor combine the reserved third of the milkweed, mint leaves, cheese, and lemon juice; pulse until a rough paste has formed. Taste for seasoning and add some Field Garlic Salt and pepper.

Serve the hot soup in bowls with a dollop of the paste on top. Stir the paste into the broth as you eat.

Common Milkweed Buds with Ginger and Soy

Serves 2

This was one of the first ways I ever prepared milkweed, and it remains a classic. The creaminess of the cooked buds and stems is delicious with sharp lime, strong soy, and fragrant ginger. (I would kill to add *miyoga* buds to this dish—I am growing them and waiting impatiently.)

12 common milkweed buds with stems
1 tablespoon unscented oil
1 thumb-sized piece of ginger, peeled and sliced into very thin matchsticks
2 tablespoons soy sauce
1 tablespoon lime juice
½ teaspoon sugar

Bring a pot of salted water to a boil. Blanch the buds and stems in it for a minute. Drain and refresh them under cold water, then roll dry in a clean kitchen towel.

In a saucepan over medium heat, heat the oil. Add the ginger and sauté gently for 4 to 5 minutes, until cooked through. Increase the heat and add the soy sauce, lime juice, and sugar, stirring briskly to dissolve the sugar. Add the blanched milkweed. Toss well. Cook for a couple of minutes, until just tender. Serve.

Common Milkweed Bud Pizza with Bacon and Pickled Turnips

Makes one 14-inch (35 cm) pizza

Scattering milkweed buds across a pizza makes the few seem like many. The pickles add last-minute crunch and brightness. High-flavor pantry basics like Lacto-Fermented Garlic Mustard and Ramp Leaf Salt send it over the top. Other tricks? Yes. Good bacon. My go-to bacon is nitrate-free, smoked, and fairly thickly sliced. Roasting it in the oven keeps it nice and flat.

PIZZA DOUGH

1 tablespoon dry yeast

1 teaspoon sugar

¾ cup (190 ml) warm water

2 cups (240 g) all-purpose flour

¾ teaspoon salt

3 tablespoons olive oil

TOPPING

3 ounces (85 g) common milkweed buds

1 jalapeño pepper

1 tablespoon Common Milkweed
    Flower Vinegar

4 slices bacon

2 medium balls (8 ounces/227 g, total)
    fresh mozzarella

6 young Japanese turnips
    (substitute radishes)

1 tablespoon salt

2 tablespoons Lacto-Fermented
    Garlic Mustard

Ramp Leaf Salt

FOR THE DOUGH: Mix the yeast with the sugar in the warm water in a jug and allow it to bubble. Place the flour and salt in a mixing bowl, pour in the yeast mixture and the oil, and stir well until a cohesive dough forms. Turn out onto a board and knead until it feels silky, supple, and elastic, and does not stick to your fingers—at least 10 minutes. Place in a clean, lightly oiled bowl and cover. Let rise until it has doubled, roughly 1 to 3 hours.

Preheat the oven to 400°F (200°C).

Punch down the risen dough. Oil a large pizza pan or baking sheet. Hold the dough up in front of you in both hands and work your way around it, holding it by the upper edge and letting the rest hang down as you move it counterclockwise (if you are right-handed). Keep moving steadily and quickly and gravity will stretch it. If one side starts to go rogue and stretches too much, lay it flat on your prepared sheet and push the dough out toward the pan edges from the middle, using your knuckles. When you have an even circle, cover the dough and allow it to rest

FOR THE TOPPING: Bring a pot of water to a boil and blanch the milkweed for 1 minute. Drain, refresh, and roll up in a kitchen towel to dry. Slice the jalapeno very thinly and place in a small bowl with the vinegar. Lay the bacon on a baking sheet or in a skillet and roast in the hot oven for about 12 to 15 minutes, until it has begun to color at the edges. Drain the fat and scoop the bacon onto a paper towel. Cut each strip into three or four pieces.

Increase the oven heat to 550°F (290°C).

Tear about ten even chunks from the mozzarella and distribute them evenly across the pizza. Lay the blanched milkweed buds on top of pieces of cheese. Scatter the drained jalapeño slices across the pizza. Add the bacon last.

Slide the pizza into the very hot oven and cook for about 25 to 30 minutes, until the edges of the pie are blistering.

While the pizza is baking, cut the turnips or radishes in quarters, keeping some green stems, and lay them in a small bowl. Douse them with the 1 tablespoon of salt and massage it in. Just before removing the cooked pizza, rinse them and pat dry.

When the pizza is done, pull it out, slide it onto a cutting board, and top at once with the salt-pickled turnips or radishes. Scatter the Lacto-Fermented Garlic Mustard sparingly over the top. Season lightly with Ramp Leaf Salt.

Slice, and snarf.

Common Milkweed, Sheep Sorrel, and Pea Purée

Makes 1½ cups (255 g)

A close cousin to the Milkweed and Fava Bean Pâté, but different. Either eat this straight up, toss it with fresh pasta, or save it for a Common Milkweed and Pea Herb Tart

6 ounces (170 g) tender common
    milkweed leaves
10 ounces (283 g) peas
8 stalks dill
1 ounce (28 g) sheep sorrel leaves
½ cup (15 g) mint leaves, chopped
1 tablespoon sugar
½ teaspoon salt
¼ cup (60 ml) extra-virgin olive oil
Lemon juice (optional)

Bring water to a boil in a pot over high heat. Drop the milkweed leaves into the pot and cook until tender, about 3 minutes. Remove the leaves and refresh in cold water. Squeeze dry.

While they are cooking, cook the peas in another pot of boiling water with the bunch of dill until barely tender and still bright green. Drain the peas. Roughly chop the dill.

In the bowl of a food processor combine all the ingredients. Pulse until thoroughly smooth. Taste. It should be well seasoned, but add more salt and a touch more lemon juice if it needs more acid.

Common Milkweed and Pea Herb Tart

Makes 1 tart

This vivid green tart vibrates with midspring flavors. It can be eaten warm or at room temperature.

PASTRY
6 ounces (170 g) flour
½ teaspoon salt
3 ounces (85 g) cold butter
2–4 tablespoons cold water
1 large egg, beaten

FILLING
1½ cups (255 g) Common Milkweed,
    Sheep Sorrel, and Pea Purée
3 large egg yolks
1 whole large egg
⅓ cup (80 ml) cream
⅓ cup (50 g) fresh goat cheese
8 mint leaves, cut into ribbons
¼ teaspoon salt
Black pepper

FOR THE PASTRY: Lightly butter an 8-inch (20 cm) springform pan. Place the flour and salt in a mixing bowl. Grate the cold butter onto the flour. Using your fingers, work the butter into the flour until the mixture resembles coarse crumbs. Add 2 tablespoons of cold water and stir. Add more if necessary until the pastry sticks together. Form into a rough disk, wrap, and chill for an hour. Roll the pastry out on a lightly floured board, then transfer it to the pan, allowing the edges to hang over. Prick the base with a fork. Place the pan in the freezer for 10 minutes to chill.

Preheat the oven to 350°F (180°C).

Remove the chilled pastry and trim its edges. Line it with foil. Bake for 30 minutes. Remove from the oven, and remove the foil very carefully. Brush the shell with the beaten egg and return to the oven for 10 minutes.

FOR THE FILLING: In a bowl mix the purée with the egg yolks and the whole egg, until smooth. Add the cream. Crumble in the goat cheese. The cheese does not have to be smoothly blended in but can remain in pieces. Add the mint, and salt and pepper to taste.

TO ASSEMBLE: Pour the filling into the baked pastry shell. Slide into the oven and bake until the middle is just set and an inserted skewer comes out clean, about 40 minutes. Let it rest for a minute, then carefully release the spring. If you are very brave and dexterous, you can transfer the whole tart from its pan base to a plate once it has cooled.

Fermented Common Milkweed Flower Cordial

Makes 6 cups (1½ liters)

I have been making a milkweed cordial in one form or another for about seven years, now. Nothing I have posted on social media has attracted as much interest as this gorgeous, rosy ferment. Is it a soda, is it a cordial, is it a mead? It's a fuzzy area, with fizzy things. I call it a cordial, because, despite the bubbles (like Fermented Elderflower Cordial), I use it diluted. With no added yeast and no citric acid to slow down yeast activity, this is a wild fermentation. It is the starting point of two fantastic vinegars.

3 cups (750 ml) common milkweed flowers
1 pound (453 g) sugar
6 cups (1½ liters) water
Peel of 1 lemon, in long strips (optional)

Use scissors to snip all the milkweed flowers from the tiny stems within the umbel.

Combine the flowers, sugar, water, and lemon peel (if using) in a clean jar. Stir well to dissolve all the sugar. Cover the jar's mouth with a layer of cheesecloth secured with a rubber band or string. You want to keep insects out and let air in.

Leave the jar at room temperature for about 3 to 6 days. Stir every day until you bottle the cordial. For the first day or three you may notice no change. But bubbles will form as fermentation becomes active, and you will hear a delightful fizzing when you put your ear to the jar's mouth. The flowers will also rise in the jar as gas pushes them up. Push them down again with a clean spoon.

When it is extremely fizzy, give the cordial one more day. Strain the liquid through a fine-mesh sieve into a clean bowl. Strain again through a double layer of cheesecloth. (Reserve the strained flowers, or pomace, for Common Milkweed Flower Vinegar – The Quick Way.) At this point the cordial is ready to make Common Milkweed Flower Vinegar – The Long Way.

Otherwise, pour the strained cordial into clean bottles. Store in the fridge: This will slow down continued fermentation. Left out, without releasing accumulated gas, a bottle can explode. The cordial is ready to drink straightaway and will keep indefinitely in the fridge.

Migration

Makes 1 drink

When the weather clears suddenly after a storm has lifted the sodden blanket of summer humidity, I feel suddenly homesick and restless. I want to go places.

3 fluid ounces (6 tablespoons) bourbon
1 fluid ounce (2 tablespoons) Northeast No. 1 Vermouth
1 fluid ounce (2 tablespoons) Fermented Common Milkweed Flower Cordial
1 teaspoon pomegranate molasses

Shake all the ingredients up with ice. Strain, and pour.

The Monarch

Makes 1 drink

I use year-old Fermented Common Milkweed Flower Cordial for this butterfly-named cocktail—it has mellowed and lost its pink glitter but glows from within in terms of flavor.

3 fluid ounces (6 tablespoons)
    Red Currant Gin*
1 fluid ounce (2 tablespoons) Fermented
    Common Milkweed Flower Cordial
1 fluid ounce (2 tablespoons) Northeast
    No. 1 Vermouth
¼ teaspoon Juniper Sugar

Shake up all the ingredients very well without ice. Once the sugar has dissolved, add ice and shake again. Strain, and pour.

* Red Currant Gin is exactly what it sounds like: Fill a jar with fresh red currants. Cover with gin. After 2 weeks, strain it (you can reuse the red currants for jelly). It keeps indefinitely.

The Perfect Host

Makes 1 drink

Common milkweed flowers pair beautifully with the grapefruit notes of ripe black cherries, macerating in rum.

2 fluid ounces (4 tablespoons)
    Black Cherry Rum
1½ fluid ounces (3 tablespoons) Northeast
    No. 1 Vermouth
1 fluid ounce (2 tablespoons) Fermented
    Common Milkweed Flower Cordial
½ fluid ounce (1 tablespoon) fresh
    lime juice

Combine in a shaker with ice. Shake, strain, and pour.

Kir Syriaca

Makes 1 drink

This cocktail was born in the early summer of 2011, the year I began experimenting with milkweed flowers. It is as simple as can be: sparkling wine—I usually use fruity Prosecco—and milkweed flower cordial. Depending on your glass you will use more or less wine. I like coupes and flutes.

1½ fluid ounces (3 tablespoons) Fermented
    Common Milkweed Flower Cordial, chilled
4–6 fluid ounces (120–180 ml) dry sparkling wine or Champagne, chilled

Pour the cordial into the glass. Top with bubbly.

Common Milkweed Flower Vinegar — The Quick Way

Makes 5 cups (1¼ liters)

To make a quick, fragrant vinegar from the flavorful pomace (basically flower dregs, in this case) left over after straining Fermented Common Milkweed Flower Cordial, I like to use honey, which complements the flowers' aroma. The resulting vinegar is great for dressings but is also refreshing sipped with sparkling water on muggy days.

4 cups (1 liter) pomace from Fermented
    Common Milkweed Flower Cordial
1 cup (250 ml) honey
3 cups (750 ml) white wine vinegar
1 cup (250 ml) water

Combine all the ingredients in a clean glass jar and stir well, until the honey has dissolved. Cover the mouth of the jar with cheesecloth secured with string or a rubber band, and let sit at room temperature for 1 week. Strain through a fine-mesh sieve, and then through a couple of layers of cheesecloth. Bottle in clean, narrow-necked bottles.

Common Milkweed Flower Vinegar — The Long Way

Makes about 5 cups (1¼ liters)

This was the first vinegar I ever made. By accident. A lid on a bottle of cordial had not been tightened. Air crept in. The cordial was transformed into excellent vinegar. I now make it on purpose, and it is surprisingly simple. Fermentation times vary widely, and the timing below is a rough guideline. Excellent tomes have been written on the subject of vinegar making.

6 cups (1½ liters) Fermented Common
    Milkweed Cordial

Instead of bottling your Fermented Common Milkweed Flower Cordial after straining, return it to its large jar or jars. It should not fill more than half the jar (air is good). Cover the mouth with cheesecloth secured with string or an elastic band. Leave it out at room temperature and allow nature to take its course. Acetobacter are everywhere.

After 3 to 5 weeks, if it smells and tastes like vinegar, it is vinegar. With some of my vinegars, a mother of vinegar forms on top around the 4- to 5-week mark, but it can take longer (or shorter). And sometimes it does not form. When the vinegar tastes good, strain it into clean, narrow-necked bottles and seal. If a visible mother of vinegar has formed (it doesn't, always), scoop it out gently and store for later use in an airtight jar, covered in any vinegar (it must be submerged to stay alive).

New Potato Salad with Common Milkweed Vinegar

Serves 4 as a side

This is the kind of salad I whip together without thinking on a day when the first summer potatoes have been dug and the garden's salad leaves and herbs look luscious. You can use the herbs of your choice; I favor peppery nasturtium, chervil, chives, and whatever salad leaves the garden is producing. The vinegar never fails to deliver a splash of uniquely seasonal foraged flavor.

1 head new, green garlic
3 tablespoons Common Milkweed
    Flower Vinegar
¼ teaspoon salt
1 teaspoon sugar
1 pound (453 g) new potatoes
2 tablespoons cream
1 tablespoon extra-virgin olive oil
3 loose handfuls fresh salad leaves
    and herbs
Black pepper

Chop the new garlic very finely. In a bowl combine the vinegar, salt, sugar, and chopped garlic. Muddle and let sit for 10 minutes. Cook the potatoes in boiling, salted water until just tender. Timing will depend on their size. Drain. Add the warm potatoes to the vinegar mixture and toss well. Pour in the cream and oil. Toss again. Now add the leaves and herbs. Toss once more. Serve right away, with black pepper cracked over the top.

Roasted Common Milkweed Pods

Serves 4 as a side

The soft interior texture of young milkweed pods is emphasized by a crisp coat of bread crumbs. If you have never eaten a milkweed pod before, this simple method is good place to start. I choose pods up to 1½ inches (4 cm) long. They are delicious straight from the oven, although an addition of cut lemon wedges or good aioli is never a bad idea.

1 pound (453 g) young common
    milkweed pods
3 tablespoons olive oil, plus extra
¼ teaspoon salt
⅓ cup (20 g) panko bread crumbs
1 tablespoon chile flakes (optional)

Preheat the oven to 400°F (200°C).

Bring a large pot of water to a boil. Drop in the milkweed pods and blanch for 2 minutes. Drain, refresh in cold water, and roll them up in a kitchen towel to absorb extra moisture—they are sponges and can turn soggy. Place them in a bowl. Drizzle the olive oil over them and toss the pods so that they are well coated. Add the salt, the bread crumbs, and the chile flakes, if using. Toss very well again.

Oil two baking sheets with some extra olive oil. Spread the pods evenly over the sheets, adding any bread crumbs that have lingered in the bowl. Roast in the oven until the crumbs and pods are beginning to brown, about 40 minutes. Serve piping hot.

Common Milkweed Pod Fried Rice

Serves 2

The first part of this recipe forms a wild summer *soffrito*—the basis of flavor on which anything else can be built (like a Creole gumbo's onion and green pepper, or Italy's onion-celery-carrot foundation). My quirk is adding fresh curry leaf—I grow potted plants and bring them indoors in our cold winters. After the rice, your larder or leftovers will yield the rest. Mushrooms, cold chicken or meat, other vegetables. For me it might be leftover Spicebush Tequila Skirt Steak, or Soy-Pickled Oyster Mushrooms. The one secret to good fried rice is sufficient oil. *Yes.* Make sure it is high quality.

WILD SUMMER SOFFRITO

4 tablespoons unscented oil, divided

1 large onion, finely chopped

1 cup (about 3 ounces/85 g) baby common milkweed pods

1 tablespoon Salted Ramp Leaves

1 branch curry leaves

1 teaspoon ground cumin

½ teaspoon ground spicebush

3 cups cooked rice

1 tablespoon soy sauce

1 tablespoon lime juice

Lime wedges, for serving

OPTIONAL ADDITIONS

1 cup (150 g) Soy-Pickled Oyster Mushrooms

1 cup (150 g) thinly sliced Spicebush Tequila Skirt Steak

Heat 3 tablespoons of the oil over medium heat in a skillet. Add the onion. Cook, stirring occasionally, for a slow 25 minutes, until it has turned sweet and golden brown. If it scorches, reduce the heat. While the onion is cooking, bring a pot of water to a boil and drop the milkweed buds in to blanch. Scoop them out after a minute and drain. Pat them dry (they soak up moisture). Add the milkweed pods to the onion with the Salted Ramp Leaves, curry leaves, cumin, and spicebush. Stir well. Cook for another 5 minutes. Increase the heat to high, add the remaining tablespoon of oil, and stir in the rice, breaking it up if it is cold and has lumps. Add the soy sauce and lime juice and stir thoroughly. It is ready when the rice is hot.

If you are adding the extras, this is the time to do it. Stir them in and incorporate well. When heated through, serve, with lime wedges on the side.

Dandelion

OTHER COMMON NAMES: None in current use in English

BOTANICAL NAME: *Taraxacum* species

STATUS: Invasive perennial in North America, also cultivated as a vegetable

WHERE: Gardens, lawns, open ground, farmers markets, supermarkets

SEASON: Early spring through fall

USE: Vegetable, salad leaf

PARTS USED: Root, crown, leaves, stem, and flowers

GROW? Yes

TASTES LIKE: Frisée meets radicchio

Dandelions are the familiar faces of the weed-eating world. Even if you have never gone hunting for wild edible plants, the chances are good that you have met a dandelion. Transplants from Europe, they are one of the most cosmopolitan weeds.

Love at first bite they are not. For many people dandelions are an acquired taste. They can be very bitter. That is not necessarily a bad thing, as many other cultures know. But try them in the transition between late winter and early spring, when they are at their mildest.

Once you have identified their ragged late-winter rosettes growing flush with the cold ground, the whole crown can be dug up. Dandelions are good to eat as soon as the ground thaws, when they are at their mildest and most succulent. Once trimmed, cleaned, and soaked in ice water (to crisp them up), dandelion crowns are one of the earliest and best treats of early spring.

Eaten raw in a salad, quick-pickled, or cooked, they are a juicy revelation if you have only tasted the mature and uncompromising green leaves.

While the root can be used after drying, for a hot beverage or an infusion, I am not personally wild about the flavor. If you would like to try it, there is a lot of information about it on the web.

In midspring sunny dandelion flowers make this useful food easy to spot in a sea of anonymous green. They also drive some lawn owners nuts. If I had a lawn, I would be happy with a salad bar right in the middle of it. Your own (untreated) lawn might be the best place to look for this versatile perennial vegetable. I nurture my single volunteered plant, growing in gravel.

The blooms appear singly on hollow stems, which bleed a white latex when picked (some dandelion look-alikes have branching flower stems and fibrous stalks). The stems themselves are a crunchy salad ingredient (especially after the ice-water-bath treatment). After being introduced to succulent and bitter puntarelle (a sought-after variety of chicory) served in a strong dressing of lemon and anchovy at Al di La, a local Italian restaurant, I realized how similar the flower stems are in texture and flavor.

If you have the patience to collect them, dandelion flowers make the whimsical dandelion wine, loved by literature. For a simpler effervescent fermentation, follow the method for Fermented Common Milkweed Flower Cordial. Perversely, for someone with a penchant for fermenting flowers, I find the flavor of the flowers to be too mild to be worth the trouble and prefer the strong-tasting flower stems. The flowers are often made into fritters; like anything fresh-fried, they are appealing. Again, I prefer flavors with a stronger presence, and so I save my frittering for elderflowers and black locust.

Dandelion leaves are dentated, meaning they have tooth-like edges (their teeth point back down toward the stem), giving rise to the French name *dent-de-lion*. Lion's teeth. A more archaic French term for dandelion is *pissenlit*: pee in bed, referring to its reported diuretic properties. This may be a plant to avoid in quantity (by juicing, for example) if you have compromised kidney function.

As spring progresses the leaves become more strongly flavored. The mildest are harvested from plants that have not yet flowered, and also from dandelions that grow in the shade. They can be eaten right through to the beginning of winter but will become more assertive as the weather warms (late fall can produce a fresh flush of mild leaves). In her beautiful and collectable book *Vegetables from Amaranth to Zucchini*, author Elizabeth Schneider writes: "The bitterness can be balanced with roasted nut oils, fruit or sherry or balsamic vinegars, and cheese with sharpness and acidity . . . or mitigate[d] . . . with citrus fruit or beets." I agree. And it is not merely about mitigation, or hiding, but about the pleasure of contrasts. Classic French *salade Lyonnaise* calls for warm bacon fat, crispy bacon, sharp vinegar, soft eggs, and crisp croutons; the accompanying wilted and bitter leaves are almost a relief.

Mature dandelion leaves—the kind I can buy in bunches from my local organic greengrocer—are best cooked. The strongly flavored greens are beloved around the edges of the eastern Mediterranean. In Greece they belong to the catchall collection of wild edible weeds called *horta*, cooked and tossed with oil, lemon juice, and salt. They are also typical pie ingredients. A dandelion and sheep's-milk cheese pie I take on my forage walks disappears almost before I can slice it.

How to Collect and Prepare

For the early-spring crowns, dig them up with small trowel or knife, trimming off most of the root below the crown and any winter-battered leaves above it. Soak the intact crowns in water. Scrub well (a toothbrush is helpful) to remove all the soil and grit that will be lodged where the leaves meet the crown after a long winter flat on the ground.

For flower stems, snap off as low down as possible. Revive flower stems in a bowl of water with some ice cubes added.

The picked leaves keep well if kept wrapped in the fridge. If they have wilted in transit, plunge them into a bowl of water to perk them up before drying and wrapping. Blanching mature leaves for a minute in boiling water tames their bitterness dramatically.

CULTIVATION TIPS
USDA Hardiness Zones 3–10

Dandelions are best grown from seed, as their long taproots make established plants hard to transplant. Sow seed shallowly in full sun or light shade in spring, after your last frost date, or in early fall, six weeks before the first frost date. They germinate best in cool temperatures.

Dandelion Crown Pad Thai

Serves 4 as an appetizer

This recipe calls for the crisp crowns that are such an ephemeral delight before the new leaves shoot up in spring. They must be washed scrupulously, as tiny bits of grit become lodged where the stems meet the crown.

NOODLES

1 box (8 ounces/227 g) pad Thai
   rice noodles
3 tablespoons unscented oil, divided
8 large bulbs field garlic, thinly sliced
2 large eggs

DANDELIONS

2 tablespoons unscented oil
16 spring dandelion crowns, squeaky-clean

SAUCE

1 tablespoon Sumac Essence
2 tablespoons tamarind paste
3 tablespoons fish sauce
3 tablespoons sugar

EXTRAS

⅓ cup (50 g) chopped, roasted peanuts
4 lime wedges

Soak the noodles in a bowl of very hot water for 8 minutes.

FOR THE DANDELIONS: Heat the oil over high heat in a pan that can accommodate the crowns in a single layer. Add the dandelions and wilt them, stirring often, for no more than 2 minutes—they will lose volume quite fast. Remove them to a plate.

FOR THE SAUCE: Combine the sauce ingredients and stir well.

FOR THE FINISHED NOODLES: Reduce the heat under the pan to medium and add 2 tablespoons of the oil. Add the sliced field garlic, cooking until the pieces are tender. Now add the remaining tablespoon of oil and crack the eggs into the pan. Immediately add the drained noodles to the eggs and toss well (it's easiest with kitchen tongs or large chopsticks), mixing the egg in. Increase the heat to medium-high and pour the sauce ingredients over the noodles. Finally, return the dandelion crowns to the pan with the noodles, and toss to heat through. Top with roasted peanuts and add a lime wedge, if you like.

Dandelion Lyonnaise Bruschetta

Serves 4

One of the nicest ways to eat young dandelions is based on the classic salade Lyonnaise, where the leaves are dressed in a warm vinaigrette and crunchy bits of bacon, rounded out by sunny egg yolks. I serve it as bruschetta. Cooking bacon in a hot oven makes it beautifully crisp and flat, and it does not spit at you. If you prefer the stove, and do not flinch when spat upon, cook your bacon there. A version of this recipe first appeared on *Gardenista*.

2 tablespoons sherry vinegar

½ teaspoon sugar

Large pinch of salt

4 strips bacon

3 large eggs

4 slices sourdough bread

2 ramp bulbs or 4 field garlic bulbs

8 ounces (227 g) dandelion leaves, washed and dried

1 tablespoon olive oil

Black pepper

Preheat the oven to 400°F (200°C).

In a small bowl mix the vinegar with the sugar and salt until those dissolve. Set aside.

Lay the bacon flat in a skillet and place in the hot oven. Roast the bacon until it is crisp—12 to 15 minutes—turning once.

Bring the eggs to a boil in a small pot of water for 1 minute, turn off the heat, and let them sit in the water for 6 minutes. Dunk in cold water and peel. Chop them roughly—the yolks should be barely set.

While the bacon and eggs are cooking, toast the bread. As soon as it is toasted, rub both sides with the raw ramp or field garlic bulbs. Set aside on a plate.

As soon as the bacon is crisp, remove it from the skillet. Pour off all but 1 tablespoon of the rendered bacon fat. Toss the dandelion leaves into the fat in the hot skillet and stir. Add the vinegar mixture at once and toss the leaves, adding the olive oil last. Pile the wilted leaves onto the toasted bread; break the bacon into pieces and scatter on top of the dandelions. Finally, add the egg, distributing the pieces evenly. If there are any pan juices left, drizzle these over the top of your bruschetta. Finish with lots of freshly ground black pepper. Serve at once.

Pickled Dandelion Stems

Makes 2 cups (500 ml)

These spicy pickles are delicious on buttered bread, or in soups and stews. You can use the stems even after the flowers have faded—they will just be more bitter, though this softens with time. The juicy midribs of large leaves can be pickled in the same way.

8 ounces (227 g) dandelion flower stems, washed

1 cup (250 ml) white wine vinegar

1 cup (250 ml) water

3 tablespoons sugar

1 tablespoon salt

8 bird's eye chiles

10 allspice berries

Trim the ends of the dandelions neatly and cut them to fit the size of the jar or jars you are using. Pack the trimmed stems into clean jars. In a large jug mix the vinegar and water with the sugar and salt. Stir until the granules have dissolved. Pour over the dandelion stems until they are covered (add more liquid, if necessary, in a 1:1 ratio of vinegar to water). Add the chiles and allspice. Seal and store at room temperature. Keep in the fridge once open. Leftover brine is excellent in vinaigrettes.

Dandelion Phyllo Triangles

Makes 27 small triangles (9 triangles per 2 phyllo sheets)

Like their counterparts the Lamb's Quarter and Beet Leaf Phyllo Triangles, these crisp pies are easy to make and even easier to store and cook. I blanch dandelion leaves to remove some bitterness.

12 ounces (340 g) dandelion leaves

2 ounces (57 g) soft goat cheese

2 ounces (57 g) ricotta

1 tablespoon Salted Ramp Leaves

1 teaspoon Ground Sumac

½ teaspoon Ramp Leaf Salt

6 sheets regular phyllo pastry

4 tablespoons melted butter, plus extra, if necessary

Trim off any tough stalks from the leaves. Bring a pot of water to a boil. Drop the dandelions into the water, bring it to a boil again, and push them under. Keep doing this for 3 minutes. Lift them out, refresh them in cold water, and squeeze them as dry as possible. Untangle the squeezed leaves and place them in a bowl. Add all the other filling ingredients, except the phyllo and butter, and mix well.

Unwrap the phyllo sheets and cover them with a damp kitchen towel to prevent them from drying. Take one sheet, lay it on a dry work surface, and brush it with butter, working from the edges in. Lay a second sheet on top and repeat.

Working quickly, cut the sheets lengthwise twice and across twice, to make nine even squares. Lay a spoonful of filling in the top right-hand quadrant of each square.

Fold 1: Fold the left half of the square over the filled side and press down. Brush the exposed phyllo with butter. Fold 2: Fold the bottom of the new rectangle over the top filled side to make a new, small square. Brush with butter again. Fold 3: Finally, fold the square's top right corner toward the bottom left corner, to form a triangle. Press down firmly to stick the phyllo together. Brush with butter. Transfer each triangle to a buttered baking sheet and cover with plastic or a damp tea towel until you are ready to bake. They can be chilled in the fridge or frozen at this point.

Repeat until you have made 27 triangles.

TO BAKE: Preheat the oven to 400°F (200°C). Bake the triangles in batches until one side is turning golden, about 8 minutes, then turn them. Bake until the second side is golden. Eat hot or at room temperature. Once cool they can be frozen.

Dandelion Stem Salad

Serves 4 as a side or appetizer

The discovery that supple dandelion flower stems have a snappy texture and bitter kick was a happy one—they remind me a lot of coveted puntarelle, an Italian chicory. Bright lemon and salty anchovies create a bracing dressing for the strongly flavored stems.

8 ounces (227 g) dandelion flower stems
4 anchovy fillets
2 tablespoons finely chopped field
    garlic bulbs
2 tablespoons red wine vinegar
½ teaspoon lemon zest
1 tablespoon extra-virgin olive oil

Refresh stems in an ice-water bath for an hour to crisp them up. Drain and dry. Chop the anchovies finely, then mash them together with the field garlic bulbs. Put them in a small bowl and add the vinegar and lemon zest. Stir well, then add the olive oil and stir again. Place the stems in a large bowl, pour the dressing over, and toss very well.

Dandelion Dagwood

Serves 4

My mother made an occasional fast-food-ish treat for us when we were little: a long thin loaf of white bread sliced in three horizontally and stuffed with layers of cheesy ham and leftover chicken with mayonnaise. It came out of the oven gooey with melted goodness. We all called it a dagwood. This is my forager's version.

TOP LAYER

8 slices good bacon
1½ pounds (680 g) dandelion leaves, washed
2 tablespoons Elderflower Vinegar
Black pepper
Salt

BOTTOM LAYER

2 cups (230 g) grated sharp cheddar
2 tablespoons Garlic Mustard Root Relish
3 tablespoons smooth Dijon mustard
⅓ cup (80 ml) mayonnaise
Salt

BREAD

1 mîche or round sourdough loaf

FOR THE TOP LAYER: Preheat the oven to 400°F (200°C). Lay the bacon strips on a sheet pan and roast until they are crisp, about 12 to 15 minutes. Save 1 tablespoon of the melted fat. Lay the bacon on a paper towel to drain.

Place the dandelion leaves in a pot over medium-high heat with ¼ cup (60 ml) water. Cover and wilt for 6 to 8 minutes. Turn the leaves a few times. When they have collapsed completely, drain any extra water from the pot. Add the tablespoon of bacon fat and the vinegar. Turn the leaves and coat well with the dressing. Crack over some black pepper and add a pinch of salt.

FOR THE BOTTOM LAYER: In a bowl combine the cheese, Garlic Mustard Root Relish, mustard, and mayonnaise. Add a pinch of salt. Mix very well.

TO ASSEMBLE: Slice the loaf horizontally into three equal pieces. Spread the cheese mixture on the bottom later. Place the middle piece of bread on top and press down lightly. Lay the dandelion leaves on top, and top those with the crisp strips of bacon. Add the top of the bread.

Lay the stuffed loaf on large sheet of foil. Wrap and close it tightly. Place it in the hot oven for 15 minutes, which will be enough to melt the cheese and toast the bread. Place on a bread board and unwrap at the table. Serve in thick slices.

Dandelion and Pork Sausage Giant Hoagie

Serves 4

We live in an Italian neighborhood where you can buy sloppy hoagies stuffed with oily rapini and chile. I love bitter flavors with heat and lemon, so when I collect a bunch of bitter summer dandelions, this is a good local way to use them. I like English-style pork sausages or chipolatas for the hoagie, but breakfast sausage with its breath of fennel is more traditional. Wilting summer dandelions in salt extracts some of their bitterness.

4 ounces (113 g) dandelion leaves, washed

¼ cup salt

3 tablespoons olive oil

1¼ pounds (567 g) pork sausage, removed from casing

4 cloves garlic, chopped

1 teaspoon chile flakes

1 tablespoon lemon juice

1 loaf crusty white bread, such as ciabatta

3 ounces (85 g) grated mozzarella

Bruise the dandelion leaves lightly by squeezing them in your hands. Place them in a bowl and cover with the salt. Massage the leaves and let them sit for 30 minutes, then rinse them very well.

Preheat the oven to 425°F (220°C).

Heat the oil in a large skillet over medium-high heat and add the sausage. Break up the meat with a spoon as it sizzles. Cook until one side is beginning to brown, about 8 minutes. Add the garlic and cook another 3 minutes. Add the chile and lemon juice and stir well. Now add the dandelion leaves and stir well. Cook another minute. Slice the bread in half, horizontally. Scoop out some of the bread's innards to create a long trough (save and dry the bread for crumbs). Pile the meat, the leaves, and any residual oil into the trough and spread out well. Sprinkle the grated mozzarella over the filling. Top with the lid of the bread. Wrap in foil and transfer to the hot oven for 10 minutes.

Serve straight from its foil, cutting into generous, sloppy slices.

Dandelion Field Garlic Short Ribs

Serves 4

I make this rich, easy stew when days are lengthening but spring nights remain chilly. It keeps very well and reheats like a dream.

1 pound (453 g) dandelion leaves

2 tablespoons white miso

4 beef short ribs (about 1 pound/453 g each), 1 rib per person

2 tablespoons soy sauce

1 cup (120 g) rhubarb cut into thick slices

1 tablespoon sugar

½ teaspoon ground spicebush

½ cup (70 g) field garlic bulbs

Preheat the oven to 400°F (200°C).

Bring a pot of water to a boil. Drop in the dandelion leaves and blanch at a boil for 30 seconds, dunking them under. Remove, drain, refresh in cold water, and squeeze lightly dry.

Thin the miso with a little water. In a Dutch oven or casserole dish, combine all the ingredients and add 2 cups of water, or enough to cover the beef. Place in the oven and cook for 2½ hours. Check on it every 40 minutes or so, pushing the dandelions beneath the surface and turning the ribs so that the tops brown evenly. If you will be eating at once, tilt the pot to one side and scoop off as much of the floating fat as possible. Otherwise, chill until Day 2, remove any congealed fat, and reheat gently.

Dandelion Pie

Makes 2 pies, 10 inches (25 cm) each

Feta and sumac are classic Mediterranean and Middle Eastern companions to any wild leafy greens. This hearty recipe works with amaranths, lamb's quarters, nettles, and quickweed, as well as spinach and chard.

DOUGH

1 tablespoon yeast

1 teaspoon sugar

1¼ cups (310 ml) tepid water

1 pound (453 g) all-purpose flour

¾ teaspoon salt

⅓ cup (80 ml) extra-virgin olive oil

FILLING

2¼ pounds (1 kg) dandelion leaves and
     tender stems, washed and still wet

½ teaspoon salt

2 tablespoons lemon juice

6 ounces (170 g) feta cheese,
     roughly crumbled

2 teaspoons Ground Sumac

¼ teaspoon black pepper

FOR THE DOUGH: Mix the yeast with the sugar in the tepid water in a jug and allow it to bubble. Place the flour and salt in a mixing bowl, pour in the yeast mixture and the oil, and stir well until a cohesive dough forms. Turn out onto a board and knead until it feels silky, supple, and elastic and does not stick to your fingers—at least 10 minutes. Place in a clean, lightly oiled bowl and cover. Allow it to rise until it has doubled, about 1 to 2 hours. Return the dough to a floured board and knead for a few seconds. Divide it in four pieces. Let it rest for 10 minutes, covered.

FOR THE FILLING: In a large covered pot over medium heat, cook the wet dandelion leaves with the salt and lemon juice until they are completely wilted, about 10 minutes. Refresh them under cold water, then drain and squeeze as dry as possible. Chop them roughly. Place the greens and feta in a bowl, add the sumac and pepper, and toss well.

TO ASSEMBLE: Preheat the oven to 450°F (230°C). Oil two baking sheets. Working with two balls at a time, roll the dough flat into 10- to 11-inch (25–28 cm) disks. Gently wrap one disk around your rolling pin and transfer to a baking sheet. Readjust its shape if it stretches in the transfer. Heap half the dandelion filling onto the dough and spread it out, leaving the outside ½ inch (1 cm) clear. Wet that edge with water. Place the second rolled-out disk on top of the first, covering the filling. Press down and crimp the edges. Cut some steam vents in the top and slide into the hot oven. Repeat with the second pie. Bake each pie until golden, 20 to 25 minutes.

Dandelion and Soy Chicken

Serves 4

Layers of flavor, with the earthiness of dandelion stems balancing the rooty sweetness of carrots and yams, make this a comfort dish worth every loud slurp.

CHICKEN

4 chicken thighs

1 thumb-sized piece of ginger, cut into matchsticks

2 long chiles, like serrano, halved lengthwise

4 shallots, sliced in half lengthwise

2 tablespoons soy sauce

1 tablespoon lime juice

¼ cup (60 ml) water

BROTH

1 tablespoon unscented oil

⅓ cup (50 g) chopped field garlic bulbs

½ medium onion, finely sliced

1 cup (140 g) finely diced carrots

2 tablespoons soy sauce

3 cups (750 ml) water or chicken broth

8 ounces (227 g) yams, in narrow wedges

2 ounces (57 g) mature dandelion stems and leaves

1 lemongrass heart, halved

1 stick kombu (dried kelp)

2 teaspoons sugar

2 heaped tablespoons bonito flakes

8 ounces (227 g) soba noodles (optional)

1 ounce (28 g) Pickled Dandelion Stems

FOR THE CHICKEN: Preheat the oven to 450°F (230°C).

Lay the chicken thighs in a skillet. Tuck the ginger matchsticks and the chiles under each piece. Add the shallots to the skillet. Pour in the soy sauce, lime juice, and water. Roast in the oven until the chicken is deep golden brown and crisp on top, about 50 to 55 minutes.

FOR THE BROTH: While the chicken is roasting, heat the oil in a pot over medium heat. Add the field garlic, onion, and carrots and sauté for 15 minutes, occasionally stirring. Add the soy and chicken broth or water, along with the yams, dandelions, lemongrass, kombu, and sugar. Increase the heat to bring the liquid to a brief boil, then reduce it to keep the broth at a simmer until the yams are tender, about 35 minutes. Place the bonito flakes in a perforated ladle, piece of cheesecloth, or small strainer and lower this into the hot liquid. Infuse for 5 minutes. Lift them out, squeezing every drop from the flakes.

TO FINISH: When the chicken is cooked, remove it to a dish and keep warm. Transfer the chiles, ginger, and shallots from the skillet to the broth pot. Deglaze the chicken pan over high heat with a ladleful of the broth. Pour the chicken pan's juices into the broth. Taste the broth for seasoning. If necessary balance it out with a little more lime juice.

TO SERVE: If you are using noodles, bring the broth to a gentle boil and add them, cooking them until just tender, about 8 minutes. Add a ladleful of broth and some of the vegetables to each bowl. With tongs add a nest of noodles. Top each nest with the crispy chicken, and arrange a bundle of spicy Pickled Dandelion Stems alongside. If you're not using the noodles, add a ladleful of broth and some of the vegetables to each bowl, top with the crispy chicken, and arrange a bundle of spicy Pickled Dandelion Stems alongside.

Daylily

OTHER COMMON NAMES: Ditch lily, common orange daylily, tawny daylily

BOTANICAL NAME: *Hemerocallis fulva*

STATUS: Invasive perennial in North America, vegetable in China and Japan

WHERE: Open ground, woodland, gardens

SEASON: Spring, summer, and fall

USE: Vegetable

PARTS USED: Tubers, young shoots, buds, and flowers

GROW? Only if you are vigilant about their spread

TASTES LIKE: Green bean meets white asparagus by way of leek

Orange daylily tubers, shoots, buds, and flowers are delicious and easy to prepare and have been eaten by many thousands, if not millions, of people, for a very, very long time: They are a common food in China. Increasingly (if you are counting in tiny increments) the shoots and buds are offered on restaurant menus, foraged and supplied by seasoned as well as newly minted professional foragers. The tender spring shoots are meltingly good when cooked slowly, like leeks. Early summer's buds are a crisp salad ingredient with a hint of scallion breath, while the open flowers add drama to any plate. The small tubers are a very good starchy vegetable.

But there is still a sense of mystery and uncertainty accompanying the edible nature of *Hemerocallis fulva*, and I feel it is important to illuminate the issue, at the risk of being verbose, as well as frustratingly inconclusive.

Scrupulous foraging writers will inform you that a few people experience gastric distress after eating daylilies. It is true. I know of four people who have been sickened (the symptoms are diarrhea, and sometimes vomiting) after eating the flowers of *Hemerocallis fulva*. One of them is wild foods author Dr. John Kallas, author of *Edible Wild Plants*. He and a friend became ill after eating a flower and six raw buds. This has not happened to me, or to countless people who have eaten them with no ill effect. Understanding why it happens is a real head scratcher. It is worth putting it into a broader context. Not all toxicities are the same,

and there are several factors to consider before you sit down to dinner.

First: Not infrequently, several different plants share a common name. When talking about ingesting plants, that can lead to trouble. Some people call daylilies tiger lilies. Tiger lily is in fact *Lilium lancifolium*, a different genus, whose flowers are reported to be toxic, at least to cats. (Perversely, the bulbs of *Lilium* species are edible, when cooked. But that is another story.) So there is that. Identify your *Hemerocallis fulva* with certainty.

And then we get to diploids, tetraploids, and triploids. Fasten your seat belts.

Most documented (important distinction) daylily poisonings—human and animal—are associated with eating species daylilies (meaning not cultivars or hybrids) in Asia, where the plants are widely consumed. The toxin responsible for these poisonings *appears* to be hemerocallin, a neurotoxin. The poisonings, some of which are fatal, are associated with the tubers and roots of specific species. *Hemerocallis fulva* is not one of them. What seems to be relevant is that the species daylilies in question are diploids. Diploids have two sets of chromosomes: one set from the egg cell and one set from the sperm in the pollen. In other words, they are fertile and make seeds.

Hemerocallis fulva, our common orange daylily, is a triploid. It has three sets of chromosomes and is usually infertile, as it does not set fertile seed (its invasive nature is due to its spreading rhizomes).

In daylily breeding, which is a massive industry, many of the *thousands* of cultivars (the word is short for "cultivated varieties," with the name always appearing in single quotation marks) created are tetraploids—they have four sets of chromosomes. Tetraploids are valued for ornamental reasons: larger flowers and sturdier leaves and stalks. You do not become a tetraploid by wishing it. A toxic alkaloid (not all alkaloids are bad for us) called colchicine—extracted from meadow crocus (*Colchicum autumnale*)—is used to induce polyploidy (more than two sets of chromosomes). It is theorized that eating daylily cultivars (bred for the horticultural trade) exposed to colchicine, rather than the good old orange ditch lily *Hemerocallis fulva*, may result in the distress that some foragers experience. But it is also extremely doubtful that the colchicine persists in a plant regenerated from tissue culture. These findings are not (yet, perhaps) supported by good science.

Finally, there are the bad reactions to daylilies that have been identified positively as *H. fulva*. Dr. Kallas says that the only pattern he has seen is that errant plants are responsible. "That is, it is not a personal food sensitivity. . . . Anyone who eats the errant plants will have symptoms. I had eaten many daylilies before . . . and have eaten many daylilies since without incident. But I have not gone back to that same patch that caused the problem." It is a compelling theory. Then again, I know of two foragers who have eaten raw daylily flowers and shoots from different patches in different states, experiencing gastric distress each time. Were those all errant plants? Are those people simply sensitive to daylilies? Would cooking render the plants harmless for them?

And what does this mean for us, the hungry and worried foragers?

It is well worth conveying that traditional Chinese methods of preparing daylilies include soaking and blanching. Tradition carries a lot of weight. And I know of one Chinese Canadian forager (Shell Yu) with a biochemical background who scrupulously soaks buds and fresh flowers *and* removes their anthers and pistils. These preparation methods have been studied in China—and even if the toxin targeted in the studies may be the wrong one, perhaps the soaking leaches the plant of another.

To summarize: Daylilies have been eaten for thousands of years and can be delicious. If care is not taken in choosing your daylilies, you may have a bad time. The triploid *Hemerocallis fulva* is the yummy one (for most people). Avoid the diploid wild species. Avoid the horticultural cultivars. And eat daylilies (or any new food) in moderation.

One day, we may know more.

How to Collect and Prepare

Tubers: Dig the tubers in early spring when the first daylily shoots are pushing above the ground. You can also dig them in early through late fall, when they have fattened up again. They will always be there waiting for you but can be more flaccid in the summer months. Wash and scrub very well, using the rough side of a sponge. They do not have to be peeled. Soak or parboil before proceeding with the recipes.

Shoots: Young tender shoots are the best to eat, and I harvest them around 3 to 8 inches in height. Their tenderness is the most important factor. Trim as you would a leek: Slit them down the middle, stopping short of the whitest end. Soak in water to dislodge any soil.

Buds and flowers: Easy, just pick.

Traditional Chinese methods advocate soaking the buds in water before eating raw or cooked. They also suggest removing the anthers and pistil from open flowers, erring on the side of caution.

Caution

If you are trying daylilies for the first time, make sure you are have identified *Hemerocallis fulva* correctly. Eat a small amount. If you are surfing online for more answers, choose your sources critically, stick to scientific papers and university sites (and read between those lines, too), and absorb what experienced foragers write.

CULTIVATION TIPS
USDA Hardiness Zones 3–10

Escaped daylilies are damagingly invasive: Although eating the tubers and shoots controls a patch well, manage a cultivated clump rigorously to prevent its sideways migration. Divide clumps if they become too large, chopping them up and composting the remains. The plants grow in full sun as well as in dappled or semi-shade.

Daylily Tubers Poached in Olive Oil

Serves 4 as a side or appetizer

Daylily tubers are fattest in early to late spring and again in late fall. Poaching them slowly with aromatics turns the little tubers buttery and soft. Serve with good bread for dipping and wiping the bowls.

2 cups (8 ounces/227 g) daylily tubers, trimmed and scrubbed

1 teaspoon coriander seeds, toasted

1 cup (250 ml) extra-virgin olive oil, divided

8 field garlic bulbs, trimmed and slit lengthwise

½ teaspoon salt

¼ teaspoon black pepper

1 tablespoon lemon juice

8 sprigs marjoram or oregano flowers or leaves

6 stalks thyme

4 fronds fennel

Place the daylily tubers in a pot of salted water and bring to a brief boil. Cook at a simmer for 10 minutes. Drain the water.

Return the dry pot to medium heat and add the coriander seeds. Toast them until they are fragrant. Add 2 tablespoons of the oil and then the field garlic bulbs. Sauté gently for 2 minutes. Add the daylily tubers and toss well. Sprinkle the salt and pepper over them, tossing again. Add the lemon juice and the herbs, stir well, and pour on the rest of the olive oil. Heat the oil until tiny bubbles form, and then keep the pot on medium-low to poach very gently—uncovered—for an hour. Serve hot.

Daylily Tuber Oven Fries

Serves 2 as a side

After the work of digging, scrubbing, trimming, and soaking, daylily tubers reward you by roasting much faster than potatoes. Watch them, or they will burn. While their edges will be deliciously crisp, roasted daylilies will be more caramelized than potato chips.

1 pound (453 g) daylily tubers, washed and cut in half lengthwise

3 tablespoons olive oil

½ teaspoon Ramp Leaf Salt

Soak the cut tubers in a basin of water for 2 hours. Drain and dry.

Preheat the oven to 425°F (220°C).

Place the tubers in a bowl with the olive oil and toss very well. Spread them out on a baking sheet and roast until they are pale brown and smelling just like roast potatoes—about 35 minutes. Season with the salt as soon as they come out of the oven.

Daylily Hash Browns

Serves 4 as a side

I add a little potato to a daylily hash to help bind the mixture with the starch from the potato. Good trimmings for this hash include eggs, cooked pokeweed shoots, the first local asparagus, crisp ham, or your favorite greens.

10 ounces (283 g) daylily tubers, washed well and sliced lengthwise

4 ounces (113 g) grated potato, rinsed and dried

½ teaspoon Field Garlic Salt

1 tablespoon butter

Cook the daylilies in boiling salted water until barely tender. Drain.

Combine the drained daylilies and the grated potato in a bowl. Add the Field Garlic Salt and mix well with your fingers to break it up. In a small skillet melt the butter over medium heat, swirling it around the edges. Pile the daylily-potato mixture into the middle of the skillet and then spread it evenly across the bottom of the pan. Reduce the heat to low and cover the skillet with a lid. Cook for 10 minutes. Gently loosen the hash all around with a knife or spatula. Flip the brown bits over to crisp the other side. Cook another 10 minutes, uncovered. Serve piping hot.

Braised Daylily Shoots

Serves 2 as an entrée, 4 as an appetizer

Daylily's spring shoots have a delicate flavor reminiscent of the sweetness of slow-cooked leeks. Eat them hot or cold as an appetizer or side dish, add them to complex broths like Wild Roast Salmon with Spring Forages, layer them with thin sheets of fresh pasta, or—my favorite by far— simply lay the meltingly soft shoots over sturdy toast with a pinch of Ramp Leaf Salt, a scattering of snipped field garlic greens, and some peppery brassica flowers.

3 tablespoons extra-virgin olive oil, plus extra
8 ounces (227 g) daylily shoots (12–20, depending on size), trimmed and well washed
¼ cup (60 ml) water
⅛ teaspoon salt
Black pepper
2 teaspoons lemon juice
4 slices sturdy bread
Pinch of Ramp Leaf Salt
Field garlic greens (optional)
Arugula or mustard flowers (optional)

Heat the oil over medium heat in a skillet. Add the shoots in a single later. Pour in the water and season with the salt and pepper. Bring the liquid to a boil, then reduce the heat to low and braise gently for 20 minutes, covered. Add the lemon juice, turn the shoots over, and cook another 15 minutes. For the last 5 minutes, increase the heat to medium-high to cook off any remaining liquid. Toast the bread and drizzle it with some extra olive oil. Lay the daylily shoots on top, season lightly with the Ramp Leaf Salt, and scatter the field garlic greens and flowers across the top, if using.

Daylily Bud Pickles

Makes 2 cups (500 ml)

Eat these either as quick pickles (they are flavorful after 30 minutes), or keep them for a later season.

8 ounces (227 g) closed daylily buds
1 cup (250 ml) white wine vinegar
1 cup (250 ml) water (or enough to cover
    buds in bowl)
1 tablespoon salt
3 tablespoons sugar
4 cloves
8 dried spicebush fruit
1 stick cinnamon
15 peppercorns

Soak the buds in a bowl of salted water for an hour. Drain the buds and pack them into a clean jar. In a large jug mix the vinegar and water with the salt and sugar. Stir very well until the granules have dissolved. Pour over the daylilies. Insert the spices. Seal.

Cold Udon Noodles with Daylily Buds, Garlic Scapes, and Prickly Ash

Serves 2 and is easily multiplied

Daylilies and garlic scapes appear when the first stickily hot weather comes knocking at the firmly closed door. This simple cold noodle salad requires 15 minutes of heat for cooking the noodles and blanching the vegetables. Then it's chill, chill, chill.

2 ounces (57 g) garlic scapes, chopped into
    ¼-inch (½ cm) pieces
6 ounces (170 g) udon noodles
2 ounces (57 g) unopened daylily buds
2 teaspoons toasted sesame oil
4 tablespoons soy sauce
2 teaspoons sugar
1 tablespoon Prickly Ash Oil
½ lime

OPTIONAL

6 ounces (170 g) firm silken tofu,
    cut into cubes
1½ ounces (40 g) Daylily Bud Pickles
6 Pickled Field Garlic Flowers or
    chive flowers
1 teaspoon Prickly Ash Paste

Bring a pot of water to a boil. Drop the garlic scapes into it. Cook for 3 minutes, then scoop them out with a slotted spoon. Refresh them in a bowl of cold water. Drain and pat dry. Place the udon noodles in the same boiling water. Cook until just tender—4 to 5 minutes. Scoop them out with tongs and place into a large bowl of ice water. Now plunge the daylily buds into, yes, the same water, for 60 seconds, no more. Scoop them out with a slotted spoon, and dunk in cold water. Remove them and pat them very dry.

Drain the udon noodles. Place them in a serving bowl and drizzle the sesame oil over them. Add the soy and sugar. Toss the noodles well. Add the garlic scapes and the daylily buds. Finally, add the Prickly Ash Oil and toss one more time. Chill the noodles for at least 30 minutes. At this point the salad is ready to eat. Serve with wedges of the lime.

For a more substantial meal, add the tofu, Daylily Bud Pickles, Pickled Field Garlic or chive flowers, and Prickly Ash Paste.

Daylily Salad

Serves 2

This strikingly beautiful salad marries the sweet crunch of pea pods with crisp daylily petals and creamy cheese. Eat the flowers in moderation.

6 daylily flowers

2 cups (160 g) snap peas or fresh garden peas in pods

2 tablespoons soft goat cheese

2 teaspoons toasted sesame oil

1 tablespoon soy sauce

1 tablespoon aged balsamic vinegar

2 field garlic flower heads, separated

With a sharp knife, slit some of the flowers down the middle. (Remove the anthers and pistil if you are following traditional Chinese preparation.) Top and tail the peapods if they have strings. Slit half of them down the middle to expose the peas. Arrange the peas and flowers on a plate. Crumble the cheese and scatter it across the salad. At this point the salad can be covered and chilled if you want to make it ahead. To serve, drizzle first the sesame oil, then the soy and balsamic vinegar, across the top. Finish with the field garlic flowers. Serve within 10 minutes.

Soy-Braised Daylily Chicken

Serves 4

This mouthwatering one-pot wonder evolved one evening late in June when our daylilies were fading, well, daily. I had to hustle to make use of them all but did not have the time for anything complicated. If you can find Ohsawa Organic Nama Shoyu Unpasteurized Soy Sauce, it adds a great deal to this dish. If you do not have fresh Thai lime leaves (I grow them), use a strip of lime zest. Serve with lime-scented rice (cook a lime leaf or some zest with the rice and squeeze lime juice over before serving) to sop up the incredible sauce.

2 tablespoons unscented oil

4 whole chicken legs

¼ cup (60 ml) soy sauce

¼ cup (60 ml) Common Milkweed Flower Vinegar

1 can (13.5 fluid ounces/400 ml) coconut milk

2 cups (500 ml) water

3 fresh Thai lime leaves

16 day-old daylilies (one day after being open)

Warm the oil over high heat in a pot that can accommodate the chicken in a single layer. Place the chicken in the pot, skin-side down. Allow it to sizzle for 2 to 3 minutes. Pour in the soy. Let it bubble for 1 minute, then turn the pieces of chicken. Let it bubble for another minute (it will smell wonderful). Now add the vinegar. After 1 more minute of bubbling, add the coconut milk and the water. The liquid should just cover the chicken. Add the lime leaves. Reduce the heat and cover the pot, keeping the dish at a simmer. Cook for 1 hour and remove the lid. Increase the heat a little to maintain a lightly bubbling simmer, add the daylilies, and cook for another 45 minutes.

Preheat the broiler. Slide the pot under the broiler and broil for 8 to 10 minutes, until the chicken is dark brown and sticky on top.

Dirty, Dirty Daylily Rice

Serves 4

Until I ate a superb version of dirty rice at Pizza Moto, a restaurant in our Brooklyn neighborhood, the phenomenon was a mystery to me. A chalky, stodgy mystery. Theirs was different: lusciously oily, salty, and pocked with bits of crackling. So I became interested, and this is the result. Daylilies are an outstanding match for the soffrito of green peppers, onion, and garlic, and the whole thing is underscored by deeply smoky bacon. It is so good that I cook rice especially to make it; but really, dirty rice is designed for leftovers. Using every stage of daylily flowers is very satisfying.

Don't rush this recipe; the early stages should cook slowly and sweetly. I like to serve it with Prickly Ash and Soy Marinated Salmon, Prickly Ash BBQ Chicken Wings, or eggs, for breakfast.

4 ounces (113 g) fatty bacon,
   cut into thin strips
3 tablespoons vegetable oil
1 large onion, very finely chopped
2 tablespoons finely chopped garlic
1 cup (142 g) finely cubed green pepper
1 cup (about 90 g) fresh daylily buds
1 cup (20 g) day-old daylily flowers
2 cups (150 g) cooked beans
½ cup (40 g) Daylily Bud Pickles
4 cups (680 g) cooked rice
1 teaspoon Ramp Leaf Salt, plus extra
2–3 tablespoons lime juice

In a large skillet over medium-high heat, place the pieces of bacon. Cook until the fat begins to render, 4 to 5 minutes. Reduce the heat to medium and add the oil to the bacon fat. Add the onion and stir well. Cook for 10 minutes, stirring occasionally. Reduce the heat to medium-low, add the garlic and green pepper, and cook another 10 minutes. Now add the fresh daylily buds and day-old flowers, and stir. Add the beans and stir to coat them with the aromatics. Cook gently for another 10 minutes (sense a pattern?). Increase the heat again to medium high, and add the pickled daylilies, the rice, and the Ramp Leaf Salt. Stir well. Cook another minute or two until the rice has heated through. Finish with 1 tablespoon of lime juice, and taste. Add more lime juice, and more salt, if necessary—you want a salty-sour-oily balance.

DRIED DAYLILIES

Daylilies are helpful in that they begin the drying process for you. One day after blooming they start to wither, clinging for a few more days to their stalks. This is the time to collect them, with the harvest period lasting two to four weeks. I simply lay them out on large sheets of parchment paper to dry, starting at one end and adding more flowers daily. They are usually completely dry within a week. Once they are crisp, I pack them upright into glass jars and seal. They have lasted a year with good flavor. Opening the jar is a treat, because they smell exactly, freakily, like chocolate. And that is the flavor they bring to any dish, too.

Add them to soups and stews where you need some more substance. In moist heat they become silky in texture.

Hot-and-Sour Soup
with Daylilies and Chicken of the Woods

Serves 4

Dry daylily flowers turn slightly viscous in warm liquid and serve to thicken soup. They are traditionally served in hot-and-sour Chinese soups and can also be bought, bagged, in Chinatowns. I make my version of the classic soup in late summer or early fall when chicken of the woods mushrooms (*Laetiporus sulphureus* and *L. cincinnatus*) are in season. Choose immature mushrooms the older fans are very dry.

MUSHROOM BASE

3 tablespoons unscented oil

8 ounces (227 g) young, tender chicken of
   the woods

¼ teaspoon salt

1 tablespoon lemon juice

1 tablespoon tomato paste

2 teaspoons sugar

SOUP

2 tablespoons unscented oil

⅓ cup (50 g) finely chopped onion

4 Ramp Pickles, slit lengthwise

2 thumb-sized pieces of ginger, peeled and
   cut into matchsticks

3 tablespoons soy sauce

1 tablespoon plus 1 teaspoon sugar

4 cups (1 liter) chicken or mushroom broth

6 tablespoons rice vinegar

16 dried daylily flowers

¼ cup snipped chive leaves

2 teaspoons red chile flakes

2 large eggs

FOR THE MUSHROOMS: Heat the oil over medium-high heat in a saucepan. Add the mushrooms, season them with the salt, give the pan a shake, and cover with a lid. Reduce the heat to medium. Stew the mushrooms for 5 minutes. Lift the lid, add the lemon juice, tomato paste, and sugar, stir well, and cover again. Reduce the heat to keep the liquid the mushrooms have exuded at a gentle simmer. Cook for 20 minutes.

FOR THE SOUP: Heat the oil in a pot over medium heat and add the onion. Sauté for 5 minutes before adding the ramps, prepared mushrooms, ginger, and soy. Allow the mixture to cook until it looks dark and caramelly, without sticking, about 5 minutes. Add the sugar, broth, vinegar, and daylilies. Stir gently and bring to a gentle simmer, still over medium heat. Cook for 15 minutes, add the chopped chive leaves and chile flakes, and taste. The soup should have a strongly acid edge balanced with sweet and salty. Turn the heat to high, and when the liquid bubbles break a couple of eggs into it. Swirl them into the soup using a chopstick, and serve at once.

Elderflowers and Elderberries

OTHER COMMON NAMES: Elderblow, elder

BOTANICAL NAMES: *Sambucus* species

STATUS: Both exotic and indigenous shrubs, widespread in North America

WHERE: Fields, streamsides, gardens

SEASON: Summer

USE: Aromatic, fruit

PARTS USED: Flowers, unripe and ripe fruit

GROW? Yes

TASTES LIKE: I can think of no flavor comparisons for the flowers or fruit; they are unique

---

For lovers of elderflowers, early summer is a happy time. The large white flowering umbels frost elder shrubs with pollen-laden blossoms, a magnet for honeybees and other pollinators. They are also irresistible to foragers: While *Sambucus* species can be an ornamental boon to the gardener, their real reward is for the cook and the home-brewing alchemist.

I encounter two elderberries in the Northeast: *S. nigra* and *S. canadensis* (which is also viewed as a subspecies of *S. nigra*). Other *Sambucus* species, like the West Coast *S. nigra* subsp. *caerulea* with blue fruit, can be used in the same ways, although their flavor will be different (and better by some accounts). I have no personal experience with the red-fruited species of *Sambucus*, but the drupes are edible once cooked. Yes, despite their common name, the fruit is really a drupe, not a berry. *Elderdrupes* just does not sound the same.

Elderflowers bloom around the time that peak serviceberry season is drawing to a close in my hood. They induce a kind of giddiness in foragers. Their flavor, released into syrups and infusions, is unique, and they taste better in translation than they smell in bloom. Summer is not summer without a fizzing jar of elderflower cordial on the brew.

For the fruit, cooking is key. Despite their gorgeously glossy appearance when ripe, these fruits' raw flavor is unimpressive. Also, the raw fruit can make some people sick. But something magical happens with heat as well as with fermentation. A cupful of relatively bland, raw elderberry juice (I do *not* recommend drinking it) brought to a boil for a few minutes turns darkly complex. Ripe fruit covered with sugar and allowed to ferment for days or weeks becomes bright and assertive. Even unripe green fruit—considered very toxic—is rendered edible by fermentation, as the Nordic Food Lab has taught us. Elderberry syrup is a proven therapy for colds and flu—it has antiviral and anti-influenza properties, among others.

How to Collect and Prepare

Remember that when you pick the flowers, you are depriving the plant of fruit. If you want fruit later, leave as many umbels behind as you take. Once you are home, spread them out to encourage any small insects to leave. Do not wash the flowers or you will lose precious pollen and wild yeast.

Elderberries are one of the easiest fruits to pick en masse and quite quickly. By the time they are very ripe, their stems snap easily. In good years their umbels are loaded with juicy fruit, and it requires little effort to carry several pounds home.

Once you have the fruit, you need to detach it from its stems. A quick way to do this is to freeze the whole umbels. Stick a bagful of fruit in the freezer for a couple of hours. Once frozen, they drop off very easily. The drawback here is that the very thin stems to individual fruits also break off easily and you end up with more stem matter than if you pick the fruit off fresh and unfrozen. If you need to use the fruit raw for fermentations, it is also better not to freeze the elderberries, as freezing will kill some helpful wild yeasts. It takes me about an hour (and something good on Netflix) to process 5 pounds of unfrozen fruit. Freezing will take half the time.

The Goo: Crushing elderberries, raw or cooked, releases a fascinating, rubbery substance that will coat your implements—usually only the part that is constantly in contact with the juice and seeds from elderberries under pressure. When the fruit is raw, the gum is clear to beige, and when cooked it is green. To clean your equipment, first rinse it, then dry it with a paper towel. Coat the surface generously with mineral oil. Leave for 10 minutes and wipe with paper towels, newspaper, cotton wool pads, or old pieces of cloth (that you never want to use again). Coat with oil again and repeat. When The Goo is gone, scrub the clean equipment with a soapy sponge and hot water (I prefer a nailbrush to dislodge the snags of the cotton wool pads I use). Good as new.

Caution

All green parts of elderberry are considered toxic. Raw ripe fruit also can be toxic in certain doses (different for everyone), so eat it with caution. Cooked is fine. If taking elderberry syrup as a medicine, do not consume more than 3 tablespoons per day. I have had a mild allergic recation to it (skin rash). Never eat raw green elderberries *unless* they have been fermented first.

CULTIVATION TIPS
USDA Hardiness Zones 3–9

Plant elderberry in full sun or partial shade (more sun means more flowers). The medium-sized shrubs prefer moist soil but tolerate a wide range of conditions.

Elderberries have a reputation for being weedy because they grow fast and spread via stolons, eventually forming colonies in spots they favor. For foragers in the urban or rural wilds, this energetic habit is good news, but for kitchen gardeners it means a little management. If you do not want elderberry to naturalize and spread, check for suckers several times in the growing season and prune them off. Prune the shrubs for shape in late winter, and cut them all the way to the ground every two to three years to refresh their yield. They often fruit best on second-year canes.

Fermented Elderflower Cordial

Makes about 8 cups (2 liters)

Elderflower cordial is a sacred early-summer ritual—brew it once, and it lasts all year. It makes exquisite frozen popsicles, long drinks, and cocktails. The cordial can also be used in baking, in salad dressings, and in fruity desserts. It can become an exceptional vinegar.

The addition of lemon juice helps to slow fermentation down (many recipes call for citric acid) and keeps the effervescent brew more stable. For an unfermented syrup, see Elderflower Syrup.

You can add other aromatic edible flowers to the ferment. Petite but profusely flowered *Rosa multiflora* is highly invasive and in bloom at the same time as elder. So is honeysuckle. Each adds its own character, and both are lovely.

6 ounces (170 g) elderflower umbels
    (approximately 30)
1 pound (453 g) sugar
6 cups (1½ liters) water
Zest of 4 lemons, peeled in strips,
    without pith
½ cup (125 ml) fresh lemon juice
    (4–5 lemons' worth)

Do not wash the flowers or you will lose the pollen and the wild yeasts. Instead, leave them outside for a few hours to allow egress for small insects. Strip the tiny white flowers from the green stems, using your fingers or a fork. (Tip: Leaving them in a paper bag overnight will encourage many of the blooms to fall off, making sorting easier.) Discard as much green as possible (in any plant it will add a tannic note, but with elderflowers the green is considered toxic).

Pack the flowers lightly into a large, clean mason jar or jars. Dump the sugar on top of them. Add the water, lemon zest, and juice. Stir well.

Screw the lid on loosely or secure a layer of cheesecloth over the mouth of the jar with a rubber band or string. At this stage the ferment actually *needs* air, which the cloth or loose lid allows, while keeping insects out.

Leave the jar at room temperature, stirring once a day.

Around Day 3 to 5 (this depends very much on temperatures and yeast), you will notice bubbles rising. Fermentation has begun. After another day or two, the elderflowers will rise and push up out of the jar; that's serious carbonation happening. Push them back down gently. Allow the jars of cordial to ferment another day or two, until the flowers no longer rise. Strain the cordial through a fine-mesh strainer and then again through cheesecloth. You can save the pomace (the leftover flowers and lemon peel) to make an elderflower vinegar or marmalade. Bottle the double-strained cordial in clean bottles. For peace of mind keep the bottles in the fridge, as fermentation will continue in the bottles; left out, they can explode. The cordial lasts indefinitely if unopened.

Ingrid Bergman

Makes 1 cocktail

Strawberries belong to elderflower season. I grow alpine strawberries, which have a very intense flavor, but any very ripe strawberry can be used for the shrub component.

Strawberry Shrub

Makes enough for 4 cocktails

½ cup (85 g) ripe strawberries
½ cup (125 ml) Elderflower Vinegar

Mash the berries in a bowl, cover with the vinegar, and leave overnight. Strain the vinegar, then bottle it. It lasts indefinitely in the refrigerator (the leftover berries are good stirred into a red wine pan glaze for duck breasts or pork chops).

Cocktail

Makes 1 drink

3 fluid ounces (6 tablespoons) gin
1 fluid ounce (2 tablespoons) Strawberry Shrub
1 fluid ounce (2 tablespoons) Fermented Elderflower Cordial

Pour the ingredients into a cocktail shaker, add ice, and shake like mad. Strain and pour.

Fade to Fall

Makes 1 drink

A contemplative drink for the fragile days in fall when the first citrus arrive and the elderflower stash is still strong.

3 fluid ounces (6 tablespoons) gin
1 fluid ounce (2 tablespoons) ruby grapefruit juice
1 fluid ounce (2 tablespoons) Fermented Elderflower Cordial

Shake all the ingredients with ice. Strain and pour.

Gin and Tonic Elderflower Jelly with Red Currants

Serves 6

For a hot summer night, or an outdoor lunch, this is the perfect dessert, suspending a hint of bubbles within each quivering spoonful. Just don't give it to the children. They will never be the same. Because of the hint of bitterness from the tonic and the pop of tartness from the red currants, this is a mildly sweet jelly—if you have a very sweet tooth, I would suggest stirring ¼ cup sugar into the cordial. It keeps well—make it up to 4 days in advance.

2¼ cups (560 ml) Fermented Elderflower
    Cordial, divided
2 tablespoons plus 1 teaspoon
    powdered gelatin
½ cup (125 ml) tonic water
¼ cup (60 ml) gin
⅓ cup (30 g) red currants

Heat ½ cup of the Fermented Elderflower Cordial in a saucepan over high heat. When it bubbles turn off the heat. Sprinkle the gelatin onto it and whisk it in immediately until it has dissolved.

In a bowl combine the rest of the cordial with the tonic and the gin. Pour the elderflower-gelatin mixture into this and stir gently with a spoon. Transfer the mixture to a Jell-O mold or rounded bowl, cover, and chill in the fridge. Add half the red currants after 30 minutes, and the rest 30 minutes later. They will sink in. Chill until set—about another 6 hours. Serve it portioned in cocktail coupes, or unmold it by dipping its base *briefly* in just-boiled water, slipping a hot knife around the edges, and inverting it swiftly onto a serving plate.

Elderflower Syrup

Makes 6 cups (1½ liters)

Elderflower Syrup is distinct from Fermented Elderflower Cordial. The syrup is more concentrated in terms of both flowers and sugar used. It is not fermented, although it is possible that a little fizzing may occur in the bottle. But the use of heat kills a lot of the bacteria (*wild yeasts* sounds sexier, doesn't it?) associated with fermentation. I easily double this recipe in good elderflower years. Bottled, it is a lovely gift and makes for good trading, too.

6 cups (1½ liters) water
3½ pounds (1.6 kg) sugar
10 ounces (283 g) elderflowers, stripped
    from stalks
2 lemons, washed and sliced
Zest of 2 washed lemons, microplaned
3 fluid ounces (90 ml) lemon juice

Combine the water with the sugar in a pot. Stir well as you bring the mixture to a boil over medium-high heat. Allow it to boil for 2 minutes, then turn off the heat. Add the elderflowers and all the lemon. Stir very well. Allow the mixture to sit, covered, for 12 hours. Strain through a fine-mesh sieve, and then again through double layers of muslin. Transfer to clean bottles.

Use the leftover pomace (the flavorful flowers and lemon pieces) to make Elderflower Pomace Marmalade or to flavor one of the Elderflower Vinegar recipes on page 128.

Elderflower Vinegar — The Quick Way

Makes 2½ cups (625 ml)

The sweet and sticky pomace left after straining Fermented Elderflower Cordial or Elderflower Syrup remains piercingly flavorful. Transferring that valuable flavor to a vinegar is good resource management and squeezes the most out of this lovely season. I think of this as a "cheat" vinegar, but honestly, it is so good that I don't believe the method matters one tiny bit. For a longer, more traditional method, see Elderflower Vinegar — The Long Way.

    The quantities will vary depending on the cordial or syrup you have just made, so those below are simply a guide.

1 packed cup (200 g) elderflower pomace
2½ cups (625 ml) white wine vinegar

Pack the pomace into a clean glass jar and cover with the vinegar. Infuse for 2 weeks, then strain. Bottle the vinegar, but save the pomace (one more time!) for Elderflower Pomace Marmalade.

Elderflower Vinegar — The Long Way

Makes just under 4 cups (1 liter)

Like Common Milkweed Cordial, elderflower cordial yields potentially stunning vinegar.

    This is less a recipe than a method. A loose method. Tomes have been written on the subject, really good ones. (You can use any of the cordial, soda pop, or fizz recipes in these pages to make vinegar.)

4 cups Fermented Elderflower Cordial

Pour the cordial into a large, widemouthed jar. It should not fill it more than halfway. Cover the mouth with cheesecloth secured with twine or a rubber band. Now allow nature to take its course. In most cases the bacteria present will create vinegar for you, with no mother of vinegar required. Taste it after 3 to 5 weeks. If it tastes and smells like vinegar, it is vinegar. Strain it through double layers of cheesecloth, and bottle in a narrow-necked bottle. If a visible mother of vinegar has formed (it doesn't, always), scoop it out gently and store for later use in an airtight jar, covered in any vinegar (it must be submerged to stay alive).

Elderflower Pomace Marmalade

Makes 6 jars, ½ pint (250 ml) each

First comes the Elderflower Syrup, or cordial, then the vinegar. The remaining pomace of flowers and lemons remain resolutely good. How's that for threefold return on foraging investment? Marmalade is the logical next and final step. I rarely use pectin for jams and jellies, but it is necessary here. The calcium water stipulated is per Pomona's Universal Pectin directions, and the calcium ingredient is included in their pack of pectin.

12 fluid ounces (340 ml)
    elderflower and lemon pomace
4 cups (1 liter) water
3 tablespoons lemon juice
4 teaspoons calcium water
10 ounces (283 g) sugar
1 tablespoon powdered pectin

Combine the pomace, water, lemon juice, and calcium water in a pot and bring to a boil over medium-high heat. Mix the sugar with the powdered pectin in a bowl. While the elderflower liquid is boiling, sprinkle the sugar-pectin mixture into it and stir vigorously for a minute at a full boil. It is very important to keep stirring to dissolve the pectin. Turn off the heat, allow the mixture to cool off for a few minutes, then ladle into clean jars. Seal when cool.

Roasted Elderflower Carrots

Serves 4 as a side

The sweetness of roasted carrots is enhanced by Fermented Elderflower Cordial and vinegar, with a zesty control of sumac and lemon to keep the flavors fresh. Either serve them whole (hot or at room temperature) or proceed per instructions for a pâté.

3¾ pounds (1.7 kg) carrots
3 tablespoons olive oil
¼ cup (60 ml) Fermented Elderflower Cordial
3 tablespoons Elderflower Vinegar
½ teaspoon Ground Elder Salt
½ teaspoon ground elder seeds
½ teaspoon Ground Sumac
½ teaspoon lemon zest

Preheat the oven to 350°F (180°C).

Peel and slice the carrots into ¼-inch (½ cm) pieces. Place them in a bowl and add the olive oil, Elderflower Cordial and Vinegar, Ground Elder Salt and seeds, sumac, and lemon zest. Toss well. Transfer the carrots to a baking sheet or roasting pan. Add ½ cup (125 ml) water, and roast in the oven until they are very tender, about 1¼ hours. If the pan scorches, add a small amount of water. Serve the carrots hot or at room temperature.

Roasted Elderflower Carrot Pâté

Roasted Elderflower Carrots, as above
1 tablespoon lemon juice
2 tablespoons extra-virgin olive oil
½ teaspoon black pepper

Place the carrots in a food processor with the lemon juice, olive oil, and black pepper, and pulse until smooth. Serve with raw vegetables, crackers, or good bread.

Carrot, Elderflower, and Spicebush Salad

Serves 4 as a side

Fresh and raw, this vivid salad is a refreshing side dish for rich stews like Garlic Mustard and Spicy Pork, or coal-grilled meats like Mugwort and Yogurt Leg of Lamb—or a stand-alone lunch in its own right (the last spoonful of tangy juices might be the best part—also good thrown into a cocktail!). If you make this in early spring, you may also be able to collect lesser celandine (*Ficaria verna*)—an edible super-invader whose shimmering petals add an iridescence to the already bright plate.

8 cups (800 g) peeled and grated or shred-
    ded carrots (about 10 medium carrots)
½ teaspoon salt
3 tablespoons Elderflower Syrup
4 tablespoons lemon juice
¾ teaspoon ground spicebush
1 tablespoon spicebush flowers (optional)
1 teaspoon lesser celandine flower petals
    (optional)

Place the carrots in a bowl and add the salt, Elderflower Syrup, lemon juice, and ground spicebush. Toss well. After a few minutes the carrots will lose some volume as the salt draws out their moisture. Just before serving, plate the carrots; if you are using the spicebush and lesser celandine flowers, sprinkle them over the top.

Elderflower-Poached Peaches

Serves 4

This delicate summer dessert requires perfect freestone peaches.

8 ripe peaches
2 cups (500 ml) water
⅓ cup (80 ml) Fermented Elderflower Cordial
1 vanilla bean
1 strip lemon zest, 3 inches (8 cm) long

Place the peaches in a pot. Add the water and cordial, vanilla bean and lemon zest. Bring the liquid to a simmer over medium heat, and keep at a gentle simmer for 25 minutes (reduce the heat when it boils). Remove the peaches from the liquid to a dish. When they are cool enough to handle, tip any accumulated juice back into the pot. Carefully peel their skins off, trying to keep their flesh smooth and free of nicks. Place the peaches in a shallow serving bowl. Bring the poaching liquid to a gentle boil over medium-high heat and reduce until it is slightly sticky. Pour this reduction over the peaches. Serve them cool.

Elderbutter Potted Shrimp

Makes 2 cups (500 ml)

Packing cooked, chopped shrimp (or trout, or salmon, or crab) in melted butter is one of my favorite ways to carry food on a picnic adventure. Californian wild foods chef Mia Wasilevich's recipe for elderbutter and poached lobster tails in her lovely cookbook *Ugly Little Greens* inspired this version of the summer picnic treat. The richness of butterfat delivers every atom of the delicate flowers' flavor, and I slip some intense cordial as well as Elderflower Vinegar into the poaching liquid for additional depth. Slather it onto crackers, Cattail Quiskets, or dense brown bread.

ELDERBUTTER

8 ounces (227 g) butter
2 ounces (57 g) elderflowers

SHRIMP

¾ pound (340 g) shelled shrimp tails
3 tablespoons Elderbutter
1 tablespoon Fermented Elderflower Cordial
1 tablespoon Elderflower Vinegar
¼ teaspoon salt

TO FINISH

2 teaspoons Elderflower Vinegar
Salt
1 tablespoon Elderbutter
4 ounces (113 g) unsalted butter
1 tablespoon elderflowers

FOR THE ELDERBUTTER: Melt the butter in a saucepan over gentle heat. Turn off the heat and pour the butter into a clean jar. Add the flowers and stir to make sure they are submerged and coated in the liquid butter. Cover and transfer to the fridge for 24 hours. Remove the cold jar and allow it to return to room temperature. Transfer the butter to a small saucepan over the lowest heat possible, and stir as it melts. When it has liquified, pour the flower butter through a double-mesh sieve into a bowl, pressing it with the back of a spoon to coax all the butter through. Store in the fridge and use within a week.

FOR THE SHRIMP: Place the shrimp tails in a saucepan that holds them snugly. Add the Elderbutter, Fermented Elderflower Cordial, and elderflower vinegar. Place the pan over medium-low heat, covered. When the butter has melted, reduce the heat to low. Cook very gently until the shrimp are pink and cooked through. Baste them with the cooking liquid occasionally. Sprinkle them with salt once cooked.

Scoop the shrimp tails and their poaching liquid into a bowl. Cover, and transfer to the fridge to chill. Once they are the cold the butter will have risen and congealed. Remove the shrimp from the bowl, keeping the butter and discarding the liquid cooking juices (or save for fish soup). Chop the shrimp finely and place in a bowl.

TO FINISH: Drizzle the elderflower vinegar over the shrimp and mix well. Taste. Add a little salt if necessary. Place 1 tablespoon of the saved Elderbutter in a small saucepan along with the regular butter and heat very gently over medium-low to low heat (too much heat will kill the delicate elder flavor). While the butter is melting, pack the shrimp meat as densely as possible into ramekins, pressing down with the back of a spoon to get rid of air pockets (the more spaces you leave, the more melted butter you will need). When the butter has melted pour it gently over the shrimp meat. It should reach the surface. If it does not, melt some more. Hey, we only live once.

Sprinkle with some elderflowers for decoration, cover, and chill. This will keep up to 4 days in the fridge if well wrapped and packed in enough butter.

Elderflower Fritters

Serves 4

Fried elderflowers are one of the better-known treats associated with these early-summer umbels. Delicious when hot and crunchy, straight from the hot oil (what wouldn't be?), they are fun to eat once a season. I up the elder ante by using the cordial in the batter. If you are not eating them within hours of picking, keep the flowers fresh by placing their fresh-cut stems in water, covering them, and storing in the fridge overnight. Otherwise they wilt and drop their flowers.

8 large elderflower umbels, attached to
    2–3 inches (5–8 cm) of stalk
4 ounces (113 g) flour
⅛ teaspoon salt
6 fluid ounces (175 ml) sparkling water
1 tablespoon Fermented Elderflower Cordial
1 large egg white
Unscented oil*
5–6 tablespoons honey
Zest of 1 lemon

* You will need enough oil to fill a pan or
  pot 1½ inches (4 cm) deep—enough to
  cover the battered elderflowers.

Do not wash the elderflowers. Evict any small insects by shaking gently.

In a bowl whisk together the flour and salt with the sparkling water and Elderflower Cordial. Place in the fridge to rest for 30 minutes. Whisk the egg white until it holds soft peaks. Just before frying, fold half the egg white into the batter, and then add the other half, blending gently.

Heat the oil in your pan over high heat. Test for sizzle by dropping in a small amount of batter. It should float and bubble at once. Reduce the heat to medium-high. Working one at a time, dip each elderflower into the batter. Coat the flower as much as possible, then lift it and shake off excess batter—tapping it against the side of the bowl helps. Lower it into the oil with one hand, separating the goopy smaller stalks with a chopstick so that the flower-head fries spread out rather than remain a solid mass. Repeat with enough elderflowers to fill the pan without crowding. Fry until the batter has turned dark golden—about 4 minutes—then lift and place on paper towels for a minute to absorb excess oil. Transfer to a serving plate. To serve, drizzle a little honey across the top of the hot fritters and strew some lemon zest over them.

Elderflower Figs

Serves 4

Late-summer and fall figs are a treat I look forward to all year. They are so perfect as a fruit (techni-cally a flower) that I interfere with them as little as possible and rarely cook them. I grew up peeling figs (sitting high up in the fig tree to do so) but am less finicky about it now. Their skins are also very pretty. Peel or don't peel—up to you. The quantities here are a suggestion. I could probably eat these figs all by myself in one sitting. Serve them in a pretty glass bowl or in individual glasses.

12 figs
½ cup (125 ml) Fermented Elderflower
    Cordial, chilled
1 cup (250 ml) Prosecco, chilled

Place the figs, each cut in half, in the bowl. Pour the cordial over them. Cover and macerate for at least 2 hours. Just before serving, add the cold Prosecco. Serve with spoons for dipping up the juice.

Elderflower Madeleines

Makes 24 3-inch (8 cm) madeleines

Almost identical to the Cattail Pollen and Honey Madeleines, these delicately flavored treats do not use brown butter, as its nuttiness would overpower the elderflower. I use 2 madeleine trays.

You can also use Fermented Honeysuckle Cordial for these madeleines—its aroma is as powerful.

3 ounces (85 g) butter
2 large eggs
3 ounces (85 g) sugar
3 ounces (85 g) all-purpose flour
¼ teaspoon salt
1 teaspoon baking powder
1 tablespoon Elderflower Syrup
2 tablespoons melted butter, for brushing

Melt the 3 ounces (85 g) butter in small saucepan over medium-low heat.

In a mixing bowl beat the eggs with the sugar until pale and fluffy about 2 minutes. In another bowl combine the flour, salt, and baking powder. Gradually fold the flour mixture into the beaten eggs. Add the melted butter and the Elderflower Syrup, and stir well but gently. Cover the batter and place it in the fridge for 10 minutes.

Paint melted butter evenly into the madeleine molds and on their edges (the madeleines may spread). Transfer the buttered tray or trays to the freezer to chill.

Preheat the oven to 425°F (220°C).

When the batter has chilled for 10 minutes, spoon it conservatively into the madeleine molds. Bake for 5 minutes, then reduce the heat to 400°F (200°C) and open the oven for 15 seconds to dispel some extra hot air. Close the door and bake another 3 to 5 minutes. Toward the end the madeleines bake fast; you must remove them as soon as the very middle of a madeleine springs back after it has been touched. Have a wire rack waiting. Flip the tray upside down and shake the madeleines out. If they stick, loosen their edges gently with a knife. Serve them warm, or wait until they have cooled completely before storing them in an airtight container. They are still very good the following day.

Fermented Elderberry Capers

Makes 3 cups (750 ml)

Unripe elderberries are toxic. Until they are fermented and pickled. Magic? Or just the slow-food tradition? After the Nordic Food Lab (those Danes—backing up culinary experimentation with science!) started writing about them in 2013, an elderberry caper trend slowly picked up, fueled in turn by Californian terroirist Pascal Baudar, who includes them in his excellent book *The New Wildcrafted Cuisine*. I like capers but do not think that every bud and berry deserves to be one. Elder is an exception. It has the inherent flavor of elderflower cordial, released somehow after 2 weeks in a light fermenting brine. The seeds also turn miraculously crisp.

FERMENTING

8 ounces (227 g) green elderberries
2 teaspoons salt

PICKLING

1 cup (250 ml) Elderflower Vinegar
½ cup (125 ml) water
2 teaspoons salt
1 teaspoon sugar

TO FERMENT: Pick the green elderberries from their stems. Soak them in water for 1 hour. Rinse and dry them, and pack them into a clean glass jar. Add the salt. Close the jar. Shake and tilt the jar until you see salt distributed all over the berries, top-to-bottom. Leave out for 2 days. Shake a couple of times. Transfer to the fridge.

TO PICKLE: After another 18 days open the elderberries (I'm sure you have, already) and give them a sniff. They should smell good. A little yeasty. But fresh. Rinse them under cool water, drain, and pack into the washed and clean jar. Add the vinegar, water, salt, and sugar. Close with a lid and shake gently to dissolve the salt and sugar. Store at room temperature.

After 10 days your capers will be ready.

Fermented Elderberry Syrup

Makes about 3 cups (750 ml)

What began as an experiment turned into a keeper. It does not take long to extract a syrup from juicy elderberries, and I find myself stealing from the fermenting jar about 5 days after the fruit and sugar have begun sitting together. The transformative process of fermentation converts the fairly bland raw elderberries into something darkly appealing with a tart backbone and a crisp sweetness around the edges.

Diluted with sparkling water—or white or red wine, for an aperitif—the syrup has a refreshingly complex flavor. It is fantastic added to savory dishes, too. I am not put off by using sugar (clearly), but this intense syrup is a concentrate, meant to be used in Aristotle's holy moderation. You are not chugging it all at once. The strained fruit can be used later in desserts, sauces, or a ketchup. And yes, take a daily tablespoonful in flu season. It's powerful stuff (to the point that when I overdosed I developed a light rash on my chest, so go easy). While the syrup is fermenting, I dip sneakily into the jar to extract the fermenting fruit, which has excellent flavor and crystalline crunch and brings depth to many dishes.

4 cups (about 1¼ pounds/567 g) ripe elderberries
1½ pounds (680 g) sugar

Place the fruit in a clean jar and cover with the sugar. Close the lid and shake the jar until the fruit and sugar are well mixed. Leave until the juices have been drawn out (I leave it for 20 days). After the fruit begins fermenting in the syrup (after 3 to 4 days, usually), open the lid daily to allow gas to escape. Strain through a double mesh sieve and then through cheesecloth, and bottle. Save the fruit in a clean jar in the fridge for adding to cooked dishes.

Sam Can

Makes 1 drink

Because of the elderberries I tell myself that this is actually healthful; the fruit's proven antiviral properties reach out to smack any incipient bugs on the nose.

2½ fluid ounces (5 tablespoons) dark rum
1 fluid ounce (2 tablespoons) Fermented Elderberry Syrup
1 fluid ounce (2 tablespoons) Sumac Vodka
½ fluid ounce (1 tablespoon) Fermented Honeysuckle Cordial

Shake it all up with ice. Strain and pour.

Elderberry Juice

Makes approximately 2 cups (500 ml)

This juice is for cooking, not drinking. It could make you sick if consumed raw. Add it to savory stews, braises, and cooked sauces; use it to deglaze roasting pans; or reduce it to make a syrup for desserts or cocktails. Save extra juice by freezing it in ice cube trays and bagging the vivid cubes.

Every cup (5 ounces/142 g) of ripe, raw elderberries yields just over ¼ cup (60 ml) of juice.

8 cups (2½ pounds/1.1 kg) elderberries

Using the finest sieve on your food mill, work the fruit through the mill into a bowl below, reversing the handle occasionally to dislodge compacted pulp. Discard the leftover seeds. You may find that after processing the raw fruit, your food mill's sieve is coated with a rubbery substance. Consult "The Goo" on page 124 for cleaning tips.

Freeze elderberry juice in ice cube trays and then bag the gorgeous cubes in smaller plastic bags for later use. If you have a lot of freezer space (lucky you), make more juice and freeze in larger containers. You will be glad of it later.

Elderberry Soup

Serves 4 as an appetizer

This easy soup's flavor is staggeringly satisfying, given its few ingredients. It owes its inspiration to Inga Byleckie, who described to me a hot soup her mother used to make in raw Danish winters. I was expecting to tinker for a while before arriving at a good flavor, but after boiling raw elderberry juice briefly I realized that very little more would be needed. The juice is transformed by cooking. This is addictive stuff. Save enough juice in the freezer to make it on a miserable winter day when you feel the sniffles coming on. In smaller amounts, use it as a sauce for puddings and ice creams.

3 cups (750 ml) Elderberry Juice
4 tablespoons sugar
3 cinnamon sticks
2 tablespoons Sumac Vodka
    (or 1 tablespoon lime juice)
⅛ teaspoon salt

Heat the juice in a saucepan until it boils. Add the sugar and cinnamon sticks; simmer for 10 minutes. Skim off any brown foam that rises. Add the Sumac Vodka and the salt. Stir. Taste the soup and add a little more salt, if necessary. Serve hot.

Cooked Elderberry Syrup

Makes 2 cups (500 ml)

Why make a cooked syrup if you have fermented syrup already? Fermented syrup has a different flavor altogether. So why not?

My husband the Frenchman and I sip a tablespoonful at a time when—if—we feel a suspicious scratch in our throat. I do not know if it works (although clinical trials would indicate that it does); we are sick rarely. And okay, I admit it: Sometimes it finds its way into a cocktail or dessert.

2 pounds (907 g) ripe elderberries
8 ounces (227 g) sugar
4 cups (1 liter) water
1 teaspoon citric acid (lemon salt)

Place the elderberries in a pot and cover with the sugar. Stir or shake to distribute the sugar better. Cover and leave overnight. Add the water and bring to a gentle boil over medium-high heat. Cook for 5 minutes at a boil. Turn off the heat and allow the mixture to cool.

Using the finest sieve on your food mill, work the berries and liquid through it, reversing the handle occasionally to dislodge stuck bits. Scrape the bottom of the mill to catch the good purée sticking there. Return the pulp and liquid to the pot and heat over medium-high heat until simmering. Cook until the liquid has reduced in volume by half. Turn off the heat and stir in the citric acid. Let cool. Pour into a clean glass bottle, and keep in the fridge.

Save any juicy bits that didn't make it through the sieve for Elderberry Gin. And to clean your equipment, consult "The Goo" on page 124.

Elderberry Gin

Makes about 4½ cups (1.1 liters)

Call it extreme economy, with benefits. Once I have pulped *cooked* elderberries after making Cooked Elderberry Syrup, there is still a lot of juicy material left on the wrong side of the food mill's sieve. It is very flavorful, so why waste it, after all that foraging and de-stemming? So I cover it with gin, add some of the strained, sweet elderberry juice, and leave it all to become acquainted for no more than 10 days before straining. Result? Purple gin. Possibly with some real health benefits, but that is not the point. Although it does make for good conversation. (You could also use white rum, vodka, or eau-de-vie in place of the gin.) Shown opposite.

4 cups (1 liter) pulp left after processing
    Cooked Elderberry Syrup
½ cup (125 ml) Cooked Elderberry Syrup
4 cups (1 liter) good gin

In a clean glass jar combine all the ingredients. Stir very well to break up the compacted elderberry pulp. Cover. After 10 days strain through a double-mesh sieve, and then again through cheesecloth. Bottle. Keeps indefinitely.

Bug Slayer

Makes 1 bug-slaying drink

Elderberries have proven antiviral properties, and I keep a jar of syrup on hand purely for dosing purposes if the Frenchman or I feel under the weather. The same jar delivers a very good mixer—astringent, sweet, very elder. Shaking it up with Elderberry Gin and lemon juice, I can hear the flu run, screaming. It's a hot-pink drink. Pink is your friend.

3 fluid ounces (6 tablespoons) Elderberry Gin
1 fluid ounce (2 tablespoons) Cooked Elderberry Syrup
1 fluid ounce (2 tablespoons) lemon juice

Shake them up well with ice. Strain and pour. Then go to bed.

Elderberry Gin and Chicken Liver Mousse

Makes 6 pots, ½ cup (125 ml) each

This mousse is light and silky in texture, and quick to assemble. If you use cream that has an additive like carrageenan in it, do not be worried by the weirdly gelatinous texture of the mixture after blending. But do try to find cream that is just cream (harder than it sounds). You can also substitute Sweetfern Bourbon or Bayberry Beach Plum Gin for the Elderberry Gin. Serve with good toast or bread and a relish of Field Garlic Marmalade, Juniper Black Currant Chutney, or Fermented Elderberry Capers.

4 ounces (113 g) butter, melted
1 pound (453 g) chicken livers, cleaned
2 large egg yolks
5 fluid ounces (150 ml) cream
1 teaspoon salt
3 tablespoons Elderberry Gin
Sweetfern leaves (optional)

Preheat the oven to 300°F (150°C).

FOR INDIVIDUAL SERVINGS: Combine all the ingredients and blend until very smooth (you may have to do this in two batches). If you are using sweetfern, place a leaf in the bottom of each ramekin. Pour the mixture into six ½-cup (125 ml) ramekins until they're three-quarters full. Place a large skillet or baking pan in the oven. Place the ramekins in it. Fill the pan with hot water until it reaches two-thirds of the way up the ramekins' sides. Place a large sheet of parchment or foil over the top of the ramekins to protect the mousse from the oven's hot air. Bake for 30 to 35 minutes, or until the mousse is firm and does not jiggle wildly in the middle when you give it a firm jab. Ideally, you're looking for a barely discernible shiver.

Once the mousses are cool, chill them in the fridge, keeping them covered. Either serve them straight from the pot, or unmold them: Dip a knife in just-boiled water and slide it around the inner edge of each ramekin. Cover with a small serving plate or board and invert. Serve cool.

VARIATION, FOR A SINGLE, SLICEABLE MOUSSE: Instead of using ramekins, pour all the mousse mixture into a baking pan or terrine approximately 8½ by 4½ inches (22 × 11 cm). Remember to line it with sweetfern leaves, if using, before you pour. Place in the bain-marie as above, and cover with parchment or foil. You will need a longer bake, about an hour. It is done when a skewer inserted all the way comes out clean. Once cool, follow the chilling and serving instructions above.

Elderberry and Spicebush Meatballs with Red Cabbage

Serves 4

I can't help thinking of Swedish meatballs when I work with elderberry syrup. Fermented elderberries are incorporated into this spicy meatball mixture where spicebush and nutmeg create a little Scandinavian-American harmony. The fermented fruits' seeds are distinctively crunchy. Elderberry syrup and vinegar play a sweet-and-sour harmony with juniper in the tender cabbage sauce.

MEATBALLS

⅓ cup (80 ml) milk

⅔ cup (40 g) panko bread crumbs

1½ pounds (680 g) ground beef

3 tablespoons fermented elderberries (see Fermented Elderberry Syrup), drained

1 teaspoon ground black pepper

1 teaspoon ground spicebush

¾ teaspoon salt

¼ teaspoon ground nutmeg

1 large egg

2 tablespoons butter, divided

SWEET-AND-SOUR CABBAGE SAUCE

3 tablespoons butter

2 cups (284 g) onion, finely chopped

3 cups (300 g) finely diced red cabbage

2 tablespoons flour

1½ cups (375 ml) red wine

1½ cups (375 ml) chicken broth

3 tablespoons Elderflower Vinegar

2 tablespoons Fermented Elderberry Syrup

15 juniper berries

⅓ cup (80 ml) heavy cream

Salt

Black pepper

FOR THE MEATBALLS: In a small bowl pour the milk over the bread crumbs. Combine the meat with the elderberries, pepper, spicebush, salt, and nutmeg. Add the soaked bread crumbs and mix well with a fork until combined. Add the egg and mix again. Wet your hands and form small meatballs, about 1 inch (2½ cm) in diameter. When they are all made, place them on a plate, cover, and set aside in the fridge while you make the sauce

FOR THE SAUCE: Melt the butter in a pot over medium-high heat. Add the onion and cabbage and stir well. Reduce the heat to medium-low and cover. Cook for 30 minutes. Remove the lid and stir well. Add the flour and stir thoroughly. Turn up the heat to high. Add the wine gradually and stir very well. Allow the wine to come to a boil, then add the chicken stock, Elderflower Vinegar, Elderberry Syrup, and juniper berries. When the liquid comes to a boil again, reduce the heat to keep it at a simmer, and cook for another 10 minutes, stirring occasionally. Add the cream and simmer for a final 10 minutes. Taste and season with salt and pepper.

MEANWHILE, BROWN THE MEATBALLS: Heat a skillet over medium-high heat, adding 1 tablespoon of the butter. Add the meatballs in batches (about three should do it, with more butter added as you work) and brown them on one side. Flip and brown the other. *Remove to a plate before they are cooked through.*

TO FINISH: When the cabbage is meltingly tender, return all the reserved meatballs and any juice they have exuded to the skillet they browned in. Pour the hot cabbage sauce over them and boil gently over medium heat for 4 to 5 minutes to cook them through, turning them once. Turn off the heat and let them sit for a couple of minutes. Serve.

Raised Pork Pie with Elderberries and Wild Herbs

Serves 4–6

Oh, this pie. It is a Very. Good. Pie. Old-fashioned raised pies are fun to eat, very delicious, and not as hard to make as they say. I have always had a thing about pork pies. They are easy to buy in my native South Africa, probably because of a British colonial and then Commonwealth culinary hangover. There, they sell mini versions, for picnics. I had to learn to make my own in New York. If you have never made a hot-water crust before, it is eye opening. Contrary to what I read and hear, I find it is easy to work with, and it *tastes* fantastic. I use the saved drippings from a duck I have roasted, which are very flavorful, but you can buy duck fat already rendered. Do not be tempted to roll the pastry very thinly—you are building a wall to contain a lot of juice; thin pastry will burst. Pork has a natural affinity with fruit, and fermented elderberries fit the bill. Juniper sugar, sage-like mugwort, resinous bayberry, and white sweet clover flowers add botanical complexity to the filling. I serve the pie cold, in wedges (with BC Ketchup and Fermented Elderberry Capers on the side), when the meat has set firmly. *If you want to eat it hot*, be aware that it will gush (very delicious) juices at you. Serve it from a dish that will contain them. It's like a pastry moat, breaking. I say chill it, overnight.

It helps to have a special, deep springform pan for this pie. Mine is 8 by 3¼ inches (20 × 8 cm) and has a little channel at the base for catching juices (which is very useful).

FILLING

2 pounds 6 ounces (1 kg) pork butt,
  cut into ¾-inch (2 cm) cubes
1 pound (453 g) ground pork (or minced
  pork belly)
2 ounces (57 g) pancetta, chopped
3 tablespoons Elderberry Gin
3 tablespoons finely chopped mugwort
1½ teaspoons Juniper Sugar
1½ teaspoons salt
½ teaspoon black pepper
3 tablespoons fermented elderberries (see
  Fermented Elderberry Syrup)
½ cup (71 g) very finely chopped onion
1 tablespoon white sweet clover flowers
12 bayberry leaves
12 juniper berries

DOUGH

15 ounces (425 g) all-purpose flour
1 teaspoon salt
6 ounces (170 g) duck fat, melted and
  kept hot
6 fluid ounces (175 ml) boiling water

FOR THE FILLING: Combine all the ingredients except the elderberries, onion, white sweet clover, bayberry leaves, and juniper berries in a large bowl. Mix very well with your hands. Cover and refrigerate overnight.

Remove the filling from the fridge 30 minutes before assembling the pie (while you make the pastry). Add the elderberries, chopped onion, and white sweet clover to the pork mixture. Mix very well.

Preheat the oven to 350°F (180°C).

FOR THE PASTRY: Combine the flour and salt in a large bowl and make a well. Pour in the hot duck fat and the boiling water. Stir to create a shaggy pastry (it will not be cohesive). Tip it out onto a clean board and knead for 2 minutes until it is very smooth (it will be hot, and that is correct!). You will find that the fat prevents it from sticking; I do not use extra flour on the board while rolling.

Cut off one-quarter of the pastry and reserve for the pie lid. Butter your baking pan.

Roll the rest of the pastry out to a circle between ¼ and ⅜ inch (6–9 mm) thick. The circle should be wide enough for its edges to overhang the pan by 1½ inches (4 cm) all around once it lines the pan. Wrap the pastry around your rolling pin and lower it into the prepared baking pan. Press it well against the sides and make sure there are no holes. (If there are, patch them with small pieces of pastry and water.)

TO ASSEMBLE AND BAKE: Fill the pastry case with the pork mixture. Pack it tightly. Arrange the bayberry leaves in a circle on top, points inward. Pace a juniper berry between each leaf. Roll out the pastry lid, and lay it on top. Trim the overhanging edges with scissors, and fold them up over

EGG WASH

1 large egg, beaten

**JELLY (OPTIONAL,
AND ONLY FOR SERVING COLD)**

1 cup (250 ml) very hot, well-flavored
chicken broth

1 tablespoon powdered gelatin

the lid. Crimp them very firmly together. Cut a hole in the center of the pie lid to allow steam to exit. Brush with the beaten egg.

Bake the pie for 1 hour and 30 minutes. Reduce the heat to 325°F (170°C) and continue to bake for another 50 minutes. (If the bubbling juices inside the pie decide to escape from the vent, or from any tears or open seams, and then escape further to drip from the moat around the baking pan, slide a tray onto the rack below the pie to catch the drips.)

Remove from the oven. If you are eating the pie hot, remember the gushing juices and unmold carefully.

If you are eating it cold (recommended), give the pie 20 minutes to cool a little, then transfer to the fridge to chill for 4 or more hours.

OPTIONAL STEP FOR A COLD PIE: The pie will be delicious without this step, but I love the wobbly jelly in a pork pie. Once the pie has chilled for 4 hours or more, heat the chicken stock until boiling. Take it off the heat and sprinkle the tablespoon of gelatin into the liquid. Stir very well to dissolve. Pour the liquid slowly and carefully into the pie through the steam vent. It should all be absorbed. Let the pie chill for an additional 2 or more hours before serving.

TO UNMOLD: Remove the chilled pie from the fridge to unmold. Dip a knife in boiling water and slide it around the whole pie, between the pan and the pastry wall. Re-dip the knife often, to loosen the hardened fat or gelatinous juices that may be sticking the pastry to the pan. Release the spring and slide the pan sides up and off. Heat the knife again and loosen the bottom of the pie from its base. Transfer gently to a serving plate.

Griesmeelpudding with Elderberry Sauce

Serves 6

Winny Vettorato, a Dutch friend whose Norwegian forest cats I stalk gently on Instagram, told me about a pudding her mother used to make. Its simplicity—and solid comfort—resonated with me. I made it, and fell in love. *Griesmeelpudding* is heavy, no denying it. I think it must be eaten by hungry people who have had a lot of winter exercise. I like it best as soon as it is unmolded. What makes it work is the simple elderberry sauce, which is actually Elderberry Soup reinvented, with a sneaky slick of Fermented Elderberry Syrup.

1 cup (190 g) cream of wheat
3 cups (750 ml) milk
¾ cup (150 g) sugar
½ teaspoon ground spicebush
⅛ teaspoon salt
2 tablespoons Fermented Elderberry Syrup
2 tablespoons fermented elderberries
1 cup (250 ml) Elderberry Soup, for serving

In a pot whisk the cream of wheat with 1 cup of the milk. Gradually add the rest of the milk, the sugar, spicebush, and the salt. Heat over high heat, whisking to keep it smooth as it thickens. Cook until it is tender, about 5 minutes. Take a 6-cup (8-inch/20-cm) pudding or Bundt mold and wet it. Pour the thick pudding mixture into it while still wet. Allow it to cool. It will set in about 2 hours, while still being tepid. Place a serving plate over the mold, flip both upside down, and shake quickly to dislodge the pudding. You should hear a slurping thump as it drops. Lift the mold off gently. Drizzle the Fermented Elderberry Syrup over it and scatter the fruit across it. Serve the elderberry soup in a jug for pouring over each helping.

Fiddleheads

OTHER COMMON NAMES: Ostrich fern, western bracken fern, eagle fern, brake

BOTANICAL NAMES: *Matteuccia struthiopteris, Pteridium aquilinum*

STATUS: Indigenous North American perennials. Ostrich fern occurs in Canada, the Midwest, and the northeastern US; bracken occurs throughout Canada and the US

WHERE: Woodland, forest margins, ostrich fern fiddleheads at farmers markets

SEASON: Midspring

USE: Vegetable

PARTS USED: Crosier or fiddlehead

GROW? Yes

TASTES LIKE: Flavor is unique

What is a fiddlehead? It is not a plant, but a part of a plant: the immature, furled frond of a fern, also called a crosier. All ferns have fiddleheads, and several species are eaten across the world. There is much debate about which ones are safe to eat, and whether there are long-term consequences for people who eat many fiddleheads of particular ferns on a regular basis. Toxicity appears to be cumulative.

Bracken fern (*Pteridium aquilinum,* also commonly called brake and eagle fern—on account of its claw-like unfurling fronds) is possibly responsible for a high incidence of oral and throat cancers in Japan and Korea, in populations who eat it regularly and in large amounts. If you want to explore the potential health effects further, wild foods author Hank Shaw sums up the gnarly and murky topic well on his website, Honest Food. Suffice it to say that eaten in moderation and properly prepared (cooked in boiling, salted water), bracken fern is a very appealing and flavorful vegetable. I include it here because it is exceptionally widely distributed, occurring on every continent except the frozen one. I first ate bracken fiddleheads in Cape Town, where the plant is invasive, and where it both benefits from and contributes to wildfires. Curiously, living near or working in dense stands of bracken could be worse for you than eating it, since its fine spores—the reason it occurs so widely—may be

carcinogenic. You can control a cooking environment, but not what you breathe.

In the United States most fiddleheads brought to farmers markets every spring belong to native North American *Matteuccia struthiopteris*, varieties of which also occur in Europe and Asia. Like bracken fern, ostrich fern fiddleheads should also be blanched prior to eating.

Unlike ubiquitous and invasive bracken, it might actually be possible to eat North American ostrich ferns out of existence. I feel unease about the increasing quantities being brought to market. I have seen basketfuls blacken at a local supermarket, unsold at $17.99 a pound, while at nearby Whole Foods they were snapped up at half the price. The freshest fiddleheads appear in quantity at farmers markets. This is fantastic for cooks, but what are the longer-term implications? While some professional harvesters may collect fiddleheads responsibly, there are anecdotal reports of entire areas being cut clean. Each cut fiddlehead means one less frond for the plant, that year. The fronds are food factories for the ferns. A small University of Maine study completed in 2008 observed that ferns harvested of all their fiddleheads every spring produced very few or no new fiddleheads after four years, while ferns harvested of half their fiddleheads remained healthy. Despite being robust plants, in New York ostrich ferns are listed by the USDA as "exploitably vulnerable." This designation describes species that are likely to become threatened if causal factors—collection for commercial or personal use—are unchecked.

The other issue with commercial harvesting is collateral damage, that euphemism associated with the killing of civilians in war. In native woodlands these potential victims are the spring ephemerals that appear when the fiddleheads do. How much stomping can they stand?

So why even include the food here? One reason is to raise awareness of what it means to bring a wild-harvested plant to market. Not everyone thinks of that when they buy a food that is considered a delicacy. Another reason is that fiddleheads can be harvested and managed responsibly. In the case of ostrich ferns, we can grow them. We *should* grow them.

CULTIVATION TIPS

USDA Hardiness Zones 3–7

The good news about ostrich ferns is that they are very vigorous in terms of establishing themselves. In my current garden I began with one potted ostrich fern; three years later I have fifteen, with the additional clones produced by vegetative production. Now that I have a colony I can observe what impact rapacious fiddlehead harvesting might have on the plants. Ostrich ferns prefer slightly acidic soil, relish shade, and require consistent moisture. Bracken likes similar conditions but can become invasive.

How to Collect and Prepare

If you are foraging for fiddleheads, watch where you walk. Respect native plants and habitats. Cut only two to three fiddleheads per mature crown (this my guesstimate). If you are collecting bracken fern, collect as many of its tightly coiled fiddleheads as you like.

Blanch both types of fiddleheads in ample, salted boiling water for at least a minute before using them in recipes.

Caution

Do not consume fiddleheads raw. Always blanch before continuing with a recipe. Eat in moderation.

Pickled Fiddleheads

Makes 4 jars, ½ pint (250 ml) each

Fiddlehead pickles do lose their brilliant green color in brine, but not their succulent texture. They are novel additions to charcuterie plates and summer rolls after their fleeting season has fled. Best eaten within six months (in terms of texture).

8 ounces (227 g) fiddleheads
1 cup (250 ml) apple cider vinegar
1 cup (250 ml) water
1 tablespoon salt
3 tablespoons sugar

Cook the fiddleheads in boiling water for 3–4 minutes, until barely tender. Remove and drain, and pick off any remaining brown scales. Pat dry. Place the blanched pickles in a clean jar or jars. Bring the pickling ingredients to a boil on the stove, stirring to dissolve the granules. Pour while hot onto the fiddleheads, and seal.

Fiddlehead Tart

Serves 4–6

The sturdy but creamy texture of blanched fiddleheads holds up superbly to a delicate custard in a crisp pastry crust.

PASTRY

1 cup (120 g) all-purpose flour
Pinch of salt
2½ ounces (71 g) cold butter
1 large egg yolk
3–4 tablespoons cold water

FILLING

7 ounces (198 g) fiddleheads,
   washed and trimmed
5 large egg yolks
1 large egg
1½ cups (375 ml) milk
¼ teaspoon salt

FOR THE PASTRY: Combine the flour and salt in a bowl. Grate the butter onto the flour and rub it in with your fingers, until the mixture resembles coarse crumbs. Make a well in the mixture. Add the egg yolk with 2 tablespoons of the water and start mixing with a fork to bring in the flour mixture. Add a little more water and continue to blend until the pastry is just cohesive. Flatten it slightly, wrap, and allow to rest in the tridge for an hour.

Preheat the oven to 400°F (200°C). Butter an 8-inch (20 cm) pie dish. Roll the rested pastry out thinly on a lightly floured board. Transfer to the pie dish and lay the pastry in it, with overhanging edges. Prick the base with a fork. Chill another 10 minutes in the fridge. Trim the edges after it has rested. Line the pastry with foil (but no weights) and bake for 20 minutes in the hot oven. Remove, and pull the foil off gently. Return to the oven for 5 minutes. Remove, and reduce the heat to 350°F (180°C).

FOR THE FILLING: Bring a pot of water to a boil. Add the fiddleheads and blanch for 2 minutes. Drain and refresh in cold water. Dry well. Place them in the pastry shell.

In a bowl beat the eggs with the milk until just combined. Add the salt and stir until dissolved. Pour the mixture gently into the pastry shell. Transfer the dish gently to the oven and cook until the custard in the middle of the tart is just set, about 30 minutes. Serve warm.

Spring Weed Summer Rolls with Fiddleheads

Makes 12 rolls

It is really strange to call such a spring thing a summer roll. These are deceptively simple to make but so beautiful that everyone thinks it takes genius to produce them. I never make summer rolls the same way twice, as every spring week brings new forages. When I can find them, I use fresh bamboo hearts (they must be cooked first). In ramp season I add the leaves. Chickweed and young wild lettuce can provide much-needed mild bulk for the rolls; shoots and greens like garlic mustard, ground elder, dandelions, and immature prickly ash leaves provide a spectrum of herbal flavors. Spring flowers like black locust, garlic mustard, violets, wintercress, and wisteria add glamour. Precious forages like fiddleheads shine, especially if you have only a handful: Including one or two in a roll looks impressive. In other words, wing it, using this recipe merely as a guide. The only constant element in my weed rolls is Soy-Pickled Oyster Mushrooms—an important flare of intense flavor and silky texture. Substitute wood ears or shiitakes for the oyster mushrooms if you like.

I have made these wrappers up to 14 hours in advance, but they must be well covered, stored in airtight containers, and kept cold. I pack them inside stackable stainless steel lunch boxes for my forage-walk picnics, placing layers of parchment between them and under the box lids, to keep them from sticking to one another.

Once all your ingredients are assembled, the rolls are simple to make. Make sure everything is ready before you begin.

SOY-PICKLED OYSTER MUSHROOMS

3 pounds (1⅓ kg) oyster mushrooms, sliced thickly (small ones can be left whole)

2 cups (500 ml) soy sauce, divided

2 cups (500 ml) sherry vinegar, divided

2 cups (400 g) sugar, divided

1 thumb-sized piece of ginger, peeled and sliced thinly

2 teaspoons prickly ash fruit, crushed

WEED ROLLS

12 rice wrappers, 8 inches (20 cm) each

6 ounces (170 g) wild lettuce and/or chickweed, washed and dried

36 baby ground elder leaves

1 cup Soy-Pickled Oyster Mushrooms, cut into medium slices

36 garlic mustard buds or flowers

12 fiddleheads, blanched for 2 minutes

1 cup (20 g) wisteria flowers

FOR THE PICKLES: Place the clean mushrooms in a large pot. In a bowl combine ⅔ cup (160 ml) of the soy sauce, ⅔ cup of the vinegar, and ⅔ cup (134 g) of the sugar. Stir well to dissolve the sugar. Pour this over the mushrooms. Add the ginger and the prickly ash. Bring the mixture to a bubble over high heat, stirring frequently (the soy and sugar cause quick caramelization). Simmer for 8 minutes, until the mushrooms are cooked through. Turn off the heat. Combine the rest of the soy sauce, vinegar, and sugar in a bowl and whisk until the sugar has dissolved.

Allow the mushrooms to cool a little before packing them into a clean jar. Cover with the rest of the pickling liquid. Seal and store in a cool spot. After opening, keep them in the fridge.

These full-bodied pickles can also be added at the last minute to soups and stews. The rich pickling liquid gives an instant boost to vinaigrettes, stews, soups, grilled meats, and stir-fried vegetables. Even raw oysters (the molluscs). In other words, everything.

TO SET UP: To the side of your work area, have a large shallow bowl or pie dish that fits one rice wrapper. Fill it with water for dipping. Stack the dry rice wrappers beside it. In the middle of your work surface, lay a clean, damp dishcloth (wet it well, then wring it out). Leaving the center area free for the wrapper you are working on, arrange the pile of lettuce or chickweed, and the other ingredients—each in their own bowl— around the edges within easy reach.

DIPPING SAUCE

2 tablespoons soy sauce

1 tablespoon lime juice

1 teaspoon sugar

¼ teaspoon powdered green prickly ash

½ cup peanut butter

TO ASSEMBLE THE ROLLS: Lay a dry rice wrapper in the water, which should cover it. Leave it there for 5 seconds. Lift it out and lay it on the damp dishcloth. Don't worry if it still feels stiff—it will soften. On the side nearest you, leaving 1 inch (2½ cm) clear on the near edge, and 1½ inches (4 cm) clear on the sides, stack several lettuce leaves and/or a tangle of chickweed (the stack should be about 1 inch high) in a row. (Tear the lettuce leaves to fit the wrapper.) This is your bulk filler. Lay three ground elder leaves in a row on top of them. Top the leaves with a single layer of two or three slices of pickled mushrooms. Top the mushrooms with a row of three garlic mustard buds. Make a new row on the rice wrapper 1 inch (2½ cm) beyond your first: Lay the pretty things, which will be visible at the top of your wrapper: two blanched fiddleheads, with flowers between them.

TO ROLL: Beginning at the edge near you, lift the soft wrapper delicately up and over the filling. Keep rolling into a tight cylinder, folding the sides up and over the filling like a burrito as you near the two-thirds mark. This will make neat edges. As soon as your roll is ready, place it on a platter, pretty-side up; cover with another damp dish towel or plastic, or it will dry out. If your first summer roll looks a bit ragged, the second will look better as you become used to the tension needed. Cover the rolls as you finish each one.

FOR THE DIPPING SAUCE: In a small bowl combine the soy sauce and lime with the sugar and stir until the sugar has dissolved. Add the prickly ash. Place the peanut butter in another bowl. Gradually add the soy sauce mixture to it, beating with a fork as it thins. If it still seems too thick, add a little water.

Fiddleheads and Peas with Prickly Ash Paste

Serves 4 as an appetizer or side

Pure green comfort food, celebrating spring . . .

2 cups (300 g) peas
6 ounces (170 g) fiddleheads,
    washed and trimmed
2 tablespoons extra-virgin olive oil, divided
Generous squeeze of fresh lemon juice
Pinch of salt
1 teaspoon Salted Ramp Leaves
2 teaspoons Prickly Ash Paste

Preheat the broiler and place an oven rack just below it.

Bring two pots of salted water to a boil. Drop the shelled peas into one and the fiddleheads into another. Cook both for 3 to 4 minutes or until barely tender. Drain.

Scatter the fiddleheads across a baking sheet. Drizzle 1 tablespoon of the olive oil over them, and add the lemon juice. Season with the salt. Slide the fiddleheads beneath the broiler and cook for 5 minutes.

Place the peas in a serving dish and top with the fiddleheads. Pour the rest of the oil across the vegetables, then season with the Salted Ramp Leaves. Finally, add a seam of Prickly Ash Paste down the middle.

Fiddleheads with Double Beurre Noisette

Serves 1

If you make just one fiddlehead dish, let this be it. It is one of those fortunate improvisations where the contents of the fridge dictated the meal. I had fiddleheads, panko crumbs, butter, and hazelnuts. I may have hummed out loud when I sat down to enjoy it. I give quantities here for one portion, because it is an excellent use of a modest forage. But the recipe doubles, triples, and so on, easily. It is an outstanding breakfast; otherwise feed it to very lucky friends as an appetizer. It is important to brown the butter gently, not to scorch it over high heat. The finishing touch of Ramp Leaf Salt with its insinuation of green garlic adds volumes in terms of flavor.

2 ounces (57 g) fresh fiddleheads, washed
    and trimmed
1 tablespoon unsalted butter
1 tablespoon panko bread crumbs (or
    coarse, toasted crumbs)
1 tablespoon chopped hazelnuts
Pinch of Ramp Leaf Salt

Bring a pot of water to a boil. Drop in the fiddleheads and cook until they are barely tender, 3 to 4 minutes (you want a little crunch left). Remove the fiddleheads, drain, and reserve. In a small saucepan heat the butter over medium heat. Let it cook until the milk solids are turning brown; this will take about 4 to 5 minutes. When you see brown bits, add the bread crumbs and chopped hazelnuts to the butter. Toss. Increase the heat to medium and add the fiddleheads. Toss them with the crumbs and nuts until they have been warmed through. Season with a pinch of Ramp Leaf Salt. Eat at once.

Fiddlehead Lasagna

Serves 2 as an appetizer or side

Abandon all thoughts of heavily sauced winter-night lasagnas. Here, crunchy spring fiddleheads are slicked with a toasted *beurre blanc* and stacked between austere sheets of pasta. The result is surprising and very good.

12 ounces (340 g) fiddleheads,
   washed and trimmed
4 sheets of egg yolk pasta, approximately
   6 by 5 inches (15 × 13 cm) each
3 tablespoons white wine vinegar
4 tablespoons butter
2 tablespoons finely chopped ramp bulbs
1 teaspoon Ramp Leaf Salt
3 tablespoons microplaned or finely grated
   Parmigiano-Reggiano

Bring a pot of salted water to a boil over high heat and drop the fiddleheads into it. Cook for 3 to 4 minutes or until just tender. Drain them, rinse under cold water, and reserve.

Bring another pot of salted water to a boil and cook the sheets of pasta until al dente. Drain and reserve.

In a small saucepan bring the vinegar to a simmer over medium-high heat. Cook down until there is only 1 teaspoon left. Reduce the heat to low. Add the butter to the saucepan along with the chopped ramp bulbs. Cook for a slow 10 minutes until the ramp pieces are very tender.

Preheat the oven to 450°F (230°C)

TO ASSEMBLE: Butter a baking sheet. Place one piece of pasta on the sheet. Top the pasta with a single layer of fiddleheads. Drizzle 1 tablespoon of the beurre blanc over the fiddleheads. Season with some Ramp Leaf Salt. Repeat with another two layers of pasta and fiddleheads. Top with the last sheet of pasta (reserve the last tablespoon of butter for the top of the last sheet). Add a dusting of Parmigiano-Reggiano.

Slide into the hot oven and bake until heated through and golden on top, about 12 minutes. Serve immediately.

Lamb, Fiddlehead, and Prickly Ash Pizza

Makes one 14-inch (35 cm) pizza

In South Africa we eat a sausage called *boerewors*, which is spiced mostly with coriander (and cloves and a few other things) and enlivened with vinegar. The ground lamb in this pizza pays tribute to it by way of the seasoning while good mozzarella and spicy seasonal fiddleheads provide a juicy backdrop. You can, of course, omit the lamb, in which case triple the fiddlehead allowance. But the lamb version has been pronounced by the Frenchman to be the best pizza he has ever eaten. For a pizza man, that is something.

PIZZA DOUGH

1 tablespoon instant yeast

¾ cup (190 ml) tepid water

1 teaspoon sugar

2 cups (240 g) all-purpose flour

½ teaspoon salt

3 tablespoons extra-virgin olive oil

TOPPING

12 ounces (340 g) ground lamb

1 tablespoon red wine vinegar

¼ teaspoon salt

1 teaspoon ground coriander

¼ teaspoon ground black pepper

Pinch of powdered cumin

Pinch of powdered cinnamon

Pinch of powdered cloves

Seeds from 1 cardamom pod

Pinch of grated nutmeg

2 tablespoons olive oil

4 ounces (113 g) fiddleheads,
     washed and trimmed

2 teaspoons Prickly Ash Paste

4–6 fat field garlic bulbs, finely chopped

1 ball (about 6 ounces/170 g)
     fresh mozzarella

¼–½ teaspoon Ramp Leaf Salt

FOR THE DOUGH: In a jug or small bowl, stir the yeast into the water with the teaspoon of sugar and allow the mixture to bubble. Combine the flour and salt in a large bowl. When the yeast mixture has frothed, pour it into a well in the flour, along with the oil. Stir well to combine, then turn this dough out on a clean surface and knead until it feels silky and very supple, about 10 minutes. Place in a lightly oiled bowl, cover, and let rise until doubled in size, 1 to 3 hours.

When the dough has doubled, remove it from its bowl and punch it down. Oil a baking sheet. Press the dough out on the baking sheet until it is 14 to 16 inches (35–41 cm) in diameter. Cover it and let it rest while you prepare the topping.

Preheat the oven to 500°F (260°C).

FOR THE TOPPING: In a bowl combine the lamb with the vinegar, salt, coriander, pepper, cumin, cinnamon, cloves, cardamom, and nutmeg. Mix well. In a skillet, heat the oil over high heat. Add the ground lamb and cook for 5 minutes, turning once. Transfer the half-cooked lamb (it continues to cook in the oven) to a bowl.

Blanch the fiddleheads in salted boiling water for 2 minutes. Drain, refresh in cold water, and pat dry. Place them in a small bowl and add the Prickly Ash Paste with the chopped field garlic bulbs. Toss well until the fiddleheads are evenly coated.

TO ASSEMBLE: Uncover the resting pizza dough. Scatter the lamb across the pizza. Break small pieces from the ball of mozzarella and distribute evenly all over the surface. Finally, add the fiddleheads and any leftover bits of paste and field garlic.

Transfer to the hot oven and bake until the pizza's edges are dark brown—about 25 minutes. Remove, dust with Ramp Leaf Salt, and eat. There will be no leftovers.

Field Garlic

OTHER COMMON NAMES: Crow garlic, lawn chives, wild chives, wild onions, wild garlic

BOTANICAL NAME: *Allium vineale*

STATUS: Bulb-forming perennial and noxious weed in eastern and western US and Canada

WHERE: Lawns, open ground, woodland, farmers markets

SEASON: Late winter to midspring, fall

USE: Vegetable, aromatic

PARTS USED: Bulbs and leaves

GROW? No

TASTES LIKE: Onions and chives

Hailing from southern Europe, field garlic is a familiar and very invasive weed in lawns, woods, fields, and agricultural lands. Its green chive-spikes appear in late fall and persist even under snow in winter—they are a rare winter forage. The tubular and pungent leaves can be collected at any time, but mid- to late spring yields the fattest and firmest bulbs. In early summer field garlic forms buds on tall stems, followed by aerial bulbils (which look like small onions with electric hair). The buds are a tender delicacy, like miniature garlic scapes. They and the later bulbils can be eaten raw, cooked, or pickled.

By late summer field garlic has disappeared into dormancy until cold weather returns.

Field garlic leaves behave just like chives, with an extra, garlicky kick. Use them finely snipped to brighten and intensify breakfast eggs, omelets, soups, buttered bread, cream cheese spread on crackers, bread and bagels, hot potatoes, cold salads, crêpes, smoked salmon, and warm fish dishes. All very simple, but intensely and easily satisfying.

Because field garlic is so prolific, I prefer to forage for it where it is unwanted, but a vigilantly monitored test patch grows in a shadier corner of my garden. It is useful when I need leaves in a hurry.

The recipes here call for *Allium vineale*, but there are other wild onions scattered across North America (and the planet). Many of them share the same or similar common names, which can be confusing. All of them are edible. They include invasive *A. triquetrum* (three-cornered leek, a European visitor) and natives such as *A. cernuum* (nodding onion), *A. canadense* (wild garlic, Canadian garlic), and *A. stellatum* (prairie onion). These wild onions each have flat—rather than hollow—leaves, but in recipes calling for field garlic they can be used interchangeably. Bear in mind that natives may be more sensitive to harvesting, and be respectful of their population sizes and habitats. The indigenous onions are easy to grow in the right conditions, just like chives or ornamental alliums.

How to Collect and Prepare

When you are collecting field garlic bulbs, it is best to sort the plants on site, saving you from a muddy mess at home. To select the fattest bulbs, target the thickest and tallest leaves in a bunch. Grab them very close to the soil and give them a series of firm tugs to pull them free. This works if the soil is loose (in woodlands, often). Shake well to dislodge any earth. If you are faced with a solid clump in packed earth, pull or dig the whole clump up, and pick out the fat ones. Invasive field garlic spreads easily and primarily from flaked-off bulblets, so clean the area before you leave and dispose of them at home. Collect more field garlic than you think you will need; they are worth the work at home, and you will want to save some to preserve for the rest of the year.

At home cut the bulbs from the tough stalks, and wash them well in several changes of water. This is a messy business and takes time. Once they are clean peel off any loose skin, and trim off the roots. Give them another rinse. Now they are ready to eat. Discard the tough central part between bulbs and leaves. The leaves themselves keep very well in a sealed bag in the fridge for up to a week. Cut them finely, like chives. Because they can be very long, they are also useful as edible string, if any of your meals need tying up, or down.

Caution

All wild onions smell like onions. Field garlic's hollow leaves make it is easy to identify, while other wild onions with flat leaves can resemble some toxic plants. Your nose is your best friend.

Field Garlic Salt

These aromatic salts transform lowly poached eggs into modest masterpieces, breathe life into humble potatoes (or daylily tubers), and lend complexity to stews that need it. You can make either a wet or a dry version. The wet, while more unwieldy to use, preserves its flavor longer.

Dry Salt

Makes about 8 ounces (227 g)

3 ounces (85 g) chopped field garlic greens
6 ounces (170 g) salt

Place the chopped greens in the bowl of a food processor and pulse until you have a stringy pulp. Transfer the pulp to a bowl, add the salt, and mix with your fingers until the greens are broken up and integrated evenly into the salt. Spread the salt over parchment paper on trays and let it dry completely, 4 to 12 hours. Turn it every hour. Bottle in clean jars. Dry field garlic salt will lose its flavor after about 3 months, so be sure to use it up.

Wet Salt

Makes 9 ounces (255 g)

3 ounces (85 g) chopped field garlic greens
6 ounces (170 g) salt

Follow the instructions for dry salt, but instead of spreading out and drying the salt, pack it straight into jars. This preserves its intense emerald color, and with time a little fermentation action enhances its flavor. Because it clumps, it is harder to use in small, sprinkling amounts, but it is very useful as a quick bouillon, when added in moderation to soups and sauces.

Field Garlic Leaf Oil

Makes 1 cup (250 ml)

Field garlic oil adds a quick green zing to soups, sauces, and spreads. Use it also as a substitute for Ramp Leaf Oil.

12 ounces (340 g) field garlic leaves
1 cup (250 ml) unscented oil

Bring a pot of water to a boil. Drop the field garlic leaves in for 30 seconds. Drain, refresh, and dry thoroughly by rolling up in a kitchen towel. Chop the leaves roughly (this will prevent them from becoming entangled in the food processor). Combine the leaves with the oil in a food processor and pulse until very smooth. Strain through a fine-mesh sieve and bottle in small, clean jars. Freeze, or keep in the fridge and use within a week.

Smooth Field Garlic Butter

Makes about 1 pound (453 g)

Richly aromatic field garlic butter is very versatile. Enjoy it on biscuits and sandwiches, inside baked potatoes and hot French bread, on breakfast eggs and in the filling for deviled eggs, melted into pasta, spread onto seared chops. The list is endless.

4 ounces (113 g) field garlic greens, well washed
12 ounces (340 g) cold butter, grated

Bring a pot of water to a boil. Drop the field garlic leaves into it and blanch for 30 seconds. Remove them, refresh in cold water, and roll up in a clean kitchen towel to absorb all extra moisture. They must be as dry as you can get them.

Chop the greens roughly and then place them in the bowl of a food processor with the grated butter. Process until the butter has turned evenly and bright green. Transfer the butter into a fine-mesh sieve. Use the back of a wooden spoon to press it through into a bowl below. Scrape the butter off the underside of the sieve periodically. Store the compound butter in small, clean glass jars or roll it into small logs in parchment paper before wrapping well and freezing. Fresh field garlic butter will last about a week in the fridge before turning stale.

Bonus: The leaves left behind in the sieve after making field garlic butter are a very flavorful and easy filling for an omelet, or a quick topping for a steak.

Cheese Bread with Field Garlic

Makes 1 loaf

The backbone of so many of my forage picnics, this savory bread also makes the best toast. Use whatever cheese you prefer. It is particularly good with feta. The beer can be switched out with dry cider, or simply with extra milk.

2¾ cups (330 g) all-purpose flour
1 tablespoon plus 1 teaspoon baking powder
¼ teaspoon Field Garlic Salt
¼ teaspoon black pepper
2 large eggs, beaten
⅓ cup (80 ml) milk
⅓ cup (80 ml) extra-virgin olive oil (or Field Garlic Leaf Oil, or Ramp Leaf Oil)
½ cup (125 ml) beer, plus extra
3 ounces (85 g) coarsely grated Gruyère
2 ounces (57 g) coarsely grated cheddar
½ cup (15 g) finely snipped fresh field garlic greens
Coarse salt, for sprinkling on the top of the loaf

Preheat the oven 350°F (180°C). Butter an 8½-inch-long (22 cm) loaf pan (or muffin trays, if you'd like individual servings; they will bake much faster).

Combine the flour, baking powder, Field Garlic Salt, and pepper in a large bowl. Add the beaten eggs, milk, olive oil, and beer. Stir gently till well mixed. Add the cheeses and field garlic, and stir until just combined. The mixture should be quite stiff, but if it is too dry to turn easily with the spoon, add another slug or two of beer or milk. Do not overmix.

Pour the bread mixture into the prepared pan, making a shallow hollow down the middle of the batter with a wooden spoon, lengthwise. Sprinkle the top lightly with coarse salt.

Bake for 50 to 60 minutes, until a skewer comes out clean. Remove from the oven and gently tip the loaf from its pan. Place on a cooling rack.

Field Garlic Mashed Potatoes

Serves 4

These beautifully potent mashed potatoes need to be made just before they are eaten or they lose their vibrant green color to heat.

6 large potatoes, quartered
4 ounces (113 g) Smooth Field Garlic Butter
½ cup (125 ml) warm milk
½ teaspoon Field Garlic Salt
3 tablespoons finely snipped field
   garlic greens
Black pepper

Bring a pot of water to a boil over high heat. Add the cut-up potatoes and cook at a high simmer until just tender, about 15 minutes. Drain the potatoes and remove their skins while still hot. Place them in batches into a potato ricer and press into the pot they cooked in. Add the Smooth Field Garlic Butter and stir into the hot potatoes. Add the milk and stir again until incorporated. Add the Field Garlic Salt, stir, and taste. Add more if you like. Finally, stir in the field garlic greens and the pepper. If the mixture seems a little stiff, add some more milk. If the mash has cooled, warm it over medium-low heat, stirring.

Field Garlic Marmalade

Makes one ½-pint (250 ml) jar

This marmalade is a delicious relish with pâtés and mousses, terrines, cheeses, and eggs. I call it marmalade, but do not expect a jelly; it belongs in the realm of relish.

4 tablespoons olive oil
4 cups (120 g) very finely snipped or
   chopped field garlic leaves
½ cup (125 ml) red wine
3 tablespoons red wine vinegar
1 tablespoon sugar
¾ teaspoon salt
½ teaspoon black pepper

Heat the oil over medium-low heat in a saucepan. Add the field garlic leaves and cook gently for 10 minutes, stirring occasionally. Add the wine, vinegar, sugar, salt, and black pepper. Stir well. Continue cooking gently until the liquid has evaporated, about an hour.

Pack the cooled field garlic marmalade into a clean jar or jars and screw on the lids. Store in the fridge and use within a month.

Field Garlic Pickles, Three Ways

Pickling is a heady subject, and I have exercised restraint in providing only three ways to pickle these useful little onions.

Field Garlic Salt Pickles

Makes 1 pound (453 g)

Doing nothing more than salting fresh vegetables is an elegant pickling technique. The results are bright, fresh, and surprising. Use sea salt. Ramps can be pickled in the same way. Serve a selection of pickles with cocktails; you can also add the salted bulbs to sandwich fillings, or to stews and braises. The drained liquid is delicious and can be added to drinks (in tiny amounts), used as an intense boost to broths, or drizzled over salads.

1 pound (453 g) field garlic bulbs, cleaned
1½ tablespoons salt

In a bowl toss the field garlic bulbs with the salt until they are thoroughly coated. Transfer to a bowl that accommodates the garlic snugly, cover, and store in the fridge for a week. Strain from the liquid before serving.

Field Garlic White Wine Vinegar Pickles

Makes about 6 cups (1½ liters)

A classic pickle provides picnic and appetizer morsels and brine for a good Gibson.

5 cups (750 g) field garlic bulbs
1¼ cups (310 ml) white wine vinegar
2½ cups (625 ml) water
3 tablespoons salt
¼ cup (50 g) sugar
3 tablespoons mustard seeds
1 tablespoon peppercorns

Wash the field garlic very well and pat dry. Skin off the outer, loose layers to reveal the firm bulbs. Place the raw field garlic into clean glass jars. In a saucepan, bring the vinegar and water to a boil with the salt, sugar, mustard seeds, and peppercorns. Turn off the heat and cool slightly. Pour over the garlic in the jars. Screw on the lids. Stored at room temperature, these are good a year later. Keep in the fridge once opened.

Pickled Field Garlic Buds or Flowers

Makes about 3 cups (750 ml)

Field garlic buds look like miniature ornamental alliums. They, and the wild-haired flowers into which they evolve, make good eating. Pickled, they add crunch and pep to cocktails and salads. (You can pickle any wild onion flowers, as well as chive blossoms, this way.)

2 cups field garlic flowers
1 cup (250 ml) white wine vinegar
1 cup (250 ml) water
2 teaspoons salt
2 tablespoons sugar

Pack the flowers into a clean jar or jars. Add the vinegar, water, salt, and sugar. Seal, and turn back and forth to dissolve the salt and sugar. The flowers are ready after a few days but keep well for over a year (I have never gone beyond the 2-year mark).

Confit of Field Garlic

Serves 4 as an appetizer

Eating an entire leek, roots and all, at Babel, the beautiful restaurant at Babylonstoren outside Cape Town, inspired me to try the same—in miniature—with field garlic. This is a simple but rich side dish, or a relish for roasts, a topping for toast, or filling for rolled pork belly. The sweet little onions are sticky and delicious. While the attached roots and stalks remain tough, they are very flavorful to chew on.

16 fat field garlic bulbs, very well washed, roots and stalks attached
Field Garlic Salt
4 tablespoons duck fat
1 tablespoon Elderflower Vinegar
¼ teaspoon black pepper

Season the field garlic with salt. In a pan heat the fat over medium heat. Add the field garlic. Cover the pan, reduce the heat to medium-low, and cook for 25 minutes (if the field garlic turns brown, lower the heat). Uncover the pan and shake the onions to turn. Add the Elderflower Vinegar. Increase the heat to medium-high and cook uncovered at a gentle simmer for another 10 minutes. The bulbs should be pale and tender. Season with black pepper. Serve hot or at room temperature.

Field Garlic Ajo Blanco

Serves 4

This white, strong Spanish soup catches people by surprise. If they have never tasted it, they are sure they will hate it. Garlic? Vinegar? *Cold?* But no one I have met fails to ask for more. It is crisp, multilayered, and very refreshing. Do not be tempted to omit the vinegar. In early spring make it with fresh field garlic (or ramps—the green leaves add a beautiful twist), but later in summer, use pickled field garlic.

⅓ cup (50 g) Pickled Field Garlic Buds or Flowers
¾ cup (72 g) almond flour
2 slices white bread soaked in milk and squeezed out
3 cups (750 ml) very good vegetable or chicken broth, divided
1 tablespoon Wisteria Vinegar
¼ teaspoon salt
1 cup (160 g) halved grapes
Ice cubes

Combine the field garlic, almond flour, bread, and half the broth in a blender and process until smooth. Pour it into a large jug or a bowl and add the rest of the broth. Stir well. Add the vinegar and stir again; taste. Now add the salt—the balance between tartness and seasoning is a fine one. You may need more salt. The texture of the soup should be creamy but easily pourable. Transfer to the fridge to chill. Before serving, stir well.

To serve, place a few grapes in the bottom of each bowl or glass, and pour the soup on top. Add a couple of ice cubes.

Pickled Field Garlic and Fennel Seed Paste

Makes ⅓ cup (80 ml)

This powerful paste adds an intense dimension to grilled meats, fresh-baked breads, or roasted mushrooms. It works very well with raw field garlic and ramp bulbs, too. You can: Dip pieces of fresh bread into a bowl of the paste, stir a spoonful into risotto, rub it into a pork shoulder roast before slow-cooking, and add it to the pan juices for fried pork chops and mushroom dishes.

¼ teaspoon salt
20 Pickled Field Garlic cloves, peeled and finely chopped
2 tablespoons fennel seeds
3 tablespoons extra-virgin olive oil
1 teaspoon dried chile flakes (optional)

On a chopping board sprinkle the salt onto the chopped field garlic. Let sit for a few minutes, then mash the garlic to a purée using the flat of a chef's knife. Add the fennel seeds and chop and mash some more. Transfer to a small bowl and add the olive oil. For extra zing add the chile flakes. Use at once or cover and keep in the fridge for up to 3 days.

Field Garlic Baguette with Fennel

Serves 2 as an entrée, 4 as a side

Classic garlic bread all toasty from the oven is given a wild kick. I like to add the tender and lush young spring fronds from the bronze fennel growing in my garden. This is a meal in its own right, for two people who love bread.

1 baguette
5 tablespoons Smooth Field Garlic Butter
3 tablespoons Pickled Field Garlic and Fennel Seed Paste
4 tablespoons finely chopped fennel fronds
2 tablespoons snipped field garlic leaves

Preheat the oven to 400°F (200°C).

Cut slices all down the length of the baguette without breaking through the bottom crust. In a bowl mash together the butter and the paste, and add the fennel fronds and field garlic. Using a knife, smear this filling in every space you have cut in the bread.

Wrap the bread in foil and place the package in the hot oven for 15 minutes. This will be enough time to melt the butter and crust up the bread.

Rabbit with Field Garlic and Morels

Serves 4

Mustard and rabbit are a classic combination; adding morels to the cooking juices early on blends their woodsy flavor thoroughly into the rich sauce, which is perked up by a flirtation of fresh Ground Elder Salt near the end. Serve with a sprinkling of Ground Elder Gremolata. (If you are butchering a whole rabbit, save the rest for a Juniper Rabbit Terrine.)

4 rabbit hindquarters (leg and thigh)
¼ teaspoon salt
1 tablespoon unscented oil
4 tablespoons smooth Dijon mustard
1 tablespoon butter
16 morels
1 cup (250 ml) vermouth or white wine
½ cup (125 ml) mushroom broth
1 cup (250 ml) cream
½ cup (75 g) field garlic bulbs, trimmed
1 tablespoon lemon juice
½ teaspoon Ground Elder Salt

Preheat the oven to 350°F (180°C).

Season the rabbit legs with salt. Heat the oil over medium-high heat in an ovenproof dish. Brown the rabbit pieces on one side—about 4 minutes—then brown the other side. Smear 1 tablespoon of mustard over each leg. Add the tablespoon of butter to the pan. When it has melted, add the morels. Pour in the vermouth or wine and allow it to boil for 30 seconds. Add the broth and cream. Cover the dish and place it in the hot oven. Cook for 1 hour. Remove the dish, add the field garlic and lemon juice, stir to distribute, spoon the sauce over the rabbit pieces, and return the dish to the oven for another hour. In the last 15 minutes, add the Ground Elder Salt. Taste the sauce for seasoning. Serve with egg noodles, rice, or good toast.

Field Garlic Skillet Chicken

Serves 4

This powerfully flavored and simple skillet special is open to endless adaptation: Add mugwort or young bayberry, potatoes, tomatoes, squash, or lemon wedges. But always include the elements of field garlic and lemon juice.

½ cup (75 g) trimmed and finely chopped
    field garlic bulbs
⅓ cup (10 g) very finely chopped
    field garlic leaves
½ cup (125 ml) lemon juice
    (about 5 lemons)
½ teaspoon salt
Black pepper
4 whole chicken legs

In a bowl mix the field garlic bulbs and leaves with the lemon, salt, and pepper. Loosen the skin of the chicken and stuff some of this mixture under the skin. Place the chicken pieces in the bowl and rub them all over with the remaining mixture.

Preheat the oven to 450°F (230°C).

Place the chicken in a cast-iron skillet or roasting dish, on top of the leftover field garlic mixture. Add ½ cup (125 ml) water. Transfer to the hot oven. Roast until the chicken is dark brown and the skin is crisping, about 60 minutes. Add a little more water if the juices start to dry up.

Remove the skillet and allow the chicken to rest for 10 minutes before serving.

Coconut Chicken with 40 Field Garlic Bulbs

Serves 4

After buying muscat vinegar one year, falling in love, and then never finding it again, I now make my own quick version by soaking cut-up muscat grapes (ripe in early fall locally, or early spring from the Southern Hemisphere, just when field garlic is ready) in good white wine vinegar for 2 weeks. Otherwise, use Elderflower Vinegar.

8 chicken thighs
2 tablespoons soy sauce
¼ cup (60 ml) muscat vinegar
1 thumb-sized piece of ginger,
    cut into matchsticks
3 tablespoons yellow or white miso
40 field garlic bulbs, trimmed
1 can (13.5 fluid ounces/400 ml)
    coconut milk
2 cups (500 ml) water
2 large sweet potatoes, cut into thick wedges

Combine the chicken, soy sauce, vinegar, and ginger in a bowl; mix well. Marinate for at least 1 hour and as long as 24.

Preheat the oven to 350°F (180°C).

In a small bowl thin the miso with 2 tablespoons water. Place the miso, chicken with its marinade, field garlic, coconut milk, and water in a Dutch oven or casserole dish. The liquid should cover the chicken. Transfer to the oven, covered. Cook for 1 hour. Add the sweet potato and cook for another hour, uncovered. Taste the broth and adjust the seasoning with a little salt if necessary.

Roadkill Chicken with Cilantro, Lime, and Field Garlic Greens

Serves 4

Pardon the name: this chicken does look as though it might have met a sudden end on a dark night. But this is a fabulous way to cook an entire chicken faster, with crispy good brown skin all around. If I were forced to choose one dish that is my ultimate in flavor and texture satisfaction, it would be this one. Field garlic and cilantro are natural allies (use the juicy cilantro stems, too), and the marinade yields tangy juice where no single flavor stands out. It all becomes a caramelized stickiness that cries out for very good bread to mop it up.

Instead of using a whole bird, you can also simply use chicken pieces; trauma averted.

1 roasting chicken
1 cup finely chopped cilantro stems
⅓ cup (50 g) finely chopped
    field garlic bulbs
½ cup (15 g) very finely snipped
    field garlic leaves
3 tablespoons fish sauce
⅓ cup (80 ml) lime juice
1 lime, sliced and chopped
¼ cup (30 g) finely chopped ginger
2 teaspoons sugar
40 twists (yes, 40) of a pepper mill

Using shears or a very sharp, small knife, cut back from the chicken cavity, all the way below the breasts to above the wing joint, severing ribs as you go. Repeat on the other side. Now hold the top side (the breasts) in one hand and the bottom in the other, and open the chicken like a new book, bending it right back to crack the wing joints. You want it to lie as flat as possible in the roasting dish.

Once you have recovered, combine all the ingredients in a large bowl with the chicken. Rub the bird thoroughly with the mixture, and tuck some of the mixture under the skin.

Preheat the oven to 450°F (230°C).

Arrange the chicken skin-side up in a roasting dish. It should be flat. Scrape the remaining marinade together and place it under the bird so that it does not scorch. Roast for 1 hour, adding a splash of water to the dish after about 40 minutes. Remove from the oven and transfer the bird to a board or platter to rest for 10 minutes. Place the roasting dish over medium heat and add a little more water, scraping up any good residue. Taste for seasoning, and then pour these pan juices into a jug to serve with the carved chicken.

Indian Roast Chicken with Field Garlic

Serves 4

The germ of this idea came long ago from Charmaine Solomon's iconic book *The Complete Asian Cookbook*. It is a regular supper in my house. You could also add sliced potatoes to the roasting dish as the bird cooks—the juices they absorb make them almost better than the chicken itself.

1 chicken

⅓ cup (50 g) trimmed and chopped field garlic bulbs, plus their leaves, intact

Salt

2 tablespoons lemon juice

1 tablespoon Field Garlic Leaf Oil

2 tablespoons grated or finely chopped fresh ginger

1 tablespoon grated or finely chopped fresh turmeric

1 tablespoon soy sauce

2 tablespoons garam masala

2 teaspoons ground spicebush

⅓ cup (60 ml) thick yogurt

Preheat the oven to 425°F (220°C).

Rinse the bird and pat it dry. Stuff the cavity with the folded leaves from the field garlic, a pinch of salt, and a squeeze of lemon juice. Truss the drumsticks together. Either add the ingredients one by one to the bird and then rub very well all over to blend them, or mix them in a bowl and then spread this over and inside the chicken. Push some of the rub—and as many of the solid pieces of field garlic as possible—between the skin and the breast meat of the chicken and massage down to cover the breast. (I use gloves when working with fresh turmeric, because nothing in this world stains as indelibly as it does.) Place the chicken in a roasting dish with ⅓ cup (80 ml) water and roast for 1¼ hours, until it's dark brown (or an inserted skewer draws clear juices). Remove and let it rest for at least 10 minutes before carving.

Field Garlic Pork Ribs

Serves 4

Sweet field garlic and assertive mustard make a divine marinade. Do not be afraid of the amount of mustard stipulated. I mean it. I like to separate the ribs in order to expose as much surface area as possible to a flavorful marinade. This is outdoor finger food: Serve with lots of napkins and a side of Spicebush Red Slaw.

5 pounds (2¼ kg) pork ribs
1 cup (150 g) chopped field garlic bulbs
½ cup (15 g) finely snipped field garlic greens
1 lime, thinly sliced
⅓ cup (80 ml) lime juice
2 tablespoons sugar
1 teaspoon salt
1 cup (250 ml) smooth mustard
2 tablespoons finely chopped fresh hot chile

Cut between each rib bone to separate the ribs. Place all the ribs in a large bowl or in large ziplock bags. In a bowl stir all the other ingredients together and pour over the ribs. Toss well, cover (or seal the bags, sucking out the air), and place in the fridge to marinate for at least 4 hours, or up to 24.

Remove the meat from the fridge 30 minutes before you are ready to barbecue or roast. If you're roasting, preheat the oven to 450°F (230°C).

For barbecuing, place the ribs about 6 inches (15 cm) above ashed-over coals, and cook until they are brown on each side—about 8 minutes per side (that's four sides).

For roasting, place the ribs in a roasting pan and broil until dark brown on one side—about 35 minutes. Turn, and repeat (yeah, we're going for well done, here).

Once the ribs are cooked, cover them and let them rest—even well-cooked ribs benefit from resting—before serving stacked on a platter.

Field Garlic Chipotle Beef Curry

Serves 4

For its distinctive smokiness this early-spring adobo-style curry relies on chipotles (dried jalapeño chiles). Have a good playlist ready for prepping the forty field garlics. Chicken steak is a perversely named economical cut of beef from the chuck. It has a distinctive seam of gristle running right through the center. It is also sold as flat iron steak. Aside from short ribs, this is by far my preferred cut of beef for slow-cooking—it really does melt in the mouth, with the gristle dissolving into a smooth creaminess.

4 chicken steaks
2 tablespoons unscented oil
1 thumb-sized piece of ginger,
    sliced lengthwise
40 field garlic bulbs, trimmed
5 chipotle chiles, soaked in hot water
    until soft
1 can (13.5 fluid ounces/400 ml) coconut milk
3 cups (750 ml) water
2 tablespoons rice vinegar
1 tablespoon sugar
4 tablespoons soy sauce

Cut each chicken steak into three pieces. In a pot heat the oil over high heat. Brown the beef in batches, 1 to 2 minutes per side. When all the meat has been browned, return all the pieces to the pot, and add the other ingredients. Stir well. Bring the liquid to a simmer and cook, covered, for 3 hours. Serve in bowls.

Field Garlic Rack of Lamb

Serves 4

Rack of lamb is very versatile when it comes to wild herbs. You will find another recipe for it under Sweetfern. Allowing the whole rack to rest for at least 10 minutes will make it easier to carve and extra tender. Other alliums can be substituted for field garlic, but in my hood this is the first wild onion that appears after winter, and this dish is an early-spring ritual.

½–1 teaspoon salt

2 racks of lamb (approximately 8 chops each), Frenched*

6 thyme branches

12 field garlic bulbs, peeled

2 tablespoons lemon juice

4 tablespoons smooth Dijon mustard

Black pepper

⅓ cup (80 ml) Northeast No. 1 Vermouth

2 tablespoons Smooth Field Garlic Butter

* *Frenched* means the tops of the rib bones are exposed after the meat and fat have been completely trimmed from them.

Preheat the oven to 500°F (260°C).

Salt the racks evenly all over. Place them meat-side down in a pan or roasting tray and transfer to the hot oven. Cook for 12 minutes. Remove the hot pan very carefully. Reduce the oven's heat to 450°F (230°C).

Turn the racks over. Arrange them so that they are not standing straight up, but resting flat, with a space under them formed by the arching rib bones. Slide three thyme branches under each rack (in the arch) along with the field garlic bulbs. Pour the lemon juice evenly over the meat—the pan will sizzle. Smear all the mustard over the meat sides of the lamb. Return to the oven for another 10 to 15 minutes. Remove the lamb from the pan and transfer to a platter or a wooden board with a groove for juices. Crack some black pepper over the meat. Cover and rest for 10 minutes.

Meanwhile, over medium-high heat, deglaze the pan with the vermouth, stirring well. Pick out the thyme, shaking it to dislodge and keep any good brown bits. When the vermouth has reduced by half, turn off the heat. Add the butter to the hot pan juices and swirl to dissolve.

Carve the lamb, slicing between each chop. Immediately pour the pan juices over the meat and serve at once.

Fir

OTHER COMMON NAMES: Balsam fir, Fraser fir, white fir, Douglas fir, and more

BOTANICAL NAMES: *Abies balsamea, A. fraseri, A, concolor, Pseudotsuga menziesii*

STATUS: Trees native to North America

WHERE: Eastern, northern, and western America

SEASON: Winter through spring, mostly

USE: Aromatic

PARTS USED: Needles, cones

GROW? Yes

TASTES LIKE: Christmas

Fir needles are a relatively recent addition to my wild foods pantry. Since I live in the big city, my first fir forage was truly urban, and quite accidental: an organically grown Christmas tree, sold on a local sidewalk by Windswept Farm, a grower from Vermont.

I did not grow up with northern Christmas trees. My childhood Christmases were spent under blazing summer skies to the sound of swimming pool laughter. Our tree was a statuesque dried agave flower (called *garingboom* in Afrikaans), painted white. Quite effective, but

perfectly dead. Thousands of miles and a hemisphere away, the intensely evocative fragrance of the firs sold on holiday sidewalks in winter Brooklyn is still intoxicating to me. I love the time of year when the tree sellers migrate down from Vermont and Québec and set up their perfumed walk-through shops with twinkly lights. One year, when I was taking down our own tree in January, I was surprised by how strongly scented the needles still were, despite being crisp. I carried a few branches into the kitchen and began plucking. Then I added vodka. That is how a new holiday winter tradition began.

The fir genus is *Abies*, and it belongs to the pine family (Pinaceae). Many species of *Abies* are distributed across North America. If their needles are aromatic, and untreated, use them. In the Northeast we most often see balsam (*Abies balsamea*) and Fraser fir (*A. fraseri*), as well as hybrids of the two. Well-known Douglas fir—also very useful and scented—is not actually *Abies*, but *Pseudotsuga menziesii*.

I now ask for fresh trimmings from organic tree sellers. These branches, clipped from trees cut for customers, are usually given away free, though I would be happy to pay a few dollars for the distinctive flavor that I preserve to use all year, back at home.

Viscously cold fir-infused vodka sends your party in a Nordic direction. And Fir Sugar is an absurdly easy way to preserve the flavor and apply to it to everything from cocktails to dessert: Added to a small batch of fermenting summer elderberries, it makes a liqueur that demands marketing; substitute Fir Sugar in a butter cookie recipe for a holiday snack with a whisper of the North; add a dab of the green sugar to the frosting, too; and use it instead of the regular sugar and vanilla to make a surprising ice cream topped with chocolate sauce.

Fir Salt is a staple in my cured salmon and works very well with duck breast, too, whether in curing or to season a sauce with late-fall chokeberries.

How to Collect and Prepare

If you are wild-harvesting, use clean pruning shears and make a clean, considerate, angled cut. At home cut the fir into lengths that fit inside a jar, and store until needed. Use the needles dried or fresh. When you are processing fresh needles in a spice grinder, wipe the blades immediately with a hot, damp cloth, as the accumulated resin from the needles is very tenacious and will dry hard.

Caution

Know your evergreens. If you are unfamiliar with trees that have green needles, you could possibly mistake toxic yew (*Taxus* species) for fir. Fir is intensely scented. Yew is not.

Fir Sugar

Makes 2¼ cups (450 g)

Fir Sugar is wonderful on cocktail glasses—dip the rims of the glasses first into lemon juice and then gently into Fir Sugar, letting the rims dry for 10 minutes before filling the glasses. (To clean these sugared glasses, stand them upside down on a plate with a little warm water until the sugar loosens.) It also perfumes syrups, ice creams, and other desserts and adds zest to savory recipes for cured duck, pork, and salmon.

½ cup (16 g) fir needles
2 cups (400 g) sugar

Process ¼ cup (8 g) of the needles in a spice grinder with ¼ cup (50 g) sugar until very smooth and bright green. Scrape down the sides of the grinder and transfer this green sugar to a bowl. Repeat with the rest of the needles and another ¼ cup sugar. This will make a very bright green, sticky, and concentrated sugar. Add the remaining 1½ cups (300 g) sugar to the green sugar in a bowl, mixing it extremely well before bottling in clean jars and storing. The green color will fade with time (sadly), but the flavor and aroma remain intense for over a year.

Fir Salt

Makes 1 cup (250 ml)

Fir salt is the savory counterpart to Fir Sugar. It adds wonderful flavor to slow-cooked duck dishes, cured duck breast and salmon, or braised vegetables (especially red cabbage).

½ cup (16 g) fir needles
1 cup (266 g) salt

In a spice grinder combine ¼ cup of the fir needles with a ¼ cup salt and process until fine. Remove to a bowl. Repeat with another ¼ cup of needles and ¼ cup of salt. Add this mixture to the bowl with the rest of the salt. Mix very well until the salt is evenly green. Spread out on parchment and allow to air-dry, turning a few times. Bottle in small, clean jars.

Fir Vodka

Makes 3 cups (750 ml)

Opening a bottle of this infused vodka never fails to suck me into a seasonal wormhole. I actually can't drink it in July. It smells like Christmas. It is the most evocative scent I know. Make it with fresh or dried fir.

¼ cup (8 g) fir needles
3 cups (750 ml) vodka

Place the needles in a clean jar and top with the vodka. Seal and leave to macerate for 1 to 4 weeks. Strain through a fine-mesh sieve, and then again through cheesecloth. Bottle in clean glass bottles.

Black Ice

Makes 1 drink

This fir-rich holiday cocktail calls for black chokeberry (*Aronia melanocarpa*) syrup, which has a dark and earthy undertow. This North American native shrub's puckery black fruit ripens from late summer through fall and persists for months into winter, becoming less tannic with time. (Red chokeberries—*A. arbutifolia*—ripen many weeks later, starting in fall. The scarlet fruit can be collected well into the new year, although it has far less juice.) See below for the syrup method.

2 fluid ounces (4 tablespoons) Northeast
 No. 1 vermouth
1 fluid ounce (2 tablespoons) Fir Vodka
1 fluid ounce (2 tablespoons) vodka
1 fluid ounce (2 tablespoons)
 Black Chokeberry Syrup

Combine all the ingredients in a cocktail shaker with 3 cubes of ice. Shake. Pour.

Black Chokeberry Syrup and Dried Fermented Black Chokeberries

You may use any quantity of fruit for the syrup—just use the same weight of sugar. The leftover fruits are a fantastic bonus. Use them like dried cranberries.

1 pound (453 g) ripe black chokeberries
1 pound (453 g) sugar

Crush the chokeberries lightly, just enough to break the skin. Place them in a clean jar and add the sugar. Cover with a lid. Shake well to distribute the sugar. The syrup will form in the jar slowly, over weeks, but it is concentrated in flavor. Allow it to steep for 3 months before straining and bottling. The syrup will ferment a little, and this adds a nice buzz to the flavor. If fermentation is very active, open the jar to allow some gas to escape every couple of days.

Dry the leftover fruit in the same way as Dried Fermented Serviceberries or use it, still sticky, in baking or in savory sauces and chutneys. It has a rich, plummy flavor. Deploy the syrup in drinks and in savory or dessert sauces.

Jump on Spring

Makes 1 drink

This tonic-like drink is shaken up with the cold holidays' Fir Vodka and a stash of summer's precious elderberry ferment.

2 fluid ounces (4 tablespoons) Fir Vodka 2 fluid ounces (4 tablespoons) vodka 1 fluid ounce (2 tablespoons) Fermented Elderberry Syrup	Shake up with ice. Strain and pour. Garnish with a thin slice of Meyer lemon.

North

Makes 1 drink

A bracing cocktail for freezing weather.

2 fluid ounces (4 tablespoons) vodka 1½ fluid ounces (3 tablespoons) Fir Vodka ½ fluid ounce (1 tablespoon) Juniper Syrup ½ fluid ounce (1 tablespoon) lemon juice	Shake it all up with ice, strain, and pour.

Firgid

Makes 1 drink

A bracing cocktail for freezing weather. Good fuel for fruitcake baking.

4 fluid ounces (8 tablespoons) whiskey 1 fluid ounce (2 tablespoons) Fir Vodka ½ teaspoon Fir Sugar	Shake it all up without ice to dissolve the sugar. Add ice, shake again, strain, and pour.

Fir-Smoked Roast Potatoes

Serves 4 as a side

These incredible and curiously woodsy potatoes are divine. They were inspired by the work of very talented Paul Robinson. I make smauxed (faux + smoked, get it?) potatoes: I have no smoker, but small batches inside a very large stockpot on the stove work superbly. You must seal the lid carefully and unseal it outdoors or your house will smell for a week. Use all the duck fat trimmings you have been hoarding or rendering for just this moment.

¼ cup (60 ml) fir needles
2½ pounds (1.1 kg) Idaho potatoes, peeled
  and cut into 1-inch (2½ cm) pieces
2 cups (500 ml) rendered duck fat
1 teaspoon salt

Lay a piece of foil in the bottom of your largest stockpot. Place the fir needles on top of it. Cover with another piece of foil. Insert a steamer basket in the pot above the foil. Lay the potatoes in the basket. Place the lid on the pot. Now use painter's tape or foil to seal the space where the lid and the pot meet. Place the pot over medium-low heat and leave it undisturbed for 45 minutes.

Preheat the oven to 425°F (220°C). Place the duck fat in a roasting tray or heavy skillet and slide into the oven.

Take the pot outside (I am not kidding) and unseal it. A lot of smoke will escape. Remove the steamer basket. Back in the kitchen, carefully pull out the pan with the hot fat. Transfer the potatoes to it. Roast for 50 to 60 minutes until they are golden brown, turning them once. Remove them from the fat and drain for a minute on paper towels. Sprinkle generously with salt. Eat while hot.

Fir-Cured Gravlax

Serves 8

I make this gravlax with a side of salmon from my annual share of wild-caught red salmon from the Iliamna Fish Company. The sides are quite small. If your salmon yields a 3-pound (1⅓ kg) side, double the quantities below. It is an impressive platter to carry to a party. Serve the gravlax with fingers of thinly sliced dense brown bread and a side of very good unsalted butter. It really needs no trimmings. Cold vodka doesn't hurt.

FIRST CURE

1 tablespoon Fir Salt

3 tablespoons Fir Sugar

1 medium side of salmon
 (about 1¾ pounds/800 g)

3 tablespoons vodka

SECOND CURE

2 tablespoons Fir Sugar

1 tablespoon Juniper Sugar

2 tablespoons Fir Salt

3 tablespoons vodka

FOR THE FIRST CURE: Sprinkle some of the First Cure salt and sugar in the bottom of a large baking dish or nonreactive metal tray. Place the salmon skin-side down in the dish. Sprinkle the rest of the First Cure salt and sugar over the salmon, pressing it gently onto the flesh. Pour the vodka over and then tilt the dish to catch the liquid that collects, and spoon that back over the fish.

Cover the salmon with a double piece of parchment paper, and then with plastic wrap. Place a wooden board or a dish that fits within the larger dish over the salmon, and then a really heavy book (I use the *Oxford English Reference Dictionary*) or heavy cans or jars of preserves on top of that. You are putting even pressure on the salmon (otherwise known as squishing). Transfer to the refrigerator.

After 24 hours, remove the salmon from the fridge and uncover. Turn the fish so that it is skin-side up. Cover again, replace the weights, and return to the fridge for a second night.

FOR THE SECOND CURE: On the third day, remove the salmon from the dish and gently rinse off the First Cure with cool water. Pat dry with paper towels. Wipe the dish, and sprinkle the Second Cure's fresh Fir Sugar, Juniper Sugar, and Fir Salt over the bottom of the dish. Place the salmon on top, skin-side down. Sprinkle the remaining sugars and salt over the fish, press them onto the flesh, and pour over the fresh 3 tablespoons of vodka. Cover the fish with new parchment paper, then with plastic wrap, and replace the board and the weights. Send it back into the fridge for its third night.

TO FINISH: On Day 4 (the end is in sight) the salmon will be firm, perfectly cured, and ready to eat. Place the salmon on a board and slice it as finely as you can on an angle, using a very sharp knife. Have a set of good tweezers handy so that you can pull out the pinbones that will be exposed as you slice (I find it easier to remove them now than before the fish is cured).

Fir- and Juniper-Cured Duck Breasts

Makes 2 cured breasts

Curing duck breasts is easy, resulting in a dark, flavorful prosciutto. My "Christmas Cure" requires 6 days of salting and flavoring before the duck is hung to dry. I am indebted to Grant Van Gameren (then-chef at Toronto's legendary Black Hoof, now owner of a restaurant empire) for sharing his bag-cure technique with me years ago. Until then I was packing the duck in salt, which made it far too salty.

FIRST CURE

2 duck breasts, about 1 pound (453 g) each
1 cup (266 g) salt

SECOND CURE

2 tablespoons salt
1 teaspoon sugar
50 juniper berries
2 tablespoons dried mugwort

THIRD CURE

2 tablespoons Juniper Sugar
1 tablespoon Fir Sugar
1 tablespoon Mugwort Salt

FOR THE FIRST CURE: Rinse and trim the duck breasts. Pat dry. Place the breasts in a ziplock bag with the salt, toss well, and refrigerate for 48 hours. After 24 hours pour off any accumulated liquid and reseal.

Remove the breasts from the bag, rinse well, and dry thoroughly with kitchen towels. Rinse out the bag and dry it.

FOR THE SECOND CURE: Place the duck breasts back in the clean ziplock bag with the salt, sugar, juniper, and mugwort. Suck the air out of the bag with a straw and seal. Place in the fridge for 24 hours. Remove the breasts from the bag, rinse them, and dry them well. Rinse and dry the bag.

FOR THE THIRD CURE: Return the duck breasts to the bag with the Juniper and Fir Sugars and the salt. Shake it up, suck the air from the bag with a straw, and seal. Place in the fridge for 72 hours. Every 24 hours tip the bag to one side and pour out the released liquid. Reseal.

TO FINISH: On Day 7 of the total cure, you are ready to wrap and hang the duck. Remove the breasts from the bag, scrape off most of the seasoning that sticks to the meat, and rinse the breasts. Pat *very* dry. Cut two pieces of cheesecloth and fold to make 2 layers. Wrap one duck breast in each piece. Truss the breasts with butcher's string, leaving a loop at one end. Hang the breasts in a cool spot for 1 to 3 weeks (I use the hanging pot rack in my unheated kitchen—a basement is ideal). The breasts will gradually stiffen, and the meat will turn dark. When the middle feels firm—not squishy—they are ready, usually after about 10 days, but it varies. Around that time you will notice a drop of fat hanging at the end of the duck breast—a happy sign.

Fir and Lemon Ice Cream

Makes 1 pint (500 ml)

The penetratingly refreshing scent of fir captured in a spoonful of lemony ice cream is not something you will forget. I like to use Meyer lemons because of their very floral zest. But this will be good with ordinary juice lemons. The ice cream is intensely flavored, and a small portion goes a long way.

4 ounces (113 g) Fir Sugar
4 ounces (113 g) ordinary sugar
½ cup (125 ml) cold whole milk
1 tablespoon Meyer lemon zest
½ cup (125 ml) cold lemon juice
1½ cups (375 ml) cold cream

Combine the sugars and the milk in a bowl and stir until the sugar has dissolved. Add the zest and the lemon juice and stir well. Whip the cream until it holds soft peaks. Fold it into the milk mixture.

If you are using an ice cream maker, pour the mixture into its bowl and churn until very thick, about 25 to 30 minutes. Transfer to a container and place in the freezer to harden. (I buy 16-ounce frozen dessert containers online for neat ice cream storage.)

If you do not have an ice cream maker, pour the mixture into a shallow container so that when it is full the mixture is about 3 inches (7½ cm) deep. Place in the freezer, covered. After 2 hours remove and use a fork to stir the frozen edges into the center. Repeat every hour until the ice cream is frozen and mixed well.

Garlic Mustard

OTHER COMMON NAMES: Wild garlic, Jack by the hedge, hedge garlic

BOTANICAL NAME: *Alliaria petiolata*

STATUS: A noxiously invasive biennial in the northern two-thirds of the US, Canada, and Alaska

WHERE: Woodlands, roadsides, shaded field edges

SEASON: Spring and late fall

USE: Vegetable, aromatic

PARTS USED: Roots, stems, leaves, flowers, seeds

GROW? Absolutely not

TASTES LIKE: Broccoli rabe with mustard and garlic

One of the most destructive invasive plants in North America, garlic mustard has invaded woodlands from South Carolina across the Northeast and eastern Canada into the Midwest, the Pacific Northwest, through British Columbia, and into Alaska.

Pull it out by the roots where you see it, and gather all its buds to prevent it from setting its prolific seed. Eat it. It is packed with flavor. One of its British common names is sauce-alone, and it can be, with little other embellishment. The leaves are pungent and remind me of broccoli rabe with an extra hit of horseradish and garlic.

Garlic mustard appears to have arrived in North America in the mid-nineteenth century, brought as a culinary herb and medicine to Long Island, New York. Apart from having no native predators, its highly successful survival strategy includes being allelopathic. It secretes chemicals

that not only compromise the germination and growth of plants around it, but possibly interfere with mycorrhizal activity on the roots of native trees, hindering their development.

Garlic mustard is a biennial, and for foragers it has two seasons of harvest. Every early spring its germinating seeds show up as microgreens growing like a tightly embroidered mat on the winter-brown forest floor and in damp, shaded places. Once you learn to recognize them, they are one of the most intense microgreens you will ever eat. Later in spring the second-year plants form a bountiful main crop, sending out lush leaves and tender flower stalks. In late fall the spring seedlings will have grown to offer hungry foragers a diminutive crop of maturing leaves.

Every part of garlic mustard is edible. The first mature leaves of the year appear on second-year plants early in the waking year. They are quite tough and are best chopped and cooked. You can harvest the plants' roots at this stage. Gnarled and not neatly carrot-like, they have the zing of horseradish, once grated. For your sanity's sake keep only the fattest specimens— they can be fiddly and time consuming to prepare. Another few weeks sees a new flush of tender leaf growth, and second-year plants will send up a juicy flower stem.

The flowering stalks appear when violets and dandelions (and lilacs and 'Kanza'

cherries) bloom. Still in bud, the tender stalks are choice, succulent, and mild. I would like to see them sold in bunches at market, as a matter of course. The stem is soft enough to snap, and it is easy to collect a copious bouquet. The buds and flowers are peppery raw additions to summer rolls and salads and remain flavorful when cooked.

Once the flowers' petals begin to drop, the stems will have turned too fibrous to eat, but you can still collect the leaves, which by now will also be less tender. Finally, if you are patient, gather garlic mustard's spindly seed heads in early summer, dry them, and collect the tiny seeds inside. When you have enough, you can use them as a mustard, pounded with vinegar and salt.

Garlic mustard has a strong affinity for the spices and condiments of Southeast and East Asia, as well as for the boldest flavors of the Mediterranean. It is a spring tonic after a long winter and is a vegetable I keep on hand in the freezer, after blanching and drying the greens. It adds quick flavor to noodles and stews and makes an assertive pesto in the dark months when summer basil has fled.

How to Collect and Prepare

Microgreens: Shear them off with sharp scissors. Or pull up entire seedling clumps, wash exceptionally well at home, and serve whole.

Roots: Keep the fattest, trimming them on-site. Scrub with a scouring pad or nailbrush, but there's no need to peel. Microplane or grate just before serving fresh.

Leaves and stems: If they wilt after being picked, refresh them by submerging in a bowl of cool water. Keep wrapped in the fridge, or blanch, squeeze out, and freeze for later use. The bitterness of garlic mustard is emphasized by sautéing, whereas blanching diminishes it.

Garlic Mustard Root Relish

Yields 6 ounces (170 g)

Gnarly garlic mustard roots are best used fresh—microplaned or grated—and eaten right away, or they lose their horseradish sting. I like to microplane the roots minutes before serving them with spicy stews and slow-cooked beef. But extending their season by preserving the grated root with acid mellows their character, and this relish adds an interesting dimension when stirred into braises and stews, paired with dishes like Japanese Knotweed and Spring Mugwort Lamb Shanks, spread onto sandwiches, or whisked into salad dressings. If you are lucky, the root will be large and fat enough to resemble a modest and convoluted parsnip.

6 ounces (170 g/about 2 cups) garlic mustard roots, washed and trimmed
5 tablespoons white wine vinegar
1 tablespoon sugar
¼ teaspoon salt

Scrub the washed roots with a brush, rough sponge, or steel wool. You don't have to get the skin off completely. Grate them finely or microplane them. Mix the grated roots with the vinegar, sugar, and salt. Pack the mixture into a clean jar and store in the fridge. It will keep its punch for up to 3 months.

Lacto-Fermented Garlic Mustard

Makes 2 cups (500 ml)

In this preparation garlic mustard really *can* be sauce-alone (an English common name for the plant). The characteristic pungency of garlic mustard is tamed by fermentation. I like to add a dollop of the delicious fermented greens to soups and bone broths, to a sandwich of whole wheat bread with butter, or to deviled eggs. My glass crocks live in the fridge indefinitely.

1½ pounds (680 g) garlic mustard greens, tender stems, and flowers
2 teaspoons salt

Wash the garlic mustard. Pick out any yellowed or dead leaves. Place the wet garlic mustard on a large board and chop, sprinkling with salt. Taste as you go. Pack the chopped greens and their juices lightly into jars. It is essential that the greens remain submerged for healthy fermentation to occur (if they're dried and exposed, mold will form). If you do not have enough juice to cover them (unlikely), add a little water. You can weigh them down with a smooth, boiled river or beach stone that fits nicely inside the jar, or a specially designed glass or ceramic fermentation weight.

Carbon dioxide will be released during fermentation, so open the jars daily to expel accumulated gas. Depending on temperatures and microbe activity, the ferment can be eaten "green" within a few days but can carry on fermenting for weeks or months. After 1 week I store my jars in the fridge, which simply slows the process way down. Mine have kept well right through to the next garlic mustard season.

Garlic Mustard with Pecans

Makes about 1½ cups (375 ml)

This versatile leafy mixture can be used to top bruschetta, as a filling for pies, or as a topping for pizzas. Or toss it with pasta.

4 ounces (113 g) pecans
10 ounces (283 g) garlic mustard leaves
3 tablespoons extra-virgin olive oil, divided
2 tablespoons lemon juice
2 tablespoons Smooth Field Garlic Butter
½ teaspoon Field Garlic Salt

Preheat the oven to 350°F (180°C).

Spread the pecans on a baking sheet and toast in the oven for about 12 minutes, taking care not to scorch them (by the time they are smelling nutty, they are ready). Remove them and allow them to cool and crisp up. Pulse in a food processor until roughly ground. Remove and reserve.

Bring a large pot of water to a boil. Dunk the garlic mustard in it for 3 minutes. Drain, refresh, and squeeze dry.

Warm 2 tablespoons of the olive oil over medium heat in a large pot. Add the garlic mustard and stir before covering and cooking for 3 minutes. Remove the lid and turn the greens. Add the lemon juice, stir well, and cook another minute. Allow the mixture to cool a little, then transfer it to a food processor. Add the field garlic butter, salt, and pecans. Pulse until well chopped and mixed. Taste and add a little more salt if necessary.

If you are not using all the mixture immediately, store in small jars or containers and freeze. Otherwise it keeps well for up to a week in the fridge.

Garlic Mustard Flower Stems with Currants and Pine Nuts

Serves 4 as a side

The sweetness of the currants in this Sicilian-style treatment provides relief for the sautéed bitterness of the greens, and the pine nuts offer a buttery crunch. Eat it alone or on toast, under an egg or with a side of thick, garlicky yogurt dressed with sumac.

3 tablespoons extra-virgin olive oil, divided
1 pound (453 g) garlic mustard
    flowering stems
¼ teaspoon salt
¼ cup water
3 tablespoons lemon juice
2 teaspoons hot chile flakes
⅓ cup (50 g) currants
⅓ cup (50 g) pine nuts
Extra garlic mustard flowers, for garnish

In a large skillet warm 2 tablespoons of the oil over medium-high heat. Add the garlic mustard and salt. Sauté for 2 minutes, turn, add the water, and cover with a lid. Allow the stems to steam for 3 to 4 minutes. Remove the lid, toss the stems, add the lemon juice, and continue to cook until the stems are tender, about 4 minutes. Turn off the heat. Add the chile flakes and currants and let sit for a couple of minutes. Transfer the greens to a bowl. Wipe the pan, return to medium heat, and add a drizzle of olive oil. Add the pine nuts and toast carefully for a few minutes, until they have deep golden edges. Remove them immediately to prevent burning in the hot pan. Add them to the greens in the bowl and toss several times. Plate, add the fresh flowers, and enjoy warm or cool.

Garlic Mustard Pesto

Makes 2 cups (500 ml)

Garlic mustard makes a pungent, slightly bitter pesto, which I love. It freezes very well. For a milder pesto, blanch the garlic mustard in boiling water for 1 minute.

6 ounces (170 g) tightly packed
   garlic mustard leaves, tender stems,
   and flowers
2 ounces (57 g) pecans
3½ ounces (99 g) grated
   Parmigiano-Reggiano
3 tablespoons butter
⅓ cup (80 ml) extra-virgin olive oil
Salt

Combine all the ingredients in a food processor and pulse until they form a rough paste. Scrape the sides down, add a large pinch of salt, and repeat. Taste. If the mixture is too stiff, add a little more olive oil.

Garlic Mustard and Spicy Pork

Serves 4

The inspiration for this oily, hot bowl of goodness is David Chang's Momofuku restaurant in Manhattan, where I have enjoyed—many times—a mind-numbingly hot version served with noodles and sweetly roasted cashews. Salt and soy and sugar are made for garlic mustard, whose sharpness is tamed when paired with flavors that can defend themselves in dark alleys.

4 tablespoons unscented oil, divided
16 Ramp Pickles
1½ pounds (680 g) ground pork
2 tablespoons chile flakes
2 teaspoons ground prickly ash
   (or 12 spring leaf stalks)
⅓ cup (80 ml) water
3 tablespoons black bean sauce
2 tablespoons soy sauce
2 teaspoons sugar
1 pound (453 g) roughly chopped garlic
   mustard greens
1 tablespoon lime juice

Warm 2 tablespoons of the oil in a skillet over medium-low heat and add the Ramp Pickles. Cover and cook, shaking occasionally, until they are soft and lightly caramelized, about 30 minutes.

Heat another skillet over high heat. Add the pork to the hot dry skillet, breaking it up with a spoon into small, uneven chunks. Cook for about 10 minutes, until it is brown. Remove and reserve in a bowl. Return the skillet to medium heat and add the remaining 2 tablespoons oil. Add the chile flakes and ground prickly ash (if you're using leaves stir them in just before serving) and cook until you can smell the spices, about 30 seconds. Return the pork to the pan with the ramps, water, black bean sauce, soy sauce, and sugar. Stir well and cook for 10 minutes at a simmer.

Meanwhile bring a pot of water to a boil. Drop in the garlic mustard and cook for 1 minute. Remove and drain. Crank the heat in the pork skillet up to high. Add the blanched garlic mustard greens. Toss well. Add the lime juice. Cook for another minute or two to concentrate the flavors. Serve in bowls.

Tomato Roulade Stuffed with Garlic Mustard

Serves 8–10

I associate this light roulade with summer lunches under the giant London plane tree in my parents' garden in Constantia, Cape Town. I adapted the recipe from the delightful and out-of-print *House and Garden Cookbook* by Alice Wooledge Salmon. It might seem perverse to make a soufflé only to roll it into a sausage. But trust me. In spring I stuff the roulade with Garlic Mustard Pesto, in summer with basil pesto, and in fall with a mushroom sauce. I carry the roulade pre-sliced and well wrapped on my forage walks, and everyone asks for the recipe, so here it is. Make it the night before you need it.

In spring I use canned tomato sauce, and in autumn the last of the season's tomato glut for a fresh homemade sauce.

5 tablespoons all-purpose flour
1½ cups (375 ml) milk
¾ cup (190 ml) tomato sauce
3 large egg yolks
¾ cup (50 g) grated Emmenthaler cheese
    (or substitute cheddar)
Salt
Black pepper
5 large egg whites
⅓ cup (80 ml) Garlic Mustard Pesto,
    room temperature

TO MAKE THE SOUFFLÉ: Preheat the oven to 375°F (190°C). Line a 9 by 15 inch (23 × 38 cm) jelly roll pan with lightly oiled parchment paper cut to extend above its sides.

Put the flour in a round-bottomed saucepan over medium-low heat and slowly add the milk, beating with a whisk until perfectly smooth. Increase the heat and keep whisking the mixture until thick, letting it boil for 60 seconds, still beating. Remove from the heat and stir in the tomato sauce. Let cool, and stir in the egg yolks. Add the cheese and stir well. Taste, and season heavily with salt and pepper (the egg whites will dilute the seasoning later, so use more now than you are comfortable with). Whisk the egg whites to peaks. Fold half the egg whites into the cool tomato mixture, then incorporate the second half, gently.

Gently pour the soufflé mixture into the prepared pan and smooth it into the corners. Bake for 40 to 45 minutes—it will rise a lot and the top will brown. An inserted skewer should come out clean.

Moisten a clean kitchen towel and wring it out (if it is not moist, the soufflé will stick). Place the towel flat on a light chopping board larger than the jelly roll pan.* Remove the soufflé from the oven. Place the kitchen-towel-covered board towel-side down over the soufflé. Deftly invert, and remove the pan from the upside-down soufflé. *Carefully* peel off the parchment paper. Cover the soufflé until you are ready to spread the pesto.

TO ASSEMBLE INTO A ROULADE: Gently spread a layer of room-temperature Garlic Mustard Pesto over the whole soufflé. Use the damp towel to roll the soufflé away from you. Once it is in a log shape, hold it firmly for a few seconds. Remove the towel gently and transfer the rolled soufflé to a flat plate or board. Cover it well in waxed paper until needed.

To serve, cut into slices.

* If you are confident and deft, you can do this without the board: Stretch the damp towel very tightly over the top of the warm soufflé, hold the edges down at each end, and flip.

Cockles with Miso and Garlic Mustard

Serves 4

Garlic mustard is a pungently pretty addition to this flavorful cockle broth, which has been sweetened by apple cider. If you can't find cockles, use littleneck clams. A healthy cockle or clam feels heavy for its size.

2 tablespoons oil

3 medium leeks (about 1 pound/453g), finely sliced

2 teaspoons berbere spice (substitute hot pepper flakes with a large pinch of cinnamon)

2 tablespoons yellow miso

1 cup (250 ml) sparkling apple cider, off-dry or sweet

1 cup (250 ml) water

2 teaspoons Sumac Essence (substitute pomegranate molasses)

5 pounds (2¼ kg) cockles

8 ounces (227 g) garlic mustard buds (or tender stems and leaves)

9½ ounces (270 g) soba noodles (optional)

In a large pot warm the oil over medium heat. Add the leeks, stir well, and reduce the heat to low. Braise them slowly, covered with a lid, until fully cooked and sweet—about 15 minutes. Increase the heat to high. Stir in the berbere. In a small bowl mix the miso with a little of the cider or water until it is pourable. Add the miso, remaining cider and water, and Sumac Essence to the leeks, stirring. When the liquid boils, add all the clams and the garlic mustard. Cover. Cook until all the cockles have opened (discard any that remain shut)—3 to 5 minutes. Serve at once, with spoons and a spare bowl for shells.

VARIATION: For a heartier option, cook the soba noodles in boiling water for 4 minutes, drain, and add to each bowl with a ladleful of broth before piling on the cooked cockles.

Roasted Pork Rib Stew with Garlic Mustard

Serves 4–6

By April I am craving this dish. Braised garlic mustard adds a surprisingly complex finishing element to the delectable, soupy stew, where double-roasted ribs ensure a deep flavor and meat that falls off the bone. If you can resist eating it for 2 days, even better—it improves with fridge time and reheating. Use ramps or shallots if you do not have field garlic.

2 racks baby back ribs
   (about 6 pounds/2¾ kg)
1 teaspoon salt
8 dried bird's eye chiles
1 cup (150 g) chopped field garlic bulbs
1 tablespoon shrimp paste
10 cups (2½ liters) water
2 tablespoons Sumac Essence
3 tablespoons sugar
½ teaspoon salt
1 pound (453 g) garlic mustard leaves
   and flower stems
2 tablespoons Garlic Mustard Root Relish

Preheat the oven to 500°F (260°C).

Cut the ribs individually and arrange in a roasting dish. Sprinkle with salt. Roast for 30 minutes.

Combine the chiles, field garlic, and shrimp paste and stomp with a pestle and mortar until a rough paste forms (you can cheat with a food processor).

Remove the ribs from the oven and place them in a large pot. Cover them with the water. Add a little water to their roasting dish, scratch up any residue, and pour that into the pot, too. Add the stomped field garlic paste, Sumac Essence, and sugar, and stir. Cover the pot and bring the liquid to a boil over high heat. When it boils reduce the heat to a brisk simmer. Cook for 30 minutes, uncovered.

Lift the ribs from the broth and return them to their original roasting dish. Add ½ cup (125 ml) of the broth to the dish. Place the ribs in the hot oven again for 40 minutes to brown. Return the broth in the pot to a boil and reduce it while the ribs roast. After 40 minutes taste the broth and add the salt if necessary. Toss the garlic mustard greens into the broth, pushing them beneath the liquid with a spoon. Cook until wilted. Add the Garlic Mustard Root Relish and stir. Remove the roasting ribs from the oven and transfer them to the pot of reduced broth. Pour a ladleful of broth into their hot roasting pan and scrape up the brown residue again, pouring it back into the pot. Douse the ribs well with the rich broth, and serve at once.

Roasted Shallot and Ramp Chicken Curry with Garlic Mustard

Serves 4

This delectable and char-deepened curry, inspired by David Thompson's stunning book *Thai Street Food*, is brought into focus at the end by a big bunch of blanched garlic mustard.

4 whole chicken legs, or 4 drumsticks
    and 4 thighs
2 large thumb-sized pieces of ginger,
    cut in half lengthwise
3 fresh turmeric rhizomes, 2–3 inches
    (5–8 cm) long, cut in half lengthwise
4 medium shallots, cut in half, with skins
4 ramp bulbs
2 pasilla peppers
1 teaspoon coriander seeds, toasted
¼ cup (60 ml) soy sauce
2 tablespoons Sumac Essence
2 teaspoons sugar
⅓ cup (80 ml) hot water
8 ounces (227 g) garlic mustard flower
    stems, washed and dried

Preheat the oven to 400°F (200°C). Place the chicken pieces side by side in a casserole or pot with a lid, cover, and slide into the oven. Cook for about an hour while the fire gets going and the vegetables char.

If you are grilling, place the ginger, turmeric, shallots, ramp bulbs, and peppers on a wire grid over ashed-over coals, or over a low gas flame. (You can also use your broiler.) Remove the peppers as soon as they smell good, then soak them in some hot water—chop them roughly when they have softened. Remove the ramps when they are soft. Leave the shallots, ginger, and turmeric until the shallots are soft—about 30 minutes. Peel the ginger and remove the shallots' skins and root end. Roughly chop the ramps, shallots, ginger, and turmeric.

Place the charred and cut-up ingredients with the toasted coriander into a blender with the soy sauce, Sumac Essence, sugar, and hot water; purée until smooth. Stop and stir periodically to redistribute ingredients.

Remove the chicken from the oven. Reduce the heat to 325°F (170°C). Add the sauce—about 1½ cups (375 ml)—to the chicken. Cover and return to the oven for another 1½ hours.

Bring a pot of water to a boil and toss in the garlic mustard. Leave for 30 seconds. Remove, and add the greens directly to the chicken pot. Scoop some sauce over them and cook for another 20 minutes. Serve alone from bowls, or with sticky rice.

Ground Elder

OTHER COMMON NAMES: Goutweed, bishop's-weed, herb Gerard, snow-on-the-mountain

BOTANICAL NAME: *Aegopodium podagraria*

STATUS: A noxious invasive perennial

WHERE: Woodland floors, gardens, and parks in northeastern US, Upper Midwest, lower provinces of Canada, and Alaska

SEASON: Spring, early summer

USE: Aromatic, vegetable

PARTS USED: Tender leaves, stems, flower buds, flowers, and seeds

GROW? No

TASTES LIKE: Lovage meets parsley and celery

Beautiful *Aegopodium podagraria*, native to Eurasia but invasive in the United States, has a flock of common names, too many to list. So many colloquial names are a good indicator of how useful humans have found a plant to be. Dating back at least to the Roman Empire (the Romans introduced it to Britain), ground elder was used as both medicine and vegetable through the Middle Ages. It is only relatively recently that it has been forgotten as a food.

I first encountered ground elder when I worked at a garden center in Manhattan. A variegated cultivar was stocked, billed as a wonderful ground cover to grow where nothing

else would. And it did. And it does. Which is why it is listed as noxiously invasive by the USDA.

Woodlands are especially susceptible to ground elder invasion because it favors high shade and moist soil. Some states in the Northeast have begun to take action. The plant is banned in Connecticut and prohibited in Vermont. It favors the northeastern part of the United States (and Canada) and the Pacific Northwest. Warmer and drier regions have been spared.

None of the methods offered on the copious websites that address the control of ground elder include eating it, although there are tentative mentions of Russians enjoying it in salad. I am with those crazy Russians. Ground elder's assertive flavor has wide application in the kitchen.

Long after that plant-selling job, I met ground elder again in Brooklyn's Prospect Park, where I was volunteering to clean litter from a large section of woodland. In the woods a high tide of green stretched as far as the eye could see, a ground elder flood rising among the trees.

Introduced to the States via gardens in the nineteenth century (and still by garden centers in the twenty-first), ground elder spreads by rhizomes, forming dense colonies where nothing else can compete. Native saplings and perennials and the biodiversity they represent are shouldered out. In May and June ground elder bursts into tall white bloom, its wide umbels held on statuesque stems above the dense foliage. This display en masse is appealing and one of the reasons it was planted as an ornamental. But can you hear the indigenous dogtooth violets, doll's eyes, cutleaf toothwort, and wake-robins screaming for help?

Removing plants from a New York City park is against the rules, even if the plant is a noxious invasive that is controlled in other ways—sometimes with herbicides such as Roundup, sometimes by mechanical means (that is to say, cutting and digging up, just like foragers would). While I worked in these woodlands, Asian women sometimes came and collected the leaves to use medicinally, furtively packing them into bags. If found, the foraged items were confiscated. I feel there may be a better way to work together to control a plant's unwanted presence. Clinical trials show that the plant is indeed anti-inflammatory and has anti-microbial properties. Those ladies in the woods knew what they were doing.

Inspired by the furtive foraging ladies, I began to nibble. Ground elder's tender early-spring leaves are delectable. The closest match in taste is lovage. Or gentle celery.

In late spring the buds appear. These are an exceptional cooked vegetable when still furled in a green sheath. The flowers—a foamy sea of them in the woods—are an interesting and pretty seasoning sprinkled over food (like carrot tops in flavor, rather than sweet). Finally, by the height of summer, the green seeds have formed. I find them useful in relishes and chutneys and collect them like fennel seed. The flowers and seeds are still used by herbalists and are said to be diuretic as well as soporific. I have yet to fall asleep in my soup, but I use the seeds sparingly.

Identify your local patches of ground elder in summer, and visit them again early in the spring. There is plenty to go around.

How to Collect and Prepare

In early spring simply shear off ground elder's most tender growth. Later in the season when the flower buds form and remain sheathed, cut their stalks just below the bud. You can use the stalk, as long as it is tender. If leaves or buds wilt in transit, refresh them by submerging in a bowl of water until they have plumped out again. The leaves and stalks last well if wrapped while damp in a paper towel or cloth and placed in a bag. Cut the flowers as you would for a wild bouquet. They last decently well with their stems in water.

Caution

Be careful when deciding to munch on umbelliferous plants. While the family's members include well-known edibles like parsley, carrots, and fennel, there are also the deadly cousins, like poison hemlock and water hemlock. If you have never collected wild plants before and are unfamiliar with their flowers and leaves, don't guess: Be 100 percent sure of what you are picking.

Ground Elder Salt

Makes 7 ounces (198 g) fresh

I add Ground Elder Salt at the last minute to a warm dish, to preserve its fresh favor. It makes a very lickable salted rim for cocktails. The salt does *not* keep its character for long. It is best used within a month and is at its finest within hours of blending, tossed over hot potatoes or just-cooked eggs.

3 ounces (85 g) spring ground elder leaves

4 ounces (113 g) salt

Place the leaves in the bowl of a food processor and pulse until chopped finely. Transfer the greens to a bowl and add the salt. Mix well with your hands. Spread the green salt over parchment paper and let it air-dry; this will take a few hours to overnight. Crumble the dried salt with your fingers to break up any clumps, and store in an airtight jar.

Ground Elder Gin

Makes 2 cups (500 ml)

The carrot notes of ground elder become pronounced in hard liquor and are bracing when paired with assertive flavors and fixin's like lemon, rhubarb, angelica, herb salts, and vegetable juices. I use Ground Elder Gin in the spectacular Mugwort and Raspberry Liqueur.

1 ounce (28 g) ground elder flowers

2 cups (500 ml) good gin

In a glass jar cover the flowers with gin and leave to infuse for 1 week. Strain through a fine-mesh sieve and again through cheesecloth, and bottle.

The Grounded Bishop

Makes 1 cocktail

Ground elder, bishop's weed, bishops behaving badly . . . Here is a botanical pun, shaken into a bracing and herbal spring cocktail.

FOR THE RIM

2 teaspoons Ground Elder Salt

1 tablespoon lime juice

COCKTAIL

1½ fluid ounces (3 tablespoons) dry gin

1 fluid ounce (2 tablespoons) Ground
   Elder Gin

1½ fluid ounces (3 tablespoons) Chartreuse

1 fluid ounce (2 tablespoons) fresh
   lemon juice

Sprinkle the salt in one saucer and pour the lime juice in another. Dip the cocktail glass's rim into the lime juice and then the salt, working it all the way around. Let it dry for a minute.

In a shaker combine all the liquids with ice. Shake, strain, and pour.

Ground Elder and Grilled Lemon Relish

Makes about ½ cup (125 ml)

When I cook over coals in early summer I often add halved lemons to the grid above the fire, even if I am not using them with that meal: Their juice mellows beautifully, and the charred rind has a sweet pungency. I then make make this vibrant relish with the green seeds of ground elder, or fennel seeds. I use it with grilled and roast chicken, rillettes and slow-roast pork belly in winter, or simply for schmearing on good, toasted sourdough with excellent olive oil; in salad dressings (especially with citrus fruit and fennel); and even in sharp cocktails.

2 large lemons, cut in half
2 teaspoons green elder seeds
1 tablespoon chile flakes
1 teaspoon Ground Elder Salt

Roast the lemons cut-side down over glowing embers until the edges become charred—about 15 minutes. Flip, and cook the other side. Cool. They can be kept covered in the fridge for up to 3 days.

When you are ready to make the relish, squeeze the juice from the lemons and reserve. Remove all the seeds and chop the lemons very finely, skin and all. Place the chopped lemon in a small bowl. Add the reserved lemon juice, ground elder seeds, chile, and Ground Elder Salt. Stir well. Pack in a small clean jar. Keep in the fridge for up to 2 weeks, or freeze until needed.

Yogurt Cheese with Wild Herbs

Serves 8–10 as an appetizer

An Instagram posting by Danielle Prohom Olson—who forages on Vancouver Island in British Columbia—inspired what has become a spring favorite in my kitchen. My version is flavored with northeastern forages, wild salts, and young garlic pulled from the garden. You can use any seasonal herb salt and fresh herbs, but I love the emphasis of four species of allium, with a dash of ground elder, in this creamy, very spreadable cheese (technically, labneh, a drained yogurt). The better the yogurt you use, the better the result.

1 pound (453 g) Greek yogurt
2 tablespoons very finely chopped tender ground elder leaves
2 tablespoons finely snipped field garlic greens
1 tablespoon dried Salted Ramp Leaves
1 tablespoon chive flowers (separated into individual flowers)
2 tablespoons finely chopped green garlic (or ramp bulbs, or field garlic bulbs)
¾ teaspoon Ramp Leaf Salt
½ teaspoon Ground Elder Salt

In a bowl combine all the ingredients and mix well. Place a double layer of cheesecloth in a strainer over another bowl. For decoration place some edible flowers or leaves—chives, mustard, sheep sorrel, dandelion—in the center of the cloth. Carefully spoon the yogurt mixture on top of them. Bring the corners of the napkin or cloth together and twist so that the yogurt is forced into a ball. Hold it there tightly for a few seconds, allowing some liquid to drip out. Undo the twist. Now gather the cloth tightly around the ball and tie off with kitchen twine. Transfer the wrapped yogurt in its strainer and bowl to the fridge.

The cheese can be enjoyed after 4 hours but is much firmer after 12. Gently remove its cloth wrapping and turn it out onto a serving board or plate. Serve with crackers, on toast, with Nettle and Ramp Biscuits and a slick of honey, or in a fresh salad.

Oven Fries with Ground Elder Gremolata

Serves 4 as a side

For homemade french fries, roasting rather than frying is less smelly, uses far less oil, and yields a crisp chip that can hold its own with a commercial french fry any day. Each delicious chip has its own character in terms of color. Reason tells me to budget one large potato per person, but chips are never reasonable. You could easily use two, even three, per person and make a meal of it, with a sharp, wild salad on the side.

CHIPS

4 Idaho potatoes
2 tablespoons unscented oil

GROUND ELDER GREMOLATA

½–1 teaspoon Ground Elder Salt
6 tablespoons chopped tender ground
   elder leaves (about 2 ounces/57 g
   whole leaves)
2 packed teaspoons lemon zest

Preheat the oven to 425°F (220°C).

Peel and cut the potatoes into chips. I tend to cut them about ⅜ inch (1 cm) wide. Rinse the chips in a bowl of water. Pat or spin them dry. Place the dry chips in a large bowl with the oil and toss very well, until every chip is coated. Spread them out in a single layer on oiled baking sheets. They will be crisper if they do not touch. Bake them for 20 to 25 minutes or until their edges are turning pale brown, then remove the trays and turn the chips over. Bake for another 20 to 25 minutes. They are done when they are deep golden with brown edges. Remove from the oven, place immediately in a large bowl, and toss with the Ground Elder Salt, chopped ground elder, and lemon zest (if they are too crowded, do this in batches). Taste a chip and add more salt if you like. Serve at once.

Ground Elder and Garlic Mustard Potato Salad

Serves 4

This powerful spring potato salad calls, in my mind, for a platter of sausages or a smoked pork chop. It also pairs very well with smoked fish.

2 pounds (907 g) fingerling potatoes
¼ cup (60 ml) Elderflower Vinegar
½ teaspoon Ground Elder Salt
2 teaspoons sugar
4 ramp leaves, cut into fine ribbons
1 tablespoon Ramp Leaf Oil
2 tablespoons extra-virgin olive oil
2 ounces (57 g) tender ground elder leaves
1 ounce (28 g) tender garlic mustard buds
   and tender stems
Black pepper

Cook the fingerlings in salted water until they are just tender when pierced with a sharp knife. Remove them and drain. Cut the larger potatoes down the middle (to allow the dressing to penetrate). In a large bowl combine the vinegar, salt, and sugar. Whisk to dissolve the granules. Add the ramp leaves and whisk in both oils. Dump the warm potatoes into the vinaigrette and toss very well. Add the ground elder and garlic mustard, toss again, and serve, with plenty of fresh pepper cracked over the top.

Strong Salad

Serves 2–4

Years ago a friend made me a salad that seemed outrageous. She included only herbs, like mint, parsley, and basil. To entice me, she put an egg on it. It worked. Now I occasionally crave what I call Strong Salad, and I eat it with crispy croutons, or pile it onto good bread. Ground elder is an ideal candidate for it, and its fellow spring invasives wintercress, garlic mustard, and sheep sorrel are equal partners, in terms of in-your-face flavor. The quantities are very loose, but I find I like it best when ground elder takes the lead. Use young leaves that have just unfurled.

2 tablespoons Wisteria Vinegar
Large pinch salt
Large pinch sugar
1 tablespoon cream
2 tablespoons extra-virgin olive oil
3 ounces (85 g) tender ground elder leaves
1 ounce (28 g) wintercress or upland cress
    leaves and flowers
½ ounce (14 g) garlic mustard buds and
    tender leaves
½ ounce (14 g) sheep sorrel leaves
Sprinkling of mixed violets, wintercress
    flowers, garlic mustard flowers

In the bottom of a large bowl, whisk the vinegar, salt, and sugar. Add the cream and oil and whisk until the vinaigrette emulsifies. Drop in all the leaves and flowers; toss lightly with your hands. Plate and serve at once.

Ground Elder Egg Salad Wraps

Serves 2–6

While this brightly fresh spring salad can be enjoyed straight up, I like to spread it on wide lavash bought from our local Damascus Bread & Pastry Shop, a short bike ride from where we live in Brooklyn. You could also stuff it into pita, or pile it onto good brown bread.

6 large eggs
⅓ cup Ramp Aioli, or mayonnaise
½ teaspoon Ground Elder Salt
Black pepper
⅓ cup (10 g) finely chopped dill
⅓ cup (10 g) finely chopped ground elder
2 tablespoons finely snipped field
    garlic greens
1–2 lavash breads
2 ounces (57 g) whole, tender ground elder
    leaves with edible flowers

Place the eggs in pot of cold water, and bring the water to a boil. Allow it to boil for 7 minutes, then remove the eggs, plunge them into cold water, peel them, and chop them roughly. Place them in a bowl and add the Ramp Aioli, Ground Elder Salt, pepper, chopped herbs, and field garlic greens. Mix very well. Taste. Add more salt or pepper.

If you are using bread, spread a layer of the egg salad over a fresh lavash. Top with an even layer of ground elder leaves and flowers. Roll up. Wrap the rolled salad sandwich well and chill until you need it.

Rhubarb and Ground Elder Soup

Serves 4–6

Local rhubarb appears around the time that ground elder forms flower buds. These tender, sheathed buds echo the celery brightness of the young leaves. This soup doesn't have the prettiest color, but the flavor makes up for it.

1½ pounds (680 g) rhubarb, cut into
    2-inch (5 cm) lengths
¼ cup (50 g) sugar plus 1 tablespoon
2 tablespoons olive oil
1 finely chopped medium onion
    (about 1 cup)
4 ounces (113 g) tender ground elder
    leaves or immature flower buds, divided
2 cups (500 ml) vegetable or chicken broth
1 cup (250 ml) buttermilk
¼ teaspoon Ground Elder Salt

Preheat the oven to 325°F (170°C).

Toss the rhubarb and ¼ cup of the sugar in a bowl, then spread out on a baking sheet. Roast the rhubarb for about 1½ hours, until soft.

Warm the olive oil in a pot over medium-high heat and add the onion. Sauté until the onion is translucent, stirring every now and then, about 6 minutes. Stir in half the ground elder leaves or buds. Add the broth and bring the liquid to a simmer. Cook at a simmer for 12 to 15 minutes, then cool to lukewarm. Purée the soup in batches until it is very smooth, adding to each batch some of the remaining raw ground elder and the buttermilk, until you have used them up. For the smoothest soup, strain the liquid through a fine-mesh strainer, pushing it though with a wooden spoon. Add the Ground Elder Salt, stir well, and taste. Add more if necessary.

Serve the soup hot or chilled.

Ground Elder and Fennel Pork Rillettes

Makes about 3½ cups (875 ml)

These rillettes are intensely flavored with summer's fennel pollen and make beautiful picnic or cool supper fare, spread on bread or crackers. Pack into individual- or group-sized jars for later use. I often save a jar for winter, too (and Thanksgiving Spicebush Goose). I choose bone-in belly for the texture that the bones' gelatin gives to the shredded meat, but it is not essential. If you cannot find or do not make verjuice, substitute dry white wine. Serve with a relish of Pickled Fiddleheads, Bayberry Plums, or Fermented Elderberry Capers.

2½ pounds (1.1 kg) bone-in, skin-on
    pork belly
2 tablespoons Ground Elder and Grilled
    Lemon Relish
1 teaspoon sugar
½ teaspoon Ground Elder Salt
10 fennel flower heads
1 cup (250 ml) verjuice (or dry white wine)
1 cup (250 ml) water

Cut the pork belly into about eight large chunks. Place them in a Dutch oven or pot along with the Ground Elder and Grilled Lemon Relish, sugar, Ground Elder Salt, fennel flowers, verjuice, and water. Bring the liquid to a brief boil over high heat. Cover the pot and reduce the heat to maintain a gentle simmer. Cook for 5 to 6 hours. Check the liquid level occasionally: At the end of the cooking time, it should be syrupy and have reduced by about three-quarters. Toward the 5-hour mark shred the pork using two forks, to expose as much meat as possible to the flavorful juices.

Allow the meat to cool a little, then work it with your hands to break up every little piece of fat and by-now-gelatinous skin. Pick out the bones (yes, you can suck them, just wash your hands before you work again!). Once the meat is evenly fine, pack it into clean glass jars. Fill to the top and seal. Keep in the fridge up to a week, or freeze.

Honeysuckle

OTHER COMMON NAMES: Japanese honeysuckle

BOTANICAL NAME: *Lonicera japonica*

STATUS: Noxiously invasive perennial vine

WHERE: Woodlands, clearings, meadows, and gardens across the US and Canada

SEASON: Late spring

USE: Aromatic

PARTS USED: Flowers

GROW? No

TASTES LIKE: Honeysuckle

Japanese honeysuckle is so familiar that it seems to belong wherever it grows. And it does grow almost everywhere. The deliciously persuasive scent of the vines' flowers encourages many gardeners to avert their eyes from its destructive, strangling nature. Widespread across the United States and Canada, as well as Europe and as far south as New Zealand, its tenaciously twining habit is responsible for significant habitat transformation as it outcompetes native plants by

shading them and stealing their lunch money (well, sucking up their nutrients from the soil). Its black fruits, ripening in autumn, are readily eaten by birds, and the seed is spread as they travel.

Stateside, Japanese honeysuckle first appeared on Long Island early in the nineteenth century (preceding garlic mustard by a few decades), encouraged to the continent by horticulturists. Like garlic mustard, war has been declared on it by almost every state.

My own romantic notions of honeysuckle have been hard to shake. I remain smitten by that scent. So when I spend a quiet hour in early summer picking its tubular flowers on an empty pathway in a city woodland, an intense sense of nostalgia is evoked by the delicate petals that I am dropping into my paper bag, which fills slowly with memories from childhood, and a subliminal chatter provided by a lifetime of literature. But the rationalist in me appreciates the fact that fewer flowers mean fewer fruits, which means a slower spread. It is a drop in the biodiversity bucket, but what a delectable drop.

Honeysuckle has one use for me: as an aromatic. The flowers make the most heady cordial I have tasted, and its seamless translation from one sense to the next—smell to taste—seems miraculous. Sweet cordial is partnered by a complex and tart vinegar, and these two simple infusions inform countless subsequent creations.

How to Collect and Prepare

Pick only the flowers (the green parts and fruit are considered toxic). This takes patience, but the reward is a few heady cupfuls. Use a paper bag for collection, as they sweat too much in plastic. Try to use them within a few hours of collection while their perfume is strongest. Do not wash them, or scent-be-gone.

Fermented Honeysuckle Cordial

Makes 5 cups (1¼ liters)

This is probably the most delightful fizzy drink I know. It tastes exactly the way that honeysuckle smells. Make it with just honeysuckle flowers, or combine with *Rosa multiflora* (which will make it slightly pink), or elderflower.

3 cups (3 ounces/85 g) honeysuckle flowers
5 cups (1¼ liters) water
2 cups (400 g) sugar

Combine all the ingredients in a large clean jar and stir until the sugar has dissolved. Cover the mouth with cheesecloth secured with string or a rubber band and stir daily. After several days, once fermentation is very active (lots of bubbles, flowers slowly rising out of the jar), push the flowers down and keep stirring. Give it an extra day, then strain through a fine-mesh sieve. Strain again through a double layer of cheesecloth. Pour into clean bottles and close. For peace of mind keep the bottles in the fridge, as some fermentation will continue. A bottle can explode, left out and warm. Reserve the strained flowers to make Quick Honeysuckle Vinegar. To make long-form vinegar from the cordial itself, see Elderflower Vinegar—The Long Way.

Quick Honeysuckle Vinegar

Makes about 2¼ cups (560 ml)

It is a crime to throw out the fragrant pomace after you have strained the Fermented Honeysuckle Cordial. Instead, transfer it to a clean jar, and cover with good white wine vinegar.

1 packed cup (about 200 g) strained
   honeysuckle flowers
2¼ cups (560 ml) white wine vinegar

Place the honeysuckle flowers in a clean jar. Cover with vinegar. Let steep for 2 weeks. Strain through a double-mesh sieve, again through cheesecloth, and bottle. This vinegar keeps indefinitely until opened (after which store it in the fridge)

Honeysuckle Sea Bass Burgers with Sweetfern Butter

Serves 4

Fat sea bass fillets are beautiful on buns. Cattail provides a toasty coating, while the sweet sourness of aromatic honeysuckle does not overpower the delicate meat. The fresh-cut-hay scent of sweetfern—which Mallory O'Donnell, a digital foraging friend, refers to as "dat fish herb"—slicks together this perfect summer supper.

2 pounds (907 g) sea bass, cut into 4 pieces
2 tablespoons Quick Honeysuckle Vinegar
1 tablespoon Fermented Honeysuckle Cordial
1 tablespoon dried male cattail flower
½ teaspoon fresh Sweetfern Salt
2 tablespoons unscented oil
2 tablespoons Sweetfern Butter
4 brioche or hamburger buns

Fifteen minutes before cooking, place the sea bass pieces in a shallow dish, skin-side down. Pour the Quick Honeysuckle Vinegar and Fermented Honeysuckle Cordial over the fish. Sprinkle the cattail flowers and some Sweetfern Salt over the top.

In a large skillet over medium-high heat, warm the oil. Add the sea bass pieces, skin-side down. Give them an immediate wiggle to prevent them from sticking. Cook for about 6 minutes (if your fillets are not very plump, decrease the cooking time), or until the edges of the fish are turning white and opaque. Turn. Season the skin with some Sweetfern Salt. Continue to cook until the fish is firm—about another 6 minutes.

While the fish is cooking, melt the Sweetfern Butter in a small, separate pot over medium-low heat. Warm or toast the buns.

When the sea bass is cooked, carefully transfer it to a plate. Add the leftover marinade to the pan and turn the heat up so that it sizzles. Cook for 30 seconds.

Place a fish fillet on each bun. Pour some Sweetfern Butter over the fish. Add some of the pan glaze. Top with the bun lid. Serve hot.

Braised Quail with Honeysuckle Vinegar and Sweetfern

Serves 4

I think of quail as fall fare, and this honeysuckle sweet-and-sour braise is scented with autumn's mature sweetfern. But make it anytime during the long sweetfern season, using clusters of spring's young catkins instead. And naturally, you have a supply of early summer's Fermented Honeysuckle Cordial and Quick Honeysuckle Vinegar in the pantry. Right? You need a skillet that is large to accommodate all the little birds, with good airflow between them so they roast in the hot oven's blast—huddled together, they will just steam.

8 quail (2 per person)

1 teaspoon fresh Sweetfern Salt

48 whole sweetfern leaves

2 tablespoons Sweetfern Butter, cold and cut into 8 slices

4 tablespoons butter, divided

⅓ cup (80 ml) Quick Honeysuckle Vinegar

¼ cup (60 ml) Fermented Honeysuckle Cordial

Black pepper

⅓ cup (80 ml) water

Salt

Preheat the oven to 500°F (260°C). Yes, hot.

Fifteen minutes before browning them, season the birds all over with the Sweetfern Salt. Stuff six sweetfern leaves into each quail's cavity along with a thin slice of Sweetfern Butter.

In a large skillet melt 2 tablespoons of the regular butter over high heat. When it is foaming add four quail, breast-side down. Brown for about 2 minutes. Turn and brown the other side for 2 minutes. Remove to a plate. Melt the rest of the regular butter and repeat with the remaining quail. When these have been browned, return the first quail to the skillet (if they do not all fit easily, transfer them to a roasting pan). Over medium-high heat pour the Quick Honeysuckle Vinegar and Fermented Honeysuckle Cordial over the quail. Transfer to the hot oven. Roast for 15 minutes.

Remove the quail to a serving platter or carving board with a runnel for juice. Season with freshly ground black pepper and let rest under a cover or foil tent for 10 minutes. Return the skillet to the stovetop and add the water to the juices. Bring to a boil over high heat. Taste. Add a little salt if necessary. Pour it off into a small jug for passing around the table.

Finger bowls and extra napkins are a good idea.

Pork Chops with Preserved Lemon and Honeysuckle

Serves 2 hungry people, 4 as part of a picnic

While I love a hefty pork chop that is still pink in the middle, I also enjoy grilling thinner chops, browning them well and serving them at room temperature with strong flavors. Sweet honeysuckle added to the pan juices with lemon and fresh figs makes a fantastic postcooking marinade.

4 medium pork chops, each ½ inch
   (1 cm) thick
Large pinch of salt
1 tablespoon rosemary needles
2 tablespoons salt-preserved lemon skin,
   cut into small pieces, divided
2 tablespoons lemon juice, divided
2 tablespoons oil
2 tablespoons Fermented
   Honeysuckle Cordial
2 tablespoons extra-virgin olive oil
Black pepper
6 figs, peeled and halved

Place the pork chops in a shallow dish and season with the salt, rosemary, 1 tablespoon of the preserved lemon rind, and 1 tablespoon of the lemon juice. Heat the oil in a skillet over high heat. Add the chops to the skillet and cook until one side is quite brown—about 5 minutes. Turn. Cook the other side, also about 5 minutes (these are well-done chops). Remove to a platter and immediately add the rest of the preserved lemon rind and lemon juice, the Fermented Honeysuckle Cordial, and the olive oil to the chops. Turn them to coat. After 10 minutes grind some fresh black pepper over them, add the figs, and serve.

Japanese Knotweed

OTHER COMMON NAMES: Fleeceflower

BOTANICAL NAME: *Reynoutria japonica*
(also referred to as *Fallopia japonica* and
Polygonum cuspidatum)

STATUS: Noxious perennial weed

WHERE: Widespread in the US near streams and
rivers, disturbed ground, and woodland

SEASON: Spring

USE: Vegetable

PARTS USED: Shoots, tender leaf tips, flowers

GROW? Absolutely not—it is one of the world's
most invasive plants

TASTES LIKE: Sorrel meets earthy rhubarb

Like so many other problem plants, Japanese knotweed, an East Asia native, was imported to the United States as a garden ornamental, before escaping. Its clusters of ivory summer flowers are scented and attractive (use them to make a cordial, per the Fermented Honeysuckle Cordial recipe). Bees love them. Its jointed stems and bamboo-like growth are graceful. It dies back to the ground every winter and rises magically in the spring. What a fantastic plant!

No. Japanese knotweed is now on many states' noxious weeds list. Michigan and New York have banned the sale, purchase, and transportation of the plant, which is reported to occur in forty-two states (the arid Southwest is exempt). Its relentlessly dense monoculture colonies compromise native plants by excluding them, and it alters local ecologies. It promotes soil erosion, even though it was originally thought to control it. It chokes streamsides and riverbanks. Japanese knotweed shoots can crack asphalt and concrete.

It is a crime to plant it in England, where you may not sell your property unless you have disclosed whether Japanese knotweed occurs on it. In urban places knotweed is more of a capitalist irritant than an environmental one (since the natural environment has already been flattened). Developers hate it.

This aggressive member of the buckwheat family has run botanical riot in habitats where it has no natural enemies. Enter the forager. By harvesting Japanese knotweed shoots in early spring, you are going right for the invasive jugular.

Chief among the herbicides used to control knotweed (and many other invasive or unwanted plants) is Roundup, containing glyphosate. The effects of Roundup on human and ecological health have inspired great controversy. The federal Environmental Protection Agency has remained relatively silent, although in 2015 California's EPA listed glyphosate as a human carcinogen. Some nations have banned sale of Roundup. What effect can the herbicide have on someone eating plants that have been sprayed in a previous season? We do not know, but I avoid sites that have been sprayed, and in my own organic horticultural life I would never use it.

Long-term biocontrol of Japanese knotweed might prove the most effective and

earth-friendly method—if it does not backfire, as often happens when one invasive is introduced to control another. A sap-sucking psyllid (say that fast) from knotweed's native Japan is a possible candidate for taming the plant's spread beyond its indigenous borders. Trials regarding its efficacy and possible drawbacks are being conducted in England and the United States. But until *Aphalara itadori* is established and starts sucking full-time, there is another way to tame this floral thug.

Digging up knotweed is ineffective; it can regrow quickly from just a small piece of left-behind root or stem. However, the regular and repeated shearing of its shoots could eventually deplete the underground rhizomes of energy and can potentially force a clump into retirement. This is where systematic, managed foraging could help.

Viewing Japanese knotweed as food could help transform the expensive-to-control weed into an income booster for landowners and farmers, provide cooks with a new and versatile vegetable, spare the environment some of the effects of mass herbicide application, and help to control the plant by creative mechanical means. It is so abundant where it occurs that it could easily fuel annual spring Japanese knotweed festivals, where craft brewers and bakers, chefs and landowners could come together to feed, educate, and entertain an adventurous eating public, always looking for the next trend in food.

The choice edible part of Japanese knotweed is its young shoot, which resembles an asparagus spear. The stockiest, plumpest shoots are the most tender and juicy. Skinny ones tend to be fibrous. (These tart stems are stuffed with resveratrol, the antioxidant polyphenol touted for its anti-inflammatory effect. Japanese knotweed—from China and Japan—is the leading source of resveratrol in supplement form.)

Japanese knotweed has an earthily sour flavor, which varies depending on where it is growing and at what stage of growth it is. More mature shoots tend to be more acidic. Raw, knotweed is less astringent than the rhubarb to which it is often compared, but it does collapse like rhubarb when exposed to heat. Moist heat makes knotweed melt, while dry heat adds a little more texture to it—left uncovered too long in an oven, it can become leathery.

When the shoots are very tender, you can use the whole stem. They are sour. Imagine licking a cut lemon. Pickle the stems. These crunchy pickles are good with Russian-style *zakuski* in dark winters when spring is a memory.

Cooked, the stalks are mellower and soft, and reminiscent of cooked sorrel. Be prepared for your beautifully vivid shoots to lose their vibrant color the minute they meet heat. Like sorrel, they turn into mudswamp green. Forgive them; they still taste good.

They work well with anything creamily bland, from dairy cream to coconut milk and eggs. Japanese knotweed is delicious in curries, in sauces, in risottos, slow-cooked in pot roasts with the last of the winter root vegetables, whipped into mashed potatoes, roasted with baby whole potatoes, and puréed into leek and potato soups. Many foragers like to use knotweed like rhubarb (although I find it more vegetal in flavor).

After the stems have matured and are too tough, the young unfurling leaf tips are still good to eat, with more crunch than the melty, cooked stems. Sauté them briefly to add to omelets, to accompany spring meatballs, as a green stew with fava beans, or as a tart side to a rich main dish.

How to Collect and Prepare

To harvest the shoots in early spring, choose a spot where the previous season's old canes stand tall or lie sprawled untidily. They are long, dry, brown, and hollow. If there are no canes, but plenty of spindly shoots, the chances are good that the clump was sprayed the year before; that's the kind of patch I would avoid.

Slice the youngest, fat-for-their-height green shoots off at the base. More mature, taller shoots can be sliced higher up. This is about harvesting meristems, the actively growing part of the plant, which will be most tender toward the tip (like an asparagus). Your knife will tell you where to slice; no effort should be required. Carry them home. There may be ants on the shoots, so leave them outside to let them escape, or dunk them in a large basin of water. Peel the membrane from tougher stems and discard the joints between each hollow section if they are tough. Very tender shoots can be eaten in their entirety. In summer the tiny, scented white flowers are besieged by bees. Cut whole flower stalks, shaking them very gently to dislodge these armed pollinators. Strip the flowers off the stalks at home. They are a sour seasoning on a salad or sashimi, or good for a fermented soda pop or cordial.

Safe Disposal of Japanese Knotweed

This may sound strange to some American readers, but residents of the United Kingdom are better acquainted with the pernicious ways of Japanese knotweed, where its presence lowers property values: It is not advisable to chuck out your knotweed debris in the compost, or in the trash. If you have pieces of knotweed stem left (after removing the tougher joints, for example), ideally they should be boiled to prevent them from taking root where they land. The tiniest pieces of stems can regenerate. Collect your knotweed trimmings in a pot, cover with water, and boil for 5 minutes until dead.

Japanese Knotweed Caprese

Serves 4 as an appetizer

In this vivid spring rendition of the classic summer salad, raw knotweed provides crunch and acid for the mellow backdrop of good mozzarella or burrata. Use very tender shoots. If you have Ramp Leaf Salt, all the better.

1 ball buffalo mozzarella
1 ounce (28 g) sliced Japanese knotweed stems and tips
2 tablespoons extra-virgin olive oil
Ramp Leaf Salt
Black pepper

Slice the mozzarella and arrange on a serving plate. Scatter the knotweed rounds across it, and drizzle with olive oil. Season with Ramp Leaf Salt and pepper to taste. Done.

Japanese Knotweed Pickles

Makes 1 quart (1 liter)

For pickles I prefer to skin my knotweed shoots, as the outer membrane can become a little fibrous after brining for a long time. I like to serve them with smoked fish and shots of viscously cold vodka.

1¼ cups (310 ml) white wine vinegar
1¼ cups (310 ml) water
1 teaspoon white peppercorns
6 allspice berries
1 tablespoon salt
2 tablespoons sugar
8 ounces (227 g) Japanese knotweed shoots, skinned and jointed, sliced into rounds or left whole

Combine the vinegar, water, pepper, allspice, salt, and sugar in a pot and bring to a brief boil. Turn off the heat. Loosely pack the knotweed rounds into clean jars (if you have left the the shoots whole, stand them up). Pour the brine over the knotweed. Seal the jars. The pickles are ready after a week and good up to a year or more.

Japanese Knotweed Omelet

Makes 1 omelet

Please don't shoot me for providing an omelet recipe! I come in peace. And I came to omelet making quite late in life. Tipsi Titoti—who taught me about South African weeds—makes the best, neatest omelets, whirling around the stove making three at a time. She taught me two tricks to the perfect omelet (golden outside, weeping inside): a very clean, well-buttered pan and higher heat than you would think. (Of course, there is the other, sneaky trick: lower heat than you would think. But let's stick to the former method.)

1 tablespoon plus 2 teaspoons butter, divided
12 Japanese knotweed tips
Salt
Pepper
3 large eggs
3 tablespoons milk
½ cup (30 g) microplaned Parmigiano-Reggiano

Melt the 2 teaspoons of butter over medium heat in a pan. Add the Japanese knotweed tips, sprinkle with a pinch of salt, and grind some black pepper over everything. Cover, reduce the heat to medium-low, and cook until the knotweed is just fork-tender, about 10 minutes. Shake the pan occasionally to turn the tips. Reserve the cooked knotweed tips in a bowl.

Beat the eggs in a bowl. Add the milk, a pinch of salt, and black pepper to your liking. Heat an 8½- to 10-inch (22–25 cm) pan over medium-high heat. After 30 seconds add the remaining tablespoon of butter, lifting and tilting the pan until the butter coats the whole bottom as well as the lower sides. Return the pan to the flame for a few seconds and then pour the egg mixture into it. Allow the eggs to cook unmolested for 60 seconds. Gently start loosening the edges with a spatula, just nudging the egg loose and tilting the pan to let the runny eggs fill the spot. When you have done that all around the pan, add your knotweed tips, scattering them in a rough line across the middle. Add the cheese and some more black pepper. Let the eggs cook another 30 seconds—they should be setting at the edges and still moist in the middle. Tilt the pan away from you and slide a spatula or blunt knife under the omelet edges closest to you, allowing gravity to help you fold this higher half over the lower half. Keeping the pan tilted, slide the folded omelet out of the pan and onto a waiting serving plate.

Quick Japanese Knotweed Sauces

Butter and Knotweed Sauce

Serves 1

In springtime the quickest thing I do with knotweed is chop it finely and melt it in some hot butter over medium heat. This quick, tart sauce is delicious on eggs, grilled chicken, and fish.

2 tablespoons butter
1½ ounces (40 g) finely chopped
    Japanese knotweed
Salt

Melt the butter over medium-high heat in a skillet. When it foams, reduce the heat to medium and add the Japanese knotweed. Cook for about 10 minutes, stirring a few times. It will turn that unprepossessing khaki color and lose its crunch. Season with salt to taste.

Cream and Knotweed Sauce

Makes 1½ cups (375 ml)

Butter, cream? Why all the dairy? I like dairy, for one thing. For another, the acid of the knotweed slices right through it. Match made in foraging heaven. This is the kind of sauce I assemble quickly after pan-frying chicken breasts, fish, or pork chops. Adding the white wine to the pan they cooked in gives you a good base for the sauce to come.

½ cup (125 ml) white wine (or vermouth)
½ cup (125 ml) chicken or vegetable broth
5 ounces (142 g) Japanese knotweed tips
    (halved), or shoots cut into thin rounds
½ cup (125 ml) cream
Salt
Black pepper

Remove what you have been cooking (chicken breasts? pork chops? salmon?) from its skillet to rest. Over high heat pour the white wine or vermouth into the skillet. Allow it to boil for about 30 seconds, then add the broth. Reduce the heat to medium-high. Cook another 3 minutes to reduce, then add the Japanese knotweed and the cream. Simmer for about 8 minutes until the knotweed "melts" into the liquid. Stir occasionally. Taste, and season with salt and pepper. Return what you were cooking to the skillet (along with any resting juices) and spoon the sauce over. Serve.

Japanese Knotweed and Field Garlic Vichyssoise

Serves 4–6

Soothing, unthreatening vichyssoise laced with tart knotweed is my secret weapon when introducing knotweed to shy persons. They are converted on the spot to weed eating. Serve hot (heresy!), or cold.

2 tablespoons butter

15 ounces (425 g) cut-up Japanese knotweed stems

2 cups (57 g) finely snipped field garlic greens

2 medium potatoes, peeled and cubed

7 cups (1¾ liters) vegetable or chicken stock

⅓ cup (80 ml) cream

Salt

In a large pot melt the butter over medium heat. Add the Japanese knotweed. Sauté for 3 to 4 minutes, stirring. Add the field garlic greens, potatoes, and vegetable or chicken stock. Bring the liquid to a boil over high heat, then reduce the heat and simmer for 30 minutes. Allow the soup to cool a little, then blend it in batches until very smooth. Strain each batch though a fine-mesh sieve into a bowl. Add the cream and stir well. Taste the soup and salt it. If you are serving the soup cold, overseason it slightly, as cold mutes the seasoning. Transfer to the fridge and chill.

Yes, it can also be served warm and is awfully good.

Japanese Knotweed Hummus

Serves 4–6 as an appetizer

Raw Japanese knotweed adds the indispensable citric note as well as a fresh green to spring hummus. Serve with dense bread, crackers, or raw vegetables.

2 cans (each 15½ ounces/439 g) chickpeas, drained

3 ounces (85 g) sliced Japanese knotweed shoots

½ cup (125 ml) tahini

10 field garlic bulbs (or 4 ramp bulbs), peeled and trimmed

¼ teaspoon salt

¼ cup (60 ml) cold water, plus extra

Place the chickpeas in a food processor and pulse until roughly chopped. Add the knotweed, tahini, field garlic, and salt. Process again. Finally add the water in a stream and process until you have a very smooth and creamy paste. Taste, adding a little more salt if necessary. If the paste is still too thick, add more water.

Japanese Knotweed and Lentil Puffs

Serves 6–8 as a canapé

A homely but mouthwatering filling of lentils and knotweed is given glamour and crunch inside a crisp puff pastry case. Instead of making a collection of small puffs, you could make individual entrée portions for four by cutting larger pastry cases.

1 cup (200 g) green lentils

3 cups (750 ml) vegetable broth

1 small onion, finely chopped

1 teaspoon Ramp Leaf Salt, divided

2 tablespoons Wisteria Vinegar, divided

½ teaspoon black pepper

1 tablespoon olive oil

8 ounces (227 g) Japanese knotweed
   shoots, trimmed and cut into ½-inch
   (1 cm) pieces

2 sheets puff pastry, chilled

1 large egg yolk

3 tablespoons milk

3 tablespoons Greek yogurt or crème fraîche

2–3 tablespoons small edible flowers,
   like mustard

Combine the lentils, broth, onion, ½ teaspoon of the Ramp Leaf Salt, 1 tablespoon of the Wisteria Vinegar, and the pepper in a saucepan. Bring to a boil over high heat. Reduce the heat to medium-low and cook until the lentils are tender, 25 to 30 minutes.

Meanwhile, warm the olive oil in a pan over medium heat. Add the knotweed pieces. Sauté for 5 minutes, and add the rest of the Ramp Leaf Salt. Add the second tablespoon of vinegar. Cook another 5 minutes. Transfer the knotweed to the lentil pot and stir. (Continue to cook until the lentils are tender.)

Preheat the oven to 400°F (200°C).

Lay your pastry sheets on a lightly floured surface. Cut out the shapes you prefer for the puffs. I like rectangles about 3 by 2 inches (7½ × 5 cm). Transfer them carefully to a buttered baking sheet. Very lightly, with the tip of sharp knife, trace a rectangle within the edges of the pastry, taking care not to cut through to the bottom. (After baking this will allow you to pop out a cavity in the pastry, for the filling.) Using even less pressure with your sharp knife, delicately do some crosshatching over this future lid. Place the baking sheet in the fridge for 10 minutes, covered. Whisk the egg yolk and milk in a small bowl. Paint this egg wash across the pastry.

Slide into the oven and bake until puffed up and deep golden, about 20 minutes.

Slide a knife along the score mark you made (it will have closed up a little), loosen all around, and then carefully lift up each rectangular lid. Spoon the filling into each cavity. Top each pile of lentils with a small dollop of yogurt or crème fraîche. Top gently with the lid, or leave them open, if you prefer. Arrange on a serving plate and garnish with edible flowers.

Wild Roast Salmon with Spring Forages in Miso Broth

Serves 4

The wild bounty of midspring is dizzying. The three stages to this celebratory dish make it a labor of love, but it will reward you with its flavor. For the broth—which you can make ahead and freeze—I use shrimp shells saved and frozen from shrimp dinners past. They add indispensable flavor. If you buy fresh shrimp, save the critters for other dishes, after peeling. Arctic char or shad are also very good body doubles for wild salmon. Offer spoons for the broth, quick pickles, and a side of sticky rice.

BROTH

1 tablespoon oil

5 ounces (142 g) shrimp shells
(from approximately 3 pounds/1⅓ kg
of shrimp)

¼ cup (60 ml) lemon juice

6 cups (1½ liters) water

¼ cup (60 ml) fish sauce

1 tablespoon plus 1 teaspoon sugar

2 tablespoons yellow miso

2 Thai lime leaves

6 slices ginger, 3 inches (7½ cm) long

15 slices fresh serrano chile

2 tablespoons sliced Japanese
Knotweed Pickles

1 ounce (28 g) young garlic mustard
leaves, plus some flowers for garnish

8 Japanese knotweed shoots, sliced into
thin rounds, tips left intact

RAMPS AND MORELS

1 tablespoon oil

12 ramp bulbs

4 ounces (113 g) morels, sliced in half

1 tablespoon soy sauce

FISH

2 tablespoons soy sauce

1 tablespoon lemon juice

4 pieces salmon, Arctic char, or shad
(6 ounces/170 g each), or a side of fish
(1½ pounds/680 g)

1 tablespoon toasted sesame oil

Leaves of 12 ramps, roughly chopped

FOR THE BROTH: In a pot over medium-high heat, warm the oil and toss in the shrimp shells. When they are pink all over, add the lemon juice. Stir. Let it cook and caramelize for a minute. Add the water, fish sauce, sugar, and miso (thin the miso with a little water). Add the lime leaves, ginger, and chile. Bring to a boil, then cook at a simmer for 20 minutes. Strain the solids from the broth. (This part can be made ahead and frozen.)

Return the broth to the rinsed and wiped pot. Heat to a simmer and add the Japanese Knotweed Pickles.

FOR THE RAMPS AND MORELS: Heat the oil over medium heat. Add the ramps and morels. Sauté for 5 minutes, then turn. Cook for another 5 minutes and add the soy sauce. Stir as the soy sauce cooks off and caramelizes. When the soy sauce has evaporated, deglaze the pan (with the mushrooms and ramps still in it) with a ladleful of the shrimp broth. Stir well, then pour the mushrooms and ramps into the pot that holds the strained broth. Bring the broth to a simmer.

FOR THE FISH: Turn on the oven's broiler. Drizzle the soy sauce and lemon over the fish's meaty side.

Use the sesame oil to oil a baking sheet, spread out the ramp leaves, and lay the fish fillets on top of them, skin-side up (the ramps should be covered by the fish, or they will scorch). Slide into the hot oven and roast for 4 to 6 minutes, until the fish's skin is blistered and the meat is *just* cooked.

TO ASSEMBLE: Drop the garlic mustard leaves and raw Japanese knotweed rounds into the simmering broth and cook for a minute at a simmer. Ladle the broth into four separate bowls. Place a piece of cooked fish in each bowl, skin side up, and add the ramp leaves in their soy glaze. Garnish with the knotweed tips and some garlic mustard flowers.

Japanese Knotweed and Spring Mugwort Lamb Shanks

Serves 4

This straightforward spring pot roast, with lamb, knotweed shoots, and the bitter herb (mugwort) prescribed for Passover, works equally well for Easter traditions, and for foragers who march to the beat of their own drum.

4 lamb shanks

10 ounces (283 g) Japanese knotweed tips and stalk, cut into 1½-inch (4 cm) lengths

1 ounce (28 g) young mugwort shoots

½ cup (125 ml) water

½ teaspoon Field Garlic Salt, divided

2 teaspoons Field Garlic Leaf Oil

Preheat the oven to 400°F (200°C).

Place the lamb in a Dutch oven or casserole dish with the Japanese knotweed, mugwort, and ¼ teaspoon of the Field Garlic Salt. Cook in the oven for 1½ hours. Remove the lid, check the juices in the bottom of the pot (it must not dry out completely), and add the rest of the salt. Cook another hour. Just before serving, drizzle the Field Garlic Leaf Oil over the meat.

Serve with good bread, or Field Garlic Mashed Potatoes to mop up the juices.

Japanese Knotweed Lamb Curry

Serves 4

This succulent early-spring curry is fragrant rather than hot, with the perfume of lemongrass complementing the earthier tang of the knotweed. As the knotweed melts in the moist heat, it blends with the coconut milk to make a smooth, plate-licking sauce. Neck chops are ideal for this dish, but shoulder chops or even stewing lamb (or mutton) works very well, too. Serve with sticky rice or naan breads.

4 lamb neck or shoulder chops (about 2¼ pounds/1 kg)

½ teaspoon Field Garlic Salt

12 ounces (340 g) Japanese knotweed shoots and tips

2 tablespoons fish sauce

1 cup (250 ml) coconut milk

12 field garlic bulbs, trimmed and sliced

1 thumb-sized piece of ginger, sliced

2 turmeric rhizomes, 2 inches (5 cm) each, peeled

1 lemongrass heart, split

4 dried bird's eye chiles, or 1 teaspoon chile flakes

Water

Preheat the oven to 450°F (230°C). Season the lamb chops with the Field Garlic Salt. Place them in a casserole or Dutch oven and cook for an hour in the oven. Reduce the heat to 350°F (180°C). Add the Japanese knotweed, fish sauce, coconut milk, field garlic bulbs, ginger, turmeric, lemongrass, chile, and enough water to reach just below the knotweed piled on top of the meat. Return to the oven and cook, covered, until the sauce has reduced to a creamy mass around the meat—about 2 hours.

Japanese Knotweed and Field Garlic Spring Meatballs

Serves 4 (makes about 36 meatballs)

This recipe is inspired by dishes with a heavy Middle Eastern spin, unapologetic with the spices and herbs. The Frenchman wolfed this the first time I made it years ago. (I only told him he was eating weeds halfway through. That's how you reel them in.) Early-season field garlic and Japanese knotweed shoots are a thrilling spring treat. The dill and cumin reward you with a fragrant puff of flavor when you bite into the meatballs.

MEATBALLS

1½ pounds (680 g) ground lamb

1 ounce (28 g) panko bread crumbs
(or homemade, coarse bread crumbs)

1 cup (150 g) finely sliced field garlic bulbs

½ cup (15 g) chopped dill

1 tablespoon cumin

½ teaspoon salt

Black pepper

1 large egg

2 tablespoons extra-virgin olive oil

SAUCE

1 pound (453 g) fava beans, shelled and
just cooked

5 ounces (142 g) tender Japanese
knotweed tips

½ cup (15 g) sheep sorrel leaves
(or 1 tablespoon lemon juice)

2 cups (500 ml) chicken broth

Salt

Black pepper

2 tablespoons extra-virgin olive oil

20 mint leaves, torn up

FOR THE MEATBALLS: In a large bowl combine all the meatball ingredients except the oil and mix well. Wet your hands with some water and form the mixture into golf-ball-sized meatballs. Put them aside on a large plate. (This can be done the day before and kept chilled.)

Heat the oil over high heat in a large skillet. Add about eight meatballs at a time, and brown them (1 to 2 minutes per side); remove to a plate and brown the next batch. The meatballs should not be cooked through.

FOR THE SAUCE: Once the meatballs have been browned, return them all to the pan and add the fava beans, Japanese knotweed, sheep sorrel, and chicken broth. Shake the pan to get the vegetables in touch with the hot liquid. Cook until the fava beans are tender, about 8 minutes. Stir every now and then to submerge the sheep sorrel leaves.

Taste the pan juices, and add salt and pepper. Just before removing the pan from the heat, drizzle the olive oil over everything and add the torn-up mint leaves. Stir to allow the oil to emulsify, and serve at once in bowls.

Spicebush and Rhubarb Knotweed Jelly Roll

Serves 10–12

A classic sponge is wrapped around tartly sweet, slightly chewy roasted Japanese knotweed and soft rhubarb to create a childhood dessert with a wild twist. Nothing has disappeared as fast on my forage walks as this sweet treat.

KNOTWEED AND RHUBARB FILLING

1 pound (453 g) Japanese knotweed
    stems, cut up into ¼- to ½-inch
    (½–1 cm) pieces
½ cup (100 g) sugar, divided
1 tablespoon ground spicebush, divided
1 pound (453 g) rhubarb stems, cut into
    ¼-inch (½ cm) pieces

SWISS ROLL

3 large eggs
3 ounces (85 g) sugar
3 ounces (85 g) all-purpose flour
Pinch of salt
¾ teaspoon baking powder
½ teaspoon ground spicebush
1 tablespoon sugar

FOR THE KNOTWEED AND RHUBARB FILLING: Preheat the oven to 325°F (170°C).

In one bowl toss the knotweed with half the sugar and spicebush. In another bowl toss the rhubarb with the rest of the sugar and spicebush. Scatter each mixture across the bottom of a large baking sheet, rhubarb on one side, knotweed on the other. Slide into the oven and roast for an hour. The knotweed dries out faster than the rhubarb, so remove it after an hour, and set aside in a bowl. Continue cooking the rhubarb for another half hour. Place the cooked rhubarb in the bowl with the knotweed. Let cool.

FOR THE SWISS ROLL: Heat the oven to 400°F (200°C).

Prepare a 13 by 9 inch (33 × 23 cm) jelly roll pan: On baking parchment draw around the pan with a pencil. Cut the parchment ½ inch (1 cm) outside the drawn line. Crease the parchment along the drawn lines. Oil or butter the pan lightly and lay the paper inside it, then lightly butter or oil the paper.

In a bowl whisk or beat the eggs with the sugar until pale and fluffy and a line is left on top of the mixture when you lift the whisk or beater. Carefully add the flour, salt, and baking powder; fold them in using a spatula. Pour the mixture into the prepared pan. Bake for 10 minutes. The mixture should spring back when you dent it with a finger.

Lift the cake in its parchment lining from the pan onto a wire rack. Invert it quickly and gently pull off the parchment paper. Cut another sheet of parchment larger than the cake, place it on a clean surface, and sprinkle with the spicebush and sugar. Transfer the cake, brown-side down, to this parchment. Make a shallow cut across the cake, 1 inch (2½ cm) from the short side closest to you—this helps make a tight roll. Sprinkle the roasted knotweed and rhubarb and any accumulated syrup evenly across the surface. This should all be done while the cake is still warm or it becomes harder to roll.

To roll, fold the cake over the cut and hold it for a few seconds. Use the sugared parchment to roll the cake firmly away from you. When it has been rolled up, hold the roll firmly in place for about 10 seconds, with the seam at the bottom, to set the shape. If you will be serving it later, transfer it to the fridge still wrapped (it keeps well for at least 12 hours); keep it covered. If you are serving at once, remove the paper and slice with a serrated knife.

Juniper

OTHER COMMON NAMES: Eastern red cedar, red cedar, common juniper, and others

BOTANICAL NAMES: *Juniperus virginiana* and other species

STATUS: Indigenous tree, distributed widely across the US and Canada

WHERE: Varying habitats, depending on species

SEASON: Early fall through spring

USE: Aromatic, spice

PARTS USED: Ripe fruit

GROW? Yes

TASTES LIKE: Sweet juniper

I find it thrilling to be able to cycle fifteen minutes one way and cycle home again with a small bagful of just-picked ripe juniper berries, collected from eastern red cedars (*Juniperus virginiana*) growing in Brooklyn. These trees are often used in city landscaping because of their hardiness, and this is a boon to urban and suburban wild spice collectors. Few city dwellers realize that this pricy spice is theirs for the picking at double the flavor. Two cupfuls will last my small household all year. Their vital, sweet taste is incomparably better (to me) than the drier, dustier version we buy in a store.

Every two to three years, the female trees bear "fruit," which are really seed cones resembling a berry. They are perfectly smooth and blue and when ripe taste like juniper candy. The males bear pale yellow-brown seed cones that have characteristic scales and points— these produce pollen in early spring. It is a flavorful ingredient, like cattail pollen in application, but much finer. (Wear a mask when working with the pollen to avoid inhaling it.) I collect ripe juniper in late winter or early spring. Raw, they are very palatable as long as they are ripe. Never be tempted to eat a handful at a time; juniper is meant to be used in small doses (like most spices), or it can be toxic. The fruit and foliage have a long history of use in Native American medicine.

Picking the juniper berries does not harm the tree, and there is plenty left for the birds (cedar waxwings love them), since who can reach all the way up, anyway?

Juniper leads to a lot of naming confusion. The crop I collect comes from *J. virginiana*— known as eastern red cedar, or red cedar. In this context the word *cedar* makes me want pull my hair out. These trees are *not* cedars, botanically speaking—those would be *Cedrus*, belonging to the Pinacea family (pines). Junipers are the genus *Juniperus*, belonging to the Cupressaceae family, which, wait for it, is

known as the cyprus family! It is worth being aware of this semantic murk so that you head for the correct tree, especially in print or online. Yes, juniper berries (which are not berries) come from a tree called cedar. Which isn't. Luckily, the fruit is very distinctive. Round, smooth, various shades of powdery blue.

Eastern red cedar is widespread east of the Rockies and all the way into Canada. But there are enough species to cover the country, and their "fruit" is edible, though each varies in flavor: *Juniperus communis*—common or dwarf juniper—has a very broad range (and includes Eurasia, unusually), but some of its populations Stateside are threatened and even endangered. *Juniperus californica* and *J. occidentalis* occur on the West Coast, and the Southwest hosts a slew of junipers in its famous piñon-juniper biome (and also often referred to as cedar or cedar berries), including *J. osteosperma, J. grandis, J. monosperma*. The Rockies? *J. scopulorum*.

There is a native juniper for everybody.

I typically include juniper in slow-cooked and wintry dishes like borscht, sweet red cabbage, meatball sauces, and game dishes, and also in desserts with fruit. But its scented resin is beautiful with early-summer strawberries—fresh or in ice cream. Baking and roasting fruit (plums, pears, quinces) and root vegetables (carrots, parsnips, beets) with juniper infuses them with its strong character. Make your own gin with vodka and juniper, or grind them with salt or sugar to perfume cured meats and fish and to enervate cocktail glass rims.

How to Collect and Prepare

Taste the "fruit" before you collect it. Eastern red cedar berries and other edible junipers should taste pleasantly resinous and slightly sweet. Collect only very ripe fruit, from late fall through winter and spring. I believe that late winter yields the best flavor. I put my juniper straight into a roomy jar without any special drying. It remains flavorful for over a year. For making syrups and infusions, I grind the juniper whole, wiping the spice grinder as soon as it has been used, as the resin tends to gum up the blades.

Caution

Juniperus sabina (known as savin juniper) is reported to be toxic and an abortifacient, meaning that it can cause abortions. I have tasted (not swallowed) the female cones from *J. sabina*, and they were completely horrible, not something I would willingly eat. This is not a native juniper and it is sold in the nursery trade, for landscaping and gardens. It is generally low growing and sprawling.

I think any juniper munched by the cupful will make you sick, and most studies delivering a toxic verdict include subjecting unfortunate laboratory animals to insane concentrations of a plant. Nothing you would ever ingest normally.

CULTIVATION TIPS
USDA Hardiness Zones 2–9, for various species

There are too many species to cover individually, but junipers do share some traits. They are water-wise and drought-tolerant. They require full sun (six hours plus). Eastern red cedar will enjoy a lot of moisture as long as the ground is well drained, but also tolerates dry soil. It is also exceptionally cold-hardy: Its range includes USDA Hardiness Zones 2 through 9. And as noted above, if you want to forage from your planting, do not plant *J. sabina*.

Juniper Sugar

Makes 1¼ cups (310 ml)

Sugar made with freshly gathered juniper adds wild aroma to baking, marinades, cures (like gravlax and duck), slow braises or stews involving duck or rabbit or pork, and cocktails. I keep a supply in the freezer, where it remains as fresh as the day it was made for over a year.

¼ cup (¾ ounce/20 g) juniper berries
1 cup (7 ounces/198 g) sugar

Grind the juniper berries in a spice grinder until very fine—this is important, as larger pieces of seed may remain and be very hard on teeth. Transfer the pulverized berries (they will actually be moist) to a bowl and mix very well with the sugar. Store a small amount in an airtight jar or food-safe container, and freeze the rest for later use.

Juniper Syrup

Makes 2 cups (500 ml)

Sweet, resinous, fruity, and a little bitter, juniper syrup is persuasively gin-y, without the alcohol. I use it in mixed drinks, of course, but it adds dimensions and aroma to roasted vegetables and fruit, and to the pan juices of roast meats.

½ cup (1½ ounces/40 g) fresh juniper berries
2 cups (500 ml) water
2 cups (400 g) sugar

Grind the juniper berries in batches in your spice grinder (wipe the blades down at once, or they gum up). Bring the water and sugar to a boil in a pot on the stove over medium-high heat; stir well to dissolve the sugar. Add the ground juniper and simmer for 5 minutes. Turn the heat off and let the mixture cool. Cover the pot and infuse overnight or for 12 hours. Strain the mixture through a fine-mesh sieve, and then again through cheesecloth. Pour into a clean glass bottle or bottles and store in the fridge, or freeze. Frozen, it will taste fresh for upward of a year.

Triple Juniper

Makes 1 drink

I created this cocktail for a Remodelista Market preview one early spring in New York, using juniper foraged in Brooklyn. The sugar rim is intensely perfumed, and this pure juniper is the first thing you taste when you sip. We made around five hundred cocktails that night, and this one brought people back, begging for more.

FOR THE RIM

2 teaspoons Juniper Sugar

1 tablespoon lime juice

DRINK

3 fluid ounces (6 tablespoons) gin

1 fluid ounce (2 tablespoons) Juniper Syrup

1 fluid ounce (2 tablespoons) Sumac Water

FOR THE RIM: Sprinkle the sugar in one saucer and pour the lime juice in another. Dip the rim of the glass into the lime juice and then very gently into the sugar, starting on one side and working it all the way around. Let it set for a minute.

FOR THE DRINK: Shake up all the cocktail ingredients with ice, strain, and pour.

Juniper Red Cabbage

Serves 4 as a side

A nest of gently spiced soft red cabbage is delicious in its own right and makes a welcoming bed for braised short ribs, duck, roast chicken, or meatballs.

2 tablespoons olive oil

1 tablespoon butter

1 medium red cabbage
   (about 2 pounds/907 g), sliced thinly

1 large red onion, sliced thinly

3 cloves garlic, chopped finely

2 tablespoons maple syrup

1 tablespoon Juniper Sugar

3 tablespoons Elderflower Vinegar

12 juniper berries

6 allspice berries

2 cinnamon sticks

1 teaspoon salt

Black pepper

1 cup (250 ml) water

In a large pot warm the olive oil and butter over medium-high heat. Add all the ingredients and stir well. Cover with a lid. Cook for 10 minutes, turning the ingredients once with a spoon. Reduce the heat to medium-low and cook for 1½ hours, stirring every 20 minutes. It is ready when the cabbage is dark, meltingly soft, and syrupy. Taste for seasoning and adjust if necessary—you want a salty-sour-sweet balance.

Juniper Black Currant Chutney

Every summer I make my version of crème de cassis by soaking musky black currants in gin, with some sugar. After the cassis is bottled, the strained fruit makes this fantastic chutney. You don't have to do the gin thing, of course, but it does add a certain something. The chutney is the perfect condiment for pork, especially ham, and rich cuts like pork belly. I love it with rabbit, game, curried lamb, pâtés, and cheeses, too. And don't forget sandwiches.

Big bonus? Use this recipe for black chokeberries, once you have allowed the fruit to ferment for a couple of weeks (see Black Ice), to diminish its tannins.

Black Currant Gin

Makes about 3 cups (750 ml)

7 cups (about 805 g) black currants
Gin to cover, about 3 cups (750 ml)
½ cup (100 g) sugar

Place the fruit in a large clean mason jar, add the gin and sugar, and screw the lid on. Tip the jar gently to dissolve the sugar. After 3 weeks strain and bottle the Black Currant Gin. Make a long drink with sparkling water, ice, and lemon; combine with tonic water and lime leaf; add a dash to a flute of sparkling wine; or shake up with fresh lime juice and silver tequila.

Chutney

Makes about 5 cups (1¼ liters)

1 cup (200 g) sugar
1 cup (150 g) raisins
7 cups (about 805 g) gin-soaked or
    fresh black currants
1 medium onion, very finely chopped
1 tablespoon Juniper Sugar
1 tablespoon ground spicebush
2 teaspoons chile flakes
1 teaspoon salt
½ teaspoon black pepper
½ teaspoon allspice
3 cloves
5 thin slices ginger, about 2 inches (5 cm)
    long, peeled
½ cup (125 ml) Common Milkweed Flower
    Vinegar (or red wine vinegar)
1 cup (250 ml) water

Combine all the ingredients in a large pot. Heat the mixture gradually over high heat, stirring early on to prevent any sticking. When foam rises, skim it. Cook at a rolling boil until the setting point is reached.

Allow the chutney to cool for a few minutes before pouring it into clean glass jars and sealing. It keeps at least for a year.

Juniper Rabbit Terrine

Makes 1 terrine

Easily sliced and loaded with flavor, terrines are excellent make-ahead food for picnics and parties. Juniper is still sweet on trees when the first field garlic can be pulled from thawed ground where I live. Otherwise, substitute conventional garlic or Ramp Pickles.

I use the forequarters and midsection of two animals, reserving the meatier hind legs for Rabbit with Field Garlic and Morels. But one bunny is fine, as long as you have the 1 pound (453 g) of meat needed. Serve the terrine with good bread, pickles, Juniper Black Currant Chutney, or roasted rhubarb.

¼ cup (20 g) juniper berries

⅓ cup (80 ml) plus 1 tablespoon vodka
  or gin, divided

3 tablespoons chopped field garlic bulbs

⅓ cup (20 g) coarse bread crumbs

1 tablespoon fresh thyme leaves

1 pound (453 g) rabbit meat,
  plus kidneys and liver

1 teaspoon Field Garlic Salt
  (or Ramp Leaf Salt)

20 twists ground black pepper

6–8 slices good bacon

Crush the juniper berries in a pestle and mortar. Reserve 2 teaspoonfuls. Put the rest of the berries in a small bowl or glass and pour ⅓ cup of the vodka or gin over them. Let macerate for 2 hours. Strain.

Crush the chopped field garlic bulbs to a paste with the pestle and mortar. Add the 2 reserved teaspoons of juniper berries along with the crumbs, the thyme, and the remaining 1 tablespoon of strained juniper vodka or gin to moisten the crumbs. Stir well.

Remove the liver and kidneys from the rabbit carcasses. Cut the livers into strips and each kidney into four pieces. Save the fat around the kidneys and cut this up into small pieces. Carve the hindquarters from the rabbits—reserve and freeze for later use. Cut the two flat flaps of meat from each torso and into small pieces. Cut out each tenderloin running along the spine. Cut each tenderloin in half, lengthwise (remove the thin membrane from its top side). Cut the rest of the meat into pieces. (Save the carcasses for broth.) Transfer all the meat except the tenderloins and offal to a food processor and pulse till roughly chopped—it will look like a messy paste.

Preheat the oven to 300°F (150°C). Fill a roasting dish or skillet with water and place it in the oven.

In a bowl combine the chopped meat, bread crumb mixture, Field Garlic Salt, black pepper, and strained juniper vodka or gin. Stir very well or mix with your hands to combine thoroughly.

Line an 8½ by 5 inch (22 × 13 cm) terrine with strips of bacon lying across its width (not lengthwise), and hanging somewhat over the edges. Spread half the chopped rabbit mixture in the bottom of the terrine. On top of it lay half the liver and kidney pieces. Lay the tenderloin pieces lengthwise over those. Add the rest of the liver and kidney pieces. Add a final layer of chopped meat mixture to finish. Press the mixture gently down with your palms. Fold the overhanging bacon pieces over the top.

Cover the terrine with parchment fitting snugly inside the edges and then with a sheet of foil, crimped tightly over the edges of the terrine. Place it carefully in the water bath in the oven. Cook for 2½ hours.

Remove the terrine from the oven and place it on a tray or dish with a lip, to catch any oozing juices. Weigh the meat down with a row of cans or a brick. Once it has cooled a little, transfer it to the fridge with its weights and chill well. It is ready as soon as it can be sliced but improves with a day or more. The weights can be removed once the meat is cold.

Juniper Spicebush Borscht

Serves 6

Borscht is a vibrant soupy stew that is as good for a main course as it is for an appetizer. I vary the recipe almost every time I make it, using beef, or mushrooms, or beans. Feel free to improvise. The wild flavors here enhance the savory sweetness of the beetroot. Serve with a side of sour cream, or with Field Garlic Butter on toast.

3 strips smoked bacon, cut into slivers

1 tablespoon olive oil

1 medium onion, finely chopped

1 medium leek, white and green parts
   finely chopped

1 large fennel bulb, finely chopped

3 large beetroots, grated

Stems and leaves (about 4.5 ounces/130 g)
   of the beetroot, washed and chopped

8 cups (2 liters) beef or mushroom broth

3 tablespoons Elderflower Vinegar

2 teaspoons ground spicebush (or 6 twigs,
   tied in a bundle)

¼ teaspoon black pepper

10 juniper berries

1 tablespoon sugar

1 bunch parsley, washed

10 bayberry leaves

1 pound (453 g) cooked or canned
   giant white beans

Salt

Heat a large pot over medium-high heat. Add the slivers of bacon and cook until their fat runs and their edges begin to brown. Add the olive oil, then the onion, leek, and fennel. Stir well and reduce the heat to medium, covering the pot with a lid. Cook for 15 minutes, stirring occasionally. Remove the lid, add the grated beetroot and its leaves, and stir well. Pour in the broth. Add the Elderflower Vinegar, spicebush, pepper, juniper, sugar, parsley (tied in a bunch), and bayberry leaves, dunking them down with a spoon. If the liquid has not covered the ingredients, add some additional water.

Bring the liquid to a boil, then reduce the heat to a simmer and cook for 1 hour (longer will not hurt). Add the beans. Taste for seasoning and add salt, a little more sugar, or another dash of vinegar if you need more salty-sour contrast. Cook for another 30 minutes. Before serving, scoop out the parsley stems.

Short Ribs Braised with Juniper, Bayberry, and Elderberry

Serves 4

Succulent comfort food, and very good surrounded by a pale green moat of Nettle Grits, Sweet-fern Polenta, or a side of Juniper Red Cabbage. In early winter I use frozen elderberry juice and the last of the tenacious bayberry leaves.

3 boneless short ribs (about 1 pound/
   453 g each), each cut into 3 pieces
½ teaspoon salt
Black pepper
2 cups (500 ml) red wine, divided
½ cup (125 ml) Elderberry Juice
   (from 2 cups elderberries)
20 bayberry leaves
16 juniper berries
8 large shallots, halved
3 large carrots, unpeeled, cut into
   thick batons

Preheat the oven to 350°F (180°C).

Season the meat with salt and pepper. Place it in a Dutch oven. Add 1 cup of the red wine along with the Elderberry Juice, bayberry, and juniper.

Transfer the covered pot to the oven. After an hour turn the ribs and add the shallots and carrots. Continue cooking for another hour, then remove the foil or lid. Cook for a third hour, until the ribs have browned and the liquid has reduced. During this hour check to make sure that the wine is not reducing completely and add some water to the pan if the level drops to a sizzle. After 3 hours of cooking, the ribs will be fork-tender.

Remove the pot from the oven. Transfer the ribs, shallots, and carrots to a serving bowl and cover. Pour off any fat floating above the delicious cooking juices. Skim off the juniper berries and remove the bay leaves. Add the cup of wine you have kept in reserve and cook off over high heat until the sauce has reduced to about a quarter of the quantity you started with. Taste for seasoning and add some salt and pepper if you feel they are necessary. Pour the juices over the waiting ribs and vegetables.

Serve from a big, warmed dish at the table, drizzling a spoonful of sauce over each portion as it is plated.

Juniper and Strawberry Frozen Yogurt

Makes 1 quart (1 liter)

Juniper gives a distinctly grown-up undertone to the first ripe, sweet, farmers market strawberries. This ice cream is best right out of the ice cream maker, where it reaches the perfect consistency after about 25 minutes. If you are storing it in the freezer, it freezes very hard, so take it out half an hour before serving, to allow it to soften.

1½ pounds (680 g) very ripe strawberries
3 ounces (85 g) Juniper Sugar
6 ounces (170 g) regular sugar
3 cups (750 ml) Greek yogurt
1 cup (250 ml) half-and-half

Cut up the washed strawberries. Place them in a bowl with both sugars and let them sit overnight, covered. In a blender purée the strawberries and sugar with any exuded juice until smooth. Transfer to a bowl and chill.

When the strawberry purée is cold, place the Greek yogurt in a bowl and add the half-and-half slowly, stirring until the mixture is smooth. Add the purée. Stir well. Transfer to an ice cream maker and churn until frozen, about 25 minutes.

Lamb's Quarters

OTHER COMMON NAMES: Fat hen, goosefoot

BOTANICAL NAMES: *Chenopodium album* and other species

STATUS: Considered a weed

WHERE: Widespread in disturbed ground, sometimes at farmers markets

SEASON: Early summer through early fall

USE: Vegetable, pseudograin

PARTS USED: Leaves, seeds

GROW? Yes

TASTES LIKE: Chard, with the textural heft of collards

In those famous journals, Meriwether Lewis recorded lamb's quarters growing near the Missouri River on July 15, 1805: "The lamb's quarter, wild coucumber, sand rush and narrow dock are also common here." Frustratingly, we do not know if he ate them. But the Lewis and Clark Expedition's members did eat much of what they found and were also fed along the way by Native Americans, who largely sustained that epic trip.

There is disagreement about whether *Chenopodium album* is a Eurasian weed (it is cultivated in India) or native to North America. Blackfoot Indians in Canada were storing the seeds hundreds of years ago. The thinking is that the species includes native American strains. All *Chenopodium* species—which include famous *C. quinoa*—are edible, and recorded nutritional information is off the charts in vitamins A, C, and K. Plus protein. For the time being *Chenopodium* belongs to the same great, edible family as amaranth: Amaranthaceae. There is much botanical quibbling about it, at a molecular level.

Along with amaranth and quickweed, lamb's quarters are a summer green, filling the

warm void between the cool seasons, when brassicas are at their best. Any recipe calling for cooked chard or spinach can be adapted to lamb's quarters, although this wild green has a more substantial texture than slightly slippery spinach. Lamb's quarters are most likely to be seen on menus as microgreens with a splash of fuchsia at the tip: 'Magenta Spreen' is a cultivar that can be bought commercially, bred mostly for its hot pink looks. But on muggy farmers market days, the more common powder-gray bunches are sometimes seen wilting on tables. Plunging the stems into cool water for a few hours revives them. The powdery residue on each mature leaf makes cooking the best choice—it disappears in heat, and they can be used in the recipes included for quickweed and amaranth. Every early summer I make one ritual pizza-like tart with an olive oil crust, topped with a mound of the steamed leaves and oil-cured olives, bound with a savory custard. And they are better than spinach in gnudi, the cooked leaves chopped finely and mixed with ricotta, bread crumbs, and eggs.

Lamb's quarters are wonderful in a simple chicken broth soup, the leaves dropped into the boiling liquid for a few minutes before being puréed smooth with some lemon juice. Perk that up with a soft poached egg. Once the flowers have set young green seeds—the unripe so-called pseudograins—these are nuttily good after a quick steam and a slick of butter.

How to Collect and Prepare

Simply cut the tender stems and leaves and carry them home. Immature stems with leaves can be eaten whole, but remove leaves from the older, tough stalks. Stripping the green seeds or flowers from the stalks is very easy— just run your fingers tightly along the plants to remove them. Always blanch lamb's quarters in boiling water before cooking.

Caution

Like amaranth, lamb's quarters can absorb a lot of nitrates if grown in soils that are highly fertilized. Avoid feeding the cooked puréed leaves to babies under the age of six months (see the "Caution" in the amaranth section, page 11). Blanch leaves before using. Like some other leafy greens (especially spinach), lamb's quarters contain oxalates, which can cause problems if you have a serious and existing kidney condition.

CULTIVATION TIPS
USDA Hardiness Zones:
All, as it is an annual

Tolerant of a wide range of soils, as long as the drainage is excellent, lamb's quarters can be grown in full sun or high, dappled shade. Sow the seed after the last frost date for your region. 'Magenta Spreen' is a beautiful cultivar with hot pink growing tips that adds glamour to the vegetable garden.

Potele

Serves 1

Potele is the Sesotho word for a dish of cornmeal (usually called mealie meal in South Africa) cooked with vegetables. Tipsi Titoti makes this particular dish with the young leaves of *umsobo*, black nightshade (*Solanum nigrum* complex)—for her it is a bowl of important comfort food. Any wild edible green can be used, and it lends itself very well to amaranth, nettles, quickweed, and sow thistle (*Sonchus oleraceus*). This is a restorative, earthy meal, a bowl of solace for when you are very hungry and tired. Or homesick.

2 ounces (57 g) washed lamb's quarters

¼ cup (1¼ ounces/35g) cornmeal

Water

Salt

1 tablespoon butter

Bring a pot of water to a boil and drop the lamb's quarters into it. Blanch for 1 minute at a boil. Remove and drain. Mix the cornmeal with some water to form a loose slurry. Pour it into the pot with a large pinch of salt and cook over medium-high heat, adding more water and stirring as it stiffens. Stir in the blanched lamb's quarter leaves and the butter. Continue to cook for about 10 minutes, when the cornmeal should be thick. Taste for salt, and tuck in.

Egg in a Lamb's Quarter Nest

Serves 1

I like to use late-summer lamb's quarter flowers for this one-dish meal. Cooked, the texture of the green flower buds and their unripe seeds is uncannily reminiscent of crunchy panko bread crumbs—lamb's quarters are just one species away from quinoa (*Chenopodium quinoa*). The flowers and seeds are very easy to collect on the spot: Just run your hand up the stalks, stripping them off as you go. To make more, simply double, triple (et cetera) the recipe, plating each nest individually.

2 ounces (57 g) lamb's quarter green
    seeds and leaves
2 tablespoons butter, divided
2 teaspoons lemon juice
1 teaspoon Salted Ramp Leaves
Salt
1 large egg
1 tablespoon soft goat cheese
Pinch of red chile flakes

Preheat the oven to 325°F (170°C).

Bring a small pot of water to a boil and dump in the lamb's quarters. Let them boil for 1 minute (press the greens under periodically). Remove them, drain, refresh in cold water, and squeeze dry.

Melt 1½ tablespoons of the butter over medium-high heat in a small skillet. Add the lamb's quarters. Sauté for a few seconds, then add the lemon juice, Salted Ramp Leaves, and a pinch of salt. Transfer the greens to a small heatproof dish, and hollow out a nest in the center. Break the egg into the nest. Season it with a pinch of salt. Break the cheese into a few small pieces and dot it around the green edges. Cut the remaining butter into small pieces and scatter those evenly over the top. Slide into the oven and bake until the white has just set, 15 to 20 minutes.

Remove from the oven, sprinkle with a generous pinch of chile flakes, and dig in.

Lamb's Quarter Soup

Serves 4 as an appetizer, 2 as an entrée

This quick and easy soup is extra good if you have flavorful chicken stock, *and* if it is correctly seasoned. Don't be afraid of salt.

8 ounces (227 g) lamb's quarters
4 cups (1 liter) chicken stock
Salt
2 tablespoons lemon juice
2 large egg yolks
Black pepper
2–4 poached eggs (optional, depending
    on number of people)

Bring a pot of water to a boil. Drop the lamb's quarters in for a minute. Remove and drain the leaves, refresh them, and squeeze them. Chop them roughly. Bring the chicken stock to a simmer over high heat. Taste it and add salt, if necessary. Add the lemon juice. Add the blanched lamb's quarters and stir. Cook for 3 minutes. Transfer the soup in batches to a blender and pulse briefly. Return to the pot and heat over medium-high heat. Do not boil. Whisk in the egg yolks and grind in some fresh black pepper. As soon as the soup is hot, it is ready to eat—any longer and you kill the beautiful chlorophyll green. If you are adding poached eggs, add each one to individual soup bowls after you have poured the hot soup (you can poach the eggs ahead of time).

Lamb's Quarter Gnudi

Serves 4 as an appetizer

I made these tender gnudi for the first time in the late spring of 2014. I remember because we had just moved to Harlem, and Central Park was a fifteen-minute walk south. One day, in its deserted northern woodlands, I stumbled across the mother lode of tender young lamb's quarters. I didn't feel bad taking a bagful of the unwanted weeds home. I based the gnudi on my memory of the timeless *malfatti* served at Al di La, a neighborhood Italian restaurant in Park Slope, where I have eaten well since I moved to New York.

GNUDI

2 pounds (907 g) fresh lamb's quarters

1 cup (230 g) fresh ricotta

½ cup (30 g) panko bread crumbs, or coarsely ground crumbs

1 large egg

½ cup (30 g) microplaned Parmigiano-Reggiano

¼ teaspoon salt

¼ teaspoon nutmeg

Black pepper to taste

½ cup (60 g) flour, for dusting and rolling

MUGWORT BUTTER SAUCE

3 tablespoons butter

12 mugwort tips (or use sage leaves)

1 gentle squeeze of fresh lemon juice, less than a tablespoon

Salt

½ cup (30 g) microplaned Parmigiano-Reggiano

Black pepper

FOR THE GNUDI: Wash the lamb's quarters. Place the leaves in a large pot of boiling water. Cook at a boil for 4 minutes, pressing them under the water when they rise. Drain, refresh in cold water, and squeeze dry. Roll them up in a kitchen towel and press out any remaining moisture. Chop the leaves finely.

In a mixing bowl, combine the lamb's quarters, ricotta, bread crumbs, egg, cheese, salt, nutmeg, and pepper, and stir thoroughly until evenly mixed. Put the bowl in the fridge for 25 minutes.

Remove the bowl from the fridge. Using two spoons—one to scoop, one to push off—make rough balls, placing each ball on a lightly floured surface. When your surface is full, roll each ball gently between your palms or on the board into oblongs about 1½ inches long by ¾ inch wide (4 × 2 cm). Dent each oblong gently along its length with a finger (this helps it catch sauce later). Put each finished piece onto a plate, also dusted lightly with flour. Repeat with any leftover mixture. Once you have used all your mixture, cover and refrigerate the gnudi for 15 minutes before cooking, or up to several hours.

In a large pot boil salted water and drop the gnudi in one at a time until there are about twelve on the bottom of the pot. Keep the water simmering. When the gnudi rise to the surface, remove each one gently with a slotted spoon, and transfer it to a warm plate while the others cook.

FOR THE SAUCE: Make this quick sauce while the gnudi are cooking. In a small saucepan over medium heat, melt the butter. Add the mugwort. Cook gently, allowing the butter to turn slightly brown. Add the squeeze of lemon, and salt to taste. Pour this sauce over the hot, plated gnocchi, sprinkle with Parmigiano-Reggiano, season liberally with cracked black pepper, and eat at once.

Lamb's Quarter and Beet Leaf Phyllo Triangles

Makes about 27 triangles

I have served these triangles at parties and on my wild plant walks, and they always vanish before I get a taste. They are well worth the effort of folding. Amaranth and quickweed work just as well as a filling.

1½ pounds (680 g) lamb's quarters
1 pound (453 g) beet greens and stems
  (from 3–4 bunches of beets)
1 tablespoon extra-virgin olive oil
12 ounces (340 g) feta cheese, crumbled
2 teaspoons Ground Sumac
4 ounces (113 g) butter
6 sheets regular phyllo dough

Bring a large pot of water to a boil and drop the lamb's quarters in for 1 minute. Remove, drain, refresh in cold water, and squeeze dry. Wash and chop the beet greens and stems. Do not dry them. In a covered pot over medium heat, cook the wet greens, about 10 minutes. Add the blanched lamb's quarters and cook until bite-tender, about 5 minutes. Turn off the heat. Refresh the cooked greens once more under cold water, then squeeze well. Place them in a bowl and add the olive oil, crumbled feta, and sumac; stir well.

Melt the butter in a small pot and keep it within reach.

Spread the unwrapped stacked phyllo sheets on one side of your work surface. Keep them covered completely at all times with a damp kitchen towel (or they dry and turn brittle).

Use two sheets of phyllo at a time, to make nine triangles:

Lay one phyllo sheet on your work surface and brush with butter, paying attention first to the edges, which dry fast. Lay the second sheet perfectly on top and brush with butter. Working quickly, cut the sheets lengthwise twice and across twice, to make nine even squares. Lay a spoonful of filling in the top right-hand quadrant of each square (it helps in the beginning to draw this out on a piece of paper first).

Fold 1: Fold the left half of the square over the filled side and press down. Brush the exposed phyllo with butter. Fold 2: Fold the bottom of the new rectangle over the top filled side to make a new, small square. Brush with butter again. Fold 3: Finally, fold the square's top right corner toward the bottom left corner, to form a triangle. Press down firmly to stick the phyllo together. Brush with butter. Transfer the first batch to a buttered baking sheet and cover with plastic or a damp tea towel until you are ready to bake. They can be chilled in the fridge or frozen at this point.

Repeat the process two more times, until you have made twenty-seven triangles

Preheat the oven to 400°F (200°C). Bake the triangles in batches until one side is turning golden, about 8 minutes, then turn the triangles. Bake until the second side is golden. Once cool they can be frozen and reheated in a 350°F (180°C) oven.

Lamb's Quarter Dashi Greens

Serves 6 as a snack

I like the assertive texture of cooked lamb's quarters, especially when they have just set seed—they have a distinct bite. The leaves are also good sponges, absorbing other flavors. This is a light appetizer or cocktail snack and can be served as part of a multiplate spread, with Japanese inflections.

GREENS

2 pounds (907 g) tender lamb's quarter
    leaves and young seeds

DASHI

4 cups (1 liter) water
2 strips kombu, about 2 by 5 inches
    (5 × 13 cm) each
½ cup (5 g) loosely packed bonito flakes
2 tablespoons yellow miso
2 tablespoons soy sauce
2 tablespoons mirin
Lime juice
1 teaspoon toasted sesame oil

FOR THE GREENS: Bring a pot of water to a boil and drop the lamb's quarters into it. Cook at a boil for 3 minutes, until the leaves are just bite-tender. Drain them, refresh in cold water, and squeeze dry. Untangle them so that they do not stay in a hard pack. Place them loosely in a bowl, cover, and chill.

FOR THE DASHI: Bring the water to a boil in a pot. Turn off the heat. Add the kombu. and the bonito flakes. Allow them to infuse for 10 minutes. Strain the dashi into a bowl through a fine-mesh sieve, removing the kombu and bonito flakes (press the sieve to get every bit of flavor out). In a small bowl thin the miso with a little of the dashi. Pour the dashi and the miso back into the pot and add the soy sauce. Stir and taste. Add the mirin and a squeeze of lime. Taste again. The flavor of the dashi should be well rounded, with no edges, and just a spike of acid to balance the various salts.

Pour 2 cups (500 ml) of the dashi into the bowl with the lamb's quarters. Marinate for 1 to 6 hours in the fridge. To serve in individual tastings, remove bite-sized clumps of the greens from the broth, squeeze, and arrange in a small pyramid on a serving plate. Repeat until you have used up all the greens. Drip a drop of sesame oil on top of each little heap. Add a slick of the dashi broth. Serve cold, with chopsticks.

Alternatively, you can serve the greens in a single pile, dressed with the sesame oil and broth.

Lamb's Quarter and Artichoke Heart Gratin

Serves 4 as a side

When I cook artichokes to eat whole, I like to dip their tender leaf bases into a beurre blanc. In this hearty gratin, using only the hearts is a luxurious way of eating the best part without all the work (at the table, that is!). This beurre blanc is a sweet-and-sour foil for the meatiness of almost crisp lamb's quarters, hiding those soft hearts.

1 pound (453 g) lamb's quarters
1 teaspoon butter, for buttering pan
8 ounces (227 g) cooked artichoke
   hearts, sliced
½ teaspoon Ramp Leaf Salt
½ cup (125 ml) Quick Honeysuckle Vinegar
¼ cup (40 g) finely chopped shallots
4 tablespoons butter
½ cured Mugwort-Cured Egg Yolk

Bring a large pot of water to a boil. Drop in the lamb's quarters and cook at a boil for 3 minutes. Drain, refresh in cold water, and chop finely. Butter an 8-inch (20 cm) pie dish or low-sided baking dish. Arrange the sliced artichoke hearts in the bottom in overlapping layers. Sprinkle some of the Ramp Leaf Salt over the slices. Top the artichoke with the cooked lamb's quarters, arranged evenly on top. Sprinkle more Ramp Leaf Salt over the lamb's quarters, reserving a pinch.

Combine the Quick Honeysuckle Vinegar and the shallots in a small saucepan and place over medium-low heat. Cook until the vinegar has evaporated and the shallots look syrupy, about 15 minutes. Add the pinch of Ramp Leaf Salt and stir. Now add 4 tablespoons of butter, beating with a whisk to emulsify.

Turn on the broiler.

Spoon the thick beurre blanc over the lamb's quarters, distributing it as evenly as possible. It will not cover them altogether. Slide the dish under the broiler and cook until pieces of shallot and the lamb's quarters begin to darken and turn crisp, about 10 minutes. Just before serving, microplane the Mugwort-Cured Egg Yolk over the top.

Lamb's Quarter and Sheep Sorrel Greenballs

Makes 10

These tender, succulent, and leafy not-meatballs are green with leaves, salty with cheese, tart with sumac, and mellowed with the gentle toasted-honey flavor of sweet clover flowers. The first time the Frenchman tasted them, he asked, "These are going into the book, right?" Right, I said. He is a meat man. But he is also a butter man, and I think the American Burnweed and Lime Butter that was frothing around in the pan may have had something to do with it.

1 pound (453 g) lamb's quarters
½ packed cup (20 g) sheep sorrel
3½ ounces (99 g) feta cheese, crumbled
⅓ cup (20 g) panko bread crumbs
2 tablespoons pine nuts
1 tablespoon white sweet clover flowers,
  stripped from stalk
1 teaspoon Ground Sumac
¼ teaspoon salt
¼ teaspoon Ramp Leaf Salt
¼ teaspoon black pepper
2 large eggs
3 tablespoons American Burnweed
  and Lime Butter

Bring a large pot of water to a boil. Drop in the lamb's quarter leaves. Cook at a boil, pushing them down, for about 3 minutes—they must be bite-tender but bright green. Drain the leaves, refresh in cold water, and squeeze dry. Chop them finely.

Preheat the oven to 425°F (220°C).

Place the chopped greens in a bowl with all the other ingredients except the American Burnweed and Lime Butter. Mix very well. Form the mixture into balls about 2 inches (5 cm) in diameter.

In a skillet over medium heat, melt half the butter. When it is foaming, add the greenballs one by one. Cook for 3 minutes, then turn over very carefully, as they are fragile. Add the rest of the butter in slices to the skillet. Immediately transfer to the hot oven for 10 minutes.

Serve hot.

Mugwort

OTHER COMMON NAMES: Common mugwort, wormwood

BOTANICAL NAME: *Artemisia vulgaris*

STATUS: Invasive perennial

WHERE: Widespread, in disturbed ground

SEASON: Spring through fall

USE: Herb

PARTS USED: Leaves, flowers, dry stems

GROW? No

TASTES LIKE: Sage and rosemary with bitterness

The chances are good that you are surrounded by *Artemisia vulgaris* or mugwort, a sage-fragrant and palatable wormwood that is highly invasive in North America but rarely used in American kitchens.

Mugwort is native to Eurasia and is well known in Korea (where it is called *ssuk*) and in Japan (*yomogi*), where a very similar species (*A. princeps*) is prevalent and familiar in cooking as well as in traditional medicines. (It is used to treat a host of ills, from depression to intestinal parasites to menstrual irregularities.) I have stumbled on references to mugwort in nineteenth-century Russian literature and cookbooks, and in Germany *Beifuß* is still used in the kitchen (but how often, I wonder?).

The first thing I heard about mugwort, from a local forager who did not suggest eating it, was that placing the herb under the pillow would induce wild dreams. I tried. Nothing unusual. I still read and hear about its dream influence (thanks perhaps to its potentially neurotoxic thujone content?), and while my dreams have always been vivid, mugwort appears to have no effect on them. Mugwort's cousin *A. absinthium* has a similar, apocryphal reputation.

My interest in mugwort is from a cook's perspective and was prompted initially by the work of West Coast forager Pascal Baudar, who was doing pioneering work with the herb in California, reviving its use in brewing. I began to experiment. Years later it is one of the culinary herbs I use routinely at home. Mugwort's long season means that it is available from early spring through late fall, with an evolving flavor profile in its shoots, leaves, flowers, and seeds. Even the dry sticks are

useful—environmentally friendly barbecue skewers, with built-in aroma. There is always mugwort salt in my tiny pantry, and I make more as the year turns and its flavor becomes stronger. Fresh, the herb is easy to find, and in late fall I gather bunches to dry for winter use.

Mugwort is also the grounding ingredient in the vermouths I make. Of all my wild food adventures, these vermouths have been the most exciting. Pure alchemy. Traditional European vermouth derives its name from *wermut*, German for "wormwood." But I only learned that after I began making it, inspired in part by the work of Kobus van der Merwe, a South African chef blazing a trail of indigenous food on that country's West Coast (what is it about that side of countries?)—who was making a vermouth with local flora.

The wild possibilities of a seasonal, hyperlocal vermouth were thrilling. I started researching vermouth making, not appreciating until then how many botanicals (twenty, by close-lipped accounts) are blended in the classic dry Noilly Prat, a staple in many cocktails and my own kitchen.

Now, opening a bottle of straw-colored Cape Vermouth, infused with crab apple and violets from my mother's Cape Town spring garden and a slew of more emphatic fynbos herbs and southern African wormwood (*Artemisia afra*), can make me cry. It transports me right to that garden in an instant. A local vermouth is redolent of time and place. I make it in every season, and wherever I am. The artemisia at the heart of these vermouths provides a herbally bitter backbone to support many other botanicals. There is something breathtaking about being able to capture a botanical environment, a landscape, a time in your life, in a bottle.

In New York the people who collect mugwort are usually Korean women, who use it to make rice dishes and desserts, but mostly medicinally. It is sometimes sold fresh in bundles on sidewalks in Brooklyn and Queens in neighborhoods with significant Chinese communities. And I have begun to see mugwort at market. At our tiny local greenmarket in Carroll Gardens, Brooklyn, Lani's Farm sells its sprigs for $24 a pound (along with other wild greens). I can't help smiling, because it is growing within reach along a chain-link fence, nearby. But I am genuinely glad that it is being found useful as a marketable crop; it is often the serious price tag itself that brings an unfamiliar ingredient to the attention of shoppers and chefs.

The more mugwort is sold, the more familiar greenmarket patrons will become with it and the more often they will recognize it where it grows in profusion, displacing native plants. It is a remarkably useful herb.

How to Collect and Prepare

In early spring mugwort leaves are one of the first forages to appear, clustering around the skeletons of the previous year's dead sticks. Collect these tender silvery leaves and wash them well, as they grow flush with the ground and tend to be gritty. As spring progresses the whole soft stem can be cut and used in its entirety. As summer intensifies the stems will become harder and tough; this is the stage when they make nifty kebab skewers. To dry mugwort for winter use, simply tie it in a bundle and hang it upside down for a couple of weeks.

Caution

To err on the side of excessive caution, steer clear of mugwort if you are pregnant, wish to be, or are nursing. But do bear in mind that medicinal applications usually use a large and concentrated amount of any herb (and in mugwort's case the root, too—always a part of a plant to avoid, if you are uncertain). Culinary quantities are far less potent.

Mugwort and Raspberry Liqueur

Makes 1 quart (1 liter)

Classic Russian Cooking (Indiana University Press, 1998) written by Elena Molokhovets in the nineteenth century is one of those rabbit hole books from whose otherworldly depths you may never return. After chancing upon a reference to mugwort in Turgenev's *A Hunter's Sketches*, I revisited its pages to look for wild herbs. Sure enough, Molokhovets includes a recipe for Lingonberry Liqueur that requires *half a pound* of dry wormwood. Her instructions are to "pour a pail of vodka" over the herbs. I knew I liked Russians. Here is my version. It yields an infusion with a spectacular, clear ruby color. No pails required. Serve neat over ice with lemon and sparkling water, or mix into cocktails.

2 ounces (57 g) fresh mugwort
12 ounces (340 g) fresh raspberries
½ cup (100 g) sugar
1 cup (250 ml) Ground Elder Gin
3 cups (750 ml) vodka

Layer the mugwort and raspberries in a clean glass jar. Add the sugar, Ground Elder Gin, and vodka. Tighten the lid. Tilt back and forth until the sugar has dissolved. Leave to infuse for 6 weeks. Strain through a fine-mesh sieve, and again through double cheesecloth or fine linen. Save the raspberries for an alcoholic dessert, or jam. (Taste one—they're good!) Bottle in a clean glass bottle—it keeps indefinitely.

The Forager

Makes 1 drink

One of the greatest pleasures of foraging is the provisions cupboard—a treasure chest after a season of preserving, infusing, and fermenting. This is a deep ruby cocktail whose sugar is kept in check by astringent sumac.

RIM

1 tablespoon lime juice

2 teaspoons Sumac Sugar

DRINK

2½ fluid ounces (5 tablespoons) Mugwort and Raspberry Liqueur

1 fluid ounce (2 tablespoons) Fermented Elderberry Syrup

1 fluid ounce (2 tablespoons) Sumac Vodka

½ fluid ounce (1 tablespoon) Sumac Essence

Pour the lime juice into a saucer. Place the Sumac Sugar in a second saucer. Dip the cocktail glass's rim into the lime and then into the sugar, working it around gently. Allow it to harden for a minute. Combine the liquids with ice in a shaker. Shake, strain, and pour.

Dame Ruby

Makes 1 drink

The tart sweetness of Bayberry Beach Plum and Red Wine Syrup adds a lick of early autumn to summer's infusions.

2 fluid ounces (4 tablespoons) Mugwort and Raspberry Liqueur

1½ fluid ounces (3 tablespoons) Sumac Vodka

1 fluid ounce (2 tablespoons) Northeast No. 1 Vermouth

½ fluid ounce (1 tablespoon) Bayberry Beach Plum and Red Wine Syrup

Combine in a cocktail shaker with ice. Shake, strain, and pour.

Northeast No. 1 Vermouth and Bitters

Makes 2⅓ quarts (2¼ liters)

Cracking a bottle of Northeast No. 1 takes me straight back to the hill in Harlem where I picked mugwort and mulberries one sticky summer—the beginning of my vermouth-making journey. This recipe, based on that first summer vermouth, is a blend of native and exotic herbs and spices as well as time-honored vermouth ingredients. It is made when mulberries turn sidewalks into crime scenes and hands a bloody purple. Thanks to the luscious fruit, it yields a pink vermouth, which may darken over time to sepia.

All my vermouths have a fortification of 1:3—one part hard liquor to three parts wine. I use a good unwooded dry white wine. It does not have to be expensive, and it should not be overly acidic or lean. I choose decent but economical vodka, preferring Stolichnaya, Wódka, or Tito's.

There are three major steps to making vermouth at home. The first is to create the collection of separate vodka infusions. The second is the brief wine infusion: Drawing on my flower-based fermentation experience, my style has evolved to include at this stage scented seasonal flowers. It is remarkable how the character of something as delicate as a violet or honeysuckle can be conveyed, years later. The third stage is blending the vodka infusions into the wine.

Vermouth is excellent served simply on ice, with no other interference, and blends very well into cocktails. I also use it often for cooking, adding it to pan juices and sauces.

Vodka Infusions

10 ounces (283 g) mulberries
4 ounces (113 g) raspberries
2 ounces (57 g) peeled lemon zest
1 liter vodka (you will have some left over)
20 bayberry leaves
8 mugwort sprigs, 5–6 inches (13–15 cm) long each
3 tablespoons Ground Sumac (in 6 tablespoons vodka)
1 ounce (28 g) whole spicebush fruits

Ten days before you plan to blend the vermouth: Infuse the mulberries, raspberries, and peeled lemon zest in individual jars, using just enough vodka to cover each ingredient (but see To Blend Vermouth instructions to ensure you have the minimum amount required).

Five days before blending: Infuse the bayberry leaves, mugwort sprigs, Ground Sumac, and spicebush in separate jars, again using enough liquor for each ingredient. (For the Ground Sumac, stir it well into its 6 tablespoons of vodka.)

Wine Infusion

2 bottles (1½ liters total) unwooded
    white wine
10 juniper berries
1 tablespoon coriander seeds,
    toasted in a pan
1 teaspoon black peppercorns
1 teaspoon pink peppercorns
½ vanilla bean
3 pieces fresh lemon zest (2 inches/
    5 cm each)
1 clove
1 stick cinnamon
1 cardamom pod
5 sprigs fresh marjoram or oregano
2 ounces (57 g) honeysuckle flowers
3 tablespoons sugar
3 tablespoons Fermented Elderflower Cordial

The day before you plan to blend the vermouth: Make the white wine infusion by combining all the ingredients *except* the honeysuckle flowers, sugar, and Fermented Elderflower Cordial in a large pot over medium heat and heat until tiny bubbles rise at the sides of the pot. *Do not boil.* Turn the heat off as soon as you see the bubbles and allow to cool. Add the honeysuckle and stir. Infuse overnight, or for 12 hours. Add 2 tablespoons of the sugar and all the cordial. Taste. The mixture should not be sweet or overtly acid, but well balanced. Add more sugar if necessary. Strain through four layers of cheesecloth (I actually prefer fine linen napkins, which I keep for straining any botanical infusions) into a large bowl.

To Blend Vermouth

5 fluid ounces (10 tablespoons)
    mulberry vodka
4 fluid ounces (8 tablespoons)
    bayberry vodka
3 fluid ounces (6 tablespoons)
    raspberry vodka
2 fluid ounces (4 tablespoons)
    lemon vodka
2 fluid ounces (4 tablespoons)
    mugwort vodka
2 fluid ounces (4 tablespoons)
    spicebush vodka
2 fluid ounces (4 tablespoons)
    sumac vodka

Measure the vodka infusions and pour them into the white wine infusion through a fine-mesh strainer lined with cheesecloth. Taste. If you like, add a little more of individual infusions—your palate is your guide. Keep tasting (hic!). When you love it, strain the combined mixture into a clean bowl through double layers of cheesecloth. The vermouth is ready to be bottled. Pour it into clean, narrow-necked bottles. It will keep indefinitely at room temperature, but once open, refrigerate.

Bitters

Blend all your leftover infusions, strain, and bottle them. These are your powerfully flavored Northeast No. 1 Bitters. The bitters keep indefinitely and create distinctive cocktails.

EXPERIMENTING WITH
YOUR OWN VERMOUTH BLENDS

If you decide you want to develop your own special vermouth blend at some point—who wouldn't?—use this recipe as a guide. Each season offers different ingredients, and a different vermouth. As you find new forages and flavors, experiment with your own, personal, and evolving blend. To begin with, create each vodka infusion in its own glass jar. (Once you have more confidence, you can combine herbs in a jar.) Use enough vodka to cover the ingredients and to give you the amount you need for blending. Of the three stages in vermouth making, the third stage—blending the vodka infusions into the wine—is where a lot could go wrong, or right. Add small amounts of the infusions at a time, and taste often. You can't undo it once it has been done, but you can always add more. As in the Northeast No. 1 recipe, you will have leftovers that you can blend into separate, and superb, bitters.

Woodsy

Makes 1 cocktail

Late autumn's evening nip demands a warming cocktail.

3 fluid ounces (6 tablespoons) bourbon
1 fluid ounce (2 tablespoons)
    clementine juice
½ fluid ounce (1 tablespoon) Northeast
    No. 1 Bitters
½ fluid ounce (1 tablespoon) Spicebush
    Clementine Cordial

Shake all the ingredients up with ice, strain, and pour.

Honey

Makes 1 drink

I shook this drink up one evening after I came home from a forage with an unexpected haul of honey mushrooms.

2 fluid ounces (4 tablespoons) Lillet Blanc
1½ fluid ounces (3 tablespoons) bourbon
1 fluid ounce (2 tablespoons) Northeast
    No. 1 Vermouth
½ ounce (1 tablespoon) Northeast
    No. 1 Bitters

Shake it all up with ice, strain, and pour.

Brown Bear

Makes 1 cocktail

A warm drink for winter nights.

2 fluid ounces (4 tablespoons) Northeast
    No. 1 Bitters
1½ fluid ounces (3 tablespoons)
    blood orange juice
1 fluid ounce (2 tablespoons) bourbon
1½ teaspoons maple syrup
	Shake up with ice, strain, and pour.

Long Goodnight

Makes 1 drink

Dark drinks match my mood in winter, and many of my cold-weather cocktails are correspondingly somber in color.

2 fluid ounces (4 tablespoons) Northeast
    No. 1 Vermouth
1½ fluid ounces (3 tablespoons)
    Black Cherry Rum
1 fluid ounce (2 tablespoons) Sumac Vodka
½ fluid ounce (1 tablespoon)
    pomegranate molasses
	Shake it all up with ice. Strain, and pour.

Mugwort Salt

Makes about 6½ ounces (184 g)

I make my first mugwort salt in early spring, when its first shoots appear beneath the previous season's long dry sticks. I continue making it through the season, ending in late fall when the seeds remain on the plants. Every month adds intensity to the flavor of the maturing leaves, flowers, and seeds. I have also made the salt by drying mugwort first and then grinding it—but this creates a lot of mugwort fluff, which must be picked off. I prefer the method below.

1 ounce (28 g) lightly packed
    mugwort leaves
6 ounces (170 g) sea salt
	Clean the mugwort by washing and drying completely.
	    Place the mugwort in a food processer and pulse until the leaves are very finely shredded. Place the mugwort in a bowl and add the salt, mixing well with your fingers to break up the clumps of the herb. Spread the herbed salt on a baking sheet or parchment paper to dry. Turn it every few hours. When it is completely dry, store in an airtight jar. Best used within 2 months.

Mugwort-Cured Egg Yolks

Makes 12

I learned from Shell Yu, a Chinese Canadian pharmacist and forager whose feed I follow on Instagram, that mugwort-flavored eggs are a traditional part of the Chinese Dragon Boat Festival. Shell wraps whole eggs with mugwort, ties them in cheesecloth, and hard-boils them. The leaves print a beautiful pattern on the shell. I riffed on this idea with egg yolks. The cured yolks are reminiscent of bottarga, and I microplane them over pasta, salads, toast, and anything else that needs a quick flick of glamour. Duck eggs are especially good; otherwise use the best quality happy-hen eggs you can find. The quantity of salt will depend on the size of the container you use. You can stack the yolks on top of one another *as long as there is sufficient salt in between* to prevent them from touching (if they touch they will stick together forever).

Sea salt
3 tablespoons sugar
2 tablespoons Mugwort Salt
12 raw egg yolks

Spread a layer of sea salt ¼ inch (½ cm) deep in the bottom of a food-safe container. Make shallow depressions in the salt—a nest to hold each egg yolk. Sprinkle some sugar across the bottom of the nests, followed by some Mugwort Salt. Place each yolk carefully in its nest. Sprinkle more Mugwort Salt on top of the yolks, followed by a sprinkling of sugar. Top with ¼ inch (½ cm) of sea salt. If your container is small and you still have egg yolks, repeat this process with another layer of eggs on top. Finish with ¼ inch (½ cm) of salt, cover the container, and transfer to the fridge.

After 4 days for chicken eggs and 5 days for duck, remove the container and carefully excavate your egg yolks. They will be quite firm. Lay them on a clean surface. Using a pastry brush, dust as much granular salt mixture off the yolks as you can. Cut a length of cheesecloth and lay the yolks on one side of it, leaving a 2-inch (5 cm) space between each yolk. Fold the empty side of the cheesecloth over the yolks. Tie a piece of butcher's twine or string between each yolk, and tie the top and bottom of the cheesecloth, so that each yolk is in its own snug little pocket. Hang them to cure for at least a week and up to 2 months (they will get harder) I like them best after about 4 weeks. Once they are as hard as you like, you can take them down and store in the fridge in a closed container (to prevent them from further drying and from taking on other fridge smells).

Mugwort Guanciale

Makes 1 cured jowl

All you need for this cured pork jowl is a good and friendly butcher. (Or your own pig.) The jowl contains the pork cheek meat, but also a huge surrounding hunk of fat, which takes on a silky texture once it is cured. Mugwort and pork are good friends, and I add juniper and spicebush, too. My favorite way to eat the cured jowl is sliced very thinly and laid straight onto a plain, very thin pizza base, with more mugwort scattered across and baked in the oven for 15 minutes. Sprinkle with a little salt and you are in heaven.

1 pork jowl, about 2 pounds (907 g)
2½ ounces (70 g) sugar
2 ounces (57 g) salt
2 tablespoons Mugwort Salt
1 teaspoon ground spicebush
10 juniper berries, lightly crushed
⅓ ounce (9 g) lightly packed fresh mugwort

Rinse the jowl and pat it dry. Trim off any untidy bits and remove any glands (compact and a slightly darker color than the fat). Place the jowl in either a ziplock bag or a shallow container and add all the cure ingredients. Massage these all over the pork. If you are using a bag (my preferred method), suck all the air out, or cover well if in a container. Place the pork in the fridge for 5 days. Every day pour off any accumulated juices. You will feel the pork becoming gradually firmer as the days pass.

Remove the pork from its cure and rinse well. Pat dry. Use a sharp knife to make a slit in one end of the jowl, thread kitchen twine through the hole, and hang the pork to air-cure. I just use the kitchen, which is quite airy. As it cures it will stiffen, and it may drip some fat with time. It will be ready after a couple of weeks (it will feel stiff); I have left it as long as 2 months before slicing.

Mugwort and Field Garlic Farmers Cheese

Makes 1 cheese ball

The quality and provenance of the milk and cream will determine the deliciousness of your cheese. You can use any vinegar. I like to use the brine from my Ramp Pickles. Other herbs, like finely chopped tender field garlic, bayberry, or spring sweetfern leaves, would work very well, too.

½ gallon (1.9 liters) whole milk
7 fluid ounces (198 ml) cream
⅓ cup (80 ml) Ramp Pickle vinegar
1 teaspoon Field Garlic Salt
　(or Ramp Leaf Salt)
1 tablespoon dried and ground mugwort
2 teaspoons Ground Sumac

Heat the milk and cream over medium heat in a large pot. Stir occasionally. When the liquid begins to simmer, very slowly pour in the vinegar while stirring gently. The moment thick curds form, you can stop adding vinegar—how much you need depends on the unique character of the dairy products. Allow the pot to sit for 15 minutes. Strain the curds through clean damp cheesecloth into a bowl. (Save the whey for baking, marinating, and braising.) Place the saved curds into a fresh bowl and add the salt and mugwort. Taste for seasoning and adjust if necessary. At this point you can use the very soft cheese to spread on bruschetta or crackers.

For a firmer, drier cheese that retains its shape, place the soft cottage cheese in a square of clean cheesecloth in a strainer over a bowl. Bring the corners of the cloth together and twist so that the cheese is forced into a ball. Cover and refrigerate. Leave to drain another 2 to 3 hours (or longer, which will make it even firmer). Just before serving, sprinkle with sumac.

Mugwort Cottage Fries

Serves 4

One of my three favorite roasted mugwort recipes, these homely and fragrant wedges are delicious served with runny eggs, juicy mushrooms, or barbecued steak.

3 large russet potatoes, cut into
   thick wedges
3 tablespoons olive oil
½ cup (15 g) mugwort leaves
½ teaspoon salt

Preheat the oven to 450°F (230°C).

   Toss the potatoes in a bowl with the olive oil, mugwort, and salt. Arrange the potatoes in a single layer in a large skillet or baking pan. Transfer to the oven and roast until they are turning brown and are tender—about 55 minutes. Turn a couple of times if you want them evenly brown.

Mugwort-Roasted Garlic

Serves 4

Whole heads of mugwort-infused garlic make a creamy spread for toast or steak. Figure on a head of garlic per person.

4 heads garlic
½ ounce (14 g) mugwort
1 tablespoon olive oil
¼ teaspoon Mugwort Salt

Preheat the oven to 375°F (190°C).

   Flake off the outer layers of dry garlic skin, leaving just a couple of layers to protect the bulbs. Slice off the tips of the cloves in one fell swoop. Arrange the mugwort leaves in the bottom of an ovenproof skillet and top with the garlic. Drizzle the oil over and season with Mugwort Salt. Roast until the fattest cloves of garlic are very tender, about 60 minutes.

Mugwort-Roasted Guavas

Serves 4

Guavas were a staple fruit when I was growing up. They are heavily perfumed and take very well to roasting, if you do not mind their seeds (clearly, I do not). I first ate roasted guavas at Babel, the inspiring restaurant on the farm Babylonstoren, near Cape Town. Those were flavored with citrus zest and thyme. Serve these guavas as a side dish with pork or as a simple appetizer.

10 small guavas, halved
½ teaspoon Mugwort Salt
Black pepper
Orange zest
½ ounce (14 g) mugwort leaves

Preheat the oven to 375°F (190°C).

   Combine all the ingredients, toss well, and arrange in an ovenproof skillet. Roast until the edges of the guavas are turning golden, about 35 to 40 minutes.

Mugwort Shortbread

Makes about 30 shortbreads

These crisp shortbreads are a regular snack on my wild food walks (in late spring I substitute tender bayberry leaves and salt). Serve with Yogurt Cheese with Wild Herbs, Mugwort and Field Garlic Farmers Cheese, Japanese Knotweed Hummus, or yogurt flavored with chopped field garlic.

1¼ cups (150 g) all-purpose flour
½ teaspoon Mugwort Salt
5 ounces (142 g) cold butter
3 ounces (85 g) grated Parmigiano-Reggiano
2 ounces (57 g) sun-dried tomatoes in olive oil, finely chopped
2 tablespoons fresh mugwort leaves or flowers, chopped
Black pepper
1 large egg yolk
3 tablespoons ice water, plus extra

Place the flour and Mugwort Salt in a mixing bowl. Cut or grate the cold butter onto the flour. Work the butter and flour between your fingers until the mixture resembles coarse crumbs. Add the cheese and chopped tomatoes; toss lightly with your fingers until combined. Add the mugwort and toss again. Crack in some black pepper. Using a fork, mix the egg yolk with the ice water in a small bowl. Add to the flour mixture and blend swiftly with a fork. Form into a rough disk with your hands, adding a very little more cold water if it is not adhering. Flatten the disk to about 6 inches (15 cm) across, wrap, and chill in the fridge for at least 1 hour.

Preheat the oven to 400°F (200°C).

Roll the pastry out evenly on a floured board. Cut into 2½-inch (6 cm) squares or rounds and place them on an oiled or lined baking sheet. Bake until the edges are turning golden or pale brown, 12 to 15 minutes. Cool on a wire rack.

Mugwort Olive Oil Crackers

Makes about 40 crackers

One of the most adaptable pastries I use is this olive oil recipe that makes a crisp base for countless pies and tarts. Rolled out even more thinly, it yields excellent crackers (as I discovered one day when babysitting friends' young sons, who were bored—we baked them together, and they wolfed them hot from the oven). Serve with Yogurt Cheese with Wild Herbs, Roasted Elderflower Carrot Pâté, or Garlic Mustard with Pecans.

2¼ cups (180 g) flour
½ cup (125 ml) extra-virgin olive oil
½ cup (125 ml) tepid water
2 tablespoons finely chopped mugwort
1 teaspoon Mugwort Salt
1 tablespoon butter

Combine all the ingredients except the butter in a mixing bowl and mix well. For ease of rolling, divide the dough into two fat disks, wrap, and chill for 30 minutes (it will never get completely hard).

Melt the butter and brush a baking sheet. Place the sheet in the freezer to chill.

Preheat the oven to 400°F (200°C).

Roll the pastry out on a floured board as thinly as possible. Now either press out crackers using a cookie cutter, or use a knife or pizza blade to hand-cut 2½-inch (6 cm) squares or rounds. Lift them carefully to the baking sheet. Bake until their edges are deeply golden, about 12 to 15 minutes. Transfer to a wire cooling rack. Once they're cool, store in an airtight container and eat within 2 days, or freeze.

Warm Mugwort and Soy Braised Tomato Salad

Serves 4

I call it a salad, but it makes an excellent entrée, tossed with sesame-slippery udon noodles. Or a topping for toast rubbed with garlic.

3 tablespoons soy sauce
2 tablespoons yellow miso
2 teaspoons sugar
2 tablespoons toasted sesame oil
1¼ pounds (567 g) cherry tomatoes
2 teaspoons Wisteria Vinegar
2 tablespoons fresh mugwort leaves,
   stripped and snipped
4 sprigs Thai basil

In a small bowl mix the soy sauce with the miso and sugar. Stir until smooth.

In a skillet heat the oil over medium-high heat. Add the cherry tomatoes. Cook them for 8 minutes, covered, shaking the pan occasionally to prevent sticking. Remove the lid and add the Wisteria Vinegar, mugwort, and Thai basil sprigs. Shake the pan a couple of times and turn off the heat (they will not be fully cooked).

Add the soy dressing to the pan and toss well. Serve warm or at room temperature.

Raw Tomato and Mugwort Salad with Miso Field Garlic

Serves 4 as a side

Tomatoes, another way, but raw. In late summer, when real tomatoes arrive at market, I dig out my nicely aging, miso-preserved field garlic bulbs (see Miso Ramps, page 340). The salty bulbs add a mellow warmth to the acidic tomatoes.

2 medium tomatoes or 1 large tomato
2 teaspoons soy sauce
3 tablespoons Miso Field Garlic
   (see Miso Ramps)
1 tablespoon mugwort leaf tips
1 tablespoon freshly snipped chives
1 teaspoon toasted sesame oil

Cut the tomato or tomatoes fairly thinly and arrange on a serving plate. Drizzle the soy sauce across the slices and scatter the Miso Field Garlic across. Add the mugwort tips, torn apart, and the chives. Finish with some drops of sesame oil.

Mugwort and Bayberry Pork Rillettes

Makes about 1½ quarts (900 g)

Spring potted pork is a useful thing for picnics to come, appetizers for a faraway supper party, no-cook meals, or flavorful additions to ragus and stuffed vegetables. It keeps up to a year in the freezer, quietly getting better all the time. Most recipes call only for poaching the meat in fat or wine, but I prefer the flavor that slow-roasting yields, with the skin basting the meat below.

ROAST PORK

1 slab pork belly, with skin,
   about 3 pounds (1⅓ kg)
½ teaspoon salt
1 teaspoon freshly cracked pepper
1 teaspoon sugar
1 ounce (28 g) fresh young mugwort
3 tablespoons bayberry buds
6 branches thyme
10 juniper berries
2 cups fruity dry white wine
2 tablespoons lemon juice
1 cup water

CONFIT OF PORK

Pork belly fat
12 field garlic bulbs, trimmed
Cooked pork belly meat, shredded finely
1 cup (250 ml) fruity dry white wine
1 tablespoon lemon juice
12 bayberry leaves
6 branches thyme
12 sprigs fresh mugwort
10 juniper berries
¼ teaspoon salt
Black pepper

FOR THE ROAST PORK: Preheat the oven to 350°F (180°C).

Score the pork belly skin deeply into the fat and rub salt and pepper into the cuts. Season the underside of the pork belly with salt, pepper, and the sugar. Place the belly skin-side up on top of the herbs and juniper berries in a roasting pan. Pour the wine, lemon juice, and water around the meat, avoiding the skin (which you may like as much as I do, as crispy crackling). Transfer to the oven and roast for 4 hours. Check periodically to make sure that the liquid does not dry up. Add a little water if it does.

When the meat is very tender when prodded suggestively with a fork, remove it from the oven and cool a little. Pour off the juices and reserve. Once you can handle the pork without pain, slide a knife between the crackling and the top layer of fat and remove. What you do with the crackling is up to you. I know what I do: It is an excellent bar snack, broken up and sprinkled with salt.

The meat and fat are in layers. Cut out the fat layers and reserve. Take all the meat and chop it finely. You could also shred it so that the long muscle fibers are preserved intact. It is a matter of texture, and I have no preference.

FOR THE CONFIT: Place all the cut-up fat you have reserved in a pot over medium heat and melt until more fat runs from it. Add the field garlic and cook for 5 minutes. Add the chopped meat and stir. Add everything else. Turn the heat up briefly to allow the wine to bubble, then reduce the heat again and cook at a very low simmer for 1 hour. Taste, and add more salt and pepper—you should season quite heavily, as it will be eaten cool, which mutes flavor. Allow the mixture to cool a little.

Pack the pork into jars or small bowls and tamp down gently. Top with melted fat. Transfer to the fridge (eat within a week) or freezer.

Mugwort Soy Beef Short Ribs

Serves 4

This is a staple dish at home for cooking over coals. Economical short ribs are every bit as good as expensive steak cuts. While this recipe is for one bone-in or boneless beef short rib per person, they are so intensely flavored that you may want to double the quantities, which is easy to do. They make the best leftovers, for everything from an Asian-inflected bone broth, to pulled beef sandwiches, to spicy ragus. The soy I prefer is Ohsawa Organic Nama Shoyu.

4 bone-in beef short ribs
   (about 1 pound/453 g each),
   1 per person
⅓ cup (80 ml) soy sauce
2 tablespoons lime juice
1 tablespoon sugar
½ ounce (14 g) mugwort leaves

TO MARINATE: Place the ribs in a large ziplock bag (or a shallow dish, in which case turn them several times). Mix all the marinade ingredients in a jug and pour into the bag. Press out all the air. Massage the bag well and leave in the fridge for the flavors to penetrate; 12 to 24 hours is ideal. Remove the ribs from the fridge 1 hour before cooking.

TO BARBECUE: Remove the ribs from their marinade and lay on a grid about 6 inches (15 cm) above the ashed-over coals. If you have a cover, use it to trap some heat. Cook until the ribs are deep brown and turn, about 6 minutes on each of four sides, but the timing will depend on your heat. If flames lick up it's fine to move the ribs around or turn them more often. The thickest part of the meat should yield slightly when prodded firmly with a finger, for a medium-rare cook. Remove to a plate and cover with foil to rest for 10 minutes. This is essential.

TO SERVE: Carve the entire hunk of meat off the bone and then slice each piece thinly across the grain. Lay the meat slices in the juices from the rested ribs. Stack the bones at one end of the plate for people who like to gnaw.

Mugwort and Yogurt Leg of Lamb

Serves 4

Butterflied leg of lamb absorbs flavors like a sponge. I cook it from early spring, when the first mugwort shoots appear, right through late fall, when the plant has grown tall and pungent. Once field garlic season is over, use either pickled bulbs or conventional garlic. In spring the leftover lamb—if there is any—makes killer sandwiches with wintercress and spicy garlic mustard greens. In summer, grill eggplants along with the lamb; their creamy insides are an excellent, smoky spread for the meat.

1½ teaspoons Mugwort Salt

1 ounce (28 g) chopped mugwort

2 ounces (57 g) chopped field garlic bulbs

½ cup (125 ml) sour cream or yogurt

1 deboned, butterflied leg of lamb,
    about 3 pounds/1⅓ kg

4 ounces (113 g) mugwort stems and leaves

Mix the Mugwort Salt, chopped mugwort, field garlic bulbs (or garlic), and sour cream or yogurt in a large bowl. Add the lamb and massage it well. Marinate from 1 hour to 1 day, in the fridge. Longer is better. Place the meat above ashed-over coals with the mugwort branches on top of it. Cover to trap the heat. Cook for about 45 minutes, total, depending on how thick the lamb is (this will deliver lamb that is slightly pink inside, but not rare). Turn the meat as each side browns.

Otherwise, cook it under a preheated broiler, for 10 to 15 minutes a side.

Allow the meat to rest for at least 10 minutes, tented under foil. Drain its accumulated juices into a little jug, slice against the grain before serving, and pass the jug around for anointing the slices.

Mugwort Spicebush Poached Pears

Serves 4

A dessert for fall. Adorable Seckel pears look beautiful in a spicebush-infused vermouth poaching liquid. The funk of mugwort grounds the sweetness.

SPICEBUSH ESSENCE

1 cup (250 ml) water

1½ ounces (40 g) whole spicebush fruit

2 ounces (57 g) sugar

PEARS

6 Seckel pears, halved and seeded

1 cup (250 ml) vermouth

½ cup (125 ml) water

½ cup (125 ml) Spicebush Essence

2 tablespoons fresh mugwort flowers
    and seeds

FOR THE SPICEBUSH ESSENCE: Combine the water, spicebush, and sugar in a small pot over high heat. When the liquid boils reduce the heat to keep it at a gentle simmer. Cook for 15 minutes and turn off the heat. Press down gently on the berries with a potato masher to release more flavor. Allow the liquid to cool. Strain through cheesecloth. (Keep any essence you do not use in the fridge; you'll find other uses.)

FOR THE PEARS: Arrange the pears in a single layer in a saucepan. Add the vermouth, water, and Spicebush Essence. Bring to a brief boil over high heat, then reduce the heat to keep the liquid at a gentle simmer. Add the mugwort. Cover with a lid and cook gently until the pears are tender when pricked with a skewer or fork, about 20 minutes. Lift the fruit from the saucepan and reserve on a plate. Reduce the poaching liquid in the saucepan over high heat until it is syrupy, about 5 minutes, then drizzle over the pears.

Nettles

OTHER COMMON NAMES: Stinging nettles, wood nettles

BOTANICAL NAMES: *Urtica dioica* and subspecies, *Laportea canadensis*

STATUS: Perennial indigenous to North America, as well as introduced

WHERE: Widespread on disturbed ground, woodlands, stream valleys, farmers markets

SEASON: Spring, winter (in mild winter rainfall regions)

USE: Vegetable

PARTS USED: Tender stems and leaves

GROW? Yes

TASTES LIKE: Mild spinach but better

One of the most widely distributed plants in North America, stinging nettles (*Urtica dioica*) occur in climates as contradictory as Alaska's and Hawaii's. But for years their allure eluded me. The thick-stalked bunches I bought at the farmers market seemed to taste like mud after the prescribed boiling. A chance encounter one spring with a verdant patch of wood nettles (*Laportea canadensis*) in the woodlands near Cold Spring, a town beside the Hudson River, converted me. Wood nettles have large, beautiful leaves, almost heart-shaped. They are an impeccable green. Gloveless and stung, I sliced as many young stems as I could with my Opinel knife and carried them home to the

city on the train. Reluctant to destroy their vivid color, I dipped them in boiling water for a minute. After I had refreshed and squeezed them, they were still brilliantly green, quite unlike the overly mature greenmarket stinging nettles that I had destroyed with overcooking. The wood nettles tasted new: silky, but not slippery, with a flavor of pure chlorophyll.

A few months later in that same year, I was enjoying a second spring in the Southern Hemisphere, walking in a fledgling olive orchard in a hamlet called Koringberg, two hours' drive from Cape Town. My friends Johan van Zyl and Peter van Noord, the orchard owners, had told me about the nettles growing there. For a forager it was a luxuriant paradise: Soaking rains had coaxed a succulent forest of edible weeds from the soil. There was mallow, nettle-leaf goosefoot (*Chenopodium murale*), and, yes, nettles. I picked until my basket could hold no more. Treated properly, they were delicious. (And I learned subsequently that South Africa has a native spotted wood nettle, *Laportea grossa*, at home in moist woodlands in that country. Its young tips are a traditional food.)

The earliest nettle shoots appear locally just before the woods have woken up in springtime. The undersides of their leaves are a gorgeous amethyst, a guarantee of absolute tenderness. I sometimes do not bother to blanch these delicacies, but drop them straight into good broth, or butter, where they practically melt. Nettle shoots are the first new edible to appear in my garden in spring, making them vulnerable to a gardener-cook-forager who is deprived of green. Picked, they keep on giving.

By the time the nettles are tall, the trees have leafed out. Stinging nettles, narrower and pointier than wood nettles, favor roughed-up ground in sun or semi-shade. They volunteer in the wake of human activity. Wood nettles love, you guessed it, woodland. They are broader plants with wide, heart-shaped leaves. My own stinging nettle patch provides me with enough for some soups and tarts, and I keep a

beady eye on it, shearing it before it sets seed. It can be invasive. It can also be clipped again and again, which encourages new growth. This is a plant that belongs in kitchen gardens.

While nettles have a uniquely silky character that warrants dishes designed for them, they translate well to any recipe calling for spinach, chard, amaranth, lamb's quarters, or quickweed.

How to Collect and Prepare

If you are picking spring tips, it is possible to do so without stinging yourself badly. But more mature stems and leaves are easier to collect if you wear gloves. Or you could follow the advice of the Frenchman's Provençal father to him as a boy: *Il faut les caresser de bas en haut.* Caress them from the bottom up (nuff said). In this way you do not, in theory, engage the stingers. For both sorts of nettles, prepare them for cooking by submerging them for a

minute in boiling water, or by pouring boiled water over them in a large bowl for a couple of minutes. Their stings dissolve. Drain them at once, refresh in cold water, and squeeze dry. Their vibrant color is preserved.

As with other greens nettles lose a lot of volume and some weight after blanching. Here is a good rule of thumb:

8 cups (about 1 ounce/28 g each) of raw nettles will yield 1 cup of blanched, squeezed nettles (about 4 ounces/113 g). So start with double the raw weight that you need cooked.

CULTIVATION TIPS
USDA Hardiness Zones 3–11

My own stinging nettle patch began with a small plant that volunteered one year in a blueberry bush's pot (perhaps from seed that accompanied a field-dug blueberry shrub). I planted it in the ground as soon as I had the space to do so. And I was warned about nettles. "They'll take over," they said. So far, they have not. Perhaps because I shear them before they set copious seed. The plant can be invasive. Stinging nettles will grow readily from a transplanted root or runner and are not choosy about semi-shade or full sun, as long as they have enough moisture. In farmyards they flourish near manure and compost piles, and old outhouses—they appreciate good feeding. Wood nettles are more of an unknown, in terms of cultivation. They occur naturally under deciduous tree cover in humus-rich soil with plenty of moisture, albeit well drained. I think they have excellent potential as a woodland or high-shade crop.

Wilted Nettles

Serves 1

If you have never eaten nettles before, start like this. It is my favorite early-spring breakfast. Despite being very simple, it is, like so many breakfasts, a small conjuring act where you need to be on top of everything at once.

1 ounce (28 g) tender spring nettle tips
2 large eggs
1–2 popadams
1 tablespoon unscented oil
1 tablespoon butter
Salt

Drop your nettles for just 30 seconds into boiling water. Fish them out and lay them on a kitchen towel to drain.

Place the eggs in boiling water for 6 minutes. Remove the eggs and peel while hot.

While the eggs are cooking, fry the popadam in the hot oil until puffed up (turn once).

While the popadam is puffing, melt the butter in a saucepan and drop the nettles into it only long enough to heat through. Season with a pinch of salt.

Halve the eggs. Plate the hot popadam with the eggs and drizzle the nettle sauce over the eggs. Finish with some hot red chile or Wintercress Green Chile Sauce. Tuck in. This is what it is all about.

Cheesy Nettle Eggs

Serves 2

My friend Bevan Christie's mother made him "cheesy eggs" when he was little—he sent me her method. We WhatsApp each other our dinners (US–Turkey), and he tells me how to make things. I add blanched nettles to this quintessential comfort food. The result is fortifying. Bevan says it is imperative to serve the eggs with toast soldiers.

1 tablespoon Smooth Field Garlic Butter
¼ cup (about ¾ ounce/20 g) grated cheese (your favorite)
2 tablespoons milk
3 ounces (85 g) blanched, squeezed nettles
4 large eggs
1 tablespoon butter
Salt
Black pepper

Preheat the oven to 325°F (170°C).

Butter two ramekins with the Smooth Field Garlic Butter. Sprinkle a thin layer of cheese into the bottom of the dishes. Add 1 tablespoon of milk to each ramekin. Distribute the blanched nettles across the milk and cheese. Crack two eggs into each dish. Add the rest of the grated cheese, top with the regular butter, and season with salt and pepper. Slide into the oven and bake until the white has just set, 15 to 20 minutes. Good luck not licking the dish.

Nettle Grits

Serves 4 as a side

American grits are like South African mealie meal and Italian polenta. Combined with stinging nettles—a unifyingly international weed—any of them makes a universal comfort food. It can be made in any season if you have kept a stash of frozen Nettle Purée.

NETTLES

1 cup (250 ml) Nettle Purée

¼ cup (60 ml) mushroom, chicken, or vegetable broth

1 tablespoon butter, melted

GRITS

1 cup (about 5 ounces/142 g) grits, cornmeal, or polenta

2 cups (500 ml) mushroom or vegetable broth

1½–2 cups (375–500 ml) milk

¼ teaspoon salt

Place the Nettle Purée in a bowl and add the warm broth. Incorporate the butter until the mixture is very smooth.

In a pot mix the grits well with 1 cup of the cool broth. Place over medium-high heat. As the liquid warms and the mixture thickens, stir. Reduce the heat to medium-low. When the mixture becomes stiffer, gradually add another cup of broth, stirring well. As it thickens add the first cup of milk. Add the salt. Taste after about 15 minutes of total cooking time and assess the thickness. Is it cooked? Do you like the texture? Add some or all of the second cup of milk if the meal still tastes raw. Stir in half the chopped nettle mixture. Just before serving stir in the rest of the nettles, cooking until it is all warm, and serve at once.

A dab of butter, or another grating of cheese, at the end is delicious.

Nettle and Pea Risotto with Mint

Serves 2 as an entrée, 4 as an appetizer

The hearty flavor of nettles is brightened by fresh peas and a lot of mint. I often make this risotto with nettles that I have frozen in purée form (it is also useful for Nettle Grits).

NETTLE PURÉE

1 cup (4 ounces/113 g) blanched, squeezed nettles

RISOTTO

2 tablespoons butter

1½ cups (10½ ounces/297 g) arborio rice

4½ cups (1.1 liters) warm vegetable or chicken broth, plus extra

2 cups (300 g) fresh or frozen peas

3 tablespoons lemon juice

Salt

1 cup (250 ml) Nettle Purée

½ cup (½ ounce/14 g) mint leaves

¾ cup (1½ ounces/40 g) microplaned Parmigiano-Reggiano

FOR THE NETTLE PURÉE: Place the nettles in the bowl of a food processor and whiz until very fine.

FOR THE RISOTTO: Melt the butter in a pot over medium-high heat. Add the rice and stir to toast for a minute or two, stirring to prevent browning. When the rice is chalky white and smelling nutty, begin adding the warm stock, a ladleful at a time, and stir until it has been absorbed. Keep adding more stock, and keep stirring. When the rice is almost cooked through, after about 20 minutes, stir in the peas and the lemon juice. Taste, and add salt. If necessary, add some more broth—you want a slightly loose mixture, not a stiff one. Cook another few minutes until the peas are just cooked but still bright green. Stir in the Nettle Purée and the mint leaves and cook another minute. Serve at once, with Parmigiano-Reggiano on the side for the cheesehounds.

Nettle and Ramp Biscuits

Makes about 14 biscuits

In the frenzied glut of late spring, I preserve nettles by freezing Nettle Purée. Drying the purée gives you a good baking ingredient.

These biscuits can be baked at once or prepared up to the pressing-out point and then frozen for later baking.

To dehydrate nettles spread out Nettle Purée on parchment laid over a baking sheet. Put the oven on its lowest setting. Place the tray in the oven for an hour, then remove and fluff out the nettles, using a fork or your fingers. Return to the oven for another hour. Continue until the nettles feel very dry—it takes me about 6 hours. Store the dried nettles in small containers or bags and freeze for later use.

1 tablespoon plus 1½ teaspoons
   Wisteria Vinegar

1½ cups (375 ml) whole milk, plus
   extra for brushing

4 cups (480 g) flour

1 tablespoon plus 1 teaspoon
   baking powder

1 teaspoon Ramp Leaf Salt

6 ounces (170 g) butter

½ cup (125 ml) dehydrated Nettle Purée

1 tablespoon crumbled Salted Ramp Leaves

Mix the Wisteria Vinegar into 1½ cups (375 ml) of the milk and let it sit for 15 minutes, to sour.

Preheat the oven to 425°F (220°C).

In a bowl combine the flour, baking powder, and Ramp Leaf Salt. Add the cold butter, cut into pieces (or grate the butter in). Rub the butter into the dry ingredients with your fingertips until the mixture resembles coarse crumbs. Add the nettles and Salted Ramp Leaves. Stir the home-made buttermilk in gradually. Pull the dough together quickly, handling it lightly and deftly.

On a lightly floured board, pat the biscuit dough out until it is about 1¼ inches (3 cm) thick. Using a 2½-inch (6 cm) cookie cutter, press out rounds. Reshape the leftover pieces of dough and press out more biscuits. Alternatively, you can also cut the entire circle of dough like a pizza into wedges. (At this point you can freeze the dough. To bake from frozen, transfer the frozen biscuits straight to the oven and add another 5 minutes to the baking time.)

Brush the tops of the biscuits with milk. Transfer to the oven and bake for 25 to 30 minutes, until well risen and golden.

Nettle Tart

Makes 1 tart

These spring tarts are more like pizzas, relying on an absurdly easy Olive Oil Pastry that bakes to a crisp. The filling and pastry can be made a day ahead, if necessary. In summer substitute lamb's quarters, amaranth, or quickweed for the nettles.

OLIVE OIL PASTRY

2¼ cups (270 g) flour
¼ teaspoon salt
½ cup (125 ml) extra-virgin olive oil
½ cup (125 ml) tepid water

FILLING

3 tablespoons extra-virgin olive oil
1 cup (150 g) chopped field garlic bulbs
1 ounce (28 g) sheep sorrel
1 pound (453 g) blanched nettles
3 large egg yolks
1 large egg
1 cup (250 ml) crème fraîche
½ cup (125 ml) cream
¼ teaspoon salt
Black pepper

FOR THE PASTRY: Place the flour and salt in a mixing bowl and make a well in the center. Pour in the oil and water and mix until the dough adheres in a ball. Flatten the ball, wrap, and chill for an hour.

FOR THE FILLING: In a saucepan over medium heat, warm the oil. Add the chopped field garlic and sauté for about 12 minutes, until it has softened and begins to take on some golden color. Add the sheep sorrel and stir until it has wilted (it will lose its beautiful green). Turn off the heat.

Place the garlic-sorrel mixture in a large bowl and add the nettles. In a smaller bowl beat the egg yolks and whole egg with the crème fraîche, cream, salt, and about 15 twists of black pepper.

Pour the cream mixture into the bowl of greens and stir gently to combine well. Dip a finger in to taste for seasoning, unless the raw eggs bother you. In which case . . . don't.

TO ASSEMBLE: Preheat the oven to 400°F (200°C). Oil an 8-inch (20 cm) fluted tart pan with spring sides or a regular springform pan.

Roll the pastry out and press it well into the pan. Trim the sides. Gently tip the filling in and spread evenly. Bake for 40 to 45 minutes until the pastry is crisp and the center of the tart is set. Remove from the oven and release the spring sides gently. Serve hot or at room temperature.

Nettle and Lamb Stew

Serves 4

My friend Bevan Christie (of the Cheesy Eggs) also introduced me to abbacchio alla Romana, a Roman lamb stew that relies on herbs with vinegar and anchovies for its distinctive flavor. It adapts very well to wild greens. Silky nettles and young sow thistle (*Sonchus oleraceus*) melt into the sauce. Serve with field-garlic-rubbed sourdough or buttered rice.

2 tablespoons olive oil
2 pounds (907 g) leg of lamb meat, cut into 2-inch (5 cm) pieces
2 cups (500 ml) water
2 cups (8 ounces/227 g) blanched nettles
1 cup (1 ounce/28 g) young sow thistle leaves
½ cup (14 g) chopped field garlic greens
8 anchovies
2 tablespoons Common Milkweed Flower Vinegar

In a saucepan heat the oil over medium-high heat. Add the lamb in batches and brown on two sides. Add all the other ingredients except the vinegar. Bring to a boil, then reduce the heat and cook on the stovetop at a simmer for 1½ hours, covered. Remove the lid and add the vinegar, stirring well. Cook at a gentle bubble for another 40 minutes, without the lid. If it threatens to dry out, add a little water. The result should be a rich, thick juice in the bottom of the saucepan, with very tender meat.

Nettle and Fiddlehead Galette

Serves 4–6

With a vibrantly spiced and crunchy crust, this spring galette is good right from the oven, or served cool at a picnic. It makes one large galette or four small ones. While fiddleheads add wonderful texture, if you do not have any, carry on without them. The galette is delicious in pure nettle form, too.

PASTRY

1 cup (120 g) all-purpose flour

½ cup (70 g) cornmeal, plus extra for sprinkling

½ teaspoon salt

1½ teaspoons black pepper

1 tablespoon Ground Sumac

8 tablespoons butter

1 large egg yolk, beaten

3 tablespoons cold water

FILLING

2 tablespoons olive oil, divided

1 very large onion, sliced thinly

¾ teaspoon salt, divided

8 ounces (227 g) blanched, chopped nettles

¾ cup (170 g) ricotta

2 large egg yolks

1 tablespoon Ground Sumac, divided

2 teaspoons Aleppo pepper (or substitute chile flakes)

1 tablespoon plus 1 teaspoon lemon juice

1 cup (100 g) blanched fiddleheads

1 large egg, beaten

3 tablespoons milk

FOR THE PASTRY: Place the flour, cornmeal, salt, and spices in a bowl. Add the cold butter, cut into small pieces (or grate it in). Using your fingers, work the butter and the flour together until the mixture resembles coarse crumbs. Add the beaten egg and stir very well; add the cold water and give another few stirs. Work deftly and quickly with your hands until you have a cohesive ball of pastry. Flatten it and chill for an hour.

FOR THE FILLING: Heat 1 tablespoon of the oil over medium-high heat in a large skillet. Add the onion with ½ teaspoon of the salt. Cover, and reduce the heat to medium-low. Cook for 15 minutes. Remove the lid and continue to cook until the onion has caramelized—about another 15 minutes. Give the onion a stir every now and then, as it can stick.

Place the blanched, chopped nettles in a bowl. Add the cooled, caramelized onion, ricotta, egg yolks, 2 teaspoons of the Ground Sumac, the Aleppo pepper, lemon juice, and the last ¼ teaspoon of salt. Stir very well. In a small bowl toss the blanched fiddleheads in the remaining tablespoon of olive oil and add the last teaspoon of sumac to them with a pinch of salt.

TO ASSEMBLE: Preheat the oven to 400°F (200°C). Oil a large baking sheet. Whisk the beaten egg and milk together in small bowl to create an egg wash. Scatter some cornmeal on a clean surface and roll out the pastry until it is about 14 inches (35 cm) in diameter. Wrap it around your rolling pin and transfer to the oiled baking sheet. Heap the nettle filling in the middle of the pastry and spread it out, leaving a good 3 inches (7½ cm) free around the edges. Top the filling with the fiddleheads. Fold the pastry over the filling and paint with the egg wash. Slide into the hot oven and bake until the pastry is deep golden, about 45 minutes. Eat hot or allow the galette to cool on a wire rack (to avoid a steamed and soggy bottom) and enjoy at room temperature.

Nettle Soufflé

Serves 4

It is a myth that soufflés are hard to make. They *do* require attention, but there is no mystery or impossible technique to master. Roux, béchamel, eggs, seasonal ingredient: soufflé!

4 tablespoons butter

6 tablespoons (45 g) flour

2 cups (500 ml) milk

1 cup (110 g) fresh goat cheese crumbled
  into small pieces

1 cup (110 g) finely grated Manchego

5 large egg yolks

1 cup (250 ml) Nettle Purée

½ teaspoon salt

20 twists of black pepper

6 large egg whites

Preheat the oven to 425°F (220°C). Butter and flour a 2-quart (2 liter) soufflé dish.

In a pot melt the butter over medium heat. Add the flour and stir very well. Reduce the heat to low and cook the resulting roux for 5 minutes, stirring occasionally.

Increase the heat to medium-high. Slowly pour some milk into the pot, stirring continuously and rapidly. The roux will seize up and become very thick. Keep adding small amounts of milk and incorporating all the liquid before adding more. Use up all the milk, and never stop stirring. By the time all the milk has been added, the mixture should be quite thin and very smooth (if lumps have remained, whisk the mixture to break them up). Reduce the heat to low and cook gently for 10 minutes. Add the crumbled goat cheese, stirring very well to incorporate it, then add the Manchego. In a bowl whisk the egg yolks lightly. Add them to the béchamel. Stir in the Nettle Purée. At this point add the salt and pepper, stir well, and taste. You want to it to be *overseasoned*—remember you will still add the egg whites, which will dilute the seasoning. Add more salt than tastes right.

In clean bowl whisk the egg whites until they retain creamy peaks. Tip half the egg whites onto the nettle mixture. Use a spatula to fold the egg whites into the mixture, turning the bowl a quarter rotation with each lift and fold you make. Add the second half of the egg whites in the same way. When the mixture is uniformly green but still bubbly and spongy, very gently tip the contents into the prepared soufflé dish. Slide it gently into the hot oven.

Cooking times will vary but after 35 minutes, when the soufflé has puffed, open the oven slowly and give the dish a little shove. If the middle of the soufflé jiggles wetly, it needs a few more minutes. Once it barely quivers it is ready. Serve immediately. Soufflés wait for no person.

Pawpaw

OTHER COMMON NAMES: Papaw, wild banana

BOTANICAL NAME: *Asimina triloba*

STATUS: Indigenous tree, southern and eastern US

WHERE: River bottoms, woodland

SEASON: Late summer through late fall

USE: Fruit

PARTS USED: Fruit

GROW? Yes

TASTES LIKE: Tropical fruit salad

Including pawpaws in these pages is an act of hope. The hope that one day we might see this now-elusive native fruit for sale in more markets, planted in more parks, and included in more gardens. How many Americans have eaten or even seen a pawpaw, a quintessentially North American fruit?

The first pawpaws I tasted were shipped to me by Integration Acres, outside the small town of Athens, Ohio. An annual Pawpaw Festival is held there in September, founded by Chris Chmiel, Integration Acres's proprietor and a pawpaw activist. That first taste was memorable, and my eyes opened wide. It was as if a platter of freshly cut, deeply ripe pineapples, guavas, passionfruit, and mangoes had been given to me in a single, smooth mouthful. For days, while the fruit was in the house, the whole place smelled fantastic.

Pawpaw's appearance when ripe may not be working in its commercial favor. Unripe, they resemble smooth green mangoes with a kidney bean curve. But when they are ready to be eaten, they have darker, bruised-looking patches, sometimes acquired by falling from the tree, as they drop when ripe. The best pawpaws can be black. The flavor of the luminous pale orange flesh is unaffected. Slice a fruit open, and inhale. The tropics. Dip a teaspoon into it. On your tongue it feels silky, like well-set custard or the smoothest, best banana. Its flavor is intense and aromatic. And it varies from tree to tree, and cultivar to cultivar.

Apart from their vivid apricot color inside, pawpaws otherwise resemble their custard apple cousins, with large, glossy brown seeds. If you are eating the fruit fresh, the seeds are easily spat out. Each one is enveloped in a little sac with a distinctive texture and taste.

Native to woodlands and river bottoms of eastern North America, pawpaws are surprisingly cold-hardy for fruit that tastes equatorial. In their colder ranges they ripen very late in the season, making them an unusual but entirely authentic counterpart to the apples we all associate with crisp weather.

More growers—private and commercial—are embarking on pawpaw cultivation as interest in the fruit grows. In pawpaw country, and as far north as Rhode Island, local farmers markets sell pawpaws in season. Observe your local pawpaw radar to see if there is a grower near you. Saplings are available from specialty nurseries. Grow pawpaw at home or in your community garden. Trees bear fruit after eight years. Start now.

Very highly recommended reading if you are interested in learning more about this delectable fruit is *Pawpaw: In Search of America's Forgotten Fruit* by Andrew Moore (Chelsea Green, 2016). It is reminiscent of a much older kind of book, where explorers went forth to search, discover, and chronicle. But written by a twenty-something in the twenty-first century.

How to Collect and Prepare

The ripe pawpaws will be on the ground. But if your timing is impeccable and the planets are aligned, they will drop into your hand from the tree at a touch. If you have found them still on the tree, squeeze them very gently. Slight give indicates ripeness. The perfume of the fruit will also be noticeable, along with a faint bloom (like white dust). Unripe fruit *will not* ripen once picked. Ripe fruit lasts unusually

well in the fridge. The puréed pulp can be frozen for later use, too, with no change in flavor.

Turning the pulp into purée for inclusion in ice creams and other dishes is genuinely time consuming. But processing a large batch at a time allows you to freeze it in portions. First chill the fruit. Then cut it open and spoon the pulp into a bowl, working the seeds loose by hand. Spin the pulp in a food processor until it is very smooth. Store in small containers or bags, and freeze as much as you can for later use. The flavor holds up exceptionally well in the freezer.

Caution

The seeds are emetic. Do not eat them, and do not get pieces of seed into your food processor when puréeing the fruit.

CULTIVATION TIPS
USDA Hardiness Zones 5–8

Pawpaw trees usually top out at about 25 feet but remain smaller if kept pruned. They require rich soil with a slightly acidic pH and plenty of moisture, as long as the drainage is exceptional. Dry sites will not do, and neither will clay. Although they are understory trees in the wild, full sun is preferable for optimal fruit production. Two trees of different named varieties are recommended for cross-pollination and fruit-set to occur. The flowers are pollinated by flies and beetles attracted to their scent. Hanging anything smelly enough to attract flies will boost pollination!

Planting a ground cover around the tree to make a nice soft carpet for the fruit to fall on will minimize bruising.

Integration

Makes 1 drink

Creamily tropical—in a cold climate way—and with a delicately tart punch, this smooth cocktail is named after Integration Acres, the outfit whose founder, Chris Chmiel, launched the annual Ohio Pawpaw Festival held every September.

RIM

1 tablespoon lime juice
2 teaspoons Sumac Sugar

COCKTAIL

2 fluid ounces (4 tablespoons) pawpaw purée
2 fluid ounces (4 tablespoons) Sumac Vodka
1 fluid ounce (2 tablespoons) silver tequila
3–4 ice cubes

FOR THE SUGAR RIM: Pour the lime juice in a saucer. Sprinkle the Sumac Sugar in another. Dip your glass's rim in the juice and then in the sugar, working it around. Allow it to set for a minute.

FOR THE DRINK: Combine all the ingredients in a blender and pulverize until smooth. Pour into the prepared glass.

Pawpaw Salsa with Fried Plantain

Serves 4 as an appetizer

Raw, ripe pawpaw is the bomb. Which means that it is so good, it is hard to find language for it. Pawpaw season coincides with the last flush of my garden-grown shiso (perilla). They make a headily aromatic combination. Balanced with acid, chile heat, and aromatic herbs, the fruit makes an incredible condiment for fried plantain, steak, curries, corn chips . . .

SALSA

10 ounces (283 g) pawpaw purée
   (from about 1 pound/453 g pawpaws)
2 tablespoons lime juice
1 serrano pepper
¼ teaspoon salt
1 cup (about 23 g) loosely packed cilantro
¾ cup (about 18 g) loosely packed red shiso
1 tablespoon chopped scallion

FRIED PLANTAIN

3 very ripe (blackened) plantains
2 tablespoons unscented oil

FOR THE SALSA: Combine all the ingredients in a food processor and spin until it is all smoothly blended. Taste and add a little more lime juice if necessary. Chill until needed.

FOR THE FRIED PLANTAIN: Peel the fruit and cut into thick slices. Use a fork to flatten each slice, pressing the tines firmly into the flesh to leave deep grooves. Do this to each side. In a skillet warm half the oil over medium-high heat and add the plantains. Fry until one side is browning and turning soft—about 4 minutes. Flip and cook the other side. Add more oil as needed. Serve hot with the Pawpaw Salsa as a dip.

Pawpaw Pork Belly with Soy and Sweetfern

Serves 4–6

Meltingly tender slablets of pork belly are first steamed with sweetfern and then roasted in an aromatic marinade of puréed pawpaw, lime juice, jalapeño, and good soy sauce (on a bed of more sweetfern, for good measure).

2 pounds (907 g) pork belly, cut into
    8 equal pieces
¼ cup (60 ml) soy sauce, divided
4 sweetfern branches 8 inches (20 cm)
    long, or about 48 leaves
1 cup (250 ml) pawpaw purée
2 tablespoons lime juice
1 medium onion, very thinly sliced
2 jalapeño peppers, very thinly sliced

Place the pork pieces in a dish and pour 2 tablespoons of the soy sauce over them. Turn them so that they are coated in soy sauce.

Place a steamer basket in the bottom of a large pot, and fill with water to just below the basket base. Place two sweetfern branches (or twenty-four leaves) in the basket and nestle the pieces of pork belly on top. Top the pork with another sweetfern branch (or twelve leaves). (You may need two pots and baskets for the steaming, depending on your setup.) Cover the pot, bring the water to a boil over high heat, and reduce the heat to low to maintain a steady amount of steam. Steam for 3 hours. Check the water level a couple of times and top up if necessary.

In a bowl combine the pawpaw purée, lime juice, the rest of the soy sauce, the onion, and the jalapeño. Stir to combine.

Preheat the oven to 350°F (180°C).

Remove the pieces of belly from the pot. Gently slice off the skin, taking away half of that top fat layer, too. (You can save the skin pieces for roasting on their own in a skillet—a good, fatty snack, or good for adding in small pieces to stews and dumplings.) Lay the leaves of the remaining sweetfern branch in an ovenproof dish or skillet. Place the pieces of belly on top. Pour over the marinade, and turn the pork pieces to coat well. Tuck any exposed sweetfern leaves back under the meat (to prevent scorching). Transfer to the hot oven and roast for 1 hour. Pull it out once to add a splash of water and to turn the meat.

To serve, cut the meat across the grain into thin slices.

Aromatic Pawpaw Chicken

Serves 4

Penetratingly aromatic pawpaw is a superb match for homegrown ginger, turmeric, cardamom leaves, and Thai lime. (I grow ginger and turmeric as shade-loving annuals in Brooklyn and overwinter the other plants indoors.) These native and exotic flavors combine to make a sensational roast chicken. Serve with sticky rice.

⅓ cup (80 ml) pawpaw purée
3 tablespoons soy sauce
1 chicken
1 tablespoon ground spicebush, divided
10 fresh ginger leaves, divided
6 fresh turmeric leaves, divided
2 fresh Thai lime leaves, divided
¼ cup (60 ml) Common Milkweed Flower
    Vinegar (or substitute apple cider vinegar)
1 cup (250 ml) coconut milk
Salt

Preheat the oven to 450°F (230°C).

Combine the pawpaw and soy sauce in a small bowl and mix well. Loosen the skin of the chicken over the breasts and spoon some of the pawpaw mixture into this pocket. Massage the skin gently to distribute it evenly. Place 2 teaspoons of the ground spicebush into the bird's cavity with half the ginger, turmeric, and lime leaves. Place the rest of the leaves in the bottom of a Dutch oven. Lay the chicken on top. Pour the remaining pawpaw mixture over the bird along with the vinegar and coconut milk. Sprinkle the rest of the spicebush over the chicken along with a large pinch of salt.

Cover, and transfer to the oven to roast for about 55 minutes. Remove the lid and allow the bird to brown as it cooks for another 25 to 30 minutes, or until a skewer inserted between thigh and drumstick draws clear juice. The skin should be very dark and crispy by this time.

Transfer the bird to a serving plate and allow it to rest for at least 10 minutes. Pour any cavity and resting juices into its roasting pan with a splash of water. Stir over medium heat and taste; adjust the seasoning if necessary. Carve the chicken and plate it with the warm roasting juices poured over before serving.

Pawpaw Fool

Serves 4

Somewhere between a fool and a syllabub, this delicate rum-and-lemon-inflected pawpaw froth will make you lick your bowl. Or glass. And spoon.

4 strips lemon zest, about 2 inches (5 cm) long
¼ cup (60 ml) rum
1¼ cups (310 ml) cold cream
3 ounces (85 g) powdered sugar
⅔ cup (160 ml) cold, very smooth pawpaw purée

At least 12 hours before making the fool, macerate the lemon zest in the rum in a small, covered bowl or jar with a lid. Keep chilled. Strain before adding to the cream.

Whip the cream with half the sugar until it holds soft peaks. Fold in the pawpaw purée. Stir in the strained rum. Taste. Because pawpaws vary in sweetness, you may want to add the rest of the sugar now. Fold it in gently. Spoon the fool into glasses or small bowls and serve at once. (If you let it sit for some hours, the cream will separate from the liquid.)

Pawpaw Ice Cream

Makes about 1 quart (1 liter)

A friend who has a well-traveled palate said that this was the best ice cream he had ever eaten when he tasted it after supper at our house one October night. That may be your reaction, too, especially if the tropical flavor of pawpaw is new to you. The first time I made it, I used no sugar at all—the fruit was overripe and intensely sweet and aromatic. Use your judgment, and let your tongue decide.

1½ cups (375 ml) pawpaw purée
¼ cup (50 g) sugar
1½ cups (375 ml) cream, chilled
1 tablespoon lemon juice
1 tablespoon plus 1 teaspoon Cachaça (or white rum)

Place the pawpaw purée in a bowl with half the sugar and mix well. Add the cream, lemon juice, and liquor and stir. Taste. More sugar may not be necessary, but if the mixture isn't sweet enough for you, stir in the rest, a tablespoon at a time. Transfer to your ice cream maker and churn until done (about 20 minutes). If you will be freezing it in a bowl, whip the cream first, before adding the other ingredients, and pour into a bowl or dish that contains the mixture to 2 inches (5 cm) deep.

Pawpaw Mousse

Makes 8 small mousses (3½ fluid ounces) or 1 large mousse (3½ cups)

⅓ cup (75 g) superfine sugar
1½ cups (375 ml) cold pawpaw purée
1 cup (250 ml) cold cream
1 cup (250 ml) cold yogurt
1 packet gelatin
¼ cup (60 ml) just-boiled water

In a small bowl mix the sugar and the pawpaw purée. Whip the cream in another bowl until soft peaks form. Stir the yogurt into the cream. Gently fold the pawpaw mixture into the cream.

Sprinkle the gelatin onto the hot water in a small bowl and whisk with a fork until it has completely dissolved. Pour the water into the mousse mixture, stirring gently but well.

Scoop the mousse into ramekins or a single mold. Cover and transfer to the fridge until set, about 3 hours.

Unmold by dipping the base of the mold into very hot water and sliding a hot knife around the edges. Invert onto a plate and shake the plate and mold vigorously until a sucking sounds signals the mousse's intention to let go.

Pawpaw Spice Cake

Makes 1 cake

This moist cake sings pawpaw. The salt in the nut topping is very important—do not forget it. Pecans, walnuts, or pine nuts could be substituted for the hazelnuts.

TOPPING

½ cup (70 g) toasted and
    chopped hazelnuts
2 tablespoons sugar
1 tablespoon ground spicebush
Large pinch of salt

CAKE

4 ounces (113 g) butter
8 ounces (227 g) sugar
1¾ cups (210 g) all-purpose flour
2 large eggs
¾ cup (190 ml) pawpaw purée
2 tablespoons yogurt
1 tablespoon bourbon
¼ teaspoon lemon zest
⅛ teaspoon salt
1 tablespoon baking powder

Preheat the oven to 350°F (180°C).

Prepare an 8-inch (20 cm) springform pan by lining the bottom with a circle of parchment paper, and lining the sides with parchment standing just above the rim of the pan.

FOR THE TOPPING: In a small bowl mix the chopped nuts with the sugar, spicebush, and salt.

FOR THE CAKE: In a large bowl beat the butter with the sugar until pale. Sprinkle a little of the flour onto the mixture and then add the eggs, beating as you go. Add the pawpaw pulp. When it is smoothly incorporated, add the yogurt, bourbon, the rest of the flour, the lemon zest, salt, and baking powder. Spoon the batter into the prepared pan.

Sprinkle the nut topping over the batter very evenly.

Slide into the oven and bake for 65 to 75 minutes, or until an skewer *inserted all the way* (the bottom can remain sticky) comes out clean.

Remove the cake from the oven and place the pan on a cooling rack. Release the spring, remove, and gently pull off the parchment. After the cake has cooled, lift it carefully from its base, remove the remaining parchment, and transfer to a serving plate.

Pawpaw and Olive Oil Loaf

Makes 1 loaf

Any bake with pawpaw is very moist, and in this aromatic loaf fresh ginger and cardamom seeds act as aromatic Asian counterweights to the wild American fruit.

1 cup (250 ml) pawpaw purée
½ cup (125 ml) extra-virgin olive oil
½ cup (125 ml) water
1 tablespoon microplaned fresh ginger
2 large eggs
1 cup (200 g) sugar
2 cups (240 g) all-purpose flour
1 teaspoon baking soda
2 teaspoons baking powder
Seeds of 2 cardamom pods
¼ teaspoon salt

Preheat the oven to 350°F (180°C). Butter an 8 by 5 inch (20 × 13 cm) baking pan.

In one bowl combine the pawpaw purée, olive oil, water, ginger (with its juice), eggs, and sugar. Beat until combined smoothly. In another bowl combine the flour, baking soda, baking powder, cardamom pod seeds, and salt. Gradually add the dry ingredients to the wet mixture and beat until the mixture is smooth. Pour this loose batter into the prepared pan and transfer to the oven. Bake for 1 hour, or until a fully inserted skewer comes out clean.

14-Karat Pawpaw Cake

Makes 1 double-layered cake

I adapted this headily spiced cake from a recipe in *The Singing Kettle Cookery Book*, published by the Union of Jewish Women in South Africa and edited by Selma Brodie. I am convinced that this cake is the prototype for all the other 14-karat cakes clogging the Internet.

CAKE

2 cups (240 g) all-purpose flour

2½ teaspoons baking powder

1½ teaspoons baking soda

1 teaspoon salt

2 teaspoons ground spicebush

1 teaspoon ground cinnamon

4 large eggs

2 cups (400 g) sugar

1⅓ cups plus 1 tablespoon (350 ml) vegetable oil

8 ounces (227 g) grated carrots

6 ounces (170 g/½ cup) pawpaw purée

1 tablespoon freshly grated ginger

4 ounces (113 g) chopped pecans

FROSTING (OPTIONAL)

8 ounces (227 g) cream cheese

2 tablespoons pawpaw purée

1 tablespoon lemon juice

2 cups (227 g) powdered sugar

12 pecan halves

FOR THE CAKE: Preheat the oven to 350°F (180°C). Butter two 8-inch (20 cm) springform cake pans and line the bottom of each with a circle of parchment paper.

In a bowl combine the flour, baking powder, baking soda, salt, spicebush, and cinnamon. In another bowl beat the eggs with the sugar until thoroughly blended. Pour in the oil and stir very well. Stir in the carrots, pawpaw, ginger, and pecans. Now add the dry ingredients slowly to the wet mixture. Pour the batter into the two prepared pans and slide carefully into the oven. Bake until an inserted skewer comes out clean, about 55 to 60 minutes.

FOR THE FROSTING: In a bowl beat the cream cheese with the pawpaw purée and the lemon juice. Add the powdered sugar and beat until it is very smooth. When the cakes are cool, frost each half and sandwich them. Garnish with the pecan halves.

Persimmon

OTHER COMMON NAMES: Common persimmon, possumwood

BOTANICAL NAME: *Diospyros virginiana*

STATUS: Indigenous tree, mostly east of the Rockies.

WHERE: River valleys and hardwood forests, parks

SEASON: Late fall and early winter

USE: Fruit, aromatic

PARTS USED: Ripe fruit, leaves

GROW? Yes

TASTES LIKE: Conventional persimmons, dried dates

As the first real cold nips at late autumn's heels, local grocery stories begin to light up with trays of bright persimmons. These are cultivars of Asian species, either the large and squat tomato-shaped fruit generally referred to as 'Fuyu', or the acorn-shaped 'Hachiya', though there are dozens of different cultivars of this eastern Asian tree, *Diospyros kaki*.

For observant nature lovers and foragers, there is another persimmon: the underappreciated native American tree, *D. virginiana*, whose small berries (technically) cling to the branches of tall trees well into winter. American persimmon is distributed through the eastern and midwestern United States and south to Florida. At the time of this writing, it is listed as threatened and of special concern in New York and Connecticut, respectively. (Farther south and west, and into Mexico, another native, *D. texana*, turns glossily and disconcertingly black when ripe.)

I associate these little persimmons with shorter days, dark afternoons, and warm light streaming from the windows of townhouses onto Brooklyn streets. The air prickles with the anticipation of quintessentially American holidays: Halloween, Thanksgiving. Fallen leaves crunch underfoot, and the air has a clarity unknown in summer. It is a lucky forager out hunting for mushrooms and acorns who comes across the tree's bright yellow leaves and wrinkled ripe fruit on the ground, and looks up: bounty. It is easy to return home with a generous sackful of this indigenous tree candy, luscious when ripe.

To preserve a windfall, push the entire, fully ripe persimmons through a medium-mesh sieve, colander, or food mill and freeze the pulp for later use. This pulp is a very friendly ingredient, delivering persimmon salsas, chiffon cakes, cheesecakes, spiced loaves, and muffins. Even cocktails.

Native Americans dried the fruit in quantity. And in late fall I love to prepare *hoshigaki*, the dried persimmons traditionally made with large Asian fruit, which sweetens magically as it hangs, even if unripe when peeled. This East Asian technique requires the fruit to be peeled, which is quite easy with the large, pointed 'Hachiya' and squat 'Fuyu', but which demands commitment with the small, native fruit. The effort is worth it, because the dried fruit lasts a year or more, flavor intact. Whereas the large fruit turn dark and rich like dates, the smaller persimmons dry much harder with a flavor reminiscent of sweetened rose water. I eat them as a luxurious snack or soak them in water (or tea, or booze) to soften them for baking and cooking. A very appealing aspect of the hoshigaki process is how pretty the persimmons look hanging as they dry, like luminous ornaments when the year is turning dark. I hang my drying persimmons in a sunny window (where my Thai limes are overwintering). Most traditional instructions say to suspend them from the "eaves," but in Brooklyn we are hard-pressed for eaves. And if left outdoors the squirrels would have a feast. Anywhere dry and airy will do.

While the small American persimmons dry in about ten days, the larger Asian fruit take weeks, aided by a light daily massage to redistribute their more ample sugars

How do you know your persimmon is ripe? The deeper orange the fruit, the riper it will be. Ripe fruit is soft, and its skin is a little wrinkled. And your tongue will tell you. In the case of the small American persimmons, you can afford to cut a few in half and do a taste test. If there is any hint of dry furriness on your tongue, leave them for a few more days before processing.

How to Collect and Prepare

Unripe native persimmons do not ripen well after being picked. Ideally you harvest them ripe from the tree or the ground below, and they can persist on the branches into winter. A good shake dislodges them and allows you to gather the fallen fruit. If you intend to make hoshigaki, try to pick them with a little piece of stem attached, to make hanging easier.

CULTIVATION TIPS
USDA Hardiness Zones 4–10

The obvious ornamental appeal of a persimmon tree is its spectacular display of fruit clinging to bare branches well after leaves have dropped. And the reward is its honey-sweet fruit. Persimmons are low-maintenance and fairly drought-tolerant. Trees in full sun produce the most fruit. *D. virginiana* is not small; it can grow to about 60 feet, so it is unsuitable for small gardens. Buy a named cultivar and ask whether it is self-fertile—meaning you only need one for fruit production. (Wild persimmons are dioecious—needing a male and a female tree.) Provide plenty of moisture (and good drainage) until the tree is established.

Twilight

Makes 1 drink

Muddling jelly-ripe persimmons with cognac yields a very flavorful, thick maceration. The shaken drink, lifted with spicebush and grounded with bitters, is the color of fall twilights, before the long nights arrive hard, and early.

PERSIMMON COGNAC

4 ripe persimmons, peeled and
   finely chopped
½ cup (125 ml) cognac or brandy

COCKTAIL

3 fluid ounces (6 tablespoons)
   Persimmon Cognac
1 fluid ounce (2 tablespoons) Northeast
   No. 1 Bitters
1 fluid ounce (2 tablespoons) Spicebush
   Clementine Cordial

FOR THE COGNAC: In a jug muddle the finely chopped persimmons with the cognac. After 1 hour strain the cognac through a fine-mesh sieve, pushing against the sieve to squeeze as much out of the fruit as possible.

FOR THE COCKTAIL: Shake all the ingredients up, strain, and pour

Persimmon, Citrus, and Roast Beet Salad

Serves 4

The beautiful farm Babylonstoren outside Cape Town in South Africa serves some of the best and most imaginative salads I have eaten. And guests staying overnight at their hotel are invited to pick whatever they like—ripe oranges, fat beets, edible weeds, and persimmons (Asian), in season—from their stunning kitchen gardens. Foraging for dinner in this playground has been one of the delights of my life.

2 pounds (907 g) baby beets
½ teaspoon ground spicebush
¼ teaspoon salt
3 oranges (pink Cara Cara are beatifically
   ideal), segmented, juice reserved
1 Meyer lemon, segmented, juice reserved
8 ripe persimmons, peeled and cut in half
3 ounces (85 g) watercress, washed
   and dried
2 tablespoons Quick Honeysuckle Vinegar
1 tablespoon Fermented Honeysuckle Cordial
⅛ teaspoon salt
3 tablespoons walnut oil
Black pepper
¼ cup Spicebush Pecans

Preheat the oven to 400°F (200°C).

Wash the beets very well and trim their tails and stems—leave ¼ inch (½ cm) of stems. Cut them in half. Arrange them on an oiled baking sheet, sprinkle with spicebush and salt, cover with foil, and roast until they are tender, about 40 minutes. Remove and reserve.

On a serving platter arrange the beets, oranges and lemon, persimmons, and watercress. Whisk together the reserved orange and lemon juice, Quick Honeysuckle Vinegar, Fermented Honeysuckle Cordial, and salt. Whisk the oil in last. Drizzle the vinaigrette over the salad just before serving, season with pepper, and scatter the Spicebush Pecans over the top.

Sunchoke Soup with Persimmon Prickly Ash Oil

Serves 4

Sunchokes are incredible native American plants. As I write this, in early fall, I look out the window and see them standing 12 feet tall at the back of our garden, not yet in bloom. I dig them in late November through December—persimmon season. Because they are aggressive spreaders, I make an effort to find and remove every single tuber. Every year I replant just three, and they bounce back.

There is one trick with sunchokes, and it is important: Like burdock root, they contain indigestible inulin, which causes gas. Before eating them slice them thinly and soak in water for an hour (if you will be eating them raw), or boil them before adding to soups and stews.

Honey-flavored persimmons flavor a sweetly piquant oil for drizzling across the top of this creamy soup. Use the same salsa for chip dipping, of course. If you have not made Prickly Ash Paste, substitute 2 roast red chiles, very finely chopped, and add those to the salsa.

SOUP

1 pound (453 g) peeled and
  sliced sunchokes
2 tablespoons oil
1 teaspoon ground spicebush
½ cup (125 ml) clementine juice
4 cups (1 liter) chicken broth
1 tablespoon lemon juice
Salt

PERSIMMON SALSA

1 cup (200 g) very ripe, peeled,
  chopped persimmons
2 teaspoons sugar
2 teaspoons lemon juice
1 tablespoon Prickly Ash Paste

PERSIMMON OIL

3 tablespoon Persimmon Salsa
2 tablespoons extra-virgin olive oil

FOR THE SOUP: Bring a pot of water to a boil and add the sliced sunchokes. Boil for 5 minutes, then turn off the heat and cover the pot. After an hour drain the water from the tender sunchokes and rinse them. Over medium-high heat warm the oil in the pot. Add the sunchoke slices, spicebush, and clementine juice. Cook until most of the juice's moisture has evaporated. Add the chicken broth, increase the heat, and cook at a simmer for 5 minutes. Add the lemon juice. Stir and taste, adding salt if desired. Allow the liquid to cool a little and purée until smooth in a blender. Pour through a strainer back into the saucepan.

FOR THE SALSA: Either chop the fruit finely by hand, and then combine in a bowl with the other ingredients, or process everything in a food processor. Taste. You are looking for the perfect balance of hot, sweet, sour, and salty. Adjust the seasoning if necessary. (The salsa will keep in the fridge for 4 days, covered.)

FOR THE OIL: In a bowl whisk together the salsa and the olive oil.

TO SERVE: Heat the soup until it simmers, scoop into bowls, and drizzle a teaspoon of the Persimmon Oil across the top.

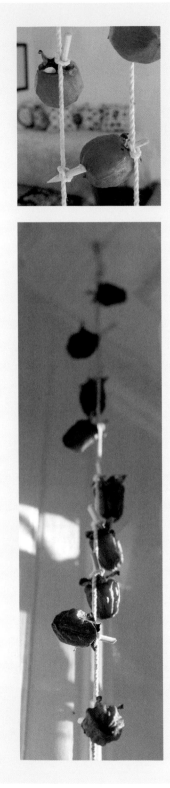

HOSHIGAKI

The traditional East Asian technique of drying substantial Asian persimmons works well with the small, native American species. The native fruit remind me of sweet rose water when dried—a flavor very different from their date-like large cousins. With native persimmons you *must* use ripe fruit: Drying unripe native persimmons does not result magically in a sweet, dried fruit, as with both the pointy 'Hachiya' and the fat-bottomed 'Fuyu'. The drying period is also shorter, and the preparation is more fiddly, and sticky. While a vegetable peeler can work with large persimmons, for the small ones you need a very sharp knife, nimble fingers, and perseverance. Having said that, it is very rewarding. I use all the fruit by the time the next windfall is ready.

What you need: Ripe persimmons, ideally with a piece of stalk attached. This is just easier for hanging. If they are windfalls, or shaken from the tree, use one small, stainless-steel screw for each persimmon, screwing it into the top of the fruit to make an attachment for the string. Also, kitchen twine.

Preparing the fruit: Peel the persimmons with a very sharp knife. If they are very ripe, you can pull the paper-thin skin off the flesh without much cutting. After peeling, dip them in just-boiled water (or vodka or gin), to clean the outside. Wash your hands well. If you are using screws, firmly screw one into the top of each fruit, leaving the head and shank protruding for your string. I tie my persimmons in long strings: Tie string around the stalk that is still attached to the fruit (or around the screw), leaving a space of one imaginary persimmon before tying on another fruit. Depending on where you will hang them, you can make long strands, like holiday lights.

Hanging the fruit: Hang the strings of fruit in a sheltered place. Outside is fine as long as no rain or animals can reach them. Mine hang indoors in a south-facing window, surrounded by sparkly winter holiday lights. Traditional hoshigaki are given a regular massage. This is a lot of fun. The idea is to distribute the sugars evenly in the fruit. It also softens the hardening exterior.

Drying the fruit: Drying times vary a lot, depending on humidity. But the small native fruit will be dry enough to store anywhere from about 10 days to 3 weeks.

Eating the fruit: The dry fruit is chewy but delicious. Eat the hoshigaki out of hand, serve them on a cheese plate (with their softer, large persimmon cousins, for contrast and fun), macerate them in booze (rum, brandy, and Calvados are good), cut them up into salads, mix them into granola, or reconstitute them by soaking and then use them in chutneys, pies, bakes, and braises.

Persimmon and Paprika Pork Stew with Sweetfern

Serves 4

Dried persimmons last so well for so long that I find myself making this autumnal stew just a month or two ahead of the new persimmon season (which is November, in my neck of the city woods). The fruit becomes luxuriously soft with soaking and slow-cooking and infuses succulent pork butt with its aroma, boosted by sweetfern. Serve with grits or Sweetfern Polenta.

4 ounces (113 g) hoshigaki, cut in half

¼ cup (60 ml) Fermented Elderflower Cordial

1 cup (250 ml) white wine

2 tablespoons butter

1½ pounds (680 g) pork butt, cut into
2-inch (5 cm) chunks

¼ teaspoon salt

8 medium shallots

5 ounces (142 g) finely chopped carrots

2 tablespoons tomato paste

1 tablespoon smoked paprika

8 sweetfern leaves

2 tablespoons lemon juice

2 cups (500 ml) chicken broth

Soak the hoshigaki for 6 hours before cooking the stew by placing them in a small bowl or jug and adding the cordial and the wine.

Melt the butter over medium-high heat in a pot. Season the pork with the salt. Add the pork to the pot and brown it on all sides, working in batches if the pot is overcrowded. Remove the browned pieces to a plate and reserve. Reduce the heat to medium and brown the shallots in the butter and fat. Cover the pot and shake it a few times as they brown— about 15 minutes. Add the carrots, tomato paste, and paprika, stirring well. Return the pork to the pot and pour in the liquid that the persimmons were soaking in. Stir very well to loosen the brown bits stuck to the bottom of the pot. Add the persimmons, sweetfern, lemon juice, and enough chicken broth to cover. Bring the liquid to a boil and then reduce the heat to maintain a gentle simmer while covered. Cook for 3 hours. Taste toward the end and add more salt if needed. When it is ready the pork will be very tender and there should be enough sauce that you can serve the dish with soup spoons.

Before serving scoop off the floating fat that will have rendered from the butt during the slow-cooking (the stew also reheats very well, so you can make this a day ahead and more easily remove the cold fat after the pot has been in the fridge overnight).

Persimmon Brandy

Makes 2 cups (500 ml)

A good batch of hoshigaki makes a wonderful infusion with brandy (or rum, or Calvados, for that matter).

2 cups (about 180 g) hoshigaki
2 cups (500 ml) good brandy

Remove any dry calyxes or stems from the fruit. Place them in a clean jar and pour in enough hooch to cover. Leave this to soak for at least a month before tasting. Strain when the brandy is well flavored, and just leave the fruit in the jar and dip from it as you need the infusion. The soaked fruit can also be cut up and used in savory stews as well as desserts.

Spicebush Duck Legs with Persimmons and Brandy

Serves 4

This is a late-fall and early-winter dish in our house, when I revel in the first persimmon forage. The native persimmons *must* be very ripe; otherwise your mouth will be left feeling furry, even after they have cooked. Serve the duck with grits, *rösti*, or mashed potatoes.

4 whole duck legs (thigh and drumstick)
¼ teaspoon salt
⅓ cup (80 ml) Persimmon Brandy
1 teaspoon ground spicebush
2 large onions, quartered
12 bayberry leaves
8 very ripe native persimmons
2 tablespoons honey
1 tablespoon lemon juice
½ cup (125 ml) water

Preheat the oven to 350°F (180°C).

Trim any excess fat from the duck legs. (You can freeze the fat for later use in Fir-Smoked Roast Potatoes.) Sprinkle the salt all over the duck and let it sit for 15 minutes. Heat a large saucepan over medium-high heat. Add the duck legs to the pan and brown for a few minutes on each side. Add the brandy and let it bubble for a few seconds. Add all the other ingredients, place a lid on the saucepan, and reduce the heat to cook at a gentle simmer for 2 hours. Scoop off the melted fat. Taste for seasoning and add salt if necessary.

Preheat the broiler. Place only the duck legs on a tray and roast them under the broiler for 8 to 10 minutes just to brown them. Return them to their hot pan and serve at once.

Persimmon Focaccia

Makes 1 focaccia

This focaccia, developed in early autumn with the previous season's hoshigaki, is moist and pillowy, with a slightly sticky crust. While this recipe works well with large 'Hachiya' or 'Fuyu,' the small native fruit have a lighter aroma and taste. Serve it simply, with good butter, or with cheese.

2 tablespoons honey

1 cup (250 ml) bergamot tea (like Earl Grey)

4 ounces (113 g) hoshigaki

Warm water as needed

1 tablespoon instant yeast

3½ cups (420 g) all-purpose flour

1 teaspoon salt

1 tablespoon butter cut up into small pieces

1 tablespoon olive oil

1 tablespoon sugar

Dissolve the honey in the hot tea. Remove any stalks or dried calyxes from the persimmons. Place the fruit in a bowl or jug and cover them with the honeyed tea. (If it does not cover them, add more tea.) Soak for 12 hours. Dried native persimmons tend to get very hard and will take some time to soften.

Remove the soaked persimmons from their tea and cut each persimmon in half. Measure the leftover tea (they will have absorbed a lot). Add warm water to this so that you have 1½ cups (325 ml), total. Add the yeast to this warm (but not hot) liquid.

Place the flour in a bowl with the salt. When the yeast froths pour it into the flour. Add the cut-up tablespoon of butter. Stir the mixture. Once it is cohesive work it in the bowl with your hand. It should be quite sticky and loose (if it is very stiff, add a little more water right after you have stirred it—flours differ). Knead the dough and pull it back and forth for about 5 minutes, stretching the glutens. Form it into a rough ball. Butter a clean bowl and transfer the dough to it. Cover and let rise until doubled in size—about an hour.

Butter and flour a skillet 10 to 12 inches (25–30 cm) across (this will give you a focaccia about 2½ inches/6 cm tall). Transfer the risen dough to a clean surface and punch it down. Add two-thirds of the persimmons to it, in stages. Push them into the dough and keep folding it over them. When all the fruit is incorporated, fold the dough into a round loaf shape. Transfer it, seam-side down, into the prepared skillet. Scatter the rest of the persimmons across the top and push them into the dough with your fingers. Cover and let rise until double in size.

Preheat the oven to 450°F (230°C).

When the dough has risen, drizzle the olive oil across the top and sprinkle with the sugar. Slide gently into the hot oven and bake for about 25 minutes. Reduce the heat to 425°F (220°C) and bake for another 20 minutes. It should be dark brown with a bit of bounce when pressed. Eat it warm, or when it has cooled. It is delicious the next day, too.

Persimmon and Mahlab Fruitcakes

Makes 12 muffin-sized cakes or 1 large round cake

A slice of fruitcake with hot, strong coffee (or Sauternes, for that matter) is a rare and seasonal treat. I age these cakes by pouring a little brandy over them every week. Our local Middle Eastern emporium, Sahadi's, stocks up on glacé fruit for the holidays, and that is where I am lucky enough to find citron as well as exceptionally lush dates. The hoshigaki, chokeberries, and serviceberries are my own, of course. Substitute dried cherries or raisins for the latter two. If you will be aging the cakes, bake them 4 weeks before icing and eating—or distributing—them.

   This recipe doubles well.

1 pound (453 g) dates

4 ounces (113 g) candied citron (or candied lemon peel if you can't source any)

4 ounces (113 g) candied orange peel

1 pound (453 g) golden raisins

6 ounces (170 g) Dried Fermented Serviceberries

6 ounces (170 g) Dried Fermented Chokeberries (see Black Chokeberry Syrup)

6 ounces (170 g) hoshigaki, cut up

½ cup (125 ml) brandy (or Persimmon Brandy)

4 ounces (113 g) pecans

4 ounces (113 g) shelled almonds

2 cups (240 g) all-purpose flour, divided

4 ounces (113 g) butter

2 cups (400 g) sugar

5 large eggs

2 tablespoons milk

1 teaspoon mahlab

½ teaspoon baking soda

1 teaspoon salt

FOR AGING (OPTIONAL)

1 cup (250 ml) brandy

FOR THE FRUIT: The day before you bake, pit the dates and cut into pieces no bigger than ½ inch (1 cm). Cut the candied citron and orange into dice no larger than ¼ inch (½ cm). Place these, along with all the other dried fruit, in a large bowl and pour the brandy over them. Mix well with your hands, cover, and leave overnight.

FOR THE CAKES: Preheat the oven to 350°F (180°C).

Spread the pecans and almonds out on a baking tray and toast in the oven for 10 to 12 minutes. When they have cooled chop them roughly.

Reduce the oven's heat to 275°F (140°C). Butter a twelve-muffin pan or one 8-inch (20 cm) cake pan.

Add ½ cup of the flour to the brandied dried fruit, and stir well or mix with your hands.

In another mixing bowl, cream the butter with the sugar. Beat in the eggs and the milk. Gradually beat in the rest of the flour along with the mahlab, baking soda, and salt. Add the fruit mixture to this bowl and use your hands (really, it is much easier than a spoon, because the mixture is so thick with fruit) to mix thoroughly.

Spoon the cake mixture into the muffin or cake pan. Do not expect a big rise, here, so fill the spaces to within ¼ inch (½ cm) of the top.

Transfer to the oven and bake for about 1 hour and 15 minutes for the muffin size. A skewer must come out clean, although with all the fruit it is harder than normal to tell.

For a round cake pan, you will need 3 hours.

TO AGE THE CAKES: For the small cakes, pour about ½ to 1 teaspoon of the brandy onto the top of each one, then wrap them in cheesecloth or linen. Place them all together in a large food-safe container where they fit snugly without being squished. Make sure there is cheesecloth between each cake so that they are not touching sides. For a large cake slowly pour ¼ cup (60 ml) over it before wrapping. Close the container and leave at room temperature for a week (a cool basement would be ideal, but mine simply live on top of the fridge). After a week unwrap them. The smell when you pop the lid is wonderful—fruity and spicy and very good. Bathe each with another ½ teaspoon of brandy (for small cakes), or 4 tablespoons of brandy (for a large cake), allowing it to seep in. Wrap, return to the container, and repeat for 4 weeks.

ROYAL ICING

1½ pounds (680 g) marzipan

⅓ cup (80 ml) rose hip or apricot jam

1 tablespoon water

1 pound (453 g) powdered sugar

3 large egg whites

½ teaspoon lemon juice

The cakes are delicious without icing, but decorating them does make them more festive.

TO ICE: Cut the marzipan into sections and roll out thinly. Make sure it is wide enough to cover the cake or cakes.

In a small saucepan warm the jam and water over low heat, stirring to loosen. Brush the warmed jam thinly over the top and sides of the first cake. Drape the marzipan over the cake and press firmly to make sure it sticks. Trim any overhanging edges around the base. Repeat until all the cakes are covered.

Sift the powdered sugar into a bowl. Add the egg whites and lemon juice and beat until very glossy and they hold a soft peak. Spread this Royal Icing over one cake at a time and top at once with your favorite edible decorations (when it dries they will not stick). Repeat with the next cake.

Once it is dry the Royal Icing turns into a hard, bulletproof shell. Now you wrap the cakes in ribbon and give to friends. But save some to eat, too.

Persimmon Spicebush Cakes

Makes 1 large cake or 8 small cakes

The color of turning leaves, this aromatic cake has autumn written all over it. While you can bake it in a round or square 8- or 9-inch (20–23 cm) pan, I like to make individual cakes as holiday gifts, baking them in pans with six slots each 3¾ inches (9½ cm) wide. Chestnut honey is ideal here, but it is mouth-melting with any honey and can be made with molasses, too. I can seldom resist breaking one open, warm from the oven, and spreading it with butter. They are denser the next day, but still wonderful.

4 ounces (113 g) hoshigaki
3 tablespoons bourbon
¼ cup (60 ml) water
1 cup (250 ml) dark honey
1 cup (250 ml) boiling water
4 ounces (113 g) butter
½ cup (100 g) sugar
1 large egg
2½ cups (300 g) flour
1½ teaspoons baking soda
½ teaspoon salt
2 teaspoons ground spicebush
1 teaspoon powdered mustard
1 teaspoon cattail pollen
1 tablespoon Sumac Sugar, for brushing
1 tablespoon water, for brushing

Preheat the oven to 350°F (180°C). Lightly butter your cake pan or pans.

FOR THE PERSIMMONS: Remove the dry stems and calyxes from the hoshigaki. Place them in a small bowl with the bourbon and water. Cover. Allow them to soak for 12 hours, turning them once so that the top fruit get a soaking, too. After they have absorbed all or most of the liquid, chop them into small pieces. The centers may still be tough, so watch your fingers.

FOR THE CAKE: In a jug or small bowl, mix together the honey and boiling water; stir to dissolve the honey. In a bowl cream the butter and sugar until light and fluffy. Beat in the egg. Gradually add the dry ingredients, alternating with the honey-water. Mix well. Stir in the persimmons.

Pour the fairly loose batter into the prepared pan or pans. Transfer to the hot oven. For a large cake bake about 35 minutes; for the smaller cakes, 18 to 20 minutes. An inserted skewer must come out clean. Turn them out carefully. Mix the Sumac Sugar and water and brush this over the tops of the cakes quickly while hot.

Pokeweed

OTHER COMMON NAMES: Poke, polk, poke salad, polk sallet, pigeonberry

BOTANICAL NAME: *Phytolacca americana*

STATUS: Indigenous perennial, considered a weed

WHERE: Disturbed ground, mostly east of the Rockies, in the southern states and sporadically on the West Coast

SEASON: Spring

USE: Vegetable

PARTS USED: Cooked young shoots and immature leaves

GROW? Yes

TASTES LIKE: Cooked green beans meet asparagus, but essentially poke

In midspring southern foragers' mouths begin to water. In Kentucky my friend Sheila Neal-Leger licks her lips. It is poke season. Every year she fries up the tender shoots and makes what her family calls Kentucky Egg Rolls. They have been eating them for generations.

In New York City I head out to my pokeweed spots in early May, scouted during the growing year, and sometimes discovered in winter, when pale canes mark the spot. The previous season's toppled stems are brittle and hollow, and skeletons of the old berry clusters are distinctive. In May in the woods and open places an edible spring is roaring, with violets and dandelions in bloom, garlic mustard

setting buds, and elm trees bending under the weight of their tender samara. At ground level succulent new poke shoots push up through the dead and crackling debris of winter leaves. I slice the supple green stems and bring them home, and we eat these juicy cooked vegetables steadily over the next two to three weeks, as different colonies emerge in their microclimates from winter hibernation.

Pokeweed is a prolific and widespread indigenous perennial, rising from bare earth to 6 feet tall and across in a matter of months. It sprouts effortlessly from fallen seed. It thrives on neglect, at home in disturbed ground in city lots and in country fields. It is the target of horticultural ire, a lot of herbicide, and more misunderstanding and mistrust.

This native American edible is in the green eye of a circling storm where opinions whip around it in a fury of contradiction. In swaths of the South and in isolated foraging pockets across the country, poke is a much-anticipated wild vegetable. Sheila, a fifth-grade science teacher, remembers her mother getting so excited she slammed on the car brakes when she saw poke coming up along the fencerows. But in agriculturally minded laboratories, pokeweed is viewed as dangerous: Horses and cows have been poisoned by pokeweed. Pigs that have snouted out the root—considered the most toxic part—have been sickened or killed. And certainly, toddlers who swallowed the berries whole have been admitted to emergency rooms. People who have eaten the plant raw have been sickened.

But for Native Americans pokeweed was food. And if it was good enough for the Cherokee and the Iroquois, it is good enough for me. I just eat it. Cooked.

As with Japanese knotweed, some foraging resources will tell you to eat shoots of a certain height, no more. This makes little sense, and wild foods author Samuel Thayer's explanation of when to eat certain plants is a balm—the meristem, the actively growing part of the plant,

is tender and snappable. That is what we should eat. To put it in context, think of the asparagus. What part of it do we eat? The tender, growing shoot, which is that meristem, actively growing and cell dividing. A good asparagus is tender. So, too, with pokeweed shoots. If they are easily snapped or sliced with no hint of tough fiber, they are good to eat. Even tall poke that has not yet branched has tender tips, and I have snapped these off as I walk by, to cook and eat at home.

The parts of pokeweed we do not eat are the roots, mature stems, mature leaves, and berries. The ripe, glossy purple berries are actually fine to eat (they are beautiful but taste horrible); it is the seeds they contain that are a problem. Unripe fruit are toxic. But to return to our asparagus comparison: Do we eat mature asparagus fronds, which resemble ferns? No. And do we eat their attractive, toxic red berries? No. We have become inured to the broader context of the vegetables we see in a supermarket aisle, and most people would not even recognize an asparagus plant. We have forgotten that vegetables are plants, and parts of a whole. And different parts behave in different ways. We do not eat green potatoes (talk about deadly nightshade!): They could kill us. We do not eat rhubarb leaves. Or uncooked kidney beans. They would make us sick.

So why do animals that eat pokeweed sicken? Mostly, they seem to be eating the rhizome. And herbivores also eat leaves and stems at all stages of growth. A *lot* of them. Raw. Cows can't cook.

But nobody (yet) is lab-testing the plant within a culinary context. And that is frustrating. Cow habits are not human habits. And humans have been eating pokeweed for a very long time.

"I openly discuss the known presence of toxins," wrote Thayer in an email, "but also acknowledge that this is perhaps the most commonly eaten wild vegetable in North America." He writes at length about pokeweed in his book *Incredible Wild Edibles*. I recommend you read it before diving in.

I usually blanch poke shoots or young leaves for a minute or two in ample boiling water before refreshing in cool water and drying (Thayer recommends cooking for longer). But for Sheila's traditional family Kentucky Egg Roll recipe, I dip the raw young shoots straight into egg and fry them up, with no parboiling. They are incredible, but read the Caution section before making them; fry them long enough to cook thoroughly, but also eat in moderate amounts. Gabrielle Langholtz, the author of *America: The Cookbook*, calls pokeweed "the best vegetable I have eaten." (Yes, I made her eat them, blanched and tossed with lime juice and olive oil.)

Enjoying this American vegetable safely is a question of knowing what part to eat, and when. And of cooking it first. Perhaps one day science will validate both our instincts and generations of native tradition.

is best described as explosive diarrhea. Neither the friend who prepared the dish, nor anyone else who ate the dish, became ill.

Eat pokeweed in well-informed moderation.

Caution

Never eat pokeweed raw. Despite one of its common names, it is *not* salad. Avoid all parts of pokeweed that are not the spring shoots or very tender young leaves. The shoots should be tender and easily sliced or snapped by hand. Again, Samuel Thayer's book *Incredible Wild Edibles* describes pokeweed preparation at length; personally, I choose to parboil pokeweed only for a minute or two, and I do not reboil. Thayer's method is to boil more than once in changes of water.

How to Collect and Prepare

Slice fat, tender young shoots with a sharp knife, or simply snap them (they will be more tender toward the unbranched, growing tip). At home the shoots last well with their bases in a bowl of water, covered in the fridge. I have also wrapped them in damp paper, placed them in a plastic bag, and left them in the crisper drawer for up to 2 weeks. They have amazing longevity. To eat, err on the side of caution and peel any red membrane from young, tender shoots. To be as safe as possible, parboil the shoots in ample boiling water. I do provide a recipe for shoots fried without boiling, but I have never stuffed myself on these Kentucky Egg Rolls, eating three or four at most. Mike Krebill, author of *The Scout's Guide to Wild Edibles*, was once persuaded to try very young, *white*-colored pokeweed shoots (possibly collected too near the rhizome?) that had been deep-fried for 45 seconds. "They tasted excellent," he said, and he gorged. What followed

CULTIVATION TIPS
USDA Hardiness Zones 4–8

Pokeweed grows tall and wide once established. Grow it if you have the space and the horticultural discipline to cut off the flowers to prevent its spread via ripe fruit. New plants germinate very readily from dropped seeds. Once established the plant is hard to remove, even by digging, and it has invasive tendencies. Pokeweed likes well drained soil with generous moisture and will grow in full sun or dappled shade. Grow from seed, sowing in spring after your last frost through late summer, when the fruits naturally ripen and fall. You could also try growing it in a very roomy container, about 16 inches or more in diameter. Each plant will give you a small handful of spring shoots to eat.

Kentucky Egg Rolls

Serves 4 as an appetizer

My foraging friend Sheila Neal Leger is a Kentucky native whose family has eaten fried poke, which they call Kentucky Egg Rolls, for decades. Nobody has dropped dead or exploded. These tidbits are juicy and addictive, a spring ritual. Sheila fries her poke shoots raw, rather than boiling them first (see the Caution section). Dropping the shoots into boiling water for a minute will not affect their flavor (the texture will differ), if you prefer to err on the side of caution. Enjoy in moderation.

16 tender pokeweed shoots
2 large eggs
3 tablespoons water
½ teaspoon salt, divided, plus extra
¾ cup (90 g) flour
¼ cup (35 g) cornmeal
½ cup (125 ml) unscented oil
4 lemon wedges

Prepare the pokeweed shoots by washing them and peeling off any red membrane. Pat dry.

Whisk together the eggs, water, and ¼ teaspoon of the salt. Pour into a shallow bowl. Mix the flour and cornmeal with another ¼ teaspoon of salt and place in another shallow bowl or plate.

In a wide saucepan, heat ¼ cup (60 ml) of the oil over medium-high heat.

Dip each pokeweed shoot in egg wash, shake off the excess, and dip into the flour mixture, coating each side. Transfer the coated shoots to the hot oil in the skillet. Add more coated shoots, up to four at a time. Fry them on each side until dark gold in color, about 5 minutes. Turn and cook the other side. The poke stem should be very tender when bitten into. Add more oil to the pan as needed.

Place the fried shoots on a paper towel and sprinkle with some extra salt. When all the shoots have been cooked, serve them immediately, with quartered lemons on the side.

BLANCHING POKEWEED

To prepare poke shoots, skin any red membranes from the stems. Bring a pot of water to a boil. Drop the poke in the water, and cook at a boil for a minimum of 60 seconds and up to 3 minutes. Haul the poke out, and plunge it into a cold-water bath. Remove and pat dry. Now you are ready to rock and roll.

Pokeweed Bruschetta

Serves 4 as an appetizer

I know, I know: Anyone can make bruschetta. But this one is really so good that it warrants being written down. The contrast between crisp, garlicky toast and succulent poke shoots is fantastic. Good bread: That is really the only knack to good bruschetta. And a dusting of concentrated Ramp Leaf Salt is the secret to bruschetta nirvana.

12 tender pokeweed shoots, lower leaves
    trimmed off
4 slices sourdough bread
3 fat field garlic bulbs
2 tablespoons extra-virgin olive oil
¼ teaspoon Ramp Leaf Salt
¼ teaspoon Aleppo pepper

Cook the poke shoots in boiling, salted water for about 3 to 4 minutes, until the stem is easily pierced with a sharp knife. Drain, refresh, and pat very dry. Toast the bread until the edges are slightly blackened. While the toast is hot, rub the field garlic cloves over the slices and drizzle them with some of the olive oil. Top the slices with the pokeweed, cutting or folding the shoots, if necessary, to fit. Top with the rest of the oil, sprinkle with Ramp Leaf Salt, and add a dusting of pepper. Serve at once.

Pokeweed Shoots Grilled with Miso Butter

Serves 4 as a side

Juicy pokeweed shoots respond well to aggressive seasoning. Combining salty miso with the slight char of grilling or broiling wraps the vegetable in flavor and preserves the succulence inside.

20 pokeweed shoots
2 tablespoons butter
2 tablespoons yellow miso

Trim all the lower leaves off the pokeweed shoots and strip off any red membrane on the stalks (save the tender leaves you pick off for a sauce or an omelet filling, after blanching). Bring a pot of water to a boil. Drop the pokeweed shoots in for 1 minute. Drain, refresh in cold water, and dry well.

Preheat the broiler, if using.

In a small bowl mash the butter and the miso to form a sticky paste. Transfer the paste to a small pot and melt over low heat. Lay the poke shoots in a dish and brush the miso paste over them. Broil or barbecue for 4 minutes on one side, then turn, brush with more butter, and broil or barbecue the other side. Serve warm or at room temperature.

Pokeweed with Anchovy Butter

Serves 4 as an appetizer

One of the best ways I know to eat raw vegetables is as *bagna cauda*—in a warm bath of olive oil, garlic, and anchovy. With pokeweed, which must not be eaten raw, I turn the idea upside down and pour the addictive sauce over the blanched stalks.

20 pokeweed shoots
3 tablespoons extra-virgin olive oil
1 tablespoon butter
6 anchovies
12 field garlic bulbs, chopped
1 lemon

Pull the lower leaves off the pokeweed (save them for another use, after blanching). Skin any red membrane from them, too. Drop the shoots into boiling water until just tender, 3 to 4 minutes. Drain, refresh under cold water, and pat dry.

Preheat the broiler.

In a small pot over medium heat, heat the oil and butter with the anchovies and field garlic. Stir to break up the anchovies. After a minute reduce the heat to low. Cook until the garlic is tender (it must not brown).

Cut two opposite sides off the lemon, leaving the center part behind. Using your hand, squeeze the juice from the center into the anchovy pot. Lay the cut sides juicy-side up under the broiler.

Lay the pokeweed on a baking sheet, drizzle all the anchovy oil mixture over the shoots, and slide under the broiler. Cook until the sauce is sizzling—about 3 minutes. Remove to a serving plate and serve at once with the grilled lemon pieces to squeeze onto the shoots, and good bread to mop up the plate.

Pasta with Pokeweed Shoot and Mushroom Sauce

Serves 2

You can substitute oyster, morel, or thinly sliced young pheasant back mushrooms if your spring forage has been especially rewarding. I like broad egg yolk noodles for this dish, but the sauce is a delicious topping for grilled chicken, poached eggs, or toast.

1 tablespoon olive oil
1 pound (453 g) button mushrooms,
    finely sliced
1 tablespoon lemon juice
½ cup (125 ml) whipping cream
Salt
8 young pokeweed shoots, blanched for
    1 minute
Black pepper
8.8 ounces (250 g) egg yolk pappardelle
    or tagliatelle
½ cup (30 g) microplaned
    Parmigiano-Reggiano

In a large pan over high heat, warm the oil. Add the sliced mushrooms and sauté, stirring, until they are turning brown and cooked through, about 12 minutes. Add the lemon juice and stir well. Pour in the cream, stirring it well to scare up any brown pan residue. Allow the cream to bubble for 30 seconds. Reduce the heat to medium. Season with salt to taste. Now stir in the blanched pokeweed shoots and allow them to heat through.

While the sauce is cooking, cook the pasta. Drain, add the al dente pasta to the pokeweed pan, and toss well. Sprinkle with Parmigiano-Reggiano and season with black pepper just before serving on warm plates.

Grilled Pokeweed Pitas

Serves 2

Moist pokeweed sandwiched inside crisp pita and a cloak of melted cheese? The best kind of fast food. I like to use pocketless pitas for these.

3 strips bacon (optional)
8 tender pokeweed shoots
1 tablespoon butter
2 pocketless pita breads
2 thick slices raclette (or your favorite melty cheese)
¼ teaspoon Ramp Leaf Salt

If you're using bacon, heat the oven to 450°F (230°C). Cut each strip of bacon in half. Lay the bacon on a baking sheet and roast in the oven until crisp, about 12 minutes. Drain on a paper towel.

Bring salted water to boil in a pot over high heat. Add the poke shoots. Cook at a simmer until just tender, 3 to 4 minutes. Drain, refresh, and dry well. In a skillet melt the butter over medium heat.

Lay four poke shoots across half of each pita. Top with the cheese. Sprinkle with Ramp Leaf Salt. Top with the bacon, if using. Fold the other half of the pita over this filling and press down very firmly to flatten. Transfer to the skillet. Use another pan or a foil-covered brick to weigh the pitas down while they cook, about 4 minutes. Turn. Weigh down again. The cheese should be melted, the pita crisp and dark gold. Eat at once.

Sloppy Josephinas

Makes 4 buns

My spicy version of a sloppy joe filling, very good on a brioche or other soft bun, or served straight up—messily good food that honors pokeweed's unpretentious culinary roots.

3 tablespoons oil
1 large onion, finely chopped
3 scallions, sliced lengthwise, then in half
8 field garlic bulbs, chopped
¼ teaspoon salt
10 tender pokeweed shoots
3 tablespoons black bean sauce (I use Lan Chi brand)
1 tablespoon sugar
3 chipotle chiles, soaked and chopped finely
1 tablespoon chile flakes
1½ pounds (680 g) ground pork
½ cup (125 ml) water
2 teaspoons lemon juice
4 brioche or potato buns

In a large skillet heat the oil over medium heat. Add the onion, scallions, field garlic, and salt. Cover and cook for 10 to 12 minutes. Remove the lid and cook another 5 minutes, until the mixture begins to brown.

While the onion mixture is cooking, boil a pot of water and add the prepared pokeweed stems. Cook until tender, about 4 minutes. Drain and reserve.

To the skillet with the onion mix, add the black bean sauce, sugar, chipotle, and chile flakes. Stir well. Cook another 2 minutes. Now push this mixture to one edge of the pan in a heap. Turn the heat to high. Add the ground pork, breaking it up with a wooden spoon. Cook for 5 minutes. Stir the meat into the onion mixture and add the water. Cook at medium-high heat until the water has evaporated. Add the pokeweed stems and the lemon juice and turn gently to coat them with sauce and heat through.

Pile the mixture onto the sliced buns and serve at once. Pass the napkins.

Pokeweed Ribolitta

Serves 4

My recipe for this reassuring minestrone relative calls for field garlic, but other wild alliums like ramps or three-cornered leeks can be substituted. Serve the stewy soup with a side of toast rubbed with a field garlic clove.

2 tablespoons olive oil

6 slices pancetta, cut into slivers

3 stalks celery, finely sliced

12 field garlic bulbs, plus leaves,
    finely chopped

2 tablespoons tomato paste

4 cups (1 liter) vegetable or chicken broth

1 teaspoon sugar

1 pound (453 g) pokeweed shoots and
    leaves, blanched

2 cups (150 g) cooked (or canned) beans

Squeeze of lemon juice

Salt

Black pepper

½ cup (30 g) microplaned
    Parmigiano-Reggiano

Heat the olive oil in a pot over medium heat. Add the pancetta pieces, the celery, and the field garlic bulbs (reserve the leaves); sauté for 10 minutes, stirring to prevent sticking. Add the tomato paste and cook for a minute to allow it to caramelize a little. Pour in the broth, add the teaspoon of sugar, and stir well. Cook for 30 minutes at a simmer, until the celery is very tender.

Cut the blanched pokeweed stems into ¼-inch (½ cm) pieces. Add these to the pot with the cooked beans, and bring back to a simmer. Add the lemon juice. Taste for seasoning and add salt and pepper. Before serving sprinkle the finely grated cheese over the soup and add a flourish of freshly ground black pepper.

Prickly Ash

OTHER COMMON NAMES: Common prickly ash, northern prickly ash, American Sichuan (my name), toothache tree, southern prickly ash, pepperwood, Hercules-club

BOTANICAL NAMES: *Zanthoxylum americanum*, *Z. clava-herculis*

STATUS: Indigenous tree

WHERE: Woodlands, meadow edges in eastern North America and southeastern US

SEASON: Spring through late summer

USE: Spice, herb

PARTS USED: Tender leaves, fruit

GROW? Yes

TASTES LIKE: Sichuan peppercorns with strong citrus zest

Prickly ash are thorny little trees whose scraggly appearance seldom invites closer attention. They often grow closely together, forming an impenetrable thicket due to their thorns. The modest fruits, ripening in early fall, do not look particularly special—until you learn that this is a species of the Asian tree that produces Sichuan peppercorns. Then you sit up and take notice.

The fruits of the Asian species of *Zanthoxylum* are the spice known variously as Sichuan peppercorns, Japanese peppercorns, and *sansho*, among other names, used in cuisines ranging from Japan east to Nepal and into India. In North America *Zanthoxylum americanum* (prickly ash) and *Z. clava-herculis* (southern prickly ash), native to eastern and southeastern North America, respectively, have very similar characteristics. When you consider that *Zanthoxylum* belongs to the intensely aromatic Rutaceae family, it makes sense: Its members include the citrus fruits we all know, and also some of the most intensely scented fynbos herbs I use in South Africa.

My local prickly ash is *Z. americanum*, which is more cold hardy than its southern cousin. Its waxy fruits ripen to red, whereas the fruit of southern prickly ash, or the toothache tree (so named for its helpful mouth-numbing properties), remain a fuzzy green.

Prickly ash's distinctive effect begins with a floral and lemony sourness on the tongue, evolves into a tingling of the lips, and ends with a disconcerting numbing of the tongue. It is

fun to watch people taste the fruit for the first time, straight off the tree. It is as much about buzzing sensation as it is of flavor. As a young man on one of my wild food walks chewed, his eyes opened wide and he asked in alarm, "What is *happening*?" It is a refreshing reaction to food.

The edible offerings begin in spring and are an ephemeral delicacy. I was taught to use prickly ash's barely unfurled leaves by a Japanese woman named Kiyoko, who attends many of my forage walks (and from whom I have learned at least as much as I may have imparted). "Sansho!" she exclaimed in real excitement when we spotted prickly ash in Brooklyn. Until then I had used only the fruit, but sansho leaves are prized in Japan as a herb. In early spring I pick tiny young leaves and include them as a final flourish in fresh summer rolls, where their lemony tingle gives a kick. Pulsed with herbs for raw sauces, their zing is unmistakable. Added to mild sashimi or assertive grilled mackerel, they are exquisite. As I played with them I began to use the mature leaves in the same way I might use curry leaf in dishes. This is not traditional, but it is very effective.

So-called Sichuan pepper trees are not related to black peppercorns (a tropical vine), but ripe, red prickly ash fruit when dry does superficially resemble pink peppercorns. When the little drupes are picked and begin to dry, the edible and flavorful pericarp splits from the glossy black seed inside. The seed itself is tasteless.

The unripe, green prickly ash fruits are as interesting as their riper iterations. The Japanese call them *mi sansho*, and their flavor is piercingly bright. I use the entire raw fruit, not worrying about the juicy seed inside. When dry the vivid green fruit turns a dull color, and its flavor mellows. If you want to remove the seeds (which harden as the fruit dries), simply shake them out when the husks split. Similarly, the dry red ripe fruit mellows to a tawny color, and its flavor remains undiminished for at least a year.

Prickly ash is listed as endangered in several states, due to land clearing and deforestation. But up in Canada, a cow-farming Instagram friend has so many on her land that she resents them: Her cows get stuck in the thickets. In Brooklyn, I have two small trees at home in pots (purchased from a nursery in Alabama), so I have a good supply of the spring leaves that I have grown to love.

One day I may have fruit.

How to Collect and Prepare

In early spring pick the tiny emerging leaflets to eat as a delicacy. They will last well in a small bowl of water in the fridge. More mature leaves can be collected after spring. Fruit can be picked unripe or ripe and left spread out on parchment to air-dry, when the husks will split from the glossy seeds. If you have a large quantity of fruit and want to separate flavorful husk from tasteless seed, sieve the dried fruit through two sizes of strainer, a large and then a medium mesh.

CULTIVATION TIPS
USDA Hardiness Zones 3–9

Prickly ash is a small tree and is suitable for urban gardens. *Z. americanum* spreads by underground runners and can form colonies. Prune off any clones that pop up if you want to contain it. Both species grow well in full sun or semi-shade, but more sun means more fruit. For fruit you need male and female trees, and often nurseries will not know what they have until the plants are more mature. The leaves are very aromatic, regardless.

Prickly Ash Oil

Makes about ⅔ cup (160 ml)

This tingling condiment—hot, fresh, and astringent—transforms salads, sandwiches, summer rolls, curries, and cold noodles. In spring use the young leaves, and later in the season use the fresh green fruit, whole. Store the oil in the fridge, *never* out on the counter; if you do, you are courting botulism. Its flavor lasts well for about 3 months.

2 ounces (57 g) tender springtime prickly ash leaves or unripe fruit

4 fresh red chile peppers (like ripe serrano), sliced

1 teaspoon salt

½ cup (125 ml) unscented oil

Pick the prickly ash leaflets from their midribs and place in a small bowl with the chiles and salt. Mix together, cover, and let sit for 48 hours at room temperature. On Day 3 pulverize the ingredients in a spice grinder or chop them exceptionally finely. Return to a small bowl and add the oil. Stir very well. Transfer to a clean jar, seal, and keep in the fridge. Stir before using.

Prickly Ash Paste

Makes ⅓ cup (80 ml)

Yuzu kosho is a hot red Japanese condiment made with yuzu (*Citrus junos*) peel and chiles. In my forager's version I add native prickly ash and substitute Meyer lemons, more easily procured than aromatic yuzu. The prickly ash's cooling astringency balances the fiery chiles. The recipe doubles well.

12 Meyer lemons

10 serrano or other hot red chiles

2 tablespoons dried prickly ash fruit

1 tablespoon salt

Microplane or peel the skin from the washed lemons. Remove the stems from the chiles and chop roughly. Transfer the lemon peel, chiles, and prickly ash fruit to a spice grinder and pulverize, stopping to scrape down the sides every few seconds. When the mixture is very fine, transfer it to a bowl and add the salt. Using a fork, mix until very well blended. Store in very small, clean jars. Keep in the fridge.

Grilled Figs with Prickly Ash Paste

Serves 4 as an appetizer

When I eat figs raw (the best way), I like them to be firm. But often store-bought figs can be overripe and syrupy. What to do? Aromatic, sweet, and salty, they become perfect cocktail snacks for late summer. Substitute basil if you do not have perfumed shiso leaves.

6 very ripe figs
2 tablespoons lime juice
2 teaspoons toasted sesame oil
1 tablespoon Prickly Ash Paste
12 shiso (perilla) leaves

Preheat the broiler.

Cut each fig in half. Drizzle with a little lime juice and a few drops of sesame oil. Top each half with about ¼ teaspoon of Prickly Ash Paste. Place the figs on a lightly oiled baking sheet and slide under the broiler. Remove them when their edges are beginning to caramelize—about 8 to 10 minutes. To serve, place each fig half on a shiso leaf and enjoy warm.

Avocado, Spring Prickly Ash, and Chive Blossom Salad

Serves 2 for lunch, 4 as an appetizer

Prickly ash leafs out when garden chives bloom. Combine their pungent flavors with creamily bland avocado for a simple but vibrant salad.

2 ripe avocados
Salt to taste
2 teaspoons prickly ash leaflets, picked from midrib
⅓ cup (10 g) chive blooms, flowers separated
2 tablespoons lime juice
Black pepper

Peel and dice the avocados and arrange in a bowl. Season with salt. Top with the prickly ash leaflets and chive blossoms. Sprinkle with lime juice and finish with freshly ground pepper.

Prickly Ash Quick Pickled Brussels Sprouts

Serves 4

Just past midsummer prickly ash fruit are fully formed but still green. Their scent is very strong—floral and citrusy. I use them often. These are my favorite quick pickles: crisp, tingling, and salty, while keeping their assertive cabbage character. Serve with cocktails or as a side to a spicy curry or rich stew. They are delicious last-minute additions to Southeast Asian–style curries, too.

1 pound (453 g) brussels sprouts, trimmed and halved

3 tablespoons soy sauce

3 tablespoons lemon juice

3 tablespoons sriracha sauce

1 tablespoon plus 2 teaspoons sugar

1½ teaspoons salt

2 teaspoons fresh unripe prickly ash fruit, crushed

2 teaspoons microplaned ginger

1 teaspoon toasted sesame oil

¼ cup (7½ g) field garlic or scallion greens

In a bowl combine all the ingredients except the field garlic and mix well. Let sit for at least 1 hour and up to 3 days in the fridge. Add the field garlic or scallion greens just before serving.

Cucumber and Green Prickly Ash Salad with Mango

Serves 4

The suggestive lemoniness (twice removed and somehow intensified) of unripe prickly ash fruit is beautiful with juicy cucumber and ripe mango and turns this salad into a smooth, crisp, sweet-and-sour flavor bomb.

1 teaspoon fresh whole unripe prickly ash fruit (or ½ teaspoon green husks)

1 teaspoon salt

4–6 Persian cucumbers

2 very ripe mangoes

2 tablespoons lime juice

1 teaspoon smoked paprika (or substitute regular paprika, ancho powder, or red chile flakes)

With the flat of a knife, crush the fresh prickly ash with the salt. (If it is dry, crush the husks in a pestle and mortar.) Whack the cucumbers with the heavy handle of a chef's knife, or a rolling pin. Cut the whacked cucumbers into 1-inch (2½ cm) pieces. Place the cucumber in a bowl with the prickly ash salt and muddle (the crushing allows the flavors to penetrate). Let sit for 30 minutes. Peel and slice the mango into slivers. Place it in a bowl with the lime juice and allow it to sit for 30 minutes.

Just before serving plate the cucumber and its juices with the mango. Sprinkle the smoked paprika across the top.

Spring Forage Eggs

Makes 22 deviled eggs

Buy good eggs from happy hens and pull together your best forages. The suggestions below are just that: Improvise! Lemony prickly ash and pungent ramp set the tone of the stuffing, but you could use whatever wild microgreens are showing up in your hood, whip Ramp Aioli and Garlic Mustard Pestos into the yolks, add Miso Ramps (or field garlic), try Fir-Cured Gravlax as a topping, or select from your collection of herb salts.

11 eggs

Leaflets from 4 tender prickly ash leaf stems, finely chopped

¼ teaspoon Ramp Leaf Salt

2 tablespoons Ramp Aioli

1 tablespoon Field Garlic Leaf Oil or Ramp Leaf Oil

Black pepper

GARNISHES

2 salted anchovy fillets, cut into slivers

8 thin slices Fir- and Juniper-Cured Duck Breasts

2 tablespoons garlic mustard microgreens

1 teaspoon Field Garlic Leaf Oil

½ teaspoon Prickly Ash Paste

Place the eggs in a pot, cover with cold water, and bring to a boil. Boil for 1 minute. Turn off the heat and leave the eggs in the water for 8 minutes. Pour off the hot water and add cold. When the eggs are cool, tap them, then roll them on a surface to loosen the shells. Peel the eggs. Cut in half.

Scoop the yolks out of half the eggs, mash them in a bowl with a fork, and add the prickly ash leaflets, Ramp Leaf Salt, Ramp Aioli, Field Garlic Leaf Oil, and pepper to taste. Arrange the eggs on a serving dish and top with slivers of anchovy, curls of duck prosciutto, the wild microgreens, drops of Field Garlic Leaf Oil, and flecks of Prickly Ash Paste.

Prickly Ash and Soy Marinated Salmon

Serves 4

This dish evolved from my serial gravlax-making experiments and yields a highly perfumed piece of grilled fish. I prefer to cook this salmon over coals, but a broiler works, too. Because moisture has been drawn from the salmon in the curing process, it will cook faster than you expect. Serve with a sharp and sweet salad, like Fast Mango and American Burnweed.

1 side salmon, about 2 pounds/907 g

1 cup (250 ml) soy sauce

½ cup (100 g) sugar

1 tablespoon finely crushed unripe prickly ash

Rinse and dry the fish well. Place it skin-side down in a dish that accommodates it without bending or folding, and pour the soy over. Sprinkle the sugar on top of the meat and top with the prickly ash. Cover the fish closely with plastic wrap or parchment paper, and transfer to the fridge.

After 24 hours, turn the salmon over, cover, and chill for another 24 hours.

Place the salmon skin-side down on an oiled grill over well-ashed coals. Cook until the skin crisps and blisters—the time will depend on the size and strength of the fire and the height above the coals—but about 8 to 10 minutes. Turn carefully. Cook the second side more briefly until barely done—about another 4 minutes.

Prickly Ash Pork with Garlic Scapes

Serves 4

Prickly ash oil adds a last-minute slick of vitality to a spicy, early-summer ground pork stir-fry. This is delicious with Cold Udon Noodles with Daylily Buds.

1½ pounds (680 g) ground pork
3 mature prickly ash leaf stalks
3 tablespoons unscented oil
¼ cup (60 ml) soy sauce
3 tablespoons lime juice
2 tablespoons sugar
2 teaspoons hot chile flakes
12 garlic scapes, tough ends and tips trimmed off
¾ cup (190 ml) water
2 tablespoons Prickly Ash Oil

Heat a skillet over medium-high heat. Add the pork and break it up with a wooden spoon. Cook until it has browned all over—about 12 minutes. Add the prickly ash leaves and the oil, and stir well. Add the soy, lime juice, sugar, and chile flakes. Stir again. Add the garlic scapes and water, and cover with a lid. Reduce the heat to low and cook until the scapes are very tender, about 12 minutes. Remove the lid, increase the heat again, and cook off any additional moisture. When the meat is a rich, oily brown, it is ready. Stir in the Prickly Ash Oil. Eat hot, or let the meat cool and then serve it chilled on a hot night with cold noodles.

Pork and Prickly Ash Ramp Leaf Packages

Makes 20 small packages

Steamed ramp leaves become sweetly edible wrappers for a pork filling where prickly ash hums its high lemony, mouth-cooling note. Serve with steamed sticky rice. The leftover steaming juices in the pot make a restorative broth: Just heat, and add all the dipping sauce ingredients!

DUMPLINGS

40 ramp leaves
1 pound (453 g) ground pork
1 tablespoon microplaned ginger
1 teaspoon Prickly Ash Paste
1 teaspoon Prickly Ash Oil
2 tablespoons soy sauce
1 large ramp bulb, grated
½ teaspoon Ramp Leaf Salt

DIPPING SAUCE

3 tablespoons soy sauce
1 tablespoon sugar
1 tablespoon microplaned ginger
1 teaspoon Prickly Ash Paste
2 teaspoons lime juice

FOR THE DUMPLINGS: Wash the ramp leaves. Leave them wet.

In a bowl mix the pork with the ginger, Prickly Ash Paste, Prickly Ash Oil, soy sauce, and grated ramp bulb.

Spoon 1 heaped tablespoonful of the pork mixture onto the end of a ramp leaf. Roll the leaf toward its empty side. Place this bundle at one end of a second leaf, with the exposed, meaty side facing down the new leaf's midrib. Roll to cover the exposed sides. Rest the finished bundle seam-side down on the work surface as you move on to the next bundle. When they are all assembled, transfer them to the fridge to rest for an hour.

TO STEAM: Place a steamer basket over water in a pot with lid. Arrange the leaf bundles snugly in the basket. Cover. Turn the heat to high and bring the water to a boil. Reduce the heat to maintain a steady simmer and constant source of steam. Steam for 8 minutes, sprinkle the Ramp Leaf Salt across the dumplings, and steam another 2 minutes, until firm.

FOR THE DIPPING SAUCE: Mix all the ingredients in a small bowl. Dip each dumpling into the sauce as you eat.

Prickly Ash Meatballs in American Burnweed Broth

Serves 4

This black-pepper-hot broth is soothing and slapping at the same time. Save the chicken meat for a marinated salad or sandwiches with Ramp Aioli. And if you don't have burnweed, substitute cilantro stalks.

BROTH

4 chicken thighs

1 medium-large onion, finely chopped (1½ cups/375 ml)

4 cloves garlic

1 cup (30 g) tender American burnweed stalks, finely chopped

2 Thai lime leaves (or 2 long pieces Meyer lemon peel)

2 teaspoons palm or unrefined sugar

1 teaspoon black pepper

3 tablespoons fish sauce

1 tablespoon lime juice

MEATBALLS

1½ pounds (680 g) ground pork

⅓ cup (20 g) panko bread crumbs

3 tablespoons fish sauce

1 tablespoon ground prickly ash

2 teaspoons sugar

2 teaspoons red chile flakes

1 teaspoon black pepper

FOR THE BROTH: Place all the broth ingredients except the fish sauce and lime juice in a pot and cover with 6 cups (1½ liters) water. Bring to a boil over high heat, then reduce the heat to a simmer. Cook for 1 hour. Strain the broth, keeping the chicken for another use, and return the broth to the pot. Add the fish sauce and lime juice. Taste for seasoning and adjust if necessary.

FOR THE MEATBALLS: Thoroughly mix all the meatball ingredients in a bowl. Wet your hands and form the meatballs into Ping-Pong ball sizes. (These can be made 24 hours in advance.)

TO COOK: Bring the broth to a boil in the pot. Drop the meatballs into the broth. They will cook in about 4 to 5 minutes. Serve straight from the pot into bowls, with a scoopful of broth poured over.

Grilled Pork and Green Prickly Ash Meatballs

Makes about 24 meatballs

I serve these aromatic meatballs with a plate of lettuce leaves, American burnweed, nasturtium leaves, and Thai basil, a dipping sauce on the side, and fire-roasted tropical vegetables like plantain and guava.

MEATBALLS

1½ teaspoons unripe prickly ash fruit
¾ teaspoon salt
2 pounds (907 g) ground pork
2 tablespoons fish sauce
½ cup (30 g) panko bread crumbs
1½ tablespoons chile flakes

FRUIT

2 limes
1 ripe plantain (optional)
12 ripe yellow guavas (optional)

LEAVES

24 large American burnweed leaves
24 nasturtium leaves
24 Boston or oak-type lettuce leaves
24 sprigs each of Thai basil, mint,
    and cilantro

DIPPING SAUCE

¼ cup (60 ml) fish sauce
2 tablespoons palm or unrefined sugar
2 tablespoons lime juice
1 teaspoon chile flakes
¼ teaspoon crushed unripe prickly ash fruit

Soak eight wooden skewers in water.

FOR THE MEATBALLS: Using a chef's knife, chop and crush the prickly ash with the salt into a paste. Place the pork in a bowl. Add the prickly ash salt paste, fish sauce, bread crumbs, and the chile flakes. Mix well. Form the meat into balls 1½ inches (4 cm) in diameter. You should have about twenty-four. String three meatballs onto each skewer and chill for 1 hour. Remove 20 minutes before grilling.

FOR THE FRUIT: Cut the limes in half. Slit the skin of each plantain on one side, top-to-bottom.

FOR THE LEAVES: Wash and dry the leaves and arrange them on a plate.

FOR THE SAUCE: Combine the fish sauce and sugar and stir until the sugar has dissolved. Add the lime juice, chile, and crushed prickly ash.

TO COOK: Wait until your coals have begun to ash over and then cook the meatballs on one side for about 10 minutes, until dark brown. Flip. Grill the other side. While they are cooking, place the whole guavas as well as the plantain over the coals. Turn a few times. They will char slightly, and the plantain will begin to split as it cooks. They are done when they are soft. Peel and slice the plantain. Arrange the meatballs and grilled fruit on a platter with the leaves or in their own bowls.

TO EAT: Wrap half a meatball in a large lettuce leaf or American burnweed leaf and add herbs—whatever combo work best for you. Top with some soft plantain, drizzle with sauce, pop in mouth, chew. Follow with a chaser of grilled guava.

Prickly Ash and Duck Meatballs

Serves 4

In midspring young prickly ash leaves are in season with the fattest field garlic. If you don't have prickly ash leaves, substitute 1 teaspoon of the dried fruit. I use fresh duck legs for this recipe, but you could also break down a single carcass.

SAUCE

2 tablespoons unscented oil

Bones from 4 whole duck legs
   (or duck carcass)

8 field garlic bulbs

1 cup (250 ml) water

1 can (13.5 fluid ounces/400 ml)
   coconut milk

1 tablespoon fish sauce

2 teaspoons ground spicebush

1 tablespoon Sumac Essence

1 tablespoon sugar

MEATBALLS

2 pounds (907 g) duck meat (from about
   4 whole duck legs), chopped

½ cup (30 g) panko bread crumbs

10 field garlic bulbs, finely chopped

2 tablespoons tender prickly ash leaflets

2 ounces (28 g) cilantro leaves, chopped

2 thumb-sized pieces of ginger,
   microplaned or finely chopped

5 tablespoons fish sauce

1 tablespoon Sumac Essence

2 tablespoons palm or unrefined sugar

1 large egg

½ cup (70 g) rice flour

2 tablespoons unscented oil

GARNISH

American burnweed

Basil

Cilantro

FOR THE CURRY SAUCE: Heat the oil in a pot over medium-high heat. Add the duck bones. Cook until they brown, turning a few times. When they smell fantastic and are dark brown, add the field garlic bulbs and cook for 1 minute. Add the water and stir very well as it bubbles. Add the coconut milk, fish sauce, ground spicebush, Sumac Essence, and sugar. Bring to a boil before turning the heat down to a brisk simmer for 1 hour. Allow the broth to cool, and strain. Discard the solids and return the broth to the pot. Taste for seasoning and adjust if necessary for salty-sour-sweet balance.

FOR THE MEATBALLS: Cut the skin and fat from the legs (save and freeze for roast potatoes or confit). Cut the meat from the bones and chop finely (you can do this in a food processor, in batches). Place the meat in a bowl with the bread crumbs, chopped field garlic, prickly ash leaflets, chopped cilantro, ginger, fish sauce, Sumac Essence, sugar, and egg. Mix very well with your hands. Cover and place in the fridge for an hour (and up to 24 hours).

TO MAKE THE MEATBALLS: Wet your hands and form Ping-Pong-sized balls. Arrange them on a plate. When they are all made, sprinkle rice flour over them. Turn, and sprinkle the other side.

Heat 1 tablespoon of the oil in a saucepan. Add one batch of meatballs and cook for just 1 minute before turning and cooking the other side. You are only browning them. Remove to a plate and brown the rest of the meatballs using more oil as needed.

TO ASSEMBLE: Heat the duck broth until it is simmering. Drop the meatballs in gently, increasing the heat to keep the broth at a simmer. Cook until the meatballs are cooked in the center, about 5 minutes.

Serve with a plateful of young American burnweed leaves, basil, cilantro, and sticky rice.

Forager's Spring Curry

Serves 4

This boldly flavored spring stew evolved from a forager's version of fridge clean-out day. Foragers have the best leftovers. It is now a spring dish I re-create every year.

1½ pounds (680 g) pork shoulder, cut into about 6 large chunks

4 ounces (113 g) young pheasant back mushroom, sliced very thinly (substitute any other mushroom)

3 tablespoons soy sauce

3 tablespoons Ramp Pickle juice

1 tablespoon sugar

1 can (13.5 fluid ounces/400 ml) coconut milk

3 hot red chiles

1 Thai lime leaf

6 radishes, cut in half, with lower stems still attached

1 tablespoon Sumac Essence

8 Prickly Ash Quick Pickled Brussels Sprouts

4 ounces (113 g) fiddleheads, blanched

2 teaspoons Prickly Ash Oil

3 ounces (85 g) watercress leaves (or substitute wintercress)

1 teaspoon Prickly Ash Paste

In a large pot combine the pork, mushroom, soy sauce, Ramp Pickle juice, sugar, coconut milk, chiles, lime leaf, and radishes. Add a little water if necessary to barely cover the meat. Bring the liquid to a simmer over high heat (stir occasionally to prevent sticking). Reduce the heat and cook at a gentle simmer for 2 hours, covered, with a crack left for some evaporation. Remove the lid and add the Sumac Essence, Prickly Ash Quick Pickled Brussels Sprouts, and fiddleheads. Increase the heat and cook uncovered at a high simmer for another 30 minutes. Stir in the Prickly Ash Oil and fresh watercress no more than 5 minutes before serving. At the table dress the top of the curry with flecks of Prickly Ash Paste.

Serve alone in bowls, or with sticky rice on the side.

Prickly Ash and Spicebush Sticky Chicken

Serves 4

Using late summer's ripe prickly ash fruit, this is addictive finger food, like Chinese takeout at home, for and by foragers.

2 large eggs
1½ cups (180 g) flour
20 chicken wings
¼ cup (60 ml) soy sauce
3 tablespoons tomato paste
¾ cup (190 ml) rice wine vinegar
½ cup (100 g) sugar
2 tablespoons ground red prickly ash fruit
1 tablespoon ground spicebush
2 ounces (57 g) baby bok choy, lettuce, or other greens

Preheat the oven to 450°F (230°C).

In a large bowl, whisk the eggs. Place the flour in a second large bowl. Place half the chicken wings in the egg bowl and mix well with your hands, making sure each piece of chicken is coated in egg.

Lift the wings from the egg bowl and place them in the flour bowl. Toss with your hands, making sure that each wing is thoroughly floured. Transfer the wings to a lightly oiled roasting dish. Repeat with the rest of the wings.

Roast the wings for 15 minutes, then turn. Roast for another 15 minutes.

Meanwhile, mix the sauce: In a bowl combine the soy sauce, tomato paste, vinegar, sugar, and spices. Stir very well until the mixture is smooth. Remove the roasting dish from the oven. Pour the sauce over the wings, coating them as evenly as possible. Roast for 15 minutes, then turn the wings and roast for another 15. (If the sauce has caramelized to the point of scorching, add a little water to the bottom of the pan. You want it to be very sticky and concentrated but not burned.)

Serve with a bite of fresh garden greens on the side.

Prickly Ash BBQ Chicken Wings

Serves 4

The familiar flavors of a summer barbecue sauce are given a feral edge by the tart tingle of prickly ash. I use whole, mature leaves (leaflets attached to the main rib) in the way that curry leaves are used (in fact, my trees grow side by side—the curry leaf trees just come indoors in the winter). Serve with Dirty, Dirty Daylily Rice; Mango, Avocado, and American Burnweed Salad; or Cucumber and Green Prickly Ash Salad with Mango.

20 chicken wings
1 cup (250 ml) soy sauce
1 cup (250 ml) ketchup
1½ tablespoons ground red prickly ash fruit
3 tablespoons Wisteria Vinegar
2 teaspoons cinnamon
⅓ cup (50 g) sesame seeds
8 prickly ash leaves

Toss all the ingredients except the leaves in a large bowl. Massage the wings well. Let them marinate for 2 hours or more, chilled.

FOR A FIRE: Place the wings above ashed-over coals and top them with the prickly ash leaves. Cook the wings until one side is beautifully brown and beginning to drip fat—10 to 15 minutes. Turn (saving the leaves) and repeat. If the fire is very hot, it's fine to turn the wings several times. Let rest for 10 minutes in a covered dish before serving.

FOR A HOT OVEN: Place the leaves in the bottom of an ovenproof skillet, top with the wings, and roast at 450°F (230°C) until the wings are dark brown, turning once—about 50 minutes, total.

Quail Stuffed with
Prickly Ash, Pheasant Back Rice, and Ramps

Serves 4

Pheasant back mushrooms (*Polyporus squamosus*) are a happy bonus when you are foraging in the springtime woods. The youngest, pig-nosed mushrooms are the most tender. Brightened with tender prickly ash leaves and the previous season's dried fruit, itty-bitty quails are stuffed with the toasty pheasant back rice and made serious with soy sauce. They are a finger-licking treat.

1 tablespoon unscented oil

6 ounces (170 g) tender pheasant back mushroom, sliced very thinly

2 slices ginger, about 2 inches (5 cm) long, cut into matchsticks

5 tablespoons soy sauce, divided

6 Ramp Pickles, cut in half

6 ramp leaves

½ teaspoon ground dried prickly ash fruit

½ cup basmati rice

1 cup water

½ teaspoon toasted sesame oil

12 quail

2 tablespoons fresh lime juice

2 teaspoons prickly ash leaflets picked from the stalk

6 whole prickly ash leaf stalks

In a pot heat the oil over medium heat. Add the pheasant back slices and sauté for a couple of minutes. Add the ginger and 2 tablespoons of the soy sauce. When it boils add the Ramp Pickles, ramp leaves, and ground prickly ash fruit. Simmer for 1 minute. Add the rice, stir to coat it with the soy sauce and aromatics, and toast the grains for a minute. Add the water. Increase the heat to bring the water to a boil, cover with a lid, and reduce the heat to its lowest setting. Cook until the liquid has been absorbed by the rice, about 12 to 15 minutes. Uncover and sprinkle the sesame oil over the rice.

Preheat the oven to 400°F (200°C).

Stuff the rice mixture into the quails' cavities. Arrange the little birds in an ovenproof dish or roasting pan. Pour the remaining soy sauce, the lime juice, and a splash of water over them. Add the separated prickly ash leaflets to the liquid in the pan. Roast for 1 hour, basting occasionally. Remove them and allow them to rest for 10 minutes before serving, with the additional prickly ash leaves scattered over them.

Purslane

OTHER COMMON NAMES: Portulaca, pigweed

BOTANICAL NAME: *Portulaca oleracea*

STATUS: Annual weed

WHERE: Widespread on disturbed ground, in agricultural fields, and gardens

SEASON: Summer

USE: Vegetable

PARTS USED: Tender stems, leaves, buds, and green seed capsules

GROW? Yes

TASTES LIKE: Succulent baby spinach, with some sourness

Most gardeners and farmers attack purslane when it infiltrates their domain. This is a shame.

The sprawling semi-succulent annual boasts the highest-yet-measured levels of omega-3 fatty acids in a plant. In my vegetable garden I transplant opportunistic purslane volunteers into tidy rows. I also grow 'Golden' purslane from seed. I know. Nuts.

Native Americans knew about purslane and used it fresh and cooked. On the other side of the Atlantic, Romans devoured it, BCE. It remains a well-known vegetable around the Mediterranean. And other North Americans are well informed: *verdolagas* (Spanish for "purslane") are appreciated in Mexico, and routinely eaten.

The common purslane we know as a weed has uncertain origins. Asia? North Africa? And while it is thought to be a post-Columbian

immigrant to North America, archaeological records have shown evidence of purslane seeds and pollen here as far back as 750 CE.

In the 1840s Henry David Thoreau was feasting on it in his Walden Pond cabin in Concord, Massachusetts. "I have made a satisfactory dinner, satisfactory on several accounts, simply off a dish of purslane (*Portulaca oleracea*) which I gathered in my cornfield, boiled and salted. I give the Latin on account of the savoriness of the trivial name," he wrote in *Walden*, published in 1854. What does "satisfactory on several accounts" mean? For a man who wrote a lot, he does not elaborate.

There are many ways purslane can be enjoyed, cooked, but boiling it is not on my list. Generally speaking, it is at its most appealing raw, with a crisp texture and faint sourness. These attributes work well with softer ingredients like ripe peaches, creamy mozzarella, and even roasted bone marrow (as a relish purslane assuages guilt and cuts the fat). Processed until smooth it lends a fullness to raw soups and green sauces. It is an edible tonic.

As with some other vegetables (Japanese knotweed, sheep sorrel), purslane's vivid color fades with heat, and it also turns slightly mucilaginous. In Cape Town, *porseleinbredie* was a traditional Cape Malay dish, a slow stew made with lamb and succulent purslane leaves. And C. Louis Leipoldt, a lauded South African poet and food writer (before there was such a thing), as well as a medical doctor and amateur botanist, liked his *porseleinblaar* stewed with butter and mace and pounded to a paste. I think the Romans would relate.

How to Collect and Prepare

You can pick purslane leaves the minute they are recognizable, as seedlings. On more mature plants the stems can also be eaten as long as they are tender (older stems are fibrous). If you can pinch the stem off between forefinger and thumbnail, it is tender enough to eat. The fat, unripe seed capsules are pleasantly succulent morsels. If you do not want purslane to spread, pick those before they release their seeds.

Purslane's flavor can be variable, as I learned from wild foods author John Slattery, author of *Southwest Foraging*: "If you gather it in the morning it will have more malic acid, and therefore be tangy in taste," he writes. "Gathered in the afternoon it will be sweeter . . . as the malic acid is transformed into glucose." I like it tangy.

Increasingly, purslane is showing up at farmers markets in late summer. When my own crop becomes too leggy, that is where I find a fresh supply. It has often wilted by the time it is sold and I plunge it into a large bowl of cool water until it has revived, snacking on the leaf tips while I wait.

CULTIVATION TIPS

USDA Hardiness Zones:
All, as it is an annual

The purslane sold frequently is 'Golden'—a cultivar with a beautiful chartreuse color and a very lush leaf habit. Sow this summer crop in late spring in full sun in well-drained soil. The plants are heat- and drought-tolerant, making this an unusually water-wise crop. If you want to control its spread, pull up the plants before they set seed.

Purslane Stem Pickles

Makes 2 cups (500 ml)

If you are using purslane leaves for another recipe, save the tender stems for umami-strong pickles. They stay crunchy and succulent indefinitely. Layer them in leafy sandwiches, add them to steamed dumpling fillings, chop them onto breakfast eggs, or drop them into soups just before serving.

4 ounces (113 g) tender purslane
   stems, washed
1 cup (250 ml) sherry vinegar
1 cup (250 ml) soy sauce
6 prickly ash fruit
4 bird's eye chiles
2 tablespoons sugar

Trim the purslane stems to fit neatly into a sterilized jar or jars. Combine all the pickle ingredients in a large jug or bowl and stir until the sugar has dissolved. Place the purslane in the jars and cover with the brine. Secure the lids and store at room temperature. Refrigerate once opened.

Salt-Pickled Purslane Leaves

Makes ½ cup (about 30 g) after wilting

A quick salt pickle yields tangy leaves that can be used immediately in endless variety. Scatter them on toasted sourdough and drizzle with olive oil, top them with a warm egg, toss them with cold udon, dress them with toasted sesame oil and Prickly Ash Paste, add them to an omelet.

1 cup (40 g) purslane leaves
1 tablespoon salt
1 teaspoon red chile flakes

Place the purslane in a small bowl with the salt. Massage it into the leaves. Add the chile and toss. Let sit for 45 minutes. Add water to the bowl, swoosh the leaves around, and drain. Turn them out onto a clean kitchen towel and roll into a sausage to dry. Unroll and fluff them up. They are ready.

Purslane and Raw Beets with Labneh

Serves 4 as an appetizer

I can't think of anything more superfood-ish than this combination. The sweet, crisp earthiness of raw beetroot is delicious with creamy labneh, while the purslane leaves provide crunch and succulence.

¼ cup (60 ml) Elderflower Vinegar
½ cup (125 ml) water
1 teaspoon salt
1 tablespoon sugar
2 medium beets, peeled and sliced thinly
½ cup (125 ml) labneh
Pinch of salt
⅓ cup (13 g) purslane leaves or tips
2 tablespoons olive oil

In a bowl stir together the Elderflower Vinegar, water, salt, and sugar. Add the beet slices and let them quick-pickle for 45 minutes. Mix the labneh in a small bowl with a pinch of salt and stir well. Remove the beets from their brine, drain, and arrange on a serving plate. Place a dollop of labneh on each beet slice, and top with some purslane. Drizzle the olive oil over everything, and serve.

Purslane and Tomato Open-Face Sandwich

Serves 1

If you make nothing else with purslane, make this. Use real, locally grown tomatoes, good mayonnaise, and hearty bread.

1 tablespoon mayonnaise
1 slice good bread
3 thick slices large, ripe tomato
Pinch of Ramp Leaf Salt
⅓ cup (13 g) purslane leaves and
    tender stems
Black pepper

Spread the mayo on the bread. Top with tomato slices. Season them with Ramp Leaf Salt. Pile on the purslane and grind some fresh black pepper over it all. Feel the omega-3s singing in your veins.

Purslane and Bean Salad

Serves 4 as a side

Straight from the summer garden, with freshly shelled beans, this is one of the nicest salads I have eaten. You can dress it up, of course, with chopped soft egg, a runny poached egg, or crumbled goat or feta cheese. I like it straight up, with no spin. The way I like my facts.

2 cups (about 230 g) freshly shelled
    mature beans
½ teaspoon salt
Squeeze of lemon juice
3 tablespoons extra-virgin olive oil
3 ounces (85 g) purslane leaves

Cook the beans in salted and simmering water over medium-high heat until they are tender. Remove the beans, saving the cooking juices. Reduce the remaining liquid over high heat until just 2 tablespoons remain. Return the beans to the pot, stir them, and taste. Season judiciously with salt. Add the lemon juice and then the olive oil. Add the purslane leaves, and turn gently into the beans. Plate and serve. Best eaten while still warm.

Purslane and Roasted Tomatillo Caprese

Serves 4 as an appetizer

Buffalo burrata's rich blandness is a soft background for acidic purslane. Late-summer tomatillos, splitting from their husks, are a good alternative to their traditional tomato cousins and become gently sweet with roasting.

8 tomatillos
Salt
2 balls (about 12 ounces/340 g total)
    burrata
1 cup (40 g) purslane leaves
2 tablespoons extra-virgin olive oil
¼ teaspoon piment d'espelette (or substitute paprika or smoked paprika)

Preheat the broiler. Oil a baking sheet. Cut the tomatillos in half, and salt the cut sides. After 5 minutes, place them on the baking sheet and slide under the broiler for 10 to 12 minutes, turning once, until they begin to take color and ooze juices. Remove and reserve.

Break large pieces from the burrata and arrange them on a serving plate. Scatter the tomatillos over the chunks of creamy burrata and top with the purslane. Drizzle the olive oil over the salad. Season with the piment d'espelette (or paprika) and a pinch of salt.

Purslane and Onion Salad with Cucumber

Serves 4

When you have perfect purslane with lots of tender stems, this simple salad makes the most of it. These quantities are a guideline; just make sure the purslane dominates.

1 medium red onion, thinly sliced

2 teaspoons salt, plus a pinch

4–5 Persian cucumbers, sliced on the diagonal

2 tablespoons Elderflower Vinegar

1 bunch (about 240 g) purslane with tender stems, washed

1 tablespoon extra-virgin olive oil

1 teaspoon Ground Sumac

Place the onion slices in a small bowl, sprinkle with 2 teaspoons of salt, and let sit for 30 minutes. Place the cucumbers in another bowl with the Elderflower Vinegar, and muddle. Cover and marinate in the fridge for 30 minutes (I like cold cucumbers). Before plating rinse the onions and dry well. Lift the cucumbers from their juices and arrange at the bottom of a bowl or serving plate. Top the cucumbers with a tangle of purslane and the onion. Sprinkle with the olive oil, the cucumbers' vinegar juices, a pinch of salt, and the Ground Sumac.

Raw Purslane and Yogurt Soup

Serves 4 as an appetizer

Succulent purslane and juicy cucumbers appear when warm weather discourages hot soup. Pack everything into a blender and 20 seconds later you have a rich, reviving, and very healthy tonic. Save tender purslane stems for pickling.

6 ounces (170 g) purslane leaves, washed

1½ pounds (680 g) cucumbers, peeled* and cut into chunks

⅔ cup (160 ml) yogurt

3 cloves garlic

2 Ramp Pickles

1 tablespoon Ramp Pickle juice

1 tablespoon Elderflower Vinegar

1 teaspoon sugar

½ teaspoon salt

3 tablespoons extra-virgin olive oil

* If you have thin-skinned Persian cucumbers, no need to peel.

Pack all the ingredients into a blender, pushing the leaves down firmly to make room. Blend until smooth, stopping occasionally to push more solid pieces down. Transfer to a jug or serving bowl and chill.

Purslane and Peach Soup

Serves 4

Fruit soups are refreshing fare for sticky summer kitchens when the thought of turning on the oven is unbearable. I grow shiso (perilla) for its fragrant, rosewater-flavored leaves, and it is often an escaped forage, depending on where you live.

4 very ripe, yellow freestone peaches, peeled and quartered
2 Persian cucumbers, sliced into chunks (about 1⅓ cups/330 ml)
½ cup (20 g) purslane leaves
1 jalapeño chile
2 scallions, finely sliced
14 basil leaves
6 shiso leaves (optional)
2 teaspoons lime juice
¼ teaspoon salt

Place all the ingredients in a blender and whiz until smooth. Taste, and adjust the seasoning if necessary. Transfer to a jug or bowl and chill.

Purslane and Tomatillo Gazpacho

Serves 4

Summer. Tall tomatillos in my garden with sprawling purslane at their feet? This soup. Most good dishes evolve from garden and foraging forays, or trips to the farmers market. The produce tells us what to do. Listen to it.

8 ripe green tomatillos, cut in half
3 Persian cucumbers, chopped (about 2 cups/500 ml)
2 green tomatoes (about 1½ cups/ 375 ml, chopped)
1 cup (40 g) purslane leaves
1 cup (35 g) cubed sourdough, crusts removed
⅓ cup (50 g) chopped onion
4 basil sprigs (or about 20 leaves)
1 tablespoon Elderflower Vinegar
1 teaspoon finely chopped jalapeño chile
1 teaspoon sugar
¼ teaspoon salt

Place all the ingredients in a blender and process until very smooth (work in batches if necessary). Taste. You may want to adjust the seasoning by adding a little more Elderflower Vinegar or sugar—I like gazpacho to be slightly tart but not mouth puckering. If the soup is too thick for your taste, add some water. Serve with ice cubes floating in each bowl.

Cold Noodle Salad with Purslane and Milkweed Hearts

Serves 4

A cold dish for hot nights. The heart of a young common milkweed pod is startling. The immature white seeds inside, sheathed like silken torpedoes, are as sweet as the flower cordial when just blanched. Trial and error will teach you when a milkweed pod is too large and mature to eat, but about thumb-sized and smaller is a good . . . rule of thumb. The seed heart should be soft and tender.

I usually budget on 3 ounces (85 g) of rice noodles per person. Use more if you are feeding wolves.

8 ounces (227 g) large and tender milkweed pods

15 ounces (425 g) ripe cherry tomatoes, halved

3 tablespoons mirin

3 tablespoons Common Milkweed Flower Vinegar

1 cup (about 64 g) finely sliced scallions, white parts only

½ cup (125 ml) soy sauce

1 thumb-sized piece of ginger, cut into fine matchsticks

2 tablespoons sugar, divided

1 Thai lime leaf, very finely sliced

6 Persian cucumbers

2 tablespoons lime juice

½ cup (15 g) mint leaves

12 ounces (340 g) rice noodles, like udon or somen

1 cup (100 g) finely sliced green beans

1 tablespoon toasted sesame oil

2 cups (80 g) purslane leaves

1 cup (64 g) finely sliced scallion greens

1 thumb-sized piece of ginger, peeled and grated

1 tablespoon chile flakes

Two 1-inch (2½ cm) thick slices silken tofu, cut into ½-inch (1 cm) rectangles

Begin marinating the milkweed and tomatoes 1 to 2 hours before you want to eat.

Bring a pot of water to a boil and drop the milkweed pods into it. Cover. They will make alarming popping noises. Ignore them. After 5 minutes scoop the pods out. Refresh, and drain. Pinch the ends off the pods and peel back the warty green covering to reveal the slender white teardrop seed capsule. Loosen it, remove, and reserve. Repeat with all the other pods. (You should really taste one, now.) Place the hearts in a bowl and add the mirin and vinegar. Transfer to the fridge.

Place the tomatoes with the scallion whites and soy sauce in a bowl. Add the ginger matchsticks, 1 tablespoon of the sugar, and shredded lime leaf. Toss, cover, and chill.

Just before cooking the noodles, whack each of the cucumbers with the heavy handle of a chef's knife to crush them slightly. Cut them into rough chunks and place in a bowl with the lime juice, the remaining tablespoon of sugar, and the mint. Drain the soy sauce from the marinating tomatoes and add it to the cucumber bowl.

Bring a large pot of water to a boil. Drop in the noodles. After 2 minutes at a rolling boil add the sliced beans. Cook another 3 minutes. Drain the contents of the pot through a fine-mesh sieve and run under cold water until the noodles and beans are cold. Drain by shaking the sieve hard. Put the noodles and beans in a large serving bowl with the sesame oil, and toss.

Add the tomato mixture, purslane, scallion greens, and grated ginger to the noodles. Add the cucumbers and their liquid. Add chile flakes and toss again. Top with the airy tofu bricks.

Porseleinbredie

Serves 4

In *Traditional Cookery of the Cape Malays* (a book published in 1954 from a posthumously discovered manuscript), the South African culinary historian Hilda Gerber recorded recipes handed down in an oral tradition among Cape Malay women—descendants of colonial slaves—living in and near Cape Town. Many of the recipes are for bredies, slow-cooked stews featuring one, or perhaps two, seasonal vegetables or fruits. In the entry for porseleinbredie, Gerber writes of a lost tradition: "Although numerous older women knew that this garden weed was edible, not one of them could give a specific recipe . . . they had an idea that fat mutton must be used, as well as 'lots of chillies to make it strong.' A few recollected that tamarind juice or *suring* [*Oxalis pes-caprae*] had been added to flavor it, but not one of them had made porseleinbredie herself."

So here is mine. I added chiles to make it strong. Serve with buttered rice.

If you happen to live where South African *Oxalis pes-caprae* is invasive (California, for example), use ½ cup (125 ml) of the chopped sour stems, or leaves, instead of Sumac Essence.

1½ pounds (680 g) stewing lamb, or shoulder or neck chops
1 teaspoon salt
3 tablespoons lard, or butter
1 pound (453 g) finely sliced onions
3 cloves garlic, chopped
2 thumb-sized pieces of ginger, grated
2 tablespoons grated fresh turmeric
6 red chiles
6 ounces (170 g) purslane leaves and tender stems
Black pepper
3 cups (750 ml) chicken broth
2 tablespoons Sumac Essence
Lemon juice

Season the lamb with the salt. In a pot melt the lard or butter over high heat. Add the pieces of meat and brown one side, 1 to 2 minutes. Turn and brown the other side. Add the onions directly to the meat, stirring everything together well. Cook for another minute. Now add the garlic, ginger, turmeric, and chiles. Stir well, still at high heat. Add the purslane, add fresh black pepper to taste, and pour in the broth, stirring to loosen any brown residue on the bottom of the pot. Add the Sumac Essence (or suring). After the liquid has come to a boil, reduce the heat to maintain a gentle simmer for 2 hours. Taste halfway through and add more salt if necessary, and possibly a squeeze of lemon juice.

Quickweed

OTHER COMMON NAMES: Gallant soldiers, guascas

BOTANICAL NAMES: *Galinsoga parviflora*, *G. quadriradiata*

STATUS: Annual weed in the US

WHERE: Gardens, open ground

SEASON: Spring to summer

USE: Vegetable

PARTS USED: Leaves, flowers

GROW? Only if you harvest before it sets seed

TASTES LIKE: Green peas (raw), sweeter nettles (cooked)

Quickweed consorts with lamb's quarters and amaranth, the wild greens of summer, so ubiquitous that one of them is usually within gathering distance of where you stand, perhaps right outside your front door.

It is a familiar and formidable gardener's enemy, called quick because it germinates and grows while your back is turned. One minute you are watering the beans, the next minute there is a menacing thicket of new plants behind you. Eat them. Allow quickweed to spread and your weeding life will be grim. When we moved to our current apartment in Brooklyn with its neglected backyard, I spent many sweaty summer hours, besieged by equally invasive day-biting Asian tiger mosquitoes, pulling it out by the bushelful. One of the two species' common names is more

summer thing, from fire-cooked steaks to garlicky grilled chicken. Their light sweetness invites a dressing of soy sauce, lime juice, and toasted sesame oil. Heat them with a little butter and top with a soft-cooked egg for breakfast. Make ajiaco. Stir the tender, sweet leaves into green pancakes and serve with herb butter.

And tell your local farmer about it. She might raise her eyebrows. But she might also begin bringing it to market. Stranger things have happened.

How to Collect and Prepare

Collect quickweed as soon as it appears in summer. Early in the season the whole plant is tender. As it grows taller and leggier, discard the wiry stems and keep only the leaves and flowers. To prevent it from spreading (it is relentless), harvest the whole plant before it sets seeds. In the kitchen use young leaves raw and wilt or blanch older, furrier leaves.

charming: gallant soldiers, an echo of its botanical name, *Galinsoga parviflora*. It makes me think of boiled eggs and strips of polite toast soldiers, saluting.

In the mountain country of Colombia, the sought-after leaves of galinsoga are called *guascas*. They are not loathed but loved, and an essential ingredient in *ajiaco*, a soupy stew of chicken, corn, and as many potato varieties as the Andes can offer. In Bogotá you can buy bunches of guascas at any supermarket. In our summer gardens we yank them out by the angry handful.

Raw, galinsoga tastes like pea greens. Cooked, it has its own flavor that is hard to define. A culinary (if not botanical) cousin of spinach, chard, nettles, and young collards, it is a sop for sauce and changes the character of stews when it is added.

Eat the youngest greens raw, in pestos with pecans and Parmigiano-Reggiano. The older leaves are furrier, but cooking smooths them. Wilt quickweed greens as a side for every

CULTIVATION TIPS
USDA Hardiness Zones:
All, as it is an annual

The hardest part about growing quickweed will be finding seed, commercially. The second hardest part about growing quickweed will be getting rid of it. I hesitated about advising readers on cultivating this flavorful green, because it can take over in the blink of an eye. One plant produces tens of thousands of seeds. The seeds require no dormancy, so they can germinate at any time. Plant quickweed *only* if you harvest the whole plant the minute you see flowers appear. You do *not* want it to set seed.

Quickweed Pesto

Makes 1¼ cups (310 ml)

Does the world need another pesto recipe? I say yes. Green peas reinforce quickweed's own sweet, pea flavor. Serve this paste with pasta, pile onto bruschetta, or insert as a pillow between poached eggs and toast. The prettiest thing you can make is a layered glassful of summer, into which you dip toast fingers: one layer of Quickweed Pesto, a layer of aioli, a layer of thick home-made tomato or red pepper sauce, and a final layer of Preserved Lemon and Pigweed Pesto.

8 ounces (227 g) quickweed, leaves and
  tender tips only
1 cup (150 g) fresh peas, blanched
2 ounces (57 g) microplaned
  Parmigiano-Reggiano
3 tablespoons butter
1 tablespoon extra-virgin olive oil
½ teaspoon lemon zest

Cook the quickweed for 2 minutes in boiling water. Strain, refresh in cool water, and squeeze the leaves dry. Combine all the ingredients in a food processor and pulse until a smooth paste is achieved. Use at once or freeze for up to 6 months.

Quickweed Griddlecakes

Makes 10 cakes, 3 inches (7½ cm) each

These green pancakes explode with flavor. Serve them with American Burnweed and Lime But-ter, salmon roe, or shaved ham. You could substitute lamb's quarters or amaranth for the quickweed, although the latter does have a distinctive flavor. In spring, if you would like to make the most of some precious ramps, substitute their leaves for scallions and a cool-weather green like mustard or young (blanched) pokeweed leaves for the quickweed.

A serving tip: I toast these just before serving, keeping the just-toasted ones hot under double-folded napkins until they are all done. They freeze well and can be toasted straight from the freezer.

8 ounces (227 g) quickweed leaves
and flowers
¾ cup (90 g) all-purpose flour
1 tablespoon plus 1 teaspoon
baking powder
½ teaspoon salt
1 teaspoon cumin
½ teaspoon ground spicebush
½ cup (125 ml) milk
¼ cup (60 ml) yogurt
3 scallions, finely chopped
1 teaspoon grated fresh turmeric
3 tablespoons olive oil

Drop the quickweed leaves and flowering tips into a pot of boiling water and cook for 3 minutes. Drain, refresh in cold water, and squeeze as dry as you can. Chop up finely.

In a bowl, combine the flour, baking powder, salt, cumin, and spice-bush. Stir to mix well. Add the milk and yogurt and stir to bring the mixture together. Add the chopped scallions and the grated turmeric and mix.

Heat a tablespoon of olive oil in a skillet over medium-high heat. Scoop about 3 tablespoons of batter at a time for one griddlecake, using a large spoon or ladle. You should be able to make three or four at a time. Make them smaller if you prefer them blini-sized. When bubbles form and begin to pop on the upper surface, turn them deftly and cook the other side. When the middle is set, they are done. Add more oil to the pan as necessary. Serve warm.

Grape Leaf and Yogurt Pie with Quickweed and Herbs

Serves 4–6 as an appetizer, 2 as an entrée

Mediterraneans have startling ways to use yogurt, as well as wild greens, to good effect. This pie is inspired in part by two recipes in Paula Wolfert's wonderful *Cooking of the Eastern Mediterranean* (in one a filling is wrapped in individual grape leaves and deep-fried; in the other, many greens are pressed into a pan on a layer of cornmeal) and by Ghillie Basan's grape leaf pie in *Classic Turkish Cooking*. None of their methods called for wild greens, but since the spirit of the edible weed is alive in that part of the world, I feel this pie would be at home beside the Aegean. This recipe also works well with amaranth, lamb's quarters, and (especially) nettles. Serve with crisp toast.

FILLING

20–26 brined grape leaves
  (depending on size)
3 ounces (85 g) quickweed leaves
  and flowers
1½ cups (375 ml) Greek yogurt
3 tablespoons finely chopped scallions
2 ounces (57 g) dill, finely chopped
1 ounce (28 g) mint, finely chopped
3 tablespoons panko bread crumbs
2 tablespoons cornmeal
1 teaspoon Ramp Leaf Salt
2 teaspoons Salted Ramp Leaves
1 teaspoon Aleppo pepper
  (or red chile flakes)

TOPPING

4 tablespoons butter
2 cloves garlic, thinly sliced
2 tablespoons pine nuts
1 teaspoon Aleppo pepper

Preheat the oven to 350°F (180°C). Soak the grape leaves in a bowl of water for 1 hour.

Chop the quickweed finely. Place all the filling ingredients in a bowl and mix until thoroughly combined.

Melt the topping butter in a small saucepan over medium-low heat.

Lightly brush some of the melted butter into a 9- to 10-inch (23–25 cm) skillet or heatproof dish. Line the dish with overlapping, radiating circles of grape leaves, allowing them to come up higher than the sides and hang over. Spoon the filling into the middle and spread it out, stopping shy of the pan edges by about ¾ inch (2 cm). Fold the overhanging grapes leaves back over the filling, adding a few more if necessary to cover it in the middle. Brush the top with melted butter. Slide into the oven for 40 minutes.

Add the garlic, pine nuts, and Aleppo pepper to the saucepan with the remaining melted butter. Heat gently over low heat for 5 minutes. Pour this over the grape leaf pie 5 minutes before removing it from the oven.

Ajiaco—An Andean Stew

Serves 4–6

In my garden the digging of a crop of potatoes coincides with the leggy stage of quickweed. The combination spells ajiaco—a traditional Colombian stew. I have taken liberties with this national dish and I hope the natives of Bogotá will forgive me: Adding a char to the chicken and the corn is not traditional, but it is delicious. If you cannot make a fire or have no barbecue, brown the corn and scallions under a broiler.

8 chicken thighs

½ teaspoon salt

2 ears corn

8 scallions, whole

2 cups (280 g) finely chopped onions

15 ounces (425 g) small potatoes, divided

4 cups (1 liter) chicken broth

2½ ounces (70 g) quickweed

2 tablespoons lime juice

⅓ cup (80 ml) sour cream

2 tablespoons capers (or Fermented Elderberry Capers)

Lime wedges

Build a small fire. Season the chicken with the salt. When the coals are ashed over, place the chicken above them, skin-side down, and grill just until the fat begins to drip and the skin browns. Turn and grill until the other side begins to brown. You are not cooking the chicken through. Remove and reserve. Place the corn and the scallions on the grill.

Transfer the browned chicken to a large Dutch oven. Add the onions, half the potatoes, and enough chicken broth to cover the ingredients. Place the pot over medium-high heat and bring the liquid to a boil. Reduce the heat to a simmer and cover. Cook for 2 hours total. Meanwhile, check on the corn, turning it so that two sides have some brown kernels. Retrieve the ears from the fire and cut them into thirds. Reserve four pieces. Slice the kernels from the remaining two pieces and add the kernels to the pot. Stir. After the stew has cooked for 1 hour, scoop out the potatoes and crush them on a chopping board with the flat of a chef's knife. Return them to the pot (where they will thicken the sauce) along with the remaining potatoes. Increase the heat until the sauce simmers again. Cook another 30 minutes. Add the quickweed and the lime juice and cook for the last 30 minutes. Serve in bowls with sour cream and capers, and lime wedges on the side.

Green Tomato and Quickweed Curry

Serves 4

Late summer, and unripe green tomatoes and relentless quickweed are dinner. This acidic sauce, laced with chiles and onion, is wonderful. The chiles wrap it in green, and the tomatoes dissolve into a gravy. The vinegar at the end is key. The tartness becomes voluptuous, enhancing the richness and throwing the aromatics into relief. If you do not have fresh curry leaf, just omit (I grow *Murraya koenigii* in a pot and bring it indoors in our cold winters).

CURRY PASTE

1 large onion, cut into quarters

3 green chiles (I like serrano here)

2 thumb-sized pieces of ginger, peeled and sliced thinly

2 teaspoons black pepper

2 tablespoons peeled and sliced fresh turmeric (or use ¼ teaspoon powdered)

½ teaspoon cumin

CURRY

2 tablespoons unscented oil

1 fresh curry leaf branch

2 teaspoons ground spicebush

5 cardamom pods

4 whole chicken legs

2 large green tomatoes, cored and chopped roughly

2 cups (50 g) loosely packed cilantro (roots, stems, leaves), chopped

3 ounces (85 g) quickweed leaves and flowers

2–3 cups (500–750 ml) chicken broth (or water)

¼ teaspoon salt

2 teaspoons sugar

3 medium potatoes, peeled and cut into thick slices or chunks

2 tablespoons Elderflower Vinegar

Load all the curry paste ingredients into the bowl of a food processor and purée until you have a fine sauce. Heat the oil in a pot over medium heat and add the wet curry paste with the curry leaf, spicebush, and cardamom pods. Stir, allowing some moisture to cook off. After 5 minutes add the chicken to the pot with the tomatoes, cilantro, and quickweed. Add enough broth or water to cover, with the salt and sugar. Bring the liquid to a boil, then reduce the heat to maintain a gentle simmer. Cook, covered, for an hour. Add the potatoes and cook for another hour, uncovered, bubbling gently, until the liquid has reduced to a thick sauce (stir from time to time). Stir in the Elderflower Vinegar 15 minutes before the curry has finished cooking.

Ramps

OTHER COMMON NAMES: Wild leeks, wild garlic

BOTANICAL NAMES: *Allium tricoccum* var. *burdickii*, *A. tricoccum* var. *tricoccum*

STATUS: Bulb-forming perennial native to northeastern North America

WHERE: Woodlands, farmers markets, grocery stores

SEASON: Early spring

USE: Vegetable, aromatic

PARTS USED: Bulbs and leaves

GROW? Yes, please

TASTES LIKE: Onions and garlic

Like their fiddlehead woodland neighbors, ramps are recognizable not just to foragers but to farmers market shoppers and even supermarket patrons. Ramps have long appeared on spring menus, celebrated as one of the first new edibles heralding the growing year.

Their popularity is leading to their demise. Ramps are listed as endangered, threatened, or vulnerable in several states. In Canada the government of Québec banned the harvest of ramps in 1995 after a steep decline in populations.

One reason for ramps' vulnerability is that they grow painfully slowly. Another is that the scale of commercial or professional harvest can be massive. Too many are being taken.

In a much-quoted study it was estimated that a conservatively harvested (10 percent taken) ramp patch required ten years to recover. *How* the ramps were harvested mattered a lot, though. Understanding that is key to appreciating how and when ramps are collected, and how that collection impacts their future.

How do ramps reproduce? Two ways. Sexual reproduction is the making of flowers and seeds. The flowers appear in late spring, maturing and setting seed after the leaves have yellowed and disappeared for a long dormancy. Ramp seeds take six to eighteen months to germinate, often requiring two winters and warm springs to emerge as spindly grass-like spikes. This new plant grows for three to five years before it can reproduce.

If you have ever been ramp collecting, you will have noticed how they often grow in clumps. This is due to asexual—or vegetative—

reproduction, which occurs in two ways: New plants (clones of the mature plant) are produced from the woody underground rootstock, a tough, rhizome-like brown structure that you will sometimes see attached to white ramp bulbs and roots (see image below). The other way is for a mature, large bulb to split into new, smaller bulbs (also clones).

Appreciating this is key to knowing how to conserve, harvest, and eat ramps sustainably. Because we are greedy, we have entered the era of what I call conservation foraging.

The digging out of entire ramps—bulbs, roots, and pieces of rootstock—as well as entire clonal clumps, will lead to the decline, or decimation, of that population, because you are leaving nothing behind for vegetative regeneration. Leaving part of the bulb and roots with rootstock will allow the plants to regenerate. Second, when whole plants are

removed, especially before they reach maturity, they cannot produce seeds. There is another factor to consider, and it affects fiddleheads, too: collateral botanical damage. When you are harvesting ramps en masse, the likelihood is good that you are stomping spring ephemerals.

What can you do? If you are out collecting a meal for your own dinner, collect one mature, fat bulb from a clump, in a place where ramps grow wall-to-wall. Cut the fat bulb well above the root. Leave the younger, thinner bulbs. *Better yet*, pick only ramp leaves, a couple from a clump. They are arousingly flavorful. They make the best salt I have ever tasted. It is like magic dust. Green MSG.

If you are a seller: Educate your customers to expect ramps that are missing part of their bulbs, or to buy leaves only.

If you are a consumer or chef: Reject wild-dug ramps that have been dug with the brown rhizome and roots attached. And tell the seller why, whether it is a professional forager, a supermarket, or a greenmarket vendor. And if you see tons of pencil-thin ramps, sold at a local emporium, holler. These are immature ramps, and it is a good indication that an entire patch has been cleaned out, for good.

Another way, the most promising way, to prevent the loss of ramps is to create an alternative to wild harvest: active cultivation.

I was surprised at how readily they grow in my urban Brooklyn backyard, in a humus-rich spot that receives sun in spring and shade in summer, when nearby ostrich ferns and jewelweed rise above them. I planted greenmarket ramps, harvested with roots and sometimes pieces of rootstock attached. After looking yellow and unhappy, they disappeared. But the following spring they were back, as though they had always grown there.

In his far larger and more mature test patches in the Wisconsin sugar maple woods, acclaimed wild foods author Sam Thayer has

RAMSONS

American ramp's European cousin has a very similar common name: ramsons (also called bear garlic, among other names). *Allium ursinum* can be used in exactly the same way as ramps amd other wild garlics. The most important distinction is that ramsons enjoy a staus of Least Concern on the IUCN Red List of Threatened Species.

seen very encouraging results. He has observed that, after nine years, a single bulb transplanted into a good habitat produces eight to sixteen mature bulbs adjacent to it, plus many seedlings. "These plants are amazingly tough," he wrote, in an email. He began with eighty-five plants. After ten years "the end tally was around 1200," and eighty-four of the original founder clumps are still surviving. Reproduction was almost exactly 50 percent by seed and 50 percent vegetative.

It is important to note that these ramps were left to grow unmolested by hungry chefs and sellers.

But this is the future of ramp foraging: grown with foresight and well managed. Current wild harvests, while feeding our still-burgeoning appetite for ramps, will ensure their demise.

Time to change.

How to Collect and Prepare

If you are wild-gathering ramps, forage from a spot where they grow prolifically. Take only one mature bulb from a clump. Cut the bulb well above the root, leaving some bulb behind. Do not gather immature, skinny bulbs. The best practice is to collect only the leaves, a few from each clump. At home, wash the ramps well. Avoid leaving them exposed to the light for a long time, as they will yellow. Cut the leaves from any harvested bulbs. If you will not be using them immediately, stack them, wrap them in a damp paper towel or cloth, and place in a bag in the fridge. They will last well for up to a week. Store the bulbs separately, in a covered bowl or bag in the fridge.

Caution

Some poisonous plants, like species of *Veratrum* (false hellebore) and *Convallaria majalis* (lily of the valley), superficially resemble ramps in the springtime. Be sure to learn the differences between them.

Ramp Leaf Salt

Makes ½ cup (about 5 ounces/142 g)

Ramp Leaf Salt is the best thing in my kitchen. Added near the end of cooking to soups, stews, roasts, and grills; deployed in aioli and fresh sauces; sprinkled on eggs and potatoes, it gives an intense and evocative spring kick long after the anticipated ramp season has passed. Using a food processor to chop the leaves yields a wetter salt that preserves the ramp flavor much longer than the hand-chopped versions I have made. Double or triple the quantities if you have enough leaves—this salt will become your most coveted seasoning. The flavor keeps well for 6 months.

4 ounces (113 g) ramp leaves
½ cup (4 ounces/113 g) sea salt

Chop the ramp leaves roughly and place them in the bowl of a food processor. Process until fine.

Transfer the ramps to a bowl, add the salt, and mix very well. Spread the green, wet salt thinly on a baking sheet or large flat surface covered with parchment paper. Allow it to air-dry, stirring and turning occasionally with clean hands or a spatula. Depending on humidity levels, this may take 24 hours. Bottle when the salt is dry.

Ramp Eggs, Baby Way

Serves 1

My mother's father was a mild man who never swore. But when he was told that his second leg would have to be amputated, due to spinal tuberculosis, he said, "Damn," and threw a teacup across his hospital room. My mother once asked him, "Dad, if you could order anything in a restaurant, what would it be?" She was a very good cook and wanted to make something special for the unassuming man, who never ate out. He thought for a while and then said, "A boiled egg, baby way."

"*Any*thing, Dad?"

"An egg," he said.

So here is a bowlful for Oupa, the grandfather I never met.

2 large eggs
2 tablespoons butter
1 teaspoon Ramp Leaf Oil
½ cup (17 g) lightly toasted torn-up bread
¼ teaspoon Ramp Leaf Salt
Black pepper

Bring water to a boil in a pot. Add the eggs in the shell and cook at a boil for 1 minute. Turn the heat off. Leave for 6 minutes for a slightly runny yolk.

Melt the butter in a small saucepan. Turn off the heat and add the Ramp Leaf Oil.

Place the warm bread in a bowl. Pour the butter over it. Scoop the eggs onto the bread. Season with the Ramp Leaf Salt and pepper.

Salted Ramp Leaves

Makes 4½ ounces (127 g) dried ramp leaves

If you are lucky enough to have a lot of ramp leaves, salting them lightly before drying delivers a stellar source of preserved flavor. Like a burst of the best bouillon cube, without the bouillon cube. The dried leaves can be eaten straight up as chips (very luxurious chips!) or, better, crumbled finely to keep as you would herbed salt. Added to stews, soups, bone broth, stuffings, sausages, or grilled mushrooms, or scattered onto pizza after it has baked (the list is endless), they offer an intense flavor boost and finish. Their flavor is preserved well for about 6 months. After this they will still add some body to broths but lose their distinctive flavor.

If your ramp leaf harvest is more modest than the amount I have given, use 8 ounces (227 g) ramp leaves to 2 teaspoons salt.

1½ pounds (680 g) ramp leaves
2 tablespoons salt

Wash and dry the leaves. Place them in a large bowl or bowls. Sprinkle the salt over them. Massage the leaves, turning them so that the salt coats them all. Bruising the leaves is fine. Allow them to sit for an hour. If you have a dehydrator, arrange them on your drying racks and dehydrate. When they are dry, store in ziplock bags or jars.

To dry in the oven, spread the leaves on baking sheets covered in parchment. You may need three or four sheets. Some overlap of leaves is okay, but it will slow the drying process.

Place the trays in the oven on its lowest setting (no higher than 150°F/66°C). Turn off the oven after 15 minutes. Leave the ramps for an hour. Turn the oven onto its lowest setting again, for 15 minutes. Turn off and let sit for another hour. Turn the leaves. Repeat these steps until you have completely dry, very crumbly leaves whose stalks snap when broken. If the leaves can bend, they are not dry enough.

Store them whole in large jars or bags, or crumble them finely and store in small jars.

Ramp Leaf Oils

Roasted Ramp Leaf Oil

Makes about 12 fluid ounces (355 ml)

Charring ramp leaves briefly over coals adds incredible depth to ramp leaf oil. It is imperative to keep this, and any oil infused with fresh produce, in the fridge or the freezer, never on the countertop. Hello, botulism. Brush it onto steaks, ribs, chops, mushrooms, and eggs, and use it in sandwiches and salad dressings. You can use any unscented oil, but for this top quality product I prefer avocado.

12 ounces (340 g) ramp leaves
1 cup (250 ml) avocado oil

Wilt the clean, dry ramp leaves over coals or on a gas barbecue until very lightly browned at the edges. Turn the leaves and give them another 1 to 2 minutes over the coals. They should *not* be crisp. Remove them to a plate and spread them out to cool.

Pulse the leaves in a food processor with the cup of oil until perfectly smooth. Now you can choose to strain through a fine-mesh sieve, or bottle directly into clean glass jars. Keep in the fridge for up to a week, or freeze until needed. Best eaten within 6 months.

Raw Ramp Leaf Oil

Makes about 12 fluid ounces (355 ml)

Raw leaves yield a brighter flavor and more vivid color than the roasted oil.

12 ounces (340 g) ramp leaves
1 cup (250 ml) avocado oil

Bring a pot of water to a boil. Drop the ramp leaves in for 30 seconds. Drain, refresh, and dry thoroughly. Chop the leaves roughly. Combine them with the oil in a food processor and pulse until very smooth. Strain through a fine-mesh sieve and bottle in small, sterilized jars. Freeze, or keep in the fridge and use within a week.

Ramp Pickles

Makes 2 jars, 1½ pints (750 ml) each

I like to keep Ramp Pickles very simple, because I deploy them later in lots of different ways. I plunge the ramps into boiling water for 30 seconds before pickling—this keeps them beautifully pink. You can skip this step (and keep an extra crispness), but the cut ends may darken after several months (this does not affect their flavor).

14 ounces (396 g) ramp bulbs and stems
    (no leaves)
2 cups (500 ml) white wine vinegar
2 cups (500 ml) water
2 tablespoons salt
6 tablespoons sugar

Have a bowl of ice water ready. Bring a large pot of salted water to a boil. Drop in the ramps and blanch for just 30 seconds. Drain the ramps, refresh in the ice water, and drain. Pat dry

In a large bowl or jug, mix together the vinegar, water, salt, and sugar. Stir well. Pack the blanched ramps into sterilized jars: Start by packing them bulb-end down, and when that crowds the bottom of the jar, switch and pack the ramps in tail-end first. Pour the pickling liquid over the ramps, to cover. Seal the jars.

Try to wait before eating them. They are ready as soon as a week later but are best after some months and good for at least a year.

Rampson

Makes 1 drink

A Gibson with ramps. (And in Europe, *Allium ursinum*—bear garlic, very similar to ramps—is also known as ramsons.)

2 fluid ounces (4 tablespoons) dry gin
1½ fluid ounces (3 tablespoons)
    Bayberry Gin
1 fluid ounce (2 tablespoons) vermouth
½ fluid ounce (1 tablespoon) Ramp
    Pickle juice
1 Ramp Pickle

Shake all the liquids up with ice, strain, pour, and garnish with a Ramp Pickle

Ramp Leaf Butter

Makes 14 ounces (396 g)

Dabbed onto grilled corn, baked potatoes, seared lamb chops, grilled steaks, sautéed mushrooms, soft polenta—a little ramp butter turns the familiar into the extraordinary. Spread it onto hot toasted sourdough, sprinkle with a pinch of Ramp Leaf Salt, and munch. Feast. Compound butters will only be as good as the butter you use.

8 ounces (227 g) butter, at room temperature
6 ounces (170 g) cleaned ramp leaves,
    well chopped

In a food processor combine the butter and the ramp leaves. Pulse until the butter and leaves are a uniformly bright green paste (scrape the sides down a few times). Pack the butter into small clean jars or roll it up into logs inside parchment paper, wrap very well, and freeze for up to 3 months. If you are using fresh do so within 3 days.

Ramp Leaf Mashed Potatoes

Serves 4

Recalibrating silky mashed potatoes with a swirl of vivid Raw Ramp Leaf Oil is irresistible. My preferred tool for a silky mash is a potato ricer. If you have frozen Ramp Leaf Oil you can make this out of season, too.

6 large potatoes (about 3½ pounds/1⅔ kg)
3 tablespoons Raw Ramp Leaf Oil
½ cup (125 ml) warm milk
1 teaspoon Ramp Leaf Salt

Cook the potatoes in salted boiling water until tender. Drain the potatoes and slip off their skins. Load them while hot into a potato ricer or food mill and press them back into the pot in which they cooked. Add the Raw Ramp Leaf Oil and warm milk and stir well. If the potatoes are too thick for your taste, add some more milk. Season with half the salt and taste. Adjust the seasoning if necessary. Reheat them gently over medium-low heat.

Miso Ramps

Makes 2 cups (500 ml) finished ramps

In her inspiring book *Preserving the Japanese Way*, author Nancy Singleton Hachisu has a recipe for garlic cloves embedded in miso. She generously allowed me to reproduce her method here. Ramps preserved this way stay crunchy (while field garlic bulbs turn meltingly soft—use precisely the same method for field garlic bulbs). The miso mellows them and adds a richer dimension. Serve as snacks or with other pickles; layer them inside slices of good bread; add them to soups, stews, and stuffings; or caramelize them with brown butter to eat with farro or crisp toast. You can reuse the delicious miso itself to embolden soups (see Wintercress Dashi) and stews.

2 cups (500 ml) white or yellow miso
2 cups (150 g) ramp bulbs, trimmed

Spread a layer of miso in the bottom of a container that will be living in your fridge for some time. Arrange a layer of ramps on top. Press the bulbs into the miso. Add more miso, and another layer of ramps. Repeat. Cover the container with its lid. Store in the fridge. The ramps are ready after 24 hours, but are way better and very mellow after 3 months.

To eat, remove the bulbs, give them a quick rinse in warm water, then pat dry.

Ramp Aioli

Makes 1½ cups (375 ml)

Aioli is a powerful way of appreciating ramps in small doses if you have had a modest forage (or are using Ramp Pickles out of season). Use the aioli as a dip for Oven Fries with Ground Elder Gremolata, or Fried Milkweed Buds; add it in dollops to fish soups; slather it on Ramp Lamb Burgers; or use it to transform simple picnic sandwiches.

1 tablespoon very finely chopped fresh
    ramp bulbs or Ramp Pickle bulbs
    (1–2 ramps)
½ teaspoon Ramp Leaf Salt
1 large egg yolk
1 teaspoon Ramp Pickle brine, or white
    wine vinegar
1 cup (250 ml) avocado oil

Using the flat of a chef's knife, mash the chopped ramps with the Ramp Leaf Salt.

In a mixing bowl, whisk the egg yolk with the mashed ramps and Ramp Pickle brine or vinegar. While whisking continuously, pour the oil into the yolk mixture, at first in drops, then in a very thin stream. Continue adding oil in a thin stream as the mixture becomes gelatinous (usually after you have used about a third of the oil). Store in a clean glass jar in the fridge.

Ramps and Smoked Trout

Serves 6 as an appetizer

Max Creek Hatchery's David Harris sells ramps along with smoked trout at the Union Square Greenmarket. The combination is irresistible. This potted trout is ideal picnic fare.

2 smoked trout
10 ramps
Squeeze of lemon juice (less than
    1 tablespoon)
8 ounces (113 g) butter

Remove the trouts' skin. Lift the meat off one side and place in a bowl. Flip the trout over and repeat. Check each piece for fine bones as you work, and remove. In the bowl, flake the trout into small pieces using two forks, one in each hand.

Cut the leaves from the ramps and save for another recipe. Slice the remaining bulbs paper-thin. Mix the ramp slices with the flaked trout and the lemon juice. Taste—add more lemon if you like.

In a small pot melt the butter over medium heat.

Place the trout and ramp mixture into small ramekins and pat down firmly with the back of a spoon. Slowly pour the butter over the ramekins, allowing it to sink down into the fish. Pour until it just covers the top of the fish (you may need more butter if the trout is not firmly packed).

Cover and refrigerate. Eat within 3 days. Serve with whole-grain brown bread, crispy toast, or crackers.

Ramp and Shrimp Ceviche

Serves 4

The combination of sweet shrimp with pungent ramps is divine. A tiny forage can be stretched this way.

If you are preparing the ceviche for varying numbers of people, figure on six medium shrimp, one ramp leaf, and 1 tablespoon of lime juice per person. (Save and freeze the shells for Wild Roast Salmon with Spring Forages in Miso Broth, or a fish soup.)

4 ramp leaves
24 medium shrimp, shelled and de-veined
5 tablespoons fresh lemon or lime juice
1 small hot red chile, finely sliced
¼ teaspoon salt
4 garlic mustard buds

Stack the ramp leaves on top of one another, roll into a tube, and slice thinly crosswise.

In a large bowl combine all the ingredients and mix well. Cover and refrigerate for 6 hours. Turn three times.

To serve, drain the juice from the shrimp (you can reuse it to make a hot broth). Arrange all the shrimp in a bowl or in individual cocktail glasses. Top with the garlic mustard flower buds.

Ramp Tart

Serves 4 as an appetizer, 2 as an entrée

This rustic, crisp tart features layers of ramp flavor and celebrates their ephemeral spring appearance.

OLIVE OIL PASTRY

2¼ cups (270 g) all-purpose flour
½ teaspoon salt
3½ fluid ounces (100 ml) extra-virgin olive oil
2 tablespoons Raw Ramp Leaf Oil
½ cup (125 ml) tepid water

TART TOPPING

20 ramps, leaves and bulbs
1 tablespoon olive oil
4 anchovy fillets
4 tablespoons Raw Ramp Leaf Oil
Squeeze of lemon juice

FOR THE PASTRY: In a large mixing bowl, combine all the pastry ingredients and stir together quickly. Form the dough into a ball, flatten a little, wrap, and chill for 30 minutes in the fridge.

Preheat the oven to 400°F (200°C).

FOR THE TOPPING: Cut very fat bulbs in half, lengthwise, so they cook evenly. Cut the leaves off half the ramps. Stack the removed leaves on top of one another, roll them up into a tube shape, and cut across the tube into thin ribbons. Heat the olive oil over medium-high heat in a saucepan. Add the whole ramps and ramp bulbs in a single layer. Sauté the bulbs for 6 minutes, then add the chiffonaded leaves, stirring. Cook another 4 minutes to wilt well. Turn off the heat.

Meanwhile chop the anchovy fillets finely. Place them in a small bowl with the Raw Ramp Leaf Oil and lemon juice; stir very well to combine. Pour this dressing over the warm ramps and stir well to coat each ramp.

TO ASSEMBLE: On a floured board roll the pastry out into a rough disk or square. Wrap the pastry around the rolling pin and transfer to an oiled baking sheet. Scatter the ramps and leaves across the pastry disk. Slide the tray into the hot oven and bake until the pastry is turning golden brown at the edges, 25 to 30 minutes. Serve hot or at room temperature.

Ramp Lamb Burgers

Makes 4 burgers

Spring burger heaven. These are big burgers. Because you would be sorry if they were small. Yes, you can top them with cheese (a soft sheep's-milk cheese is a good choice), but I prefer them straight up.

2 pounds (907 g) ground lamb
16 ramp leaves
½ teaspoon Ramp Leaf Salt
1 tablespoon lemon juice
Black pepper
4 tablespoons cold Ramp Leaf Butter,
    cut in 8 equal slices, divided
2 tablespoons unscented oil
1 tablespoon plus 1 teaspoon Roasted
    Ramp Leaf Oil
4 burger buns

Put the ground lamb in a mixing bowl. Stack the ramp leaves on top of one another, roll them into a tube, and cut them into fine ribbons. Then chop. Add the chopped ramp leaves, Ramp Leaf Salt, lemon juice, and as much ground pepper as you like to the lamb. Mix very well with your hands and form into four fat patties. Make a big dent in each patty and insert a slice of the Ramp Leaf Butter. Close up the hole. Like it was never there.

Preheat the oven to 400°F (200°C).

Heat a large skillet on the stove over high heat and add the oil. Add the four burgers. Sear them for 3 minutes, then reduce the heat to medium-high. Cook for another 2 minutes and then flip, carefully. Cook the other side for 6 minutes. Top each burger with a teaspoonful of vivid Roasted Ramp Leaf Oil, and with a slice of Ramp Leaf Butter. Transfer the burgers to a dish and cover.

Place the split burger buns in the hot oven for 1 to 2 minutes to crisp up.

Remove the hot buns from the oven and top each bottom with a burger. Spoon any accumulated juices over the burgers and add the tops. Attack.

Ramp and Beef Curry with Coconut Milk

Serves 4

Ramp season evenings are cool enough to warrant warming and complex curries. Sweet ramps balance salty soy beautifully.

3 pounds (1⅓ kg) bone-in beef short ribs, sawn across the bone into 3- to 4-inch (7½–10 cm) pieces

3 tablespoons soy sauce

2 tablespoons unscented oil

2 tablespoons tomato paste

16 ramp bulbs

1 thumb-sized piece of ginger, grated

1 dried Persian lime (or substitute a lime leaf)

1 can (13.5 fluid ounces/400 ml) coconut milk

1 tablespoon fish sauce

4 cardamom pods

5 cloves

1 cinnamon stick

2 tablespoons Sumac Essence

2 teaspoons sugar

2 tablespoons chile flakes

10 bayberry leaves

4 small red potatoes, halved

Combine the beef pieces and soy in a bowl and marinate in the fridge for at least 4 hours (or overnight). Remove from the fridge an hour before cooking.

In a large pot heat the oil over high heat. Add the beef pieces and brown them, about 1 minute per side. Reduce the heat to medium-high and add the tomato paste, stirring to let the paste caramelize. Add the ramps and stir again, cooking 1 minute. Add all the other ingredients except the potatoes. Stir well. Add water to just cover the beef. Bring the liquid to a boil. Reduce the heat to keep the liquid simmering, and cook for 2 hours, covered. Remove the lid, add the potatoes, and cook for another 45 minutes, uncovered (increase the heat slightly to keep the liquid at a high simmer; it should be bubbling slightly).

Serve in deep bowls with spoons to make the most of the sauce.

Ramp Lamb Chops

Serves 4

Fragrant ramp leaves and fire-grilled lamb make a mouthwatering early-spring meal.

8 lamb loin or rib chops

Salt

6 ramp leaves

2 tablespoons Roasted or Raw Ramp Leaf Oil

Prepare a barbecue fire. When the coals are ashed over, you are ready to grill.

Meanwhile season the lamb chops on both sides with salt to taste. Stack the ramp leaves on top of one another, roll up top-to-bottom, and slice thinly across. Place the chops in a shallow dish along with the ramp leaves and marinate until the fire is ready.

Grill the chops until they are brown on each side, and a firm finger-poke meets with some resistance in the thickest part of the meat (about 12 minutes total, depending on the thickness of the chops). Remove to a dish, baste with the Raw Ramp Leaf Oil, and cover for 10 minutes to rest.

Ramp and Pork Cassoulet

Serves 4

Pork cheeks are a delicacy, cooked low and slow. If your local butcher can't provide them, use pork shoulder or pork belly, cut into 2-inch (5 cm) pieces.

2 tablespoons butter

12 ramps, cut in half

6 slices pancetta (or substitute
   3 slices bacon)

2 pounds (907 g) pork cheeks

2 cups (400 g) green lentils, rinsed

1 teaspoon Ramp Leaf Salt

1 tablespoon Raw Ramp Leaf Oil

2 cups (500 ml) fruity dry white wine

3 cups (750 ml) chicken broth

Preheat the oven to 350°F (180°C).

In a Dutch oven heat the butter over medium-high heat and add the ramps. Sauté them just long enough to take on some color, about 6 minutes. Remove and reserve. Sauté the pancetta slices until they exude some fat. Push the pancetta to one side of the pot and add the pork cheeks. Brown them on both sides, about 1 minute per side. Remove all the meat to a bowl or plate, leaving the fat behind. Turn off the heat. Add ½ cup (100 g) of the lentils to the pot. Return a third of the pork and a third of the pancetta, spreading them evenly over the lentils. Add a third of the ramps in an even layer. Add another ½ cup (100 g) lentils. Repeat. Just before you add the last lentil layer, sprinkle the Ramp Leaf Salt and the Raw Ramp Leaf Oil over the last layer of ramps and shallots. Finish with a layer of lentils. Pour in the white wine and enough broth to cover. Bring the liquid to a gentle boil over medium-high heat, then transfer the pot carefully to the oven. Cook for 4 hours, covered. For the last hour, remove the lid to brown the top.

Serviceberry

OTHER COMMON NAMES: Saskatoon, juneberry, shadblow, shadbush, chuckley pear

BOTANICAL NAMES: *Amelanchier* species and hybrids

STATUS: Trees and shrubs, native to North America

WHERE: Relatively widespread across the US and Canada, often used in civic plantings

SEASON: Early summer

USE: Fruit, aromatic

PARTS USED: Fruit

GROW? Yes

TASTES LIKE: Sweet apple and marzipan

I met this American fruit tree one beautiful June day in Manhattan, on a Battery Park City terrace in 2007. With garden-designing friends I was taking a taking a tour of the Solaire, the first LEED-accredited high-rise in the United States and a paean to green design, whose green roofs look out over the Hudson River to the west, to rooftops below and beyond, and, at the time, to the raw construction at Ground Zero, rising in the cleft between two skyscrapers.

Loose-limbed trees were planted on one of the Solaire's terraces, their branches bowed by a heavy crop of small red fruits. I recognized them. The previous summer I had picked and eaten them in a jasmine-scented garden in the town of Ayvalik, on the Aegean. Then, nobody could tell me what they were, only that they were good to eat. On the roof of the Solaire I sneaked one into my mouth and surreptitiously pressed my teeth together. Juice far sweeter than a blueberry's spread over my tongue. I edged back toward the trees, upping the dose.

After the tour we found more of the trees on a little promontory in Teardrop Park, a green inlet in Battery Park, hidden by tall buildings. We stood like birds ready to startle, picking ripe fruit and laughing through red mouthfuls. Back home I hit the web and discovered the genus *Amelanchier*. My New York berrying had begun. Except they are not berries. Like apples, they are pomes.

Widely distributed and numbering around 25 species, these tough North American trees and shrubs withstand brutal winters to blossom in early spring. On the East Coast their bloom coincides with the running of the shad, earning them the common names shadblow and shadbush. To Canadians they are Saskatoon and are sometimes marketed as such. I like Juneberries (except when our local trees ripen early, in late May!). William Clark of the Lewis and Clark Expedition referred to them as "sarvis buries" in that extraordinary travel journal, which inspires equal parts awe and cringe. Native Americans knew serviceberries well. The pounded fruit was an ingredient in regional pemmicans. The original road food. I have dried the fermented fruit, and it is addictively good.

The fruit I ate in Turkey perhaps belonged to the one European species, *Amelanchier ovalis*, which occurs right into central Russia, although the American *A. lamarckii* has naturalized on that continent (where it is known in English as snowy mespilus). And there is one Asian serviceberry, *A. asiatica*.

Despite their native status and widespread natural distribution, their excellent shelf life (ripe fruit will be in good condition after two refrigerated weeks), and often outstanding flavor—serviceberries are almost never to be seen at market.

At first I ate serviceberries fresh, out of hand. Their flavor is frankly sweet, like cooked apples. Then I made pie. When exposed to heat the tiny seeds release a frisson of bitter almond: Amelanchier pie is redolent of marzipan. So is cake. I preserve the fruit by extracting a fermented syrup and later dry those serviceberries to use in baking.

Despite the broad occurrence of various species and hybrids across the United States, many people have never encountered an amelanchier. Happily, New York City is rich with the trees, and I have picked them in many places, including two parks designed by Michael van Valkenburgh Associates (whom I thank): Teardrop Park and Brooklyn Bridge Park (with permission). Happily, the trees, shrubs, and named cultivars are increasingly available at

nurseries. And the day I see little cardboard boxes of ripe serviceberry fruit standing shoulder to shoulder with cherries at the local farmers market, you will hear my yahoo cross-country.

How to Collect and Prepare

There is no trick. The sweetest fruit is purple, but red pomes are good to eat, too. Avoid any that have been afflicted by the fascinating fungal growths of cedar apple rust. At home the fruit lasts well, covered in the fridge, for weeks, should you have gathered a glut and come to a preparation standstill.

Caution

Like apple seeds, serviceberries' tiny seeds contain minute amounts of substances that are converted to hydrogen cyanide in our digestive system. Eating a whole pie on your own will not hurt you. The parts to be concerned about are the twigs, buds, and leaves, especially if they have wilted. These have sickened livestock and killed deer.

CULTIVATION TIPS
USDA Hardiness Zones 2–8

Various species, hybrids, and cultivars of serviceberry are increasingly available at nurseries. They range from plants that are tolerant of drought (*A. alnifolia*) to those preferring moist but well-drained sites (*A. canadensis*). Research the amelanchier adapted to your region. Although they are shade-tolerant, these shrubs and trees will produce the most abundant fruit in full sun.

Fermented Serviceberry Syrup

Makes about 2 cups (500 ml)

Using the cold extraction method I learned when making traditional *ume* (unripe Japanese apricot) syrup, serviceberries and sugar are allowed to sit as the sugar draws out the juices. Once bottled and strained, the syrup keeps very well. A tablespoon flavors soft as well as alcoholic drinks, savory pan juices, and desserts. It is one of the many delights of serviceberry season, and an easy way to preserve the harvest. The measurements below are a guideline—but you need as much sugar as fruit by weight. The leftover fruit is a delicacy in its own right.

2 pounds (907 g) ripe serviceberries
2 pounds (907 g) sugar

Combine the fruit and sugar in a large glass jar or jars. Add the lid and shake and tilt the bottle to distribute the sugar evenly. Shake it up every day, and after about a week you will see the red syrup gathering in the bottom. When fermentation begins to take place—you will hear a hiss when you open the jar—it is a good idea to allow gas to escape once a day (or just cover the jar's mouth with cheesecloth secured with string or a rubber band). More syrup will form until it covers the fruit. I like to leave this fermentation with fruit to mature for a few weeks, but you can strain it as soon as you have enough syrup. Bottle in clean glass jars.

The fruit left behind after straining the syrup can be used while it is still moist and syrupy in baking, and in savory dishes (especially with duck). It can also be dried (see Dried Fermented Serviceberries).

Dried Fermented Serviceberries

Quantity depends on how much you used for Fermented Serviceberry Syrup

If you have made Fermented Serviceberry Syrup, the strained fruit can be dried. The result is a delicacy, and easy to polish off in one sitting if you do not hold back. Serviceberries in general have huge potential as a dried snack, but I think they are much nicer after fermentation, which turns the seeds very soft as well as flavorful. Add the dried serviceberries to scones, fruit breads, fruitcakes, and trail mixes.

To dry the fruit, spread it out evenly on parchment lined baking sheets. It will be very sticky. Cover with an insect net to keep critters out. Shake the pan a couple of times a day to turn the fruit. Use clean hands to spread them out again. In a humid summer the drying process can take a week or more. Naturally, if you have a dehydrator, use it. I have tried my oven-drying method (on the lowest setting, turning it on and off every hour—I use this for ramp leaves), but it requires constant attention and is too time consuming, in this case.

When it is ready the fruit should be as moist as small raisins, rather than desiccated. Store in food-safe containers or in glass jars, or freeze.

Secret Service

Makes 1 drink

Frisky, amber, and alive with botanicals . . .

2 fluid ounces (4 tablespoons) gin
1 fluid ounce (2 tablespoons) Sumac Vodka
1 fluid ounce (2 tablespoons) vermouth
1 fluid ounce (2 tablespoons) Fermented
Serviceberry Syrup

Shake it all up with ice. Strain, and pour.

Serviceberry Breakfast Bread

Makes 1 loaf

This bread makes excellent use of Dried Fermented Serviceberries. You could substitute mahlab for the spicebush, too (in which case *use 1 teaspoon only*).

DOUGH

7 fluid ounces (200 ml) milk
2 teaspoons sugar
2 teaspoons instant yeast
12 ounces (340 g) all-purpose flour
4 ounces (113 g) whole wheat flour
1 tablespoon ground spicebush
    (or 1 *teaspoon* mahlab)
3½ ounces (99 g) cold butter
2 ounces (57 g) sugar
½ teaspoon salt
2 large eggs, whisked
5 ounces (142 g) Dried Fermented
    Serviceberries

EGG WASH

1 large egg, beaten
2 tablespoons milk

GLAZE

2 tablespoons Fermented
    Serviceberry Syrup

Warm the milk until just tepid in a saucepan over medium heat. Whisk in the sugar and yeast.

Combine the flours and the spicebush in a large bowl. Grate or cut the butter into the flour. Using your fingers, rub the butter into the flour until the mixture resembles coarse crumbs. Add the sugar and salt and mix gently.

Make a well in the flour mixture. Pour in the whisked eggs and then the yeasted milk. Stir until the dough comes together. Use your hands to bring the dough into a cohesive ball and turn it out onto a floured board. Knead for at least 10 minutes, until it becomes smooth and silky and very pliable.

Lay the kneaded dough in a lightly buttered bowl and cover. Let it rise until doubled in size, 1 to 3 hours.

Butter a 9 by 5 inch (23 × 13 cm) loaf pan.

Once the dough has doubled, punch it back down again and lay it back on your board. Sprinkle about a quarter of the Dried Fermented Serviceberries onto the dough, press them into the surface, and then knead it once or twice until the fruit has been absorbed. Repeat until all the fruit has been incorporated. (Some escapees are inevitable.) Form the dough into a rough log shape.

Lower the dough gently into the pan, seam-side down. Cover the pan and allow the dough to double in size.

Preheat the oven to 375°F (190°C).

Whisk the egg and milk together in small bowl. Brush the surface of the loaf with the egg wash.

Slide into the hot oven and bake for 35 to 45 minutes, until golden brown. Tip the bread from the pan and tap the bottom. It should sound hollow. Place it on a cooling rack with a paper towel or parchment beneath. Brush the Fermented Serviceberry Syrup onto the loaf while it is warm.

When the loaf cools, tuck in, with lots of good butter.

Grilled Peaches with Fermented Serviceberry Syrup

Serves 4

It was one of Marcella Hazan's books that taught me to grill fruit on a cooling fire. A hot skillet works very well, too. The seasonal overlap of local peaches and serviceberries is very slim, so I usually use peaches from southern states when I make this lusciously simple dessert.

4 ripe freestone peaches

1 tablespoon olive oil

2 tablespoons Fermented
Serviceberry Syrup

2½ ounces (70 g) ripe serviceberries

Split the peaches in half and remove their stones. Heat a skillet over medium-high heat, add the oil, and place the peaches in it cut-side down. Cook for 8 to 10 minutes, then very carefully turn them over. Spoon the Fermented Serviceberry Syrup into their cavities. Cook another 8 minutes (you are not cooking them through). Transfer to a serving plate and scatter the fresh serviceberries over them.

Pan-Seared Duck Breasts with Fermented Serviceberry Syrup

Serves 4

Duck, with its gamy, liverish undertones, is a natural match for the sweetness of fruit, while the dark meatiness of good soy provides ballast. Adding the near-candied, lightly alcoholic fruit brings a touch of marzipan (from the seeds) to the finished sauce.

4 duck breasts (about 1 pound/453 g each)

¼ cup (60 ml) Fermented
Serviceberry Syrup

¼ cup (60 ml) soy sauce

½ teaspoon salt

1 cup (130 g) Dried Fermented
Serviceberries

Marinate the duck 2 hours before you intend cooking.

Score the fat side of the duck breasts into diamonds, with your drawn lines about ¼ inch (½ cm) apart. Cut just shy of the meat. Combine the Fermented Serviceberry Syrup, soy sauce, and salt in a shallow dish and add the duck. Transfer to the fridge. Halfway through the marinating time, turn the meat so that all sides are well flavored. Remove the duck from the fridge half an hour before you want to cook it.

Place two dry skillets over high heat (if you have a huge pan that can accommodate all four, use one). Remove the duck breasts from their marinade (reserve it). Place two in each pan, fat-side down. Immediately reduce the heat to medium (this will allow the fat to render without burning the bleep out of the duck). Cook for about 10 minutes, as the melted fat accumulates in the pan. Remove the breasts, and pour off this fat. Increase the heat to medium-high. Return the duck breasts to the pan, meat-side down. Cover each pan with a very large lid and cook for another 5 minutes. Add the Dried Fermented Serviceberries and the rest of the marinade. There will be smoke. Cook for another 3 minutes, uncovered. The center of each breast should have some give when poked firmly with a finger. This means pink inside. Remove the breasts to a platter and cover to rest for at least 10 minutes. When the breasts have rested, carve them into slices across the grain and return them to the pan with their accumulated juices. Serve at once.

Serviceberry Ice Cream

Makes 1¼ quarts (1½ liters)

Cooking serviceberries releases their distinctive marzipan aroma. The smooth tartness of top-quality balsamic vinegar blends lusciously with the fruit. In late summer or early autumn, if there is any left, I like to serve this with Bayberry Beach Plum and Red Wine Syrup.

1½ pounds (680 g) serviceberries
    (makes about 1 cup/250 ml purée)
8 ounces (227 g) sugar
2 cups half-and-half, cold
1 cup (250 ml) cream, cold
2 tablespoons balsamic vinegar

Combine the serviceberries and sugar in a saucepan. Place over medium heat and cook until the juice begins to run, stirring occasionally to prevent sticking. Allow the oozed juices to boil for 1 minute, then turn off the heat. When the mixture has cooled, press it through a food mill to extract the seeds and any leftover stems. (If you do not have a food mill, purée the fruit in a blender and work the mixture through a fine-mesh sieve into a bowl.)

You should be left with 1 cup (250 ml) of purée. Chill it thoroughly in the fridge.

When the purée is cold, mix it with the half-and-half and cream in a bowl. Add the balsamic vinegar. Transfer to the frozen bowl of an ice cream maker and churn until thick.

Serviceberry Clafoutis

Makes 1 clafoutis

Serviceberries are so appealing straight off the tree that I sometimes hesitate to cook them. But I love marzipan and clafoutis, too, and this classic dessert embodies the best of both.

2 cups (280 g) ripe serviceberries
1 large egg
2 large egg yolks
3 tablespoons sugar
⅛ teaspoon salt
3 tablespoons flour
1 cup (250 ml) cream
¼ cup (60 ml) milk

Preheat the oven to 375°F (190°C). Butter a 9½-inch (24 cm) tart dish.

Scatter the serviceberries evenly in the dish. In a mixing bowl whisk the eggs with the sugar and salt. Add the flour and whisk until smooth. Add the cream and milk and stir until blended. Pour the batter into the tart dish. Bake the clafoutis for 35 to 40 minutes, until the custard has barely set in the middle and an inserted skewer comes out clean.

Summer Serviceberry Pudding

Serves 6

Disarmingly simple and startlingly good, the charm of an English pudding lies in very ripe, barely cooked fruit. The flavor of marzipan from the serviceberry seeds carols like Christmas from the midsummer juices, making this one of my husband's favorite desserts. I use soft, store-bought potato bread, but most white breads work. Serve with whipped cream or crème frâiche.

1½ pounds (680 g) very ripe serviceberries

¼ pound (113 g) black raspberries
    (or black currants, or raspberries)

5 ounces (142 g) sugar

⅛ teaspoon salt

1 tablespoon lemon juice

2 tablespoons brandy (optional)

8 slices (plus extra, in case) white bread,
    crusts removed

Place the fruit with the sugar in a pot and cook it over medium heat. Stir gently to dissolve the sugar. Allow the mixture to come to a boil for 10 seconds, then immediately turn off the heat. Stir in the salt, lemon juice, and brandy, if using.

Lightly butter a 1-quart (1 liter) bowl and line it with two sheets of plastic wrap or cheesecloth, allowing it to overlap the sides by 4 inches (10 cm).

Using a cookie cutter or scissors, cut a round from one bread slice to fit the bottom of the bowl. Place it in the bottom. Place four slices around the edges of the bowl. A triangular space is left between each slice. Cut matching triangles from the remaining bread to fit the spaces. If there are any holes left, patch them with extra bread.

Pour the berry mixture into the bowl. Cover the top of the filling with a slice of bread and fill in the four gaps left with pieces from another slice. Gather the plastic wrap or cloth over the top of the pudding, to cover. Place a small plate that is the same size as the pudding on top of the bread to press the filling down. Place a weight (a heavy can or jar of pickles works well) on top of that. Lift the pudding bowl into a dish with low sides to catch any oozing juices. Transfer to the fridge to chill for at least 6 and up to 24 hours.

To unmold the pudding remove the weights and peel back the plastic or cloth. Place a serving plate over the top of the pudding and quickly invert the pudding onto the plate. Carefully lift the bowl up to release the pudding. Remove the wrap, and there is your pudding. Garnish the edges with more berries, if you like.

Serviceberry Forest Cake

Makes 1 cake

North American serviceberries fill the luscious layers of this airy genoise sponge, extrapolated from Europe's famous black forest cake.

BAKING PAN

1 tablespoon melted butter

SPONGE

½ cup (60 g) flour

¼ cup (30 g) cocoa

½ teaspoon ground spicebush

¼ teaspoon salt

6 large eggs

¾ cup (150 g) sugar

3 tablespoons melted butter

FILLING

10 ounces (283 g) serviceberries

¼ cup (50 g) sugar

1½ cups (375 ml) cream

2 tablespoons powdered sugar

1 cup (120 g) black raspberries
(or use more serviceberries)

3 tablespoons Fermented
Serviceberry Syrup*

* If you have not made Fermented Service-berry Syrup, draw off and use the juice from the cooked serviceberries instead.

FOR THE SPONGE: Preheat the oven to 350°F (180°C).

Brush melted butter lightly over the bottom and sides of an 8-inch (20 cm) springform pan. Line the pan with parchment paper, making sure the parchment comes up 1½ inches (4 cm) above the sides. Place the pan in the freezer to chill.

Mix the flour, cocoa, spicebush, and salt in a small bowl.

Place the eggs and sugar in a large bowl and beat until the mixture has tripled in volume and is very pale and creamy—8 to 12 minutes. These tiny bubbles will lift the cake, as there is no other rising agent. Sprinkle the dry ingredients into the eggs in three stages, gently folding them in with a spatula after each addition. Finally, pour in the butter, folding it in gently and deftly. Pour the batter into the prepared cake pan and bake for 55 to 60 minutes, until the top of the sponge feels firm.

Remove from the oven and place on a wire rack, still in the pan, for 10 minutes. Remove the pan and carefully peel the paper from the cake. Allow it to cool upside down. *Do not cut it until it has thoroughly cooled.*

FOR THE FILLING: Combine 8½ ounces (241 g) of the serviceberries with the sugar in a saucepan. (Reserve 1½ ounce/40 g for the top of the cake.) Place over medium heat and cook, stirring gently, until the fruit is glistening with exuded juice. Allow the juice to bubble at the edges of the pan for a few seconds. Turn off the heat and let the fruit cool.

Whip the cream with the powdered sugar until stiff peaks form.

TO ASSEMBLE: Using a sharp bread knife, carefully cut the cooled sponge into three equal layers. Brush each layer with some Fermented Service-berry Syrup. Place the bottom layer on a cake stand or serving plate. Top with one-third of the cream, then scatter one-half of the cooked service-berries across it, along with one-third of the black raspberries, if using (or substitute uncooked serviceberries). Add the second cake layer, and repeat. Add the last layer, and top with reserved fresh serviceberries and black raspberries.

If you will not be eating the cake at once, keep it in the fridge, covered, until you are ready. It keeps well for 3 days.

Ricotta Serviceberry Cake

Makes 1 cake

Assembled in 10 minutes, this slow-baking and moist berry cake combines the marzipan of cooked serviceberries with the prickle of lemon zest. It keeps very well and is delicious with coffee for breakfast. If you have not made Fermented Serviceberry Syrup, just leave it out. I have baked it both ways.

4 ounces (113 g) butter, melted, divided
1½ cups (180 g) all-purpose flour
¾ cup (150 g) sugar
2 teaspoons baking powder
¼ teaspoon salt
3 large eggs
12 ounces (340 g) fresh ricotta
1 tablespoon Fermented Serviceberry Syrup
1 teaspoon microplaned lemon zest
8 ounces (227 g) serviceberries

Preheat the oven to 350°F (180°C).

Brush an 8-inch (20 cm) springform baking pan with a little of the butter. Line it with parchment paper. Butter the parchment paper lightly.

In one bowl combine the flour, sugar, baking powder, and salt. Whisk to mix evenly. In another bowl whisk the eggs with the ricotta, Fermented Serviceberry Syrup, and lemon zest. Gently add the dry ingredients to the wet, mixing as you go. Stir in the remaining melted butter, and then add most of the serviceberries, leaving a few for the top. Transfer the batter to the prepared pan, jiggle the pan gently to distribute evenly, and top with the remaining serviceberries. Slide into the oven and bake for 65 to 75 minutes, until an inserted skewer comes out clean.

Remove the cake from the oven and let it sit on a wire rack for 10 minutes before releasing the springform pan.

Serviceberry Tartlets

Makes 24 tartlets, 3 inches (7½ cm) each

I make these jammy little three-bite tarts to pack on picnics. They are a favorite on my June forage walks and are often the first taste anyone has had of serviceberries. Julia Sforza, a talented cook and baker who lives in the Hudson Valley, shared her pastry recipe with me (she uses it for peach galettes).

PASTRY

3 cups (360 g) flour

½ teaspoon salt

8 ounces (227 g) cold butter

8–11 tablespoons ice water

4 tablespoons melted butter, for the
    muffin pans

FILLING

1½ pounds (680 g) serviceberries

1½ cups (300 g) sugar

2 tablespoons cornstarch

GLAZE

3 tablespoons milk

FOR THE PASTRY: In a bowl combine the flour and salt. Grate the cold butter onto the flour. Using your fingers, work the butter into the flour until the mixture resembles coarse crumbs. Add 6 tablespoons of the ice water to the flour mixture and stir quickly with a spoon. Keep adding tablespoons of water until the dough just sticks together. I prefer to use my hands for the final mixing as they can tell faster than a spoon can. Divide the pastry in two, flatten into rough disks, wrap, and chill in the fridge for an hour.

FOR THE FILLING: Mix this just before filling the tarts (if it sits for a long time, the sugar draws out the juices and your tart will be soggy). In a bowl combine the serviceberries and sugar. Add the cornstarch and toss well.

TO BAKE: If you have one muffin tray, work in batches; if you have two, bake all the tarts at once. You can use larger-sized muffin trays, of course, but will have fewer tarts.

Preheat the oven to 400°F (200°C).

Butter two muffin pans with 3-inch (7½ cm) slots for muffins. Place them in the freezer to chill while you roll out the pastry

Working with one pastry disk at a time, roll out the pastry thinly on a floured board. Use a 3¾-inch (9½ cm) pastry cutter to press out the bottoms of the tarts. Gather the pastry remnants, press them together again, wrap, and chill. Gently place a round of pastry into each muffin slot, pressing it evenly around the edges. It will not come all the way to the top. Spoon a tablespoon of serviceberry filling into each pastry case. Transfer the filled pan to the freezer to chill while you press out the tops using a 2½-inch (6 cm) cutter. Use the chilled pastry remnants to cut out the last shapes.

Remove the chilling trays from the freezer and place a top on each tart. Press the edges together and use a fork's tines to crimp the edges all around. Pierce the top of each tart with a sharp knife to make a steam vent.

Just before baking, brush the tops of the tartlets with milk. Transfer to the hot oven and bake for about 20 minutes, until the pastry has begun to brown and some of the tarts have begun to bubble with red juice. Remove the trays, gently slide a knife around each tart's edge, and loosen each tart from its slot, transferring to a wire rack.

Serviceberry and Cherry Pie

Makes 1 pie

As American as serviceberry pie? Cherries and serviceberries share early summer and make a ruby juiced pie. Serve with very good vanilla ice cream or whipped cream.

FILLING

12 ounces (340 g) serviceberries
12 ounces (340 g) cherries, pitted
    and halved
4 ounces (113 g) sugar
Pinch of salt
2 tablespoons tapioca

PASTRY

6 ounces (170 g) butter
2½ ounces (70 g) sugar
1 large egg, lightly beaten
10½ ounces (297 g) flour
2 teaspoons baking powder
Pinch of salt

FOR THE FILLING: Combine the fruit in a pot with the sugar and salt and place over medium heat, covered. Shake the pan occasionally, taking care that the mixture does not scorch. Once juice has formed and begins to bubble, cook gently for another 5 minutes. Drain the fruit through a sieve over a bowl, reserving the syrup that collects. (When it is cool bottle the syrup—you'll have about a cupful/250 ml—and keep refrigerated for adding to drinks and cocktails.) Allow the filling to cool. Just before adding it to the pie pan, stir in the tapioca.

Preheat the oven to 350°F (180°C). Butter an 8-inch (20 cm) spring-form pan.

FOR THE PASTRY: In a bowl beat the butter and sugar until light and fluffy. Add the egg. Beat again. Gradually stir in the flour, baking powder, and salt. Gather the pastry together and tip it out onto a lightly floured board. Pinch off a quarter of it for the lid. Roll the rest of the pastry out thinly (it does not have to rest). Wrap it around your rolling pin and transfer to the cake pan, allowing it to overlap the edges by 1 inch (2½ cm). Add the serviceberry and cherry filling. Roll out and cut a pastry disk to cover the pie. Crimp the edges together, make several slits for steam, and transfer to the hot oven. Bake until the pastry is pale golden and crisp, about 35 minutes.

Serviceberry Loaf

Makes 1 loaf

I bake this addictive loaf often—it is very versatile and open to many variations.

3½ ounces (99 g) butter
3½ ounces (99 g) sugar
2 large eggs
4 tablespoons sour cream (or plain yogurt)
1 tablespoon lemon juice
5 ounces (142 g) all-purpose flour
5 ounces (142 g) whole wheat flour
1½ teaspoons baking powder
½ teaspoon baking soda
¼ teaspoon salt
1 teaspoon mahlab
⅓ cup (80 ml) milk, plus some extra
1 cup (140 g) ripe serviceberries

Heat the oven to 350°F (180°C). Butter a 9-inch (23 cm) loaf pan.

In a bowl cream the butter and sugar until pale and fluffy. Beat the eggs into the mixture, adding a little flour if it separates. Add the sour cream and lemon juice, and mix well. Add the flours, baking powder, baking soda, salt, mahlab, and milk, mix thoroughly. The batter will be quite stiff. Finally, add the serviceberries, stir again, and transfer to the loaf pan, smoothing a slight hollow down the length of the batter.

Bake for 50 minutes. Use a sharp skewer to test the interior. If it comes out sticky, return to the oven for a few minutes. Turn the loaf out of the pan and let it cool on a wire rack.

Variations

Use spicebush and fresh cranberries or blueberries instead of mahlab and serviceberries.
Use ½ cup (125 ml) cooked, puréed Japanese knotweed and omit the lemon juice and sour cream
Use 1 mashed banana and scale the milk back to ¼ cup (60 ml)
Add 3½ ounces (99 g) of chopped pecans at the end.

Serviceberry and Peach Cake with Almonds

Makes 1 cake

I freeze some early-summer serviceberries and use them in this moist cake when local peaches flood the farmers markets. This cake is divine, and I often make two and stack them on top of each other. You could also use Dried Fermented Serviceberries instead of fresh (and, for that matter, Dried Fermented Black Chokeberries—see Black Chokeberry Syrup).

4 ounces (113 g) butter
4 ounces (113 g) sugar
2 large eggs
4 ounces (113 g) all-purpose flour
4 ounces (113 g) almond flour
2 teaspoons baking powder
1 teaspoon mahlab
⅓ cup (80 ml) milk
7½ ounces (212 g) serviceberries, frozen or fresh
1 ripe peach, cut into small pieces

Preheat the oven to 350°F (180°C). Butter a springform pan.

In a bowl cream the butter and sugar until pale and fluffy. Beat in the eggs, adding a little flour to prevent the mixture from separating.

Gradually fold in the rest of the flour with the almond flour, baking powder, and mahlab. Add the milk and stir well. Last, add the serviceberries and chopped peaches. The mixture will be fairly firm by this time. If it seems dry add a little more milk.

Turn the cake mixture into the cake pan and bake for about 60 minutes, or until an inserted skewer comes out clean. Leave the cake to cool for 10 minutes in the pan, then loosen the edges, remove, and cool on a wire rack.

Serviceberry Pancakes

Makes 6–8 pancakes, 6 inches (15 cm) each

The best early-summer breakfast. Serviceberries bleed beautiful scarlet juice into these gorgeous pancakes. Serve with warm maple syrup and wedges of lemon.

4 ounces (113 g) whole wheat flour
4 ounces (113 g) all-purpose flour
2 tablespoons sugar
1 tablespoon baking powder
¼ teaspoon salt
2 large eggs, separated
1¼ cups (310 ml) milk
¼ cup (60 ml) buttermilk
2 tablespoons butter
5 ounces (142 g) serviceberries

In a large bowl mix the flours, sugar, baking powder, and salt. In a second bowl whisk the egg whites until they are fluffy and holding soft peaks. Make a well in the flour bowl and add the egg yolks, milk, and buttermilk, stirring the mixture together well. Fold in half the egg whites. Once they are incorporated fold in the rest.

Heat a skillet over medium-high heat and melt a tablespoon of butter in it. Drop two to three large spoonfuls of pancake batter into the skillet. Once they have spread out to about 6 inches (15 cm) drop some serviceberries onto them. When bubbles have risen in the batter and are bursting, turn each pancake over and cook the other side. Transfer the cooked pancakes to a plate and keep warm while you cook the rest of the pancakes. Continue until all the pancakes are cooked, adding butter to the pan as needed.

Sheep Sorrel

OTHER COMMON NAMES: Sour weed, red sorrel

BOTANICAL NAME: *Rumex acetosella*

STATUS: Perennial weed, invasive in North America

WHERE: Widespread in moist disturbed ground, lawns

SEASON: Spring through fall

USE: Vegetable

PARTS USED: Leaves

GROW? With extreme caution, due to its invasive nature

TASTES LIKE: Sorrel and lemons

The small, arrow-shaped leaves of sheep sorrel easily escape attention—unless they are growing in someone's manicured lawn. They are hard to remove because the colonies' roots spread very sneakily underground. A small piece left behind can regenerate. Which is why sheep sorrel occurs pretty much all over North America and is widely distributed globally. *Rumex acetosella* is native to Eurasia and was introduced to North America with early European settlement. It has proliferated to the extent that it is banned for sale in at least one state (Connecticut) and is listed as a noxious invasive in others.

adding acid to sauces or soups, and turning a dull green that is a disappointing contrast with its fresh color. Because they are neatly small, I include the leaves whole in mixed salads (saving their color), and love to drop them at the last minute into dishes that call for acid.

The leaves are always an excellent alternative to lemon juice.

How to Collect and Prepare

Sheep sorrel is very easy to collect if you do not mind kneeling. Pick the leaves by the handful. It is a good idea to avoid the large public lawns where it sometimes grows, as most lawns have been treated with synthetic chemical fertilizers or herbicides. Once you are home revive the leaves in a bowl of cool water and then wrap and store in the fridge. Sheep sorrel is prettiest when raw, turning a drab khaki once exposed to heat, although it loses none of its flavor.

CULTIVATION TIPS
USDA Hardiness Zones 3–7

Sheep sorrel is invasive. I grow a highly managed patch, shearing off the flowering stems it sends up in early summer before it sets seed. I contain its vegetative spread by cutting down into the soil in a straight line around my 3-square-foot patch, using a sharp-toothed trowel. This severs exploratory rhizomatous roots. If new plants emerge beyond this zone, I weed them out by hand. As a cooking gardener, the effort is rewarded by the fresh leaves that appear well before other greens in the early-spring vegetable patch.

Taste a leaf. It is powerfully sour, just like garden or so-called French sorrel. And we plant *that* on purpose. In the kitchen it behaves in the same way, too, dissolving in moist heat (like Japanese knotweed, to which it is related),

Sheep Sorrel Soda Pop

Makes 6 cups (1½ liters)

I make this pop—like a leafy lemonade—when I shear off the sheep sorrel flowers in late spring or early summer. It can be drunk as soon as it begins to fizz, but I have also kept bottles and found that they mellow agreeably with time.

4 ounces (113 g) sheep sorrel leaves
    and flowers
1 cup (200 g) sugar
6 cups (1½ liters) water

Combine the ingredients in a clean glass jar, stir well, and cover with cheesecloth secured with string or a rubber band. Stir daily. After a few days (I find sheep sorrel highly variable with fermentation—it has taken 6 days before I see any action) there will be bubbles rising when you stir. Sniff it; you will smell the yeasts working. Keep it fermenting for another 3 days and then strain it through a fine-mesh sieve, and again through cheesecloth into a clean bottle. Keep it in the fridge to be on the safe side. A bottle left out can potentially explode if the yeasts are still very active.

Drink straight up, or mix with a dash of gin and add good tonic.

Sheep Sorrel and Artichoke Dip

Serves 2 as a light meal, 4 as an appetizer

To me, artichoke dip is a clear October afternoon on Grouse Mountain in British Columbia, where my husband asked me to marry him, a month after we met. After we had both calmed down, we went into the touristy restaurant and celebrated with cold beer and a hot artichoke dip that had 1963 written all over it. In the spirit of the '60s, use canned or bottled artichoke hearts—they are seasoned differently, so take that into account before you add salt. The sheep sorrel provides cutting acid within the rich cheese and mayonnaise context. I prefer hand-chopping for this dip, but a food processor works well.

6 ounces (170 g) cooked, roughly chopped
    artichoke hearts
1½ ounces (40 g) sheep sorrel
3 ounces (85 g) grated sharp cheddar cheese
¼ cup (60 ml) mayonnaise
¼ teaspoon red chile flakes
Salt to taste
Black pepper

Chop the artichokes very finely. Chop the sheep sorrel very finely. Place both in a bowl with the cheese, mayonnaise, and chile. Mix well, and taste. Add salt and pepper.

Or: Process everything in a food processor until well mixed. Taste, and season.

Preheat the oven to 400°F (200°C).

Pack the dip into an ovenproof bowl (if it is small, leave some space at the top for hot, molten bubbling). Place the bowl in the hot oven and heat until the edges bubble, about 15 minutes. Serve with good toast.

Sheep Sorrel Smoked Fish Pâté

Makes 2 cups (500 ml)

Based on a traditional South African *snoek* pâté that I loved so much I requested it for my first grown-up birthday supper (I was twelve, my mother was the chef), this version works well with smoked mackerel, whitefish, or trout. It is an unpretentious party pleaser, where the sharpness of sheep sorrel balances the creaminess of the cheese and mayonnaise and brightens the rich smokiness of the fish. Serve with the Sambal on the side and good toast.

PÂTÉ

10 ounces (283 g) smoked fish
2 tablespoons butter
1 medium onion, finely chopped
½ teaspoon paprika
2 tablespoons tomato paste
1 teaspoon sugar
6 ounces (170 g) cream cheese
⅓ cup (80 ml) mayonnaise
1½ ounces (40 g) sheep sorrel leaves
2 tablespoons fresh lemon or lime juice
2 teaspoons fresh hot red or green chile, finely chopped
Salt
Black pepper

SAMBAL

1 small red onion, exceptionally thinly sliced
1 jalapeño pepper, very thinly sliced
Large pinch of salt
20 sheep sorrel leaves

FOR THE PÂTÉ: Remove the skin from the fish. In a bowl, flake the fish into small pieces using two forks, one in each hand. Remove any bones as you go.

Melt the butter in a saucepan over medium heat. Add the onion and cook, stirring, until it is lightly caramelized, about 15 minutes (reduce the heat if the onion scorches). Add the paprika, tomato paste, and sugar and stir well. Cook another 3 minutes. Let it cool a little before proceeding.

In the bowl of a food processor combine the cooked mixture with all the remaining pâté ingredients, except the salt and pepper. Pulse, scraping down the sides occasionally, until the mixture is smooth. Taste for salt and add if you like (it may not be necessary). Crack a generous amount of black pepper into the bowl. Pulse again. Pack the pâté into small pots, cover, and chill until needed. (Eat within 3 days.)

FOR THE SAMBAL: Just before serving, mix all the sambal ingredients well in a small bowl and serve in a small bowl alongside.

Sheep Sorrel Bruschetta

Serves 4–6 as an appetizer

This is method more than recipe, but it is too nice not to share.

Make Yogurt Cheese with Wild Herbs, but add 2 tablespoons of finely chopped sheep sorrel to the yogurt with the other herbs. When the cheese is ready, smear it onto toasted sourdough, top with more sheep sorrel leaves, and drizzle with fine extra-virgin olive oil, or honey.

Fava and Garlic Scape Bruschetta with Sheep Sorrel

Serves 2 as an entrée, 4–6 as an appetizer

Early-summer fava beans appear with the first green garlic, when the sheep sorrel is lush. These brilliant green toasts are beautiful picnic fare; pack toasts and topping separately and assemble on-site. It is not essential to skin the fava beans, but the purée will be impeccably green if you do. And frozen beans work well, too.

10½ ounces (297 g) fresh fava beans
8 garlic scapes, tough ends trimmed off
1 head young garlic, peeled
2 ounces (57 g) sheep sorrel leaves
20 mint leaves
3 tablespoons extra-virgin olive oil
½ teaspoon salt
Black pepper
6 slices sourdough bread

Bring water to a boil in two pots. Add the fava beans to one pot and cook until tender, 6 to 10 minutes, depending on their size. Remove, drain, and refresh under cold water. Slip their skins off. Cook the scapes in the other pot until just tender, about 8 to 10 minutes. Remove, drain, and refresh. Cut off their pretty flower heads and reserve to garnish.

Place the beans, garlic scape stems, garlic cloves (reserve 2 cloves), sheep sorrel, mint, olive oil, salt, and pepper to taste in a food processor. Pulse until roughly blended (or longer, if you want a perfectly smooth topping).

Toast the sourdough and rub each hot slice with the green garlic cloves. Cut the slices in half. Spread the topping onto each slice, and garnish some of the slices with the scape buds. Otherwise, serve the toast separately and allow friends to help themselves.

Sheep Sorrel and Garlic Mustard Chicken

Serves 4

Lemon and mustard work very well together, and I often use sheep sorrel for acid instead. In this last-minute sauce, the horseradish bite of garlic mustard root cuts through the cream.

4 whole chicken legs

4 ounces (113 g) pancetta, chopped

¼ teaspoon salt

¼ cup (60 ml) water

4 heaped tablespoons smooth Dijon mustard

½ cup (125 ml) white wine

⅓ cup (80 ml) cream

2 cups (60 g) sheep sorrel leaves

Salt (optional)

Black pepper

2 tablespoons garlic mustard root, scrubbed and microplaned (or Garlic Mustard Root Relish)

Preheat the oven to 400°F (200°C).

Work the skin of the chicken loose with your fingers and stuff the chopped pancetta between the skin and the meat. Season each leg lightly with salt. Place the legs in a skillet, add the water, and slide into the hot oven. After 40 minutes pull the skillet out and spread 1 tablespoon of mustard over each leg. Reduce the heat to 350°F (180°C). Return the chicken to the oven for another 30 minutes.

Remove the skillet and transfer the chicken to a plate—cover. Place the hot skillet on the stove over medium-high heat and add the wine. Stir well, allowing it to boil. Add the cream and let it boil again. Add the sheep sorrel. Stir. Cook at a simmer for about 2 more minutes. Taste for seasoning, adding salt (if necessary) and some pepper. Just before serving, stir the garlic mustard root into the juices from the resting chicken. Return the chicken leg juice to the skillet to serve.

Sheep Sorrel and Anchovy Chicken

Serves 4

This is a one-skillet special. A time-saving and frequent usual kind of supper in our house. Adding the sheep sorrel raw to the hot pan preserves its color as well as its lemony crunch.

4 chicken breasts

⅛ teaspoon salt

3 tablespoons unscented oil, divided

4 cloves garlic (or 2 Ramp Pickles), thinly sliced

½ cup (125 ml) vermouth or white wine

8 salted anchovy fillets, finely chopped

⅓ cup (40 g) capers

Black pepper

1–2 teaspoons Salted Ramp Leaves

2 ounces (57 g) sheep sorrel leaves

Preheat the oven to 500°F (260°C).

Season the breasts lightly with the salt. Add 2 tablespoons of the oil to a large skillet and heat it over high heat. When it is very hot, add the breasts to the pan. Transfer it at once to the hot oven for 15 minutes, turning the breasts halfway through. Remove them to a plate, and cover them while they rest (10 minutes).

Place the skillet on the stove and add the last tablespoon of oil. Add the garlic or Ramp Pickles. It will cook for a couple of minutes from residual heat. Add the vermouth or wine, and turn the heat to high. When the liquid bubbles add the anchovies, stirring well. Cook at a simmer for 2 minutes, then turn off the heat and add the capers and black pepper to taste. Pour any resting juices from the breasts into the pan and stir. Return the chicken to the skillet. Sprinkle the breasts with the Salted Ramp Leaves. Just before serving, place the bunch of raw sheep sorrel on top of the meat.

Sheep Sorrel and Lamb Meatballs

Makes about 25 meatballs

These succulent meatballs are good served very simply, with a flurry of raw sheep sorrel, or with the additional and creamy tartness of Sheep Sorrel Avgolemono Sauce.

1½ pounds (680 g) ground lamb
¼ cup (15 g) panko bread crumbs
1 medium onion, grated
4 field garlic bulbs (or 2 cloves garlic), grated
2 ounces (57 g) sheep sorrel leaves, roughly chopped
½ cup (15 g) finely chopped parsley
¾ teaspoon salt
3 tablespoons olive oil

Combine all the ingredients (except the oil) in a bowl and mix very well. Form the mixture into 1¼-inch (3 cm) balls. This step can be done hours ahead if you chill them.

Preheat the oven to 450°F (230°C).

Heat half the oil in a skillet over medium-high heat. Fry the meatballs in batches until brown on one side and then flip to brown the other side. Use the rest of the olive oil as the pan dries out. Transfer the browned meatballs to a baking sheet and roast in the oven for about 8 minutes until cooked through.

Sheep Sorrel Avgolemono Sauce

Makes about 1 cup (250 ml)

Greek avgolemono sauce is a frothily savory version of sweet Italian zabaglione. It is a tart and silky finish for dishes like lamb meatballs, lamb stews, pan-fried fish, crab cakes, and eggs. And it will exercise your whisking arm.

4 large egg yolks
1 tablespoon lemon juice
1 cup (250 ml) chicken stock, warm
⅛ teaspoon salt
1 ounce (28 g) sheep sorrel, chopped

In a bowl whisk the eggs. Add the lemon juice and whisk again. Pour the egg mixture into a saucepan set over low heat. Slowly pour in a little of the warm chicken stock, whisking continuously. Add the salt. Keep whisking over low heat. After about 10 minutes the sauce will have thickened. Patience. If there is even a suggestion of bubbling or boiling, the sauce will overcook and separate. Keep it low and keep whisking. Sprinkle the chopped sorrel into the hot sauce at the last minute and give it a quick stir. Taste for seasoning and adjust, if necessary.

Spicebush

OTHER COMMON NAME: Appalachian allspice

BOTANICAL NAME: *Lindera benzoin*

STATUS: Large shrub, indigenous to North America

WHERE: Deciduous woodlands east of the Rockies

SEASON: All year, fruit in early fall

USE: Spice, aromatic

PARTS USED: Twigs, leaves, flowers, fruit

GROW? Yes

TASTES LIKE: Orange zest and pine with some fresh pepper

Pretty *Lindera benzoin* bursts into bloom at the end of winter, when the woods are still resolutely brown and pale with dead leaves. Its preferred habitat is in the understory, growing below deciduous hardwoods whose branches remain bare early in the new season. Shimmering with yellow blossoms, spicebush is a harbinger of spring and holds the promise of a new season of flavor.

These North American shrubs or small trees produce an exciting aromatic that remains virtually unknown beyond foraging fringes. I use it more often in my kitchen than familiar cinnamon, or cloves, or allspice. Despite one of its common names (Appalachian allspice), spicebush does not taste like allspice, at least not to me. Instead, it suggests orange peel, with a little fresh black pepper and a backdrop of delicate resin. This throws open a lot of culinary doors. It is as useful in savory applications as it is in sweet baking, dessert making, or drinks.

The most readily used part of the plant is the fruit, appearing on female plants in summer, and ripening in late summer and early fall. It can be used fresh (green and unripe, or ripe and scarlet), or dried and ground. It is an indigenous spice that holds universal potential. It belongs in every working kitchen.

But other parts are edible, too: The marvelous thing about spicebush is that even its winter twigs are intensely aromatic, flavorful enough to use in cooking and infusions. Drop them into a simmering stew, or place them in a jar of sugar; they will imbue both with their

citrusy aroma. A fermented cordial of late-winter spicebush twigs and apples is a treat.

Early spring's little yellow flowers are a delightful raw ingredient, tasting mildly of the fruit to come. Where the shrubs are prolific, it is easy to gather a couple of handfuls by stripping the blossoms from a branch on different individuals. Never denude one shrub. It's just rude. When the leaves appear, their flavor is slightly stronger. Add them to ephemeral spring salads while they are tender and chewable. By summer the spicebush shrub has retreated into green, inconspicuous anonymity. I identify it easily now, but I used to stop to scratch its summer twigs, to make sure I had the right plant. It is a refreshing scratch-and-sniff stop on the forage walks I lead. Later, small branches with mature leaves add flavor to grilled meats or infusions. And then the main event: the fruit. Midsummer's green drupes on female plants

are brightly flavored, and by late summer they have ripened to brilliant crimson. Both stages are useful, with distinctive aromas.

While delicious fresh, the fruit should be dried and then frozen to use throughout the year. It maintains its flavor exceptionally well. I grind mine as needed, using a spice grinder. For those who live beyond the range of spicebush, or whose local spicebush populations are meager, this unique American flavor is within reach via the Internet. Integration Acres, based in Ohio, sells packages of the dried fruit, and the quality is excellent.

Spicebush could be on everyone's spice rack. It should be. Grow your own, if you have the space. The small trees are good additions to semi-shady gardens, and their presence will help boost local biodiversity.

How to Collect and Prepare

Twigs: Use a sharp, clean knife or pruning shears and cut above a leaf node. Twigs flavor stews, infuse liquors, and also perfume sugar, like a vanilla bean.

Flowers: Strip them from a branch and collect them in a small paper bag. At home keep them covered in the fridge. Limit your stripping to a couple of branches per shrub.

Fruit: Once picked, the fruit—especially the unripe green drupes—darkens quickly, although the flavor remains intact. Dry the fruit by spreading it out loosely on parchment paper and either air-drying over several days or dehydrating in a dehydrator or in the oven, using the lowest setting—200°F (93°C) or lower. If you use the oven method, *turn the oven off after 30 minutes, leave off for 1 hour, then on again for 30,* until the fruit is dry. You do not want to roast it. Freeze the dried fruit in airtight bags or small jars. It keeps its flavor exceptionally well in the freezer. Grind it up as needed.

CULTIVATION TIPS

USDA Hardiness Zones 4–9

If the goal is fruit, both male and female shrubs are needed. The flowers on males are showier, and only the females carry fruit. Spicebush prefers moist but well-drained soil and will grow in high shade, semi-shade, or full sun. It is tolerant of acidic and slightly alkaline soils. The fruit provides food for birds, and the shrub is the exclusive host for the larvae of the spicebush swallowtail butterfly.

Spicebush Sugar

Makes 2 cups (200 g)

Spicebush twigs infuse sugar in the way that vanilla beans do. Use it to sprinkle on parchment before rolling up a jelly roll, and scatter it across the top of fresh bakes while they are still hot. Add a splash of water for a quick, brushed glaze. Or just beat it into the batter of the pancakes, cakes, or breads. Winter and early-spring twigs are best.

8 spicebush twigs, about 8 inches (20 cm) long

2 cups (400 g) sugar

Trim the twigs to fit the jar you are using. Drop them in and cover with sugar. It will take about a week for the sugar to taste noticeably like spicebush.

Spicebush Clementine Cordial

Makes 4½ cups (1.1 liters)

Suzaan Hauptfleisch, the owner of Kaia, a popular South African wine bar on Manhattan's Upper East Side, asked me to a devise a cordial for her adventurous bartender one winter. I decided to combine clementines (*naartjies* in South Africa and an iconic fruit there) with all-American spicebush. I now make this versatile cordial in quantity in winter. It is best friends with bourbon. Double the recipe if you would like to give bottles away as holiday gifts.

5 ounces (142 g) dried spicebush fruit

6 cups (1½ liters) water

1½ cups (375 ml) clementine juice (about 12 clementines)

1½ cups (300 g) sugar

Zest of 4 clementines

Combine all the ingredients except the zest in a large pot over medium heat. Stir to dissolve the sugar. Allow the liquid to come to a boil. Reduce the heat to maintain a very gentle boil. Continue to cook until the liquid has reduced by half. Turn off the heat and add the clementine zest. Allow the liquid to cool, covered, overnight, as the zest infuses.

Strain through a fine mesh sieve and again through cheesecloth. Bottle in sterilized jars. Keep in the fridge.

Autumn Called

Makes 1 drink

The flavors of this earthy, somber cocktail are powerfully good. Pomegranate molasses provides a rich base note without being cloying.

3 fluid ounces (6 tablespoons) cognac

1½ fluid ounces (3 tablespoons) Spicebush Clementine Cordial

2 teaspoons pomegranate molasses

Shake all the ingredients up with ice, strain, and pour.

Spicebush Cranberry Syrup

Makes 3 cups (750 ml)

When local cranberries flood the markets, I make this easy and festively crimson syrup for holiday cocktail shaking. (You can also make a cold-extraction cranberry syrup—with the bonus of the leftover, candied fruit—by following the recipe for Fermented Serviceberry Syrup—just add spicebush and make sure to crush the cranberries, which have thick skins.)

12 ounces (340 g) cranberries, crushed
6 ounces (170 g) sugar
1 tablespoon ground spicebush
3 cups (750 ml) water

Place the cranberries, sugar, spicebush, and water in a pot over medium-high heat. Bring the liquid to a boil, then reduce the heat to a simmer and cook for 10 minutes. Turn off the heat and let the mixture cool. Strain twice through cheesecloth, bottle, and keep in the fridge. It lasts well for 1 month. Use the fruit to garnish drinks like Wild Sweetfern and Citrus Toddy.

Spicebush Cranberry Fizz

Makes 5 cups (1¼ liters)

This ferment has a strong spicebush presence and blends beautifully with applejack, bourbon, whiskey, dark rum, and tequila. It also has a great affinity for apple cider, citrus, ginger, and tea. Think hot toddies (such as Thaw and Wild Sweetfern and Citrus Toddy). Use it to deglaze a roasted carrot pan, and add it to tropical fruit salads. Because cranberries ferment slowly I add apples to my mixture to help the yeasts along.

12 ounces (340 g) cranberries,
    lightly crushed
½ apple, cut up (not peeled or cored)
1 cup (200 g) sugar
¼ cup (30 g) ground spicebush
5 cups (1¼ liters) water

Place the fruit in a clean jar. Add the sugar and spicebush, and top with the water. Stir well. Cover the jar's mouth with cheesecloth and stir daily. Small bubbles rising after a day or two are a sign of fermentation. After the bubbles have been active for 5 days, strain the fruit from the liquid through a fine-mesh strainer and again through double cheesecloth. Bottle the strained liquid and keep it in the refrigerator until needed.

Long Nights

Makes 1 drink

Winter's impenetrable nights inspire dark drinks.

2½ fluid ounces (5 tablespoons) bourbon
1 fluid ounce (2 tablespoons) Spicebush
    Cranberry Fizz
1 fluid ounce (2 tablespoons) dry sherry
2 teaspoons pomegranate molasses

Combine all the ingredients with ice in a cocktail shaker. Shake, strain, and pour.

Spicebush Pecans

Makes 2 cups (8 ounces/227 g)

My Aunt Yvonne, who is ninety as I write this, used to make roasted soy pecans using nuts from her own tree in Paarl, South Africa. They were often a gift at Christmastime. Like my aunt's, these pecans, flavored with just-ground spicebush, make very good holiday gifts and are a coveted cocktail and picnic snack. And they turn very plain salads fancy at once.

8 ounces (227 g) pecans

2 tablespoons maple syrup

2 tablespoons soy sauce

2 teaspoons ground spicebush

2 tablespoons unscented oil

Preheat the oven to 350°F (180°C).

In a bowl combine the pecans with the maple syrup, soy sauce, spicebush, and oil. Toss until the nuts are thoroughly coated. Place them in a skillet or on a small baking sheet and roast until they are sizzling and smelling very good—about 15 minutes. Shake them loose a couple of times. Take care that they do not burn. Spread them out on a sheet of parchment paper to cool.

Spicebush Ginger Pickled Carrots

Serves 6–8

You could bottle these pickles, but I like to eat them the next day as part of a pickle buffet, with smoked or roasted meats. If you make this in spring, garnish with tender spicebush leaves. Keep the brine for more pickles, vinaigrettes, or braising.

¾ cup (190 ml) white wine vinegar

1 cup (250 ml) water

1 tablespoon salt

⅓ cup (67 g) sugar

2 thumb-sized pieces of ginger, peeled and microplaned (or grated)

16 spicebush berries

10 black peppercorns

3 cloves garlic, cut into matchsticks

1¼ pounds (567 g) carrots, peeled and cut into batons

Combine the vinegar, water, salt, sugar, ginger, spices, and garlic in a large bowl. Stir until the sugar and salt have dissolved. Add the carrots and toss with your hands. Transfer to a jar. Cover and store in the fridge. Halfway through marinating, turn the jar over. Drain to serve.

Spicebush Red Slaw

Serves 4

Slaw's creamy crunch is addictive, and raw beetroot is one of my favorite earthy flavors. Appropriate in any season, this bright salad, fortified with antiviral elderberries, is one of my cold-weather tonics. If you are using Fermented Elderberry Syrup, omit the sugar.

2 tablespoons Fermented Elderberry Syrup
   or Elderberry Gin
2 tablespoons fresh lime or lemon juice
1 tablespoon blood orange or orange juice
¼ teaspoon salt
½ teaspoon ground spicebush
2 teaspoons sugar
3 tablespoons mayonnaise
12 ounces (340 g) red cabbage,
   thinly sliced
1 medium beet, peeled and coarsely grated

In a bowl combine everything except the mayonnaise, cabbage, and beet. Whisk until the sugar and salt have dissolved. Add the mayonnaise and whisk again. Toss in the shredded cabbage and grated beetroot. Mix well. Chill, and serve.

Spicebush Carrot Puff Pastry Tarts

Makes 4 small tarts

So often an afterthought or a sidekick in classic sauces and stews, carrots are the stars of these mouthwatering and vividly beautiful tarts. Make them any size you prefer; the ones below make nice appetizer portions.

PURÉE

1 pound (453 g) carrots, scrubbed
    and roughly chopped
1 cup (250 ml) cream
½ cup (125 ml) water
½ teaspoon salt
1½ teaspoons ground spicebush
2 tablespoons maple syrup

SAUCE

1½ cups (375 ml) fresh orange juice
    (about 3 large oranges)
2 pieces orange peel, 2 inches (5 cm)
    long each
½ cup (125 ml) chicken or vegetable broth
Salt (optional)

ASSEMBLY

1 large egg
2 tablespoons cream
1 tablespoon water
2 sheets prepared puff pastry

FOR THE PURÉE: Place the carrots in a pot with the cream, water, salt, spicebush, and maple syrup (the carrots should be just covered by the liquids). Bring to a boil over high heat, then reduce the heat to maintain a simmer. Cook until the carrots are tender, about 10 minutes. Strain the carrots. Save the cooking liquid for another use (savory ice cream!). In a food processor, purée the carrots until very smooth. Reserve.

FOR THE SAUCE: In a pot combine the orange juice, orange peel, and broth. Reduce the liquid over high heat until only ¼ cup (60 ml) remains (skim off any foam). Taste, and add a pinch of salt if necessary. Strain through a fine-mesh sieve, and return to a small pot.

TO ASSEMBLE: Preheat the oven to 500°F (260°C). Butter a baking sheet. In a small bowl beat together the egg, cream, and water for an egg wash.

Press out eight circles from the puff pastry, using a 4½-inch (11½ cm) cutter. Use a 1½-inch (4 cm) cutter to press out a hole in the middle of four of the circles. Place the four intact circles on the buttered baking sheet. Place a generous scoopful of cool carrot purée in the middle of each. Spread the purée out evenly, leaving the edge of the pastry uncovered. Brush the exposed edges with egg wash. Top the carrot filling with remaining 4½-inch circles (leaving the carrot purée exposed in the center). Press the outer pastry edges together with the tines of a fork and brush the pastry tops with egg wash.

Slide into the oven and bake until the puff pastry is puffed up and golden brown—about 12 minutes. Warm the orange sauce over medium heat while the tarts bake. Serve each tart on its own plate with drizzle of the sauce.

Spicebush Pork Shoulder Cooked in Milk

Serves 6

This is cold-weather comfort food, cooked low and slow. I use dried spicebush berries and mugwort from the previous season, and fresh field garlic if the ground is not frozen. You can substitute other wild onions or use garlic cloves if you have no field garlic. Instead of pork shoulder you could also use bone-in pork shanks, about 1 pound (453 g) per person.

Serve with mashed potatoes, boiled barley, or crisp bread. Or pull the meat apart as a sauce for egg yolk noodles. Or eat it simply in a bowl, with spoons for the sauce. Leftovers make a great ragu.

1 pork shoulder, deboned (about 5
   pounds/2¼ kg)

1 teaspoon salt

1 tablespoon butter

2 tablespoons olive oil

6 cups (1½ ml) full-cream milk

2 teaspoons spicebush berries, crushed

4 tablespoons dried mugwort
   (or 8 fresh sprigs)

Lemon zest peeled in strips from 2 lemons

2 tablespoons lemon juice

16 field garlic bulbs (or substitute small
   garlic cloves)

Rub the pork all over with salt. Let it sit for 10 minutes. Heat the butter and oil over medium-high heat in a Dutch oven that can accommodate the pork (you can cut the meat into two sections and snuggle them closer). Brown all sides of the pork in the hot fat, turning each side after a minute.

Add the rest of the ingredients. Bring the liquid to a boil over medium-high heat, then turn the heat to low, cover with a lid, and keep at a constant, low simmer. After 2 hours leave the lid ajar and increase the heat slightly. Cook another 2 hours. The milk and meat juices should have formed a curdled sauce, rich with lemon, mugwort, and spicebush. If the sauce is still too thin, reduce it further over medium-high heat. Serve from the Dutch oven, using a large spoon to break up the meat.

Spicebush Tequila Skirt Steak

Serves 4

Economical and relatively lean skirt steak begs for a marinade with a backbone. Spicebush's citrus flavor profile blends seamlessly with powerful tequila and sharp lime juice. Rest the steak well, and slice thinly before serving. Serve with American Burnweed Green Sauce.

2 skirt steaks, about 1¼ pounds
    (567 g) each
3 tablespoons tequila
2 tablespoons lime juice
1¼ tablespoons ground spicebush
1½ tablespoons ancho powder (or substitute smoked paprika or powdered chile)
½ teaspoon salt
½ teaspoon sugar

Lay the steaks in a shallow dish. Sprinkle the tequila, lime juice, spicebush, ancho powder, and salt over them. Turn the steaks a few times to makes sure each side of the meat is covered with flavor. Marinate for a minimum of 2 hours.

Heat a large heavy skillet (or two skillets, if necessary) over high heat. Cut the long steaks to fit. When the skillets are smoking, add the meat—no oil is necessary. Sear the meat until each side is a dark, delicious-smelling brown—about 5 minutes. Flip. Add some of the marinade while they cook. The thickest parts of the steak should still have a little give in their centers when you take them off the heat—this will ensure that they are medium-rare in the middle. Remove the steaks to a platter, sprinkle with the sugar, and cover. Let them rest for at least 10 minutes. When they have rested, slice them fairly thinly. Return the meat to the juice-filled platter, and top it with a helping of American Burnweed Green Sauce.

Spicebush Soy Bone-In Rib Eye

Serves 2, with leftovers

Steak-with-a-handle is marketed as a tomahawk. The handle is the huge rib bone, and it is probably silly to pay extra for a meatless bone. But for sheer style it is hard to beat. Use your favorite aged cut of steak, or even short ribs, but make the cut a thick one. I love Ohsawa's unpasteurized and organic soy sauce for serious soy use. The only other flavor at play here is aromatic green spicebush with late-summer spicebush leaves and green branches. It is a magical combination.

1 bone-in, aged steak, cut 2 inches (5 cm)
thick, about 2½ pounds (1.1 kg)
2 tablespoons crushed fresh green
spicebush fruit
1 cup (250 ml) good soy sauce
2–3 spicebush branches with leaves,
12 inches (30 cm) long

Place the steak in a shallow baking dish or bowl. Mix the spicebush fruit into the soy sauce and pour over the steak. Let it sit, turning once, for 2 hours before you want to cook.

Build a fire that will give your steak good heat for 30 minutes.

When the coals have ashed over, begin grilling. I start about 6 inches (15 cm) above the heat, and lower the grid once the fire cools. Turn the meat when the first side is brown. Cook each side for 8 to 10 minutes (this will vary hugely depending on how hot your fire is). Once each side has browned, lay the spicebush branches below the steak for the next two turns of the meat. Baste with the remaining soy sauce and spicebush as you cook (use a leafy branch to brush the meat). When the thickest, middle part of the meat gives slight resistance to a firm prod with a finger, the steak should be whipped off the grill if you want medium-rare meat. Allow it to rest, covered in a dish to collect any juices, for 15 minutes before carving. Lay the slices in the resting juices to serve.

Thanksgiving Spicebush Goose

Serves 6

Cooler weather brings out the big birds. My Vietnamese friend Mimi Hoang converted me to the idea of goose, rather than turkey, for Thanksgiving. Herbal vermouth with the citric and peppery notes of oranges and spicebush are lean allies for the unctuous goose. Field garlic leaves, reappearing after summer's dormancy, add fresh pungency to the stuffing.

1 medium goose (about 11 pounds/5 kg)

1½ teaspoons salt

2 teaspoons black pepper

1 cup (250 ml) Northeast No. 1 Vermouth

1 cup (250 ml) blood orange or
 orange juice

STUFFING

3 tablespoons butter

2 ounces (57 g) finely chopped scallions

1 ounce (28 g) finely chopped Ramp Pickles

⅓ cup (80 ml) Ground Elder and Fennel or
 Mugwort and Bayberry Pork Rillettes*

1 cup (60 g) panko bread crumbs

1 cup (about 200 g) cooked rice

1 ounce (28 g) finely snipped field
 garlic leaves

2 teaspoons ground spicebush

2 tablespoons Meyer lemon juice

* If you do not have the rillettes, use
 3 strips of good bacon instead.

Five hours before you plan on eating, preheat the oven to 350°F (180°C).

Season the goose inside and out with the salt and pepper. Place it in a large roasting pan. Transfer to the oven to cook for 1 hour.

FOR THE STUFFING: Meanwhile, melt the butter in a saucepan over medium-high heat. Add the chopped scallions. Reduce the heat to medium-low. Sauté the scallions for 15 minutes, before adding the Ramp Pickles and rillettes or bacon. Stir well and cook another 5 minutes. Add the bread crumbs, rice, field garlic leaves, and spicebush; stir very well to combine. Sprinkle the lemon juice over and stir once more. Reserve.

After 1 hour remove the goose from the oven. Reduce the heat to 300°F (150°C). Pour off any rendered fat from the pan (save for roast potatoes or a hot-water pastry crust for Raised Pork Pie with Elderberries and Wild Herbs, or Bayberry Meat Pies). Spoon the stuffing into the cavity. Add the vermouth and orange juice to the pan. Cover the roasting pan tightly with foil and return to the oven for another 3 hours (remove the foil twice and draw off the melting fat, being careful to leave the good brown juices behind)

After 3 hours, remove the foil from the goose. Return the heat to 350°F (180°C). Roast the goose for 1 last hour, uncovered. Add ½ cup (125 ml) water (or more vermouth) to the pan if the juices are drying out. You will need at least ½ cup (125 ml) of finished pan juices to drizzle over the carved pieces of meat.

Remove the goose from the roasting pan, and lift to a serving platter or carving board with a runnel. Tent with foil and let it rest for 30 and up to 45 minutes—this is important. Remove any more fat from the roasting tray and taste the juices. They should be rich and concentrated. Pour them into a small saucepan. When the goose has rested, add its juices to the saucepan and heat before serving.

Carve the goose into joints, remove the breasts and carve those into slices, and arrange the meat on a serving platter alongside the spooned-out stuffing. Drizzle the heated pan juices over everything.

Spicebush Roast Duck

Serves 4

Stuffing the duck with the season's first field garlic and spicebush twigs infuses the rich bird with aroma. Instead of Peking-style pancakes to wrap around morsels of meat, I prefer large, floppy lettuce leaves, like Boston or oak. With peppery wintercress the parcels of fatty duck seem positively healthy.

SAUCE

½ cup (125 ml) clementine (or orange) juice

¼ cup (60 ml) Meyer lemon juice

3 tablespoons Fermented Serviceberry Syrup

3 slices ginger

1 lemongrass heart, halved

2 Thai lime leaves

2 tablespoons soy sauce

2 teaspoons ground spicebush

½ cup (125 ml) Nigori sake or water

DUCK

1 duck, about 6 pounds (2¾ kg)

½ teaspoon salt

2 tablespoons soy sauce

30 spicebush fruit

10 field garlic bulbs

1 bunch field garlic leaves, about 1 inch
    (2½ cm) in diameter, bent in half and tied

6 spicebush twigs, 6 inches (15 cm)
    long each

FOR SERVING

24 large Boston- or oak-type lettuce leaves

2 cups (500 ml) Spicebush Ginger
    Pickled Carrots

3 ounces (85 g) wintercress or
    watercress leaves

1 ounce (28 g) very tender spicebush
    leaves or flowers

½ cup (30 g) field garlic leaves,
    snipped finely

Sauce (see above)

FOR THE SAUCE: Combine all the ingredients except the sake or water in a small saucepan over medium-high heat and bring to a boil. Turn off the heat and infuse for 30 minutes. Strain the sauce and reserve in a jug.

FOR THE DUCK: Preheat the oven to 450°F (230°C).

Season the duck all over with the salt. Place the soy sauce, spicebush fruit, field garlic, and spicebush twigs in the cavity. Position a roasting dish or skillet on a low rack in the oven. Place the duck *directly* above it on a higher rack, allowing the bird to brown all over. Roast for 45 minutes.

Reduce the heat to 325°F (170°C). Continue to roast the duck for 1 hour. Remove the duck carefully from the oven. Tilt it gently over a bowl to catch the accumulated cavity juices. Add these to the reserved sauce. Place the duck on a platter, tent with foil, and rest for 15 minutes.

Carefully remove the roasting dish or skillet with fat from the oven. Pour the melted fat off and save for another use. Deglaze the pan over high heat with the sake or water, stirring well. Add the reserved sauce with duck juices. Cook for a minute at a simmer. Pour into a jug or small bowl and keep warm.

Carve the rested duck by jointing it. With a very sharp knife, cut all the meat from the thighs and drumsticks, then cut into slices. Carve each breast into slices. Cut off all remaining meat and skin. Arrange all the carved duck and its skin on a platter beside a pile of wintercress or watercress.

TO EAT: Take a lettuce leaf, top with some duck, Spicebush Ginger Pickled Carrots, wintercress, spicebush leaves, and snipped field garlic, and drizzle with the sauce. Wrap, fold, and bite.

You may need finger bowls.

Spicebush Olive Oil Cake

Makes one 9-inch (23 cm) loaf, one 10-inch (25 cm) Bundt, or four 6-inch (15 cm) loaves

For this recipe I am indebted to my friend Julia Miller, a garden designer and superb baker who lives a few blocks from us in Brooklyn. Her house smelled glorious one morning when I visited—she was just pulling a Sicilian olive oil cake from the oven (her husband, Carmelo, is the Sicilian). She has generously allowed me to adapt it. With a very fine, moist crumb and crisp crust, it is a popular treat on my plant walks. It keeps exceptionally well and is good a week later.

2 teaspoons extra-virgin olive oil, for oiling the pan(s)
5 large eggs
1¼ cups (250 g) sugar
2 cups (500 ml) extra-virgin olive oil
1 tablespoon ground spicebush
2 cups (240 g) all-purpose flour
½ teaspoon salt
1¼ teaspoons baking powder

Preheat the oven to 325°F (170°C)

Oil your baking pan or pans. Wipe away any pooled oil.

In a mixing bowl beat the eggs with the sugar until very pale and fluffy, about 2 minutes. Add the olive oil in a thin stream while beating. The result should be a shiny batter.

Add the combined dry ingredients to the batter in three batches, beating at a slow speed. Pour the batter into the prepared pan or pans. Bake a single cake or loaf or Bundt for 50 minutes and up to 60 minutes. Test after 50 minutes to see if an inserted skewer comes out clean. If not, place back in the oven, checking every 5 minutes to see if it is done. Bake small loaves for 40 minutes.

Before turning the cake out to cool, run a knife very carefully all the way around the edges, as it tends to stick.

Slice when cool.

Spicebush and Clementine Savarin

Makes 1 cake

This airy, yeasted cake drenched with sweet and boozy winter flavors is a sumptuous end to a meal. Choose a light meal! Serve with whipped cream.

CAKE

1 tablespoon yeast

1 cup (250 ml) lukewarm milk

2 ounces (57 g) sugar

14 ounces (396 g) all-purpose flour

1 tablespoon ground spicebush

½ teaspoon salt

3 large eggs

1 teaspoon blood orange zest

6 ounces (170 g) butter, melted and cooled

1 teaspoon butter, for the pan

SPICEBUSH BOURBON SYRUP

6 ounces (170 g) sugar

5 tablespoons (75 ml) maple syrup

5 tablespoons (75 ml) water

5 tablespoons (75 ml) clementine or
   orange juice

1 tablespoon lemon juice

1 tablespoon whole spicebush fruit, crushed

⅓ cup plus 1 tablespoon (95 ml) bourbon
   or applejack

Stir the yeast into the lukewarm milk with a teaspoonful of the sugar. Allow it to sit until it froths. In a mixing bowl combine all the dry ingredients. Pour in the yeasted milk and beat until smooth. Add the eggs and the orange zest, stirring until completely incorporated. Pour in the melted butter, stirring until the batter is homogeneous (it will seem impossible at first, but keep going). Cover the bowl and allow the batter to rise until it has doubled (about an hour).

While it is rising prepare the Spicebush Bourbon Syrup. Combine all the ingredients except the bourbon in a saucepan over medium-high heat. Stir to dissolve the sugar. Cook at a boil for 30 seconds. Turn off the heat and let the mixture infuse for 30 minutes. Strain the syrup into a bowl or jug and stir in the bourbon or applejack.

Butter a 10½-inch (27 cm) Bundt pan.

When the batter has risen, give it a thorough stir to deflate it. Pour into the Bundt pan and spread so that it is evenly deep. Cover, and allow it to rise again (about an hour). When it is an inch (2½ cm) shy of the top of the pan, slide it gently into a preheated 350°F (180°C) oven.

Bake for 30 to 35 minutes or until an inserted skewer comes out clean. Gently remove the hot cake from the pan. Pour two-thirds of the prepared syrup into the pan. *Carefully* return the cake to the pan to soak. Pour half the remaining syrup over the top of the cake. Let it soak for 10 minutes. Place some paper towels beneath your cooling rack and invert the soaked savarin onto the rack to cool—watch for spills! When it is cool, serve with whipped cream. Pass the leftover syrup for friends with an extra-sweet teeth (or shake it up into a cocktail!).

Orange Spicebush Loaf

Makes 1 loaf

I bake this sticky citrus tea loaf from winter through spring, when clementines and blood oranges are plentiful. It makes excellent toast.

LOAF

6 ounces (170 g) unsalted butter

6 ounces (170 g) sugar

1 teaspoon grated clementine zest

3 large eggs

1 tablespoon ground spicebush

8 ounces (227 g) all-purpose flour

½ teaspoon salt

1 tablespoon baking powder

2 tablespoons clementine juice

SYRUP

1 cup (250 ml) mixed fresh clementine and blood orange juice (about 6 clementines plus 1 orange)

2 tablespoons sugar

6 crushed spicebush fruit

¼ cup (60 ml) bourbon

FOR THE CAKE: Preheat the oven to 350°F (180°C). Butter a 9-inch (23 cm) loaf tin.

In a mixing bowl cream the butter with the sugar and zest until light and fluffy. Add the eggs, with a dusting of flour to prevent separation. Mix well. Add the ground spicebush. Gradually add the flour, salt, baking powder, and clementine juice until well mixed.

Spoon the thick batter into the loaf pan. Use the back of the spoon to draw a furrow down the middle. Bake for 50 to 55 minutes or until a sharp skewer inserted comes out clean. Remove from the oven and leave in its baking pan.

FOR THE SYRUP: Combine the orange juice, sugar, and spicebush fruit and cook over high heat in a small saucepan until reduced by two-thirds— about 15 minutes (watch it carefully after 10 minutes, as it caramelizes fast). Turn off the heat. Add the bourbon and stir. Strain the syrup.

Use a skewer to stab a dozen holes in the warm loaf. Drizzle half the syrup slowly over the loaf in the pan. After 10 minutes loosen the edges with a knife, and transfer the sticky loaf onto a wire rack set over paper towels or parchment. Allow the leftover syrup to cool a little, and then pour the rest over the loaf. (If you do not want to use all the syrup, save some for glazing roast chicken or sweet potatoes.)

Spicebush Coffee Cake

Makes 1 cake

Spicebush and apples belong together. This is a dense, moist cake, perfect for a post-forage refueling.

TOPPING

⅓ cup (40 g) flour

⅓ cup (67 g) sugar

Pinch of salt

1 tablespoon ground spicebush

2 ounces (57 g) cold butter

CAKE

2 ounces (57 g) butter

½ cup (100 g) sugar

2 large eggs

1¼ cups (150 g) flour

⅓ cup (80 ml) milk

¼ cup (60 ml) sour cream

¼ teaspoon salt

2 teaspoons baking powder

1 apple, peeled and grated

Preheat the oven to 375°F (190°C). Butter an 8-inch (20 cm) springform pan.

FOR THE TOPPING: Combine the flour, sugar, salt, and ground spicebush in a bowl. Grate the cold butter into the mixture, then use your fingers to rub the ingredients together until they resemble large, unevenly sized crumbs. Set aside in the fridge.

FOR THE CAKE: In a mixing bowl cream the butter and sugar. Add the eggs with a dusting of flour (to prevent the eggs from separating). Mix well. Add more flour, alternating with the milk and sour cream, until all the flour has been incorporated. Add the salt and baking powder and mix well. Finally, stir in the grated apple.

Pour the batter into the prepared pan. Sprinkle the topping gently and evenly over the top.

Bake for 35 to 40 minutes, until the center is set and an inserted skewer comes out clean. Loosen the edges of the cake from the pan with a knife, release the spring, and turn out to cool on a wire rack.

Spicebush Apple Pie

Makes 1 pie

The textures of this fall pie are clear and ungoopy (technical term). The fruit is intact, and the frank American flavors of spicebush and maple syrup are allowed to speak for themselves.

PASTRY

10½ ounces (297 g) all-purpose flour

2½ ounces (70 g) sugar

¼ teaspoon salt

6 ounces (170 g) cold unsalted butter, cut up

4–8 tablespoons ice water

1 large egg yolk, lightly beaten

FILLING

2½ pounds (1.1 kg) Granny Smith or other baking apples (about 5 large apples)

⅓ cup (67 g) sugar

3 tablespoons maple syrup

¼ cup (40 g) currants, craisins, or Dried Fermented Serviceberries

2 teaspoons ground spicebush

Pinch of salt

FOR THE PASTRY: Place the flour, sugar, and salt in a large bowl. Grate the cold butter into the mixture. Rub the butter into the dry ingredients until it resembles uneven coarse crumbs. Add 2 tablespoons of the ice water to the mixture and stir with a fork. Add another 2 tablespoons and the egg yolk and mix again. Squeeze a handful of pastry firmly together. If it does not stick together, add more water. Once you have a cohesive but not sticky ball of dough, cut off a third of it for the pie top. Flatten both pieces into disks, wrap, and chill for an hour.

FOR THE APPLE FILLING: Peel, core, and quarter the apples. Cut each quarter in half. In a large pot place a steamer basket over water. Place the apple pieces in the basket, cover with a lid, and bring the water to a boil over high heat. Reduce the heat to medium-high and steam until the apples are slightly soft (not cooked all the way through), about 8 minutes. Remove the basket and allow the apples to cool. Place them in a bowl with the sugar, maple syrup, currants, spicebush, and salt. Stir gently to combine.

ASSEMBLING THE PIE: Preheat the oven to 375°F (190°C). Butter an 8-inch (20 cm) springform baking pan.

Roll out the larger pastry disk on a floured board. Fold the dough over your rolling pin and transfer it carefully to the pan, laying it across so that the sides hang over. Press down and against the sides of the pan. Patch any breaks or tears with extra pastry and a little water—it is forgiving. Transfer to the fridge to chill while you roll out the top.

When the top has been rolled, remove the baking pan from the fridge and fill evenly with the apple mixture. Place the lid over the fruit and crimp the edges. Pierce a few steam vents. Place in the heated oven and bake for about 1 hour, or until the top is browning. Serve hot or at room temperature.

Spicebush Fruit Buns

Makes 12–16 buns or 1 loaf

I could eat fruit buns until I pop. They were a regular childhood treat along with raisin bread. This recipe also makes superb bread—simply use a loaf pan.

BUNS

¾ cup plus 1 tablespoon (205 ml) warm milk

1 tablespoon yeast

3 tablespoons sugar

1 pound (453 g) all-purpose flour

½ teaspoon salt

1 tablespoon ground spicebush

½ teaspoon ground cinnamon

¼ teaspoon ground nutmeg

¼ teaspoon ground cloves

3½ ounces (99 g) butter

2 large eggs, beaten

2 ounces (57 g) Dried Fermented Serviceberries or Black Chokeberries (or substitute raisins)

2 ounces (57g) dried currants

EGG WASH

1 large egg yolk

3 tablespoons milk

SUGAR GLAZE

1 tablespoon sugar

1 tablespoon water

FOR THE DOUGH: In a jug or small bowl, combine the warm milk with the yeast and 1 teaspoon of the sugar. Let the mixture bubble.

Place the flour, salt, the rest of the sugar, and all the spices in a large mixing bowl and grate the butter into the mixture. Rub the butter and flour between your fingertips until the texture resembles coarse bread crumbs.

Add the beaten eggs to the bowl, then add the yeasted milk. Stir very well to make a loose dough. Turn the dough out onto a floured board and knead for about 10 minutes, until smooth and very supple. Lightly grease a large bowl, place the dough inside, and cover. Set aside until the dough has doubled in size—1 to 3 hours.

Transfer the dough to a floured surface, flatten it out a little, and scatter some of the fruit across it. Fold the dough over itself to incorporate the fruit. Repeat, adding a little fruit every time, folding the dough over and kneading.

Butter a 14½ by 10 inch (37 × 25 cm) baking pan with high sides. If you do not mind more free-form buns, use a regular baking sheet. For a single loaf butter a 10½ by 5½ inch (27 × 14 cm) pan.

For buns, roll and lightly stretch the dough into a long log shape about 2½ inches (6 cm) in diameter. Cut it into twelve pieces. Fold each piece into a bun shape, leaving any seams on the underside of each bun. For a loaf form into a single log about 8 inches (20 cm) long. Place the buns or loaf into their pan seam-side down. Cover and proof until doubled in size.

Preheat the oven to 400°F (200°C).

FOR THE EGG WASH: In a small bowl, beat together the egg and milk. Brush this mixture over the risen buns or bread.

Slide the dough into the hot oven. Bake buns for about 25 minutes, until golden. Bake the loaf for 35 minutes. When it's removed from the pan, the loaf should sound hollow when you knock it on the base.

FOR THE GLAZE: Mix the sugar and water. Brush the buns or loaf with the sugar glaze while they are piping hot, then transfer them to a rack to cool.

Blueberry Buttermilk Spicebush Scones

Makes 8 large triangular scones

Summer blueberries and zesty spicebush make beautiful scones. I like to serve them with a topping of Greek yogurt and jam. You could also use fermented or fresh serviceberries.

4 cups (480 g) all-purpose flour
1 cup (200 g) plus 1 tablespoon sugar
1 tablespoon plus 1 teaspoon
    baking powder
¾ teaspoon salt
2 teaspoons spicebush
4 ounces (113 g) unsalted butter
2 cups (500 ml) buttermilk
1½ cups (340 g) blueberries

Preheat the oven to 400°F (200°g). Cover a baking sheet with a piece of parchment.

In a mixing bowl combine the flour, 1 cup of sugar, baking powder, salt, and spicebush. Cut or grate the butter onto the dry ingredients and rub it in with your fingers until the mixture is very fine. Stir in the buttermilk and the blueberries and work the dough briefly with your hands just until it adheres to itself. Lift it onto a lightly floured board and pat it gently into a circle about 10 inches (25 cm) across by 1½ inches (4 cm) high.

Transfer the dough circle carefully to the baking sheet. Using a sharp knife or a serrated bread knife (I find the latter easier), gently slice the circle into quarters. Now cut each quarter in half; you will have eight wedges. Gently pull each wedge out so that it is about 1 inch (2½ cm) away from the next at the widest end, allowing for expansion as the scones bake. Sprinkle the remaining tablespoon of sugar over the top of the scones.

Slide into the oven and bake for 45 to 50 minutes, until the scones are pale brown at the edges and cooked all the way through.

Spicebush Coffee Crème Brûlée

Serves 4

This easy but elegant dessert goes a long way served in small cups or glasses. The citrus element of spicebush makes it feel like a classic coffee spice.

CUSTARD

1⅔ cups (400 ml) whipping cream

7 tablespoons (100 ml) milk

5 large egg yolks

5 tablespoons sugar

1 teaspoon ground spicebush

½ cup plus 1 tablespoon (140 ml)
   prepared espresso

SUGAR CRUST

4 tablespoons sugar

1 teaspoon ground spicebush

Preheat the oven to 300°F (150°C). Make a bain-marie by pouring hot water into a roasting dish; slide the dish into the oven.

Heat the cream and milk in a saucepan over medium heat. Whisk the egg yolks and sugar in a bowl until light and creamy. Add the ground spicebush. Pour the hot—but not boiling—cream mixture onto the egg yolks, whisking. Add the coffee.

Pour the mixture into demitasse cups or sturdy glasses that hold about ½ cup (125 ml). Place the cups into the bain-marie—the water should reach three-quarters of the way up their sides. Lay a sheet of parchment or foil across the top of the cups to protect the custards from dry heat. Bake until the center of the custards no longer quivers wildly when jiggled (a tiny shiver is perfect), about 60 minutes.

Remove and cool, out of the water. Once cooled, chill in the fridge, covered.

TO BRÛLÉE: Grind the sugar with the spicebush for a few seconds in a coffee grinder. Before serving, sprinkle the tops of the set, cold custards with about 2 teaspoonfuls of this spicebush sugar per cup and melt with a kitchen blowtorch.

Alternatively, sprinkle the sugar over the custards and place them on a baking sheet below a hot broiler. Watch *very carefully*, as the line between caramel and scrambled custard is a very fine one.

Spicebush Rhubarb Ginger Custard

Makes 6–8 pots, ⅓ cup (80 ml) each

Rhubarb and spicebush seem like a timeless combination. They are perfect together. Using more milk than cream for these custards keeps them quivering and delicate. They are a delightful end to a spring meal.

CUSTARD

2½ cups (625 ml) milk

¼ cup (60 ml) cream

1 teaspoon ground spicebush, or a bundle
 of 10 spring twigs

3 slices ginger

5 large egg yolks

Pinch of salt

⅓ cup (75 g) Spicebush Sugar

RHUBARB TOPPING

12 ounces (340 g) rhubarb, cut into ¼-inch
 (½ cm) slices

⅓ cup (67 g) sugar

¾ teaspoon ground spicebush

FOR THE CUSTARD: In a saucepan combine the milk, cream, spicebush, and ginger. Bring to a simmer over medium heat, then turn the heat off and let cool to room temperature. Strain the mixture through a fine-mesh sieve to remove the spicebush fragments and ginger. Return the milk mixture to the pot and heat gently. In a mixing bowl whisk the egg yolks, salt, and Spicebush Sugar until pale and thick. Slowly pour the hot milk mixture onto the eggs, stirring all the time with a spoon (whisking at this stage generates too many bubbles) to dissolve the sugar. Carefully pour the mixture into small glasses or espresso cups holding ⅓ cup (80 ml).

Preheat the oven to 300°F (150°C).

Make a bain-marie by pouring hot water into a roasting dish; slide the dish into the oven. Place the custard pots or glasses in the bain-marie—the water should reach three-quarters of the way up their sides. Cover the custards with a sheet of foil or parchment paper. Bake for 50 to 60 minutes, until the custards are just set and jiggle slightly when nudged. Remove them from the hot water to cool, then chill in the fridge.

FOR THE RHUBARB: Preheat the oven to 325°F (170°C).

In a bowl toss the rhubarb with the sugar and spicebush. Spread the mixture on a baking sheet and roast for about 1½ hours. The rhubarb should be soft but retain its shape. If the pan juices dry out, add a little water to the pan. Remove the rhubarb to a bowl and reserve.

TO SERVE: Top each chilled custard with some rhubarb pieces. Serve at once.

Spicebush Hot Milk Sponge with Rhubarb Filling

Makes 1 double-layered cake

A pillowy hot milk sponge is turned into a luxurious spring treat with the addition of roasted rhubarb and tart lemon curd. If you are in no mood to hold back, add sliced strawberries and a layer of Greek yogurt (or whipped cream!).

FILLING

1 pound (453 g) rhubarb, trimmed and
   sliced into 2-inch (5 cm) pieces
6 tablespoons sugar
1 teaspoon ground spicebush
½ cup (160 g) Spicebush Lemon Curd
1 cup (170 g) sliced strawberries (optional)
½ cup (125 ml) Greek or strained yogurt
   (optional)
Spicebush Sugar

SPONGE

1 cup (250 ml) milk
4½ ounces (127 g) butter
2 teaspoons ground spicebush
4 large eggs
14 ounces (396 g) sugar
8½ ounces (241 g) all-purpose flour
¼ teaspoon salt
1 tablespoon plus 1 teaspoon baking powder

FOR THE FILLING: Preheat the oven to 325°F (170°C).

In a bowl toss the rhubarb with the sugar and spicebush. Spread it out on a baking sheet and roast for about 1½ hours. The rhubarb should be soft but retain its shape. If the pan juices dry out, add a little water to the pan. Remove the rhubarb to a bowl and reserve.

FOR THE CAKE: Butter and flour two 8-inch (20 cm) springform cake pans.

Pour the milk into a saucepan. Add the butter and the spicebush. Over medium heat bring the milk to a boil and then turn off the heat. Let the mixture cool to tepid. In a mixing bowl beat the eggs with the sugar until pale and creamy. Fold the flour into this batter in stages, then add the salt and baking powder. Gradually pour the tepid milk-butter mixture into the batter (it will become very loose). Pour the batter into the cake pans.

Bake for 60 to 70 minutes or until an inserted skewer comes out clean. Slide a knife around the cakes' edges to loosen (they tend to stick), then release them from the pans. Cool on a wire rack. When cool, spread the Spicebush Lemon Curd over the lower cake and top with the reserved rhubarb. If you're using the strawberries and yogurt, add them now, and sandwich with the top cake. Sprinkle the top cake with some Spicebush Sugar.

Spicebush Condensed Milk Ice Cream

Makes 1 quart (1 liter)

This pared-down and dangerously appealing ice cream begs for a shot of espresso to be poured over it. The combination is my husband's idea of nirvana.

1 can (8 fluid ounces/236 ml)
   condensed milk
2 cups (500 ml) cream
2 teaspoons ground spicebush

Pour the condensed milk, the cream, and the spicebush into a bowl and stir with a spoon until smoothly mixed. Chill in the fridge. Either pour into an ice cream maker and churn until done, or pour into a container where the mixture lies 3 inches (7½ cm) deep. Transfer to the freezer. If it is in a container, stir it every 3 hours, bringing the frozen outer edges toward the middle.

Serve with hot, strong coffee poured over it. Instant ice cream float. Or affogato, if you want to be Italian about it.

Spicebush Rhubarb Ice Cream

Makes 1½ quarts (1½ liters)

This is the best ice cream I have ever tasted. The soft pieces of rhubarb create gentle detonations of tartness within the ice cream as it melts in your mouth.

2½ pounds (1.1 kg) rhubarb, trimmed and
    cut into 2-inch (5 cm) slices
1½ cups (300 g) sugar, divided
2 teaspoons ground spicebush
1½ cups (375 ml) half-and-half
½ cup (125 ml) cream

Preheat the oven to 325°F (170°C).

In a bowl, toss the rhubarb with ½ cup (100 g) of the sugar and the spicebush. Spread the mixture out on a baking sheet and roast for about 1½ hours until the rhubarb is very soft. *Check on it* after 1 hour. If you see signs of scorching, add a very small amount of water to the pan and tilt to distribute. Transfer the rhubarb to a bowl and let it cool, then mash it with a wooden spoon until it is a pulpy mess. The yield should be 2 cups (500 ml). Chill in the fridge. When the rhubarb is cold, combine the half-and-half and remaining 1 cup (200 g) sugar in a bowl. Whisk until the sugar has dissolved. Stir in the cream and the rhubarb.

Pour the rhubarb mixture into the machine and churn until very thick (mine takes 20 to 25 minutes). Spoon the ice cream into containers, cover, and freeze.

If you do not have an ice cream maker, pour the mixture into a bowl or container where the mixture is not more than 3 inches (7½ cm) deep. Cover and transfer to the freezer. After 2 hours, begin scratching the edges toward the center of the container, using a fork. Repeat every hour until it is frozen.

Spicebush Lemon Curd

Makes 20 ounces (567 g)

The tang of this lemon curd is sunny and long lasting. Spread it on muffins, fruit buns, or cakes (like Spicebush Hot Milk Sponge with Rhubarb Filling); plop it in baked pastry shells, or mix with cream and spring prickly ash leaflets to make Spicebush Lemon Curd Ice Cream. The lemon curd lasts for about 6 months in the fridge.

1 cup (250 ml) freshly squeezed
    lemon juice
Zest of 2 lemons
6 large egg yolks
2 large eggs
14 ounces (396 g) sugar
Pinch of salt
12 tablespoons unsalted butter, cut up
4 teaspoons ground spicebush

Combine all the ingredients in a saucepan over medium heat, whisking to blend the ingredients and to dissolve the sugar. *Whisk continuously.* Once the butter has melted, turn the heat to medium-low. Keep whisking. After 6 to 8 minutes you will notice the mixture growing thicker, and if you tip the pot to one side it will be coating the bottom. *Keep whisking.* After a couple more minutes, when it is quite thick (it will never be stiff), remove the pot from the heat.

Push the mixture through a fine-mesh sieve into a bowl and transfer into a clean jar. Cool and refrigerate.

Spicebush Lemon Curd Ice Cream

Makes 2½ cups (625 ml)

This tongue-whipping ice cream is unforgettably delicious.

1 cup (250 ml) cream
11⅓ ounces (326 g) Spicebush Lemon Curd
½ ounce (14 g) tender prickly ash leaflets
    (or 1 ounce/28 g basil)
6 tablespoons gin

Whip the cream in a bowl. Combine the Spicebush Lemon Curd with the prickly ash or basil in a food processor and process until thoroughly mixed and fine. Scrape the mixture into a bowl, then gently fold it into the cream. Add the gin and stir gently. Transfer to an ice cream maker and churn until done. It also freezes very well poured 2 inches (5 cm) deep into a dish in the freezer.

Sumac

OTHER COMMON NAMES: Staghorn sumac, smooth sumac, fragrant sumac, winged sumac

BOTANICAL NAMES: *Rhus typhina*, *R. glabra*, *R. aromatica*, *R. copallinum*, and other species

STATUS: Shrubs native to North America

WHERE: Widespread, in open, dry sunny ground, roadsides, woodland edges

SEASON: Late summer

USE: Aromatic, spice

PARTS USED: Ripe fruit

GROW? Yes

TASTES LIKE: Lemon juice, red currants

For many Americans, sumacs are so ubiquitous that they are invisible until they burst into fall radiance—the leaves of most species are vividly beautiful. This late-season brilliance ensured that North American staghorn sumac (*Rhus typhina*) was described in Britain as early as 1679, with smooth sumac (*R. glabra*) following a century later. These American shrubs brought heat to the gentle colors of European gardens in autumn.

As a food, sumac is widely perceived as a Middle Eastern spice (the Mediterranean *R. coriaria*), even though many indigenous species of Rhus are spread across North America (not to mention Africa and Asia). Sumacs ripen conspicuously in summer, their bright fruit clusters marking the middle of the foraging year. Smooth sumac has the widest North American distribution, while there is a species for practically every region. Their red, amber, and orange fruit may be used interchangeably,

although experience will teach you that each has its own flavor profile, within the parameters of Really Tart. While that sour red powder sold in stores belongs to the Mediterranean species, New Jersey forager Tama Wong uses staghorn sumac to produce an all-American powder that you can buy from her website, Meadows and More. We should all be enjoying regional sumac.

It is the intrinsic sourness that is the appeal. I rely on tart flavors in cooking and mixology, and sumac's sharpness can be caught wet or dry, making it very versatile. Cooking with sumac is like cooking with lemon juice, or tamarind. One of the easiest ways to capture its character is to soak the ripe fruit in water, to make the well-known Sumac-Ade, or what I call Sumac Water. While most people use the sour liquid as a tart drink, I go a step further and reduce it, creating a concentrated and surprisingly nuanced Sumac Essence that can be used in small amounts in many ways. Another wet method is to infuse vodka (or another liquor), which preserves the flavor. Strained and bottled, it keeps that sumac brightness alive indefinitely and is very versatile in cocktails as well as sauces. Ground sumac is the spice we recognize from the spice aisle, or when enjoying Middle Eastern food. The dried fruit is ground and sifted (although not always), and voilà: spice.

If I had to pick a favorite local species, it would be fragrant sumac (*R. aromatica*) for its plump, oil rich fruits, the ease with which they come off their dry twigs in the hand, and

Caution

What about *poison* sumac? It is the first thing I am asked on forage walks when we find sumac. Good question. It is a different plant (*Toxicodendron vernix*), although in the same family, and with that confusingly similar common name. Poison sumac does not have the orange or red fruit of the edible sumacs: Its fruit is helpfully white and hangs down (rather than being held upright, like edible sumacs) in loose clusters. But you should learn to identify its leaves since they are also compound and a horrible irritant.

Because sumacs are related to cashews, pistachios, and mangoes, anyone who has a severe allergy to those foods should test their tolerance of sumac with caution. And anyone who is so allergic to poison ivy (*Toxicodendron radicans*) that contact requires a trip to the emergency room and a shot of epinephrine should steer clear of all sumacs, or treat them with extreme caution.

for their bright, red-currant-like and saturated flavor. But every species has its season and flavor profile, within its particular summer window, offering variety and foraging satisfaction all summer long.

How to Collect and Prepare

Sumacs ripen from mid- to late summer. Fragrant sumac begins earlier than the others, and, at least locally, winged sumac—*Rhus copallinum*, with its browner fruit—is the last to ripen. The fruit clusters are ready to pick when they are intensely colored, ranging from orange to burgundy. Touch one and then lick your fingers. The tartness should be profound. To collect staghorn, smooth, and winged sumac, slice an entire, conical cluster cleanly with a knife or a pair of pruning shears. At home snip the fruit free of any green stalks. Fragrant sumac is easy to strip from its clusters by closing your hand over it and pulling toward you, stripping the drupes from the dry twigs that hold them. Your hands will become very sticky, as this sumac's oil is particularly abundant. Discard any black or spoiled fruit (insects can invade the clusters).

CULTIVATION TIPS
USDA Hardiness Zones 3–9

Sumacs should be planted in full sun and will tolerate dry conditions, once established. They are not fussy about soil, unless it drains poorly. Staghorn sumac can grow to a relatively statuesque 30 feet, winged and smooth sumacs reach around 15 feet, and fragrant sumac is a more modest 6 feet in height, at maturity. Sumacs tend to colonize an area, spreading rhizomatously. If this is a problem, shear off their clonal suckers when they appear. Read up on the best sumac for your region.

Sumac Water (or Sumac-Ade)

Makes 5 cups (1¼ liters)

This is the first thing you should make with your dewy-fresh sumac clusters. While I give quantities below, sumac water is really just the ripe fruit covered with water and strained. Sweeten it, or not, as you like. Quantities and concentrations will vary according to your forages. The ratio below yields a very sour drink.

12 ounces (340 g) ripe sumac drupes,
   stripped from stalks (about 2 cups/500 ml)
5 cups (1¼ liters) water

Combine the fruit and water in a large clean jar. Leave at room temperature for 24 hours if you mean to drink it right away. Leave for 48 hours if you are going on to make Sumac Essence.

Strain the liquid through a fine-mesh sieve and then again through a double layer of cheesecloth. You will notice that the fruit is now much paler than before soaking.

Sweeten if you like, and drink after chilling. It keeps for a couple of weeks in the fridge.

Silverlake Punch

Makes 10 drinks

Improvised dockside beside a beautiful lake in upstate New York one Labor Day weekend, this is a deceptively refreshing drink. Don't go swimming alone afterward.

20 fluid ounces (592 ml) dry gin
15 fluid ounces (444 ml) watermelon juice*
10 fluid ounces (296 ml) Sumac Water
5 fluid ounces (148 ml) Chartreuse
3 whole limes, sliced

* To make the watermelon juice, cut a very
   ripe and sweet melon into chunks and
   pulverize in a blender. Strain the juice
   into a bowl.

To make the cocktails, pour all the ingredients into a large glass jug or punch bowl (you need to see the stunning color), leaving plenty of room for ice. Add the lime slices and a lot of ice. Stir well, and pour.

Sumac Sour

Warming, herbal, and bracing. For a frosted rim, dip the glasses in a Spicebush or Sumac Sugar.

1 DRINK

2 fluid ounces (4 tablespoons) rye
1 fluid ounce (2 tablespoons) Northeast
    No. 1 Vermouth
1 fluid ounce (2 tablespoons) Sumac Water
½ fluid ounce (1 tablespoon) Northeast
    No. 1 Bitters
½ fluid ounce (1 tablespoon) maple syrup

10 DRINKS

20 fluid ounces (592 ml) rye
10 fluid ounces (296 ml) Northeast
    No. 1 Vermouth
10 fluid ounces (296 ml) Sumac Water
5 fluid ounces (148 ml) Northeast
    No. 1 Bitters
5 fluid ounces (148 ml) maple syrup

TO MAKE 1 DRINK: Shake up all the ingredients with ice, strain, and pour.

TO MAKE 10 DRINKS: Measure the ingredients into a glass pitcher and add chipped ice 3 minutes before serving. Stir well, and pour.

Sumac Essence

Makes 1½ cups (375 ml)

This is the sumac summer version of spring's Ramp Leaf Salt: like gold, to be eked out, or traded when times are tough. This wildly tart reduction is just shy of being a syrup and is a building block in my kitchen. Think of it as a native tamarind, pomegranate molasses, lemon juice, or special vinegar. Its flavor is unique.

4½ cups (1.1 liters) Sumac Water
3 tablespoons sugar

Bring the Sumac Water with the sugar to a boil over high heat. Boil until the liquid has reduced to 1½ cups (375 ml)—about 30 minutes. Transfer to a clean jar and keep in the fridge for up to 3 months, or freeze in cubes.

The Baker

Makes 1 drink

Perhaps you should not drink and bake, but I do.

3 fluid ounces (6 tablespoons) bourbon
1 fluid ounce (2 tablespoons) Sumac Essence
½ fluid ounce (1 tablespoon) Spicebush
    Clementine Cordial
½ fluid ounce (1 tablespoon) maple syrup

Shake these all up with ice. Strain, and pour.

Sumac Sugar

Makes 2 cups (500 ml)

This is special stuff. Sumac Sugar tastes just like foaming white sherbet that was in the center of my childhood lollipop candies. It is crazy sour, but sweet. I use it for frosting the rims of cocktails, and in baking. Even to coat fire-cooked beef. It is magical. Use any intensely ripe, fresh and moist sumac (I like fragrant sumac as it is very oily). This process takes time, but you can just pack it in a jar and forget about it until it is ready to use.

12 ounces (340 g) ripe sumac
    drupes, stripped from the stems
    (about 2 cups/500 ml)
1 cup (200 g) sugar

Pack the fruit with the sugar into a jar with a little headroom. Secure the lid. Shake well. Leave for 6 weeks, shaking occasionally. The sugar will become slightly damp and *very* sour.

    To strain, place the sumac and sugar in a medium-mesh sieve (fine mesh is too fine for the sugar to sift through) and sift into a bowl. When no more will sift through, use a spoon to work the fruit and sugar against the mesh. Once you have collected as much as possible, bottle it in small jars. I use ½-cup (125 ml) jars, and screw the lids on tightly. You can reuse the sugary fruit: Either pour water over it for a sweet Sumac-Ade, or douse it in good vodka, leave for 48 hours, double strain, and pour.

Sumac Vodka

Makes 2 cups (500 ml)

This tart infusion is very versatile in a cocktail shaker (and in some sauces and soups). If you are using fragrant sumac, let it sit for 4 weeks; if you are using smooth or staghorn sumac, strain it after 2 weeks (or it becomes more tannic).

4 ounces (113 g) sumac drupes,
    stripped from the stalks
2 tablespoons sugar
2 cups (500 ml) vodka

Pack the sumac into a glass jar and add the sugar and vodka. Shake to dissolve the sugar. After 2 weeks strain through a double-mesh sieve and then again through cheesecloth. Bottle.

Sourpuss

Makes 1 drink

For those days when you really couldn't give a . . .

3 fluid ounces (6 tablespoons) gin
1½ fluid ounces (3 tablespoons)
    Sumac Vodka
½ fluid ounce (1 tablespoon) lemon juice

Combine all the ingredients in a shaker with ice. Shake, strain, and pour.

Autumn Recluse

Makes 1 drink

It's hard to go out for cocktails when the afternoons are dark and the drinks are better at home.

2½ fluid ounces (5 tablespoons) bourbon
1 fluid ounce (2 tablespoons) Sumac Vodka
1 fluid ounce (2 tablespoons) blood
    orange juice
1 teaspoon maple syrup

Shake all the ingredients up with a lot of ice. Strain and pour.

That'll Do

Makes 1 drink

The amber asperity of Sumac Vodka is smoothed by a spring syrup.

3½ fluid ounces (7 tablespoons)
   Sumac Vodka
1 fluid ounce (2 tablespoons) Concentrated
   Wisteria Syrup
½ fluid ounce (1 tablespoon) Sumac Essence

Shake everything up with ice. Strain and pour. Add some sumac drupes as a garnish.

Night Crawler

Makes 1 drink

When autumn evenings fall early and it is pitch dark by six o'clock, I prowl the garden with a flashlight, stalking stubborn slugs eating my cool-weather greens. They get beer, I get the cocktail.

2 fluid ounces (4 ounces) Sumac Vodka
1 fluid ounce (2 tablespoons) plain vodka
1 fluid ounce (2 tablespoons) Elderberry Gin
1 fluid ounce (2 tablespoons) Black
   Chokeberry Syrup

Shake it all up with ice, strain, and pour.

GROUND SUMAC

The flavor of dried sumac is mellower than the taste that is caught in liquid, but it remains acidic. Dehydrating the fruit is easiest with a dehydrator, but I still use the oven, with a labor-intensive on-off cycle. The lowest setting (about 155°F/68°C) is *not* low enough to simply leave on for hours, so do not be tempted—you will alter the flavor of the fruit too much. Also, different sumac species dry at different rates. My favorite fragrant sumac actually takes the longest, while winged sumac is the quickest to dry.

Begin with as much fruit as you have time to process—the yield is fairly low:

2½ ounces (70 g) just-dried sumac drupes (about ½ cup)
= 3 tablespoons Ground Sumac

Pick all the ripe drupes from your sumac clusters, and snip off as many stems as you can. Spread the fruit out on parchment-lined baking trays and transfer to the oven on the lowest setting. After 1 hour turn the oven off. Leave off for 1 hour. Turn it on again for 1 hour. Off again for an hour. On again. Repeat, my friends, until those little suckers are dry. They will still feel a little oily.

Yes, this does require your full attention.

Welcome to foraging.

Or just buy a dehydrator. I don't have the space. Or maybe I do. I'm still thinking about it.

Transfer the dried and by now slightly darker fruit in batches to a spice grinder. Grind conservatively, pressing down on the button for a second at a time. Check often to see what is happening. When you notice the pale seeds revealed, test by sieving some through a medium-mesh sieve (fine mesh will get you absolutely nowhere). If the red, sour pericarp is sifting through, leaving behind the hard flavorless seed, then you're good to go. If it is still too bulky, grind some more. You will find that you sift in batches, returning the leftover pieces to the grinder and sifting again.

Some of the seeds that have been chewed up more finely by the grinder will sift through, but this is not the end of the world. They are tasteless but won't hurt you.

Once the sumac has all been sifted, grind the sifted part more finely in your spice grinder (this will also pulverize any of the pesky seed escapees).

Bottle in small jars. Keep one for immediate use and freeze any extra.

Sumac Red Pepper Salad

Serves 4-6 as a side

Served as a meal or a starter with toasted tortillas or flatbreads, this vivid salad vibrates with sumac and heat. The key to its texture is the very fine chopping of the pepper and onion.

4 large sweet red peppers
1 small red onion, very finely chopped
1 tablespoon Sumac Essence
1 tablespoon hot red pepper flakes
2 teaspoons Ground Sumac
½ teaspoon salt

Preheat the broiler. Cut two of the red peppers in half, remove their seeds, and lay them on a baking sheet. Broil until their skins are black. Peel the peppers and chop them exceptionally finely.

Seed and chop the two remaining raw peppers very finely. Combine all the ingredients in a bowl and mix very well.

It is ready.

Sumac Babaganoush

Serves 4 to 6 as a side

This creamy summer spread goes well with bread, crackers, warm eggs, grilled lamb, and sausages. A fire or gas burner imparts the characteristic smoky flavor.

4 medium eggplants
2 cloves garlic
1 teaspoon sugar
¼ teaspoon salt
1 tablespoon Sumac Essence
⅓ cup (80 ml) tahini
½ teaspoon Ground Sumac

Cook the eggplants directly on gas burners turned low, or over hot coals. Turn them as their skin blisters. Keep cooking until the eggplants begin to collapse and feel soft when you squeeze them.

When they are cool enough to handle, peel off the skin. Place the pulp in the bowl of a food processor with all the other ingredients except the sumac. Pulse until the mixture is smooth, then taste. Add more salt if necessary. Scoop the babaganoush into a serving bowl and sprinkle with Ground Sumac.

Potato and Garlic Scape Cigars with Sumac and Mugwort

Makes 12 cigars, about 4 inches (10 cm) long each

Ready-made phyllo offers limitless ways to wrap wild foods. I like to make these cigars when garlic scapes come to market, mugwort is already close to 5 feet tall, and sumac is ripening. I use only two sheets of phyllo at time for these *boreki*, or cigars—you can easily add another sheet if you like more crackle. If you do, use more melted butter and paint at least one sheet of the three with butter, or they will be too dry.

FILLING

12 ounces (340 g/about 2 medium)
   Idaho potatoes, quartered
4 ounces (113 g) garlic scapes, tough ends
   and points trimmed
8 ounces (227 g) feta cheese
1 large egg yolk
1 tablespoon Sumac Essence
2 teaspoons Ground Sumac
¼ teaspoon Mugwort Salt

CIGARS

6 tablespoons butter
6 sheets regular phyllo pastry
24 mugwort sprigs

FOR THE FILLING: Bring a pot of salted water to a boil and drop in the quartered potatoes. Cook until the potatoes are tender when pierced. Scoop them from the water and drain them. Now put the garlic scapes in the potato water and boil until they are just tender—about 6 minutes. Drain and refresh the garlic scapes and chop them very finely.

Skin the potatoes and process them into a bowl through a potato ricer or food mill (or just mash them as finely as possible). Add the chopped scapes, crumbled feta, egg yolk, Sumac Essence, Ground Sumac, and Mugwort Salt. Stir very well until thoroughly combined. Taste. Feta cheeses vary in saltiness.

FOR THE CIGARS: Melt the butter over medium-low heat in a small pot. Brush a baking sheet with some of the melted butter.

Unwrap the phyllo pastry and lay it on a clean surface. Cover it completely with a damp towel (or the phyllo will dry and break). Work with two sheets of phyllo at a time: Lay one on top of the other on a second clean surface. Cut the phyllo in half down the middle and then in half across the middle. You now have four rectangles measuring 12 by 7¼ inches (30½ × 18 cm).

Brush the edges of the phyllo with butter. Working along the long side, spoon 3 tablespoonfuls of filling along the end of each rectangle, leaving about ¼ inch (½ cm) at the sides empty. Lay two leaves of mugwort along the opposite end of the rectangle, ½ inch (1 cm) from the end. Carefully roll the phyllo over the filling, pressing down gently to encourage a sausage shape. Just before you reach the mugwort, butter the empty sides of the roll and fold them up and toward the middle, enclosing the filling. Continue to roll over the mugwort to complete the cigar. Brush the seam with butter. Place the cigar seam-side down on the buttered baking sheet. Cover the sheet at all times to prevent drying out. Repeat with the rest of the cigars. Once they are all prepared, you can chill or freeze them until you need to bake them.

TO BAKE: Preheat the oven to 400°F (200°C). Slide the tray into the hot oven and bake until the cigars are golden brown and crispy, about 35 minutes (45 if they have been frozen).

Sumac-Spiced Squash

Serves 4 as a side

Serve this dish of fragrantly spiced and velvety squash as part of a vegetarian smorgasbord or as a side with Bayberry Meatballs with Field Garlic Salt or Field Garlic Rack of Lamb.

2 pounds (907 g) peeled and cubed orange
    squash (butternut, pumpkin, Gold Nugget)
2 cups (500 ml) water
3 ounces (85 g) brown sugar
2 fresh Thai lime leaves (or a piece of lime
    zest 2 inches/5 cm long)
1 tablespoon lime juice
1 tablespoon Sumac Essence
½ teaspoon ground cumin
1 teaspoon Ground Sumac
¼ teaspoon salt
Black pepper

Arrange the squash in a single layer in a saucepan. Add the water, sugar, and lime leaves (or lime zest) and bring to a boil over high heat. Reduce the heat and continue cooking gently for 20 to 30 minutes, or until the water has almost evaporated. Shake the pan occasionally to prevent the squash from sticking.

When the liquid starts to turn syrupy, add the lime juice, Sumac Essence, cumin, and Ground Sumac. Shake the pan gently again and tilt to spoon the juices over the squash pieces. Season with salt and pepper, and taste. Cook some more until all the liquid disappears, taking care not to scorch.

Transfer the squash to a serving dish (use a spatula, so the squash is not . . . squashed—it is very soft). Eat at once or at room temperature.

Sumac and Mugwort Lamb Ribs with Lemon

Serves 4

In South Africa, where I grew up, pasture-raised lamb ribs are a supermarket staple and quite economical. Stateside, this delicious cut has not caught on yet. I hope that changes. They are worth hunting for, and I am lucky to have a halal butcher nearby who has a good supply. The tartness of the layers of lemon and sumac neutralizes lamb's fattiness. If Meyer lemons are not available, use lemons or limes.

16 lamb ribs (roughly 5 pounds/2¼ kg—
    the weight varies a lot)
½ teaspoon salt
4 Meyer lemons
2 tablespoons Sumac Essence
1 tablespoon Ground Sumac
5 tablespoons dried mugwort
    (15 sprigs, fresh)
6 cloves garlic, grated
2 teaspoons sugar
1 cup (250 ml) Greek yogurt

Arrange the ribs in a single layer in a shallow container. Salt them. Add the juice of two lemons, the Sumac Essence, Ground Sumac, mugwort, grated garlic, sugar, and Greek yogurt. Massage the ribs well until they are coated.

Marinate for at least an hour and up to 24 hours (in the fridge).
Preheat the oven to 450°F (230°C).*
Remove the lamb from the fridge an hour before cooking.

Place the ribs in single layer in a large cast-iron skillet or on a roasting tray. Slide into the oven. Roast for 30 minutes, then turn. Add the two remaining lemons to the roasting dish, each cut in half. Roast another 30 minutes. The ribs should be dark brown with some black edges, and most of their fat should have been rendered. Cook longer if necessary. Remove to a serving platter. Serve after the lamb has rested for 10 minutes. Squeeze the roasted lemon juice over the lamb as you eat.

* The ribs can also be barbecued: Cook 4 to 6 inches (10–15 cm) above ashed-over coals for 20 minutes, and turn. Cook for another 20. Rest as above before serving.

Sumac and Bayberry Spiced Lamb Pie

Serves 4

Inspired by a South African dish of mildly curried lamb called *bobotie*, this is a more assertively spiced savory pie for early fall. Crisp puff pastry traps its aromatic goodness. The complex tartness of sumac provides a backbone for the fragrance of spicebush, cinnamon, and bayberry.

2 tablespoons unscented oil

1 large onion, grated

4 cloves garlic, finely chopped

14 ounces (396 g) grated carrot

2 pounds (907 g) ground lamb, or coarsely
    chopped leftover cooked lamb (or beef)

2 teaspoons ground spicebush

2 teaspoons ground cinnamon

½ teaspoon black pepper

3 tablespoons tomato paste

1 tablespoon plus 1 teaspoon Aleppo pepper

3 cups (750 ml) vegetable or chicken broth

2 tablespoons soy sauce

1 teaspoon sugar

3 tablespoons Sumac Essence

12 bayberry leaves

1 sheet prepared puff pastry, chilled

1 large egg yolk

2 tablespoons water

Heat the oil in a pot over medium heat. Add the onion, garlic, and carrot; cook for 10 minutes, stirring occasionally. Increase the heat to medium-high and add the ground meat, breaking it up with a spoon. When it is incorporated, add the spicebush, cinnamon, and black pepper, and cook for another 5 minutes. Add the tomato paste and Aleppo pepper, stirring well. Pour in the broth, soy sauce, sugar, and Sumac Essence. Add the bayberry leaves. Bring the mixture to a boil, cover the pot, and reduce the heat to maintain a steady simmer for 1 hour. Uncover the pot, and increase the heat to encourage a brisk bubbling. Cook for 15 minutes to reduce the liquid. The mixture should be thick and glossy. Taste for seasoning, and add a little salt if necessary.

Preheat the oven to 400°F (200°C).

Transfer the meat mixture to a pie dish or 10-inch (25 cm) skillet.

Trim the chilled puff pastry sheet to fit the top of the dish with some overlap for crimping. Place the pastry over the top of the filling and crimp the edges. Pierce a few steam vents. Whisk the egg yolk with the water and brush over the pastry. Slide the pie dish into the oven. Bake for 45 minutes, or until the pastry is puffed and golden and smelling very good.

Sumac and Meat Open Pies

Makes 6 pies

Sumac is a traditional sharp note, with lamb or beef, in crisp Middle Eastern pizzas. The topping should be thinly and evenly spread out. Serve these pies with a lashing of Greek yogurt, chopped cucumbers and tomato, mint, Sumac Babaganoush, or Sumac Red Pepper Salad.

DOUGH

1 tablespoon yeast

1 teaspoon sugar

1¼ cups (310 ml) tepid water, divided

1 pound (453 g) all-purpose flour

¾ teaspoon salt

⅓ cup (80 ml) extra-virgin olive oil

TOPPING

1 pound (453 g) ground beef or lamb

1 medium onion, grated

1 tablespoon dried mugwort, crumbled

1 tablespoon tomato paste

1 tablespoon Sumac Essence

1 tablespoon Ground Sumac

1 teaspoon ground cumin

½ teaspoon black pepper

¼ teaspoon salt

FOR THE DOUGH: Mix the yeast with the sugar and ¼ cup of the tepid water in a small bowl or jug, and allow it to bubble. Place the flour and salt in a mixing bowl, pour in the yeast mixture with the rest of the water and the oil, and stir well until a cohesive but supple dough forms. Turn out onto a floured board and knead, stretch, and pull, until it feels silky and elastic, about 10 minutes. Place in a clean bowl and cover. Let rise until it has doubled, about 1 to 3 hours. Return the dough to a floured board and knead for a minute. Divide into six balls.

FOR THE TOPPING: In a bowl mix the ground lamb or beef with the onion, mugwort, tomato paste, Sumac Essence, Ground Sumac, cumin, pepper, and salt.

TO ASSEMBLE: Preheat the oven to 500°F (260°C).

On a floured board flatten each ball into a 5- to 6-inch (13–15 cm) disk. Cover all the disks with a damp cloth and allow them to relax for 10 minutes. Roll each disk into an oblong about 12 inches (30 cm) long. Transfer the rolled-out dough to a lightly oiled baking sheet (make them in batches if they will not all fit at once). Distribute the meat topping evenly over the dough (about 6 tablespoons per pie). Smooth and flatten the meat gently until it forms a thin, continuous layer. Slide the baking sheets into the hot oven and bake until the dough's edges are crisping and the middle is still pliable, about 10 minutes. Eat at once (or cool and freeze, with a sheet of parchment paper between each stacked pie).

Sweetfern

OTHER COMMON NAMES: None in common use

BOTANICAL NAME: *Comptonia peregrina*

STATUS: Shrub indigenous to eastern North America

WHERE: Coniferous forests, sandy barrens, disturbed woodlands

SEASON: Spring to fall

USE: Aromatic, spice

PARTS USED: Catkins and leaves

GROW? Yes

TASTES LIKE: Fresh-cut hay and some pine resin but mostly sweetfern

---

It's not every day you brush up against a forgotten flavor.

One summer in 2011 I visited a lake in Pennsylvania, surrounded by woodland. The dry edges of the dirt road where we walked on our way to swim in the lake were textured with low bushes, their slender leaves indented like ferns. When I rubbed them, I smelled it for the first time. Sweetfern. An intense new scent.

A year went by. But I remembered that fragrance under the trees when I spotted the same plants at Brooklyn Bridge Park. This good smell had to belong to something edible. I began to read.

There were almost no references to *Comptonia peregrina* being used in a culinary context. Sweetfern is indigenous up and down the East Coast and west of the Great Divide. It was well known to Native Americans, who used it

medicinally as an anti-itch treatment, an inhalant to clear the lungs, a diarrhea remedy, and a smudge to repel mosquitoes or aid in religious ceremonies. There was one tantalizing mention of "seasoning," with no elaboration; there were bland instructions for tea making and a tidbit about nibbling the spine-encased green fruit.

My sweetfern experiments began with bourbon (when in doubt, infuse). For the American herb I chose American booze, which, when strained later, smelled spicily good.

When I added the sweetfern bourbon to a chicken liver mousse, a world of food-pairing possibilities lit up.

Despite its common name, sweetfern isn't. A fern, that is. It is a shrub and belongs to the fragrant Myricaceae family (like bayberry), growing in habitats ranging from barrens to bog edges and lake shorelines. It is highly cold-tolerant. Sweetfern prefers an acidic environment, subsisting in poor soils because it teams up with bacteria to fix atmospheric nitrogen, a feat for which legumes usually take the credit. It is listed as either threatened or endangered in at least four states, but many populations are secure, and their colonies can be prolific.

In cities you are likely to find sweetfern growing only in highly managed urban sites, like public parks, and at some enlightened nurseries. I bought my own specimens at the local Gowanus Nursery in Red Hook, Brooklyn. They are now part of my herb collection, growing near my acid-loving blueberries. Unless you have access to sustainable sources, I recommend growing your own.

In early spring catkins appear on male plants. They are tender and very aromatic. Turn them into fresh rubs, or keep them whole to perfume slow-cooked, gamy meats like duck legs and venison.

The catkins infuse alcohol very quickly—strain them out after a week or the liquor becomes too tannic. For a woodsy syrup, combine a simple syrup (cooled) with the catkins and infuse overnight. The catkins ferment easily and create a herbal fizz (follow the Sheep Sorrel Soda Pop recipe to make one). Sweetfern makes an appearance in my seasonal vermouths.

My kitchen adventures with sweetfern have not ended, and I hope yours are about to begin. This unassuming and overlooked native plant warrants rediscovery and respect.

How to Collect and Prepare

To harvest the spring catkins, pick or snip them individually from the plant, which then goes on to produce leaves. To harvest leaves, use a sharp pair of pruning shears to cut off a leaf at a time, or a branch at an angle just above another leaf. In the kitchen tender catkins and early-spring leaves can be chopped up just as you would chop parsley, but mature leaves (harvested through late fall) can be used whole, more like bay leaf or thyme.

CULTIVATION TIPS
USDA Hardiness Zones 2–7

Sweetfern is beginning to appear at native plant nurseries. Online, Prairie Nursery is a good source. I suspect that the plant is adaptable to a wider range of conditions than most current literature will allow, which usually calls for acidic soil. Grow it in either full sun or semi-shade. It will withstand dry soil once established. It also grows well with a lot of moisture as long as drainage is very good. My own shrubs grow in a low pH, with all-winter shade, but a lot of sun in summer.

Sweetfern Salt

Makes ½ cup (169 g)

Beautiful sweetfern makes a rich compound salt. Use it to season grilled trout and shad, scallops and crab cakes, or to sprinkle onto fire-cooked lamb. It is best used fresh or within a week, turning stale later.

2 ounces (57 g) tender sweetfern leaves
 or catkins
4 ounces (113 g) sea salt

In a food processor blend the leaves until very fine. Remove and spread across parchment paper on a large baking sheet. Add the salt. Toss the salt and sweetfern together and spread out over the sheet. Use immediately or air-dry (6 to 12 hours, unless it is very humid). Bottle in small, clean glass jars.

Sweetfern Butter

Makes 5 ounces (142 g)

This aromatic compound butter can be made with sweetfern catkins or with tender spring leaves. Sweetfern butter is aromatically perfect with grilled lamb, as well as with seafood. Best eaten within a week.

1 ounce (28 g) tender sweetfern leaves
 or catkins
½ cup (4 ounces/113 g) unsalted butter,
 cut into pieces

Place the sweetfern in a food processor and process until very fine. Add the cut-up cold butter. Blend again until the butter is evenly green. Pack into a small clean jar and keep in the fridge or freezer.

 Alternatively, roll the butter into a log shape in a layer of parchment or waxed paper. Twist the ends to seal. It can be frozen and sliced as you need it.

Sweetfern Bourbon

Makes 2 cups (500 ml)

Sweetfern bourbon works especially well in pâtés and potted meats and adds complexity to pan juices when deglazing. Try it with duck and pork.

2 ounces (57 g) sweetfern catkins or leaves
2 cups (500 ml) bourbon

Place the catkins or leaves in a jar and cover with bourbon. Let the mixture infuse for 1 week. Strain through a fine-mesh sieve and then through cheesecloth and bottle. It lasts indefinitely.

Wild Sweetfern and Citrus Toddy

Makes 1 drink

Powerful Sweetfern Bourbon adds a warm backbone to an aromatic cold-weather toddy that draws upon the year's forages. Serve in a heat-friendly glass or mug.

FOR THE RIM

1 tablespoon orange juice
¼ teaspoon orange zest
¼ teaspoon ground spicebush
1 tablespoon sugar

TODDY

2 fluid ounces (4 tablespoons)
 Sumac Essence
2 fluid ounces (4 tablespoons) Fermented
 Elderflower Cordial
½ fluid ounce (1 tablespoon) fresh lime juice
½ fluid ounce (1 tablespoon) fresh
 orange juice
½ fluid ounce (1 tablespoon) Spicebush
 Cranberry Syrup
2 fluid ounces (4 tablespoons)
 Sweetfern Bourbon
2 spicebush cranberries (see Spicebush
 Cranberry Syrup, page 375)

FOR THE RIM: Pour the orange juice into a saucer. Mix the orange zest, spicebush, and sugar together, and sprinkle into a second saucer. Dip the rim of your glass into the juice and then into the sugar mixture, working it all the way around. Let it dry for a couple of minutes.

FOR THE TODDY: In a small saucepan combine all the toddy ingredients except the Sweetfern Bourbon and spicebush cranberries. Bring to a vigorous simmer over medium-high heat. Turn the heat off and add the Sweetfern Bourbon to the hot liquid. Pour at once into your serving glass or mug. Garnish with spicebush cranberries.

Thaw

Makes 2 drinks

Bayberry and sweetfern lose their leaves very late in the season and infuse this toddy with their wild flavor. Serve in heat-friendly cups or glasses.

¾ cup (190 ml) Spicebush Cranberry Fizz
10 bayberry or southern bay leaves
8 sweetfern leaves, plus extra for garnish
4 matchsticks of Meyer lemon zest
¼ cup (60 ml) Sweetfern Bourbon

Combine the Spicebush Cranberry Fizz with the herbs and lemon zest in a small saucepan over medium-high heat. When the mixture boils reduce the heat and allow it to simmer for 5 minutes. Turn off the heat. Pour in the Sweetfern Bourbon. Remove the herbs and pour the toddy into heat-proof glasses or mugs. Garnish with fresh sweetfern leaves.

Sweetfern Polenta

Serves 4 as a side

Any compound butter gussies up a dish of creamy polenta. The ephemeral fragrance of sweetfern is especially nice here, as it is not destroyed by high heat. Traditionally polenta is made by adding cornmeal to boiling liquid, but I start with cold water. You can use grits, too, but increase the cooking time.

1 cup (138 g) cornmeal
3 cups (750 ml) water
1 cup (250 ml) milk
2 teaspoons salt
3 tablespoons Sweetfern Butter

In a saucepan, mix the cornmeal with the water and milk, pouring the liquids in gradually and stirring to keep the batter smooth. Add half the salt. Turn the heat to medium-high and stir the cornmeal mixture. When the first molten bubbles pop, reduce the heat to medium-low. Stir every few minutes to prevent sticking and keep a skin forming on top.

The polenta is cooked when it is creamy and no grittiness remains, about 20 to 25 minutes. If it is still too thick, or uncooked, add more milk or water and cook a little longer. Just before serving, stir in the Sweetfern Butter, and add more salt to taste, if necessary. Eat at once.

Sweetfern Scallop Packages

Serves 4

When I started researching uses for sweetfern some years ago, the single food reference—apart from tea—was to fish, and that was tentative. But it was a good clue. Here, the meltingly sweet character of scallops holds up to deeply herbal sweetfern's influence. The aromatic butter turns a deep curry-powder-yellow color, infused by the heating leaves. You could also make one large package and break that open at the table.

20 sweetfern leaves
½ teaspoon fresh Sweetfern Salt
8 plump scallops
4 tablespoons Sweetfern Butter

Preheat the oven to 350°F (180°C).

To make each package, fold a 12-by-12-inch (30 × 30 cm) piece of parchment paper over onto itself for a double layer. In the middle of one half of the paper, lay five sweetfern leaves with a sprinkle of Sweetfern Salt. Set two scallops close to each other on top of that nest. Sprinkle more Sweetfern Salt over the scallops and top them with 1 tablespoon of Sweetfern Butter. Fold the empty paper over the scallops to meet the bottom paper layer. Then fold the edges over firmly toward the scallops, starting on one side and working your way around. If they pop open have no mercy and staple them shut. When all the packages are prepared, place them on a baking sheet and slide into the oven for 15 minutes.

Remove the packages and serve them at once, while they are still steaming.

Sweetfern Bourbon and Duck Liver Pâté

Makes 1½ cups (375 ml)

I love having pâté in the fridge or freezer for days when I do not feel like cooking, or when we want to escape quickly to a park for a picnic. With good bread, and pickles on the side, it is a meal.

4 ounces (113 g) butter, divided
1 tablespoon lemon juice
1½ pounds (680 g) duck liver, cleaned
    and trimmed
1 teaspoon salt, divided
½ cup (75 g) field garlic bulbs, chopped
¼ cup (60 ml) Sweetfern Bourbon
1 cup (250 ml) cream
6 branches thyme
Black pepper

Melt 1 ounce of the butter in a pot over medium heat. Sprinkle lemon juice over the duck livers and season them with ¼ teaspoon of the salt. Add the pieces of duck liver to the hot pan in batches and sauté them on each side for about 3 minutes. Turn. Sauté for another 3 minutes or until the thickest part of the liver is dark pink in the middle. Remove to a plate. Add another ounce of butter to the pan and sauté the field garlic bulbs gently for 15 minutes, until cooked. They should be golden but not brown. Meanwhile melt the remaining butter in a small saucepan over medium heat. Deglaze the pan with the Sweetfern Bourbon, stirring like mad (keep your face away in case the alcohol ignites). Return the livers to the pan and add the cream. Allow the cream to bubble for about 30 seconds, then turn off the heat. Add the thyme leaves, the rest of the salt, and pepper to taste (I use a lot).

Transfer the slightly cooled mixture to a food processor, add the melted butter, and pulse briefly for a roughly chopped pâté. Taste one more time. Scoop the chopped liver into a bowl and serve alongside toasted sourdough soldiers and a dish of finely snipped field garlic greens for a topping.

Sweetfern Bourbon and Spicebush Potted Foie Gras

Makes two ½-cup (125 ml) jars

Locally produced foie gras is a rare treat in our house. It is flavored with Sweetfern Bourbon and ground spicebush. I like to spread it on toasted slices of Orange Spicebush Loaf, rather than traditional brioche.

6 ounces (about 2 slices, 170 g total)
    foie gras, frozen or fresh
1 tablespoon Sweetfern Bourbon
¼ teaspoon salt, plus a pinch
½ teaspoon ground spicebush

If the foie gras slices are frozen, let them thaw. While they are still cold, break the slices gently where you see any veins. Remove the veins and any membrane with the tip of a sharp knife. Lay the pieces of foie gras in a shallow bowl and pour the bourbon over them. Sprinkle with the salt and spicebush. Leave for 60 minutes, turning once. Pack the pieces of foie gras into two small clean jars, pressing down with your fingers to remove any air pockets. Screw the lids on.

Place both jars in a pot filled with water that reaches just beneath the top of their lids. Cover the pot with a lid. Bring the water to a simmer. Cook at a *very* gentle simmer for 10 minutes. Turn off the heat and remove the lid from the pot. Leave the jars in the hot water for another 15 minutes. Remove and refrigerate until their melted fat has set.

Sweetfern Monkfish Stew

Serves 4

In this spring stew the firm texture of monkfish holds up very well to slow-cooking, absorbing flavors and becoming tender. Sweetfern catkins and tender leaves appear with ramps, but you can make the stew later in the year using mature sweetfern (in which case deploy your preserved Salted Ramp Leaves). For a more substantial dish, I like to add potatoes and peas. It is delicious served with an aioli spiked with smoked paprika. Microplaned bottarga over the top of each bowlful is sublime.

2 tablespoons butter
10 ramp leaves, finely chopped
    (or 2 tablespoons Salted Ramp Leaves)*
2 medium leeks, green and white parts,
    thinly sliced
1 fennel bulb, quartered and
    chopped finely
½ ounce (14 g) sweetfern catkins or very
    tender leaves (or 8 mature leaves)
1½ pounds (680 g) monkfish, cut into
    1½-inch (4 cm) thick medallions
2 teaspoons sugar
¼ teaspoon fresh Sweetfern Salt
¼ teaspoon Ramp Leaf Salt
1 cup (250 ml) white wine
⅓ cup (80 ml) cream
Pinch of saffron
Black pepper

OPTIONAL EXTRAS

6 baby potatoes, cut in half
1½ cups (225 g) peas
Aioli, with some smoked paprika stirred in
Bottarga

* If you are using Salted Ramp Leaves,
  taste before adding additional salt.

Melt the butter over medium heat in a pot. Add the ramps and leeks. Cover and sweat for 10 minutes. Add the fennel and stir well. Add the sweetfern, monkfish, sugar, Sweetfern and Ramp Leaf Salts. Increase the heat to high and pour in the wine with enough water to almost cover the fish. Allow the liquid to bubble. Reduce the heat and cook at a gentle simmer over medium-low heat for an hour. Add the cream and saffron threads, and stir. Cook for another 30 minutes. Taste, and add some pepper.

If you are adding potatoes and peas for a more substantial stew, add the potatoes now (after 1½ hours), and cook another 30 minutes over medium heat. Add the peas 5 minutes before you mean to serve.

Sweetfern Chicken with White Sweet Clover and Grapes

Serves 4

Mature sweetfern, white sweet clover (*Melilotus albus* flowers and honeysuckle vinegar add seasonal complexity to one of my favorite combinations: chicken and grapes. I like to use sultanas (also known as Thompson Seedless) for this late-summer dish.

8 chicken thighs

2 cups (320 g) grapes

3 strips bacon, finely chopped

¼ cup (60 ml) Quick Honeysuckle Vinegar

2 tablespoons white sweet clover flowers (about 40 flower stalks)

10 sweetfern leaves

½ teaspoon fresh Sweetfern Salt

Black pepper

Preheat the oven to 450°F (230°C).

Place the chicken in a shallow Dutch oven that can accommodate the pieces in a single layer. Add the grapes, bacon pieces, vinegar, white sweet clover flowers, sweetfern, and ¼ teaspoon of the Sweetfern Salt. Add enough water to cover the chicken and grapes. Transfer to the oven and cook for 45 minutes. Remove the lid and continue to cook for another 45 minutes. Remove the dish and taste the pan juices, which should have reduced by about half. Add the rest of the Sweetfern Salt if necessary, and the pepper. If the chicken skin is not a deep brown by this time, raise the oven shelf and place the dish under the broiler for 5 minutes to crisp up the skin.

Sweetfern and Mugwort Roast Beef Spareribs with Black Cherry

Serves 4

Fragrant mugwort and sweetfern pair up in this simple roast where black cherry adds depth to the pan juices (I keep a stash of Black Cherry Juice ice cubes in the freezer).

½ teaspoon Mugwort Salt

10 beef spareribs (about 5 pounds/ 2¼ kg total)

½ ounce (14 g) mugwort leaves

20 sweetfern leaves

¼ cup (60 ml) Black Cherry Juice

½ cup (125 ml) red wine

Black pepper

Preheat the oven to 425°F (220°C).

Salt the ribs generously. Scatter the mugwort and sweetfern leaves in the bottom of an ovenproof skillet or roasting pan. Place the ribs on top. Roast for 40 minutes. Now add the Black Cherry Juice and wine and about 15 twists of black pepper. Roast another 15 minutes, and turn the ribs over. Roast a final 15 minutes.

Take the skillet from the oven and transfer the ribs to a serving board or platter. Scoop out any floating fat from the pan, as well as the leaves, and place it over medium-high heat. Add ⅓ cup (80 ml) of water (or more red wine, or cherry juice—although that is usually in short supply) and stir well, cooking at a brisk boil until it is a little syrupy. Taste for seasoning and add a little more Mugwort Salt if necessary. Pour the pan juices over the ribs and serve. You'll need lots of napkins.

Sweetfern Butterflied Lamb Adobo

Serves 4

The combination of soy and vinegar (inspired by Filipino adobo) with the addition of rich coconut milk makes coal-grilled lamb delectable. Late spring's tender sweetfern leaves add a freshness to the marinade (and mugwort leaves, while very different in flavor, are an excellent substitute).

1 small butterflied leg of lamb
   (4 pounds/1¾ kg)
⅓ cup (50 g) field garlic bulbs, cut into
   short matchsticks
1 can (13.5 fluid ounces/400 ml)
   coconut milk
½ cup (125 ml) soy sauce
¼ cup (60 ml) Elderflower Vinegar
1½ ounces (40 g) spring-tender
   sweetfern leaves
½ teaspoon Sweetfern Salt

Arrange the lamb in a dish that holds the meat snugly. Pierce it in a dozen or more places with a sharp knife and slide the field garlic pieces into each opening. Pour the coconut milk, soy sauce, and Elderflower Vinegar over the meat. Massage this in and around until thoroughly coated. Marinate for a minimum 4 and up to 24 hours (much better) in the fridge.

Two hours before you are ready to grill, chop the sweetfern leaves exceptionally finely. Remove the lamb from its marinade and rub all over with the sweetfern. Return it in its marinade to the fridge for another 1½ hours.

FOR A FIRE: When the coals have just ashed over, place the lamb about 6 inches (15 cm) above the heat. Cook for a total of about 30 to 50 minutes, depending on the weight and thickness of the lamb. Move the leg to a cooler spot if dripping fat invites flare-ups. Turning it several times is fine. Rest the lamb, covered, for at least 15 minutes before carving.

FOR THE BROILER: Preheat the broiler. Lift the lamb from its marinade and place the meat spread out in a roasting dish directly beneath the broiler. Cook until the meat is brown and smelling very good, about 15 to 20 minutes. Remove the pan and turn the lamb. Cook until the other side is brown, about 15 to 20 minutes. The thinner edges will be more well done than the meaty parts, but this always suits the people who like brown bits. Cover the lamb and let it rest for 15 minutes before slicing and serving.

Sprinkle the sliced meat with Sweetfern Salt just before serving.

Sweetfern Sumac Lamb Steaks

Serves 4–6

Aromatic sweetfern combined with Sumac Essence is a tartly sweet counterpart to lamb's light gaminess. You could marinate a whole butterflied leg—but grilling individual steaks from a deboned leg gives you more of the caramelized, seared exterior of the meat, which I think is the best part.

1 ounce (28 g) tender sweetfern leaves

1 can (13.5 fluid ounces/400 ml) coconut milk

3 tablespoons Sumac Essence

1 butterflied leg of lamb (5–6 pounds/2¼–2¾ kg), cut into 1-inch (2½ cm) thick slices

½ teaspoon salt

Chop the sweetfern leaves very finely. Place them in a bowl with the coconut milk and Sumac Essence and stir well. Lay the slices of lamb in a shallow dish and pour the marinade over them, rubbing it in to make sure that each piece of meat is coated well. Transfer to the fridge and marinate overnight or for 24 hours.

For charcoal grilling make sure you have enough coals to spread over a wide surface, as the steaks take up a lot of room. Remove the meat from the fridge 30 minutes before you start to cook. When the coals have ashed over, place the steaks about 4 to 6 inches (10–15 cm) above them. Season with some salt. Cook until one side is brown, then flip (it is fine to turn them more often if your fire is still too hot). Season with more salt. Cook the other side. Cooking times vary—but this will take approximately 20 minutes, total. A firm prod with a finger into the middle of the lamb steak should have slight give. If there is no give, it is overcooked (not a crime, with this marinade, actually); if it is very soft, it is still very rare. Once cooked place the lamb in a covered dish or on a board with a channel to catch the juices. Rest for 10 minutes.

Sweetfern Rack of Lamb

Serves 4

Succulent lamb chops basted with the fresh hay scent of sweetfern are superb. Spreading the butter over the lamb late in the roasting preserves its aroma. Serve the lamb on a bed of soft polenta finished with Sweetfern Butter.

¼ teaspoon salt

2 racks of lamb (about 8 chops or
   1 pound/453 g each), Frenched*

2 small branches young sweetfern leaves,
   or about 30 leaves

4 tablespoons Sweetfern Butter

OVEN ROASTING: Preheat the oven to 500°F (260°C).

Salt the racks evenly all over. Let them rest 30 minutes at room temperature. Place them meat-side down in a pan or roasting tray and transfer to the hot oven. Cook for 12 minutes. Remove the hot pan. Reduce the oven's heat to 425°F (220°C).

Place a bed of sweetfern leaves on the bottom of the pan and pour ⅓ cup (80 ml) water over them. Return the lamb to the pan, bone-side down, resting on top of the leaves, making sure that the racks cover the leaves as much as possible. Roast for another 10 minutes. Remove the lamb from the oven again. Spread the room-temperature Sweetfern Butter over both racks in an even layer. Return to the oven for another 5 minutes. Remove the lamb to a platter, cover, and rest for 10 to 15 minutes. Carve the meat, spooning the melted butter in the pan over the chops.

COAL GRILLING: Wait until the bed of coals has ashed over. Cook the salted lamb bone-side down for about 12 minutes. (On my open barbecue I cover the meat with a domed lid to trap heat and smoke.) Turn and cook the meaty side, being vigilant for leaping flames as the fat hits the fire. Spread the Sweetfern Butter over the meat and remove to a platter to rest for 10 to 15 minutes before carving.

* *Frenched* means the top of the rib bones are exposed after the meat and fat have been completely trimmed from them.

Wintercress

Two species of invasive cress are included here, and I refer to them interchangeably, as they are so very similar. What I call wintercress is *Barbarea vulgaris* (*vulgaris* usually refers to a species being very common). *Barbarea verna* (*verna* means "vernal," or "spring") is often called early wintercress. This is the only problem with these useful plants: They have a slew of common names that are used indiscriminately. The cresses also look almost identical and are very easy to confuse with each other. Fortunately, this has no bearing on their edibility. For eating purposes both are peppery and have a firm leaf.

I prefer to call *B. verna* upland cress, and it is often sold under that name as seed, although it is also marketed as creasy greens! If you would like to tell them apart, upland cress's basal (lower) leaves have four or more lateral lobes on each side of a leaf's midrib—the leaves are generally also less robust. Wintercress's basal leaves *usually* have four or fewer lateral lobes, and the leaves are sturdy in appearance.

There is a wrinkle. And the wrinkle is an American species of cress, *B. orthoceras*—American yellow-rocket. Its distribution is mostly on the western side of the continent, but it is considered endangered in upper New England. It occurs only in wetlands. It is very similar to wintercress.

Wintercress leaves are often the first edible leaves I find in spring. I always smile when I chance upon them on a walk. Wintercress tends to grow in damp patches, like shallow depressions where rain or snowmelt pools, in full sun. Upland cress copes with less water. By midspring their stems have shot up to produce acid-yellow flowers, which are as peppery as the

leaves and a delight in summer rolls and salads. The supple, tender stems with buds are the plant's most choice (and mildest) edible part.

The hot leaves are excellent raw, especially with strong partners like citrus or tropical fruits, raw onion, soy sauce, or fermented black beans. Tuck them into a grilled cheese sandwich or ferment them to appreciate how that brassica sting evolves in the company of good bacteria. They mellow a little with heat but still provide a backdrop of spice to creamy soups or slow-cooked stews.

Essentially, they are a spring tonic, an invigorating wake-up call after a long hibernation.

How to Collect and Prepare

Nothing easier: Snip off the leaves or flowering stalk with a sharp knife. If they have wilted en route home, submerge them in a basin of water for a few hours until they plump up again. Store them wrapped in damp paper or a cloth inside a bag in the fridge. Eat raw or cooked.

CULTIVATION TIPS
USDA Hardiness Zones 5–9

Upland is very easy to grow from seed and is one of the hardiest greens in my vegetable plot. It remains robust even in humid summers, which is not typical of the Brassica family. It germinates easily and tolerates occasional dry spells. Grow in full sun to semi-shade, sowing a couple of weeks before the last frost date in your area, through late fall. Wintercress requires more water but will also produce leaves through the year, peaking in the chilly seasons, if you keep cutting it back and do not allow it to bloom.

Wintercress Butter

Makes one 6 oz (170 g) log

Punchy with peppery wintercress, this is a mouthwatering spread for assertive bread, or a topping for grilled mushrooms and meats.

8 ounces (227 g) fresh watercress
4 ounces (113 g) butter, room temperature
1 tablespoon mustard
⅛ teaspoon Ramp Leaf Salt

Bring a pot of water to a boil and drop in the wintercress to blanch for 1 minute. Remove, drain, and refresh in cold water. Squeeze dry and roll up in a kitchen towel or paper towels. Chop exceptionally finely.

Combine all the ingredients in a bowl and work together with a spoon or fork. When blended, place the butter on a sheet of parchment and roll up into a log. Twist the ends together and chill. Use within 3 days.

Wintercress, Mango, and Avocado Salad

Serves 4 as a side

Wintercress's spring season coincides with the appearance of mangoes, shipped into chilly northern cities from tropical climes. I prefer the flavor of the curved Champagne mangoes, but any ripe mango will do.

2 teaspoons lemon juice
1 teaspoon pure toasted sesame oil
1 tablespoon chopped preserved lemon rind
1 medium avocado, cut into cubes or slivers
2 Champagne mangoes, cut into strips
2 ounces (57 g) wintercress leaves
1 teaspoon hot chile flakes (optional)

Just before serving, whisk the lemon juice with the oil and preserved lemon in a large bowl. Add the avocado and mango and toss very gently—don't crush the avocado— with your hands. Arrange in a heap in a serving bowl or plate. Top the fruit with the wintercress leaves. Drizzle the rest of the dressing over the top. For extra heat sprinkle the chile flakes over the top.

Pomelo and Wintercress Salad

Serves 4

Peppery cresses are exceptionally good with citrus. Once you have bushwhacked your way through pomelo's thick skin, the compact fruit hidden inside keeps its juice like a surprise until it pops in your teeth. Having said that, use grapefruit if pomelo is unavailable. The dressing can go different ways, depending on the rest of dinner: I give two options.

SALAD

2 tablespoons unscented oil

½ cup (75 g) very finely chopped shallots

⅛ teaspoon salt

1 pomelo

3 ounces (85 g) lightly packed wintercress
(or substitute watercress)

DRESSING 1

1 tablespoon Sumac Essence

1 tablespoon fish sauce

2 teaspoons sugar

½ teaspoon finely chopped fresh red chile

1 teaspoon toasted sesame oil

DRESSING 2

1 tablespoon Wisteria Vinegar

¼ teaspoon salt

½ teaspoon sugar

2 tablespoons walnut oil

FOR THE SALAD: Heat the oil in a pan over medium-low heat and add the shallots. Cook, stirring occasionally, until they are brown and very crisp—about 30 minutes. Transfer them to a paper towel and sprinkle well with salt.

Remove the skin and pith from the pomelo. Peel off all the outer membrane, leaving the pink segments naked. It is worth the trouble.

TO DRESS AND SERVE: Just before serving, whisk the dressing of your choice in a large bowl. Add the cress leaves and toss well. Arrange the cress and pomelo on a serving plate, and scatter the crispy shallots over them. Serve at once.

Wintercress Green Chile Sauce

Makes ½ cup (125 ml)

Hot sauce takes on an early-spring dimension when you stumble across a patch of luscious wintercress. Serve it with chicken dishes or eggs, in tacos, or on your favorite cheese sandwich.

3 ounces (85 g) wintercress leaves,
    very tender stems, or buds
5 jalapeño chiles
1 large shallot, unpeeled
5 cloves garlic, unpeeled
1 tablespoon unscented oil
1 cup (250 ml) chicken stock
1 teaspoon sugar
1 tablespoon white wine vinegar
¼ teaspoon salt

Preheat the broiler.

Bring a pot of water to a boil. Drop in the wintercress and blanch for 30 seconds at a rolling boil. Remove, drain, and refresh in cold water. Squeeze dry.

Halve the jalapeños and the shallot and lay them with the garlic on a baking sheet. Slide the sheet beneath the hot broiler and cook until the peppers' skin blisters all over (if the garlic begins to burn, remove it earlier). Remove the tray, and peel and chop the chiles. Peel and chop the shallot and garlic.

Heat the oil in a pot over medium heat. Add the peppers, shallot, and garlic and cook for 10 minutes, stirring. Add the stock, sugar, vinegar, and the cress. Cook until the liquid reaches a simmer. Remove from the heat. Taste. Add salt, and possibly a smidgen more sugar. Allow the mixture to cool, then transfer to a blender to purée. Blend until smooth. Taste for seasoning one more time. Use at once or within a week.

Wintercress Grilled Cheese Sandwiches

Makes 2 sandwiches

Peppery cress, melted cheese, some garlic mustard for tang. Serve with tomato soup.

2–3 tablespoons butter, room temperature
4 slices sourdough bread
4 teaspoons Garlic Mustard Root Relish
4 ounces (113 g) grated cheddar cheese
⅛ teaspoon Ramp Leaf Salt
2 ounces (57 g) wintercress leaves or buds

Heat a skillet over medium-high heat.

Butter one side of each bread slice. Flip the slices over. Add the Garlic Mustard Root Relish, cheese, Ramp Leaf Salt, and wintercress to the bare side of two slices. Top with the remaining slices, butter side out. Transfer the sandwiches to the hot skillet. Reduce the heat to medium. Squash the sandwiches down with a spatula. Cook for 4 to 5 minutes, then turn the sandwiches and repeat for another 4 to 5 minutes. If they are becoming dry, add more butter to the pan. When the sandwiches are golden and the cheese is escaping, they are ready.

Wintercress Dashi with Miso Ramps and Pickled Dandelions

Serves 2

This is a delicate, briny spring tonic. I think of it as food for sadness, and spring fever. I keep my Miso Ramps for a long, long time. They simply get better. Using the miso they are packed in adds extra body to the dashi.

3 cups (750 ml) water

3 tablespoons ramp or field garlic miso

1 piece kombu, about 6 inches by 1 inch (15 cm × 2½ cm) dry

6 Miso Ramps (or 3 tablespoons Miso Field Garlic bulbs)

¼ cup (2½ g) bonito flakes

1 ounce (28 g) wintercress leaves and stems

2 tablespoons Pickled Dandelions Stems, cut into ¼-inch (½ cm) pieces

Heat the water in a pot over medium-high heat and whisk the miso into it. Add the kombu and the Miso Ramps or Field Garlic. Cook at a simmer for 5 minutes. Using a slotted spoon, small sieve, or cheesecloth, lower the bonito flakes into the broth and turn off the heat. Allow to infuse for 5 minutes. Lift the flakes out and squeeze them to extract every drop of flavor. Bring the heat back up to medium and drop in the wintercress leaves. Add the Pickled Dandelion Stems and a chile from their pickling liquid. Cook for no more than 2 minutes, then serve in mugs or bowls, for sipping.

Wintercress and Scallion Dim Sum Dumplings

Makes 20 dumplings

Dim Sum Go Go in Manhattan's Chinatown serves delicate all-green snow pea shoot and parsley dumplings, which inspired these. Serve with freshly grated ginger moistened with some toasted sesame oil, or with Prickly Ash Paste.

12 ounces (340 g) wintercress

1 ounce (28 g) finely chopped scallions (or field garlic greens)

1 tablespoon microplaned fresh ginger

1 tablespoon soy sauce

½ teaspoon sugar

¼ teaspoon toasted sesame oil

20 dumpling wrappers (like Nanka Seimen)

Bring a pot of water to a boil and drop the wintercress in for a minute, dunking it below the surface. Remove and drain, and refresh in cold water. Squeeze dry. Chop the wintercress roughly. Place it in a bowl with the chopped scallions or field garlic and the ginger. Add the soy sauce, sugar, and sesame oil, and stir well.

Keep a small dish of water on your work surface for sealing the wrappers.

Place about 2 teaspoonfuls of filling in the middle of each wrapper. Run a wet finger around the edge of the whole wrapper. Bring the edges to the center to create a triangle, with three seams across the top of the dumplings. Press together well to seal. Once all the wrappers are made, bring a pot or pots of water to a boil with steamer baskets inserted. Place the dumplings in the baskets and steam until the wrappers are translucent—about 4 minutes. Serve hot.

Two Tea Sandwiches

Open-Face Tea Sandwiches

Makes 6 open sandwiches

Good with any peppery leaf, the essential goodness of simple, buttered bread is sometimes overlooked.

3 tablespoons Wintercress Butter
1 tablespoon Smooth Field Garlic Butter,
    or Ramp Leaf Butter
6 slices good bread
⅛ teaspoon salt
2 ounces (57 g) wintercress leaves and buds

Mix the butters in a small bowl. Butter the bread generously. Sprinkle with a little salt. Pile on the leaves and buds. Eat at once, or cover and chill until needed.

Rolled Tea Sandwiches

Makes 12 sandwiches

My Aunt Yvonne brought rolled sandwiches to picnics, stuffed with canned white asparagus. I adored them. Snappy wintercress is a Spartan partner for supersoft white bread. (Tender, cooked pokeweed shoots are a fantastic stand-in for those asparagus . . .)

12 slices soft white sandwich bread,
    crusts cut off
⅓ cup (80 ml) mayonnaise
1 teaspoon Ramp Leaf Salt
2 ounces (57 g) wintercress leaves and
    tender stems
12 *cooked* tender pokeweed shoots
    (optional)

Spread each slice of bread with mayonnaise, and season with Ramp Leaf Salt. Lay wintercress across each slice (top with cooked pokeweed, if using) and roll up quite tightly, settling each sandwich seam-side down. Cover the sandwiches as soon as they are ready.

These can be made half a day ahead as long as they are kept covered and cold.

Wintercress Sauté

Serves 1

This is the kind of thing I wolf greedily for a solitary early-spring lunch. Of course you can pile it onto farro, or rice, or submerge it beneath a soft egg.

2 teaspoons olive oil
1 tablespoon small field garlic bulbs, trimmed
1 strip lemon zest, julienned
¼ cup (60 ml) water
6 ounces (170 g) wintercress greens, tender stems, and buds
2 teaspoons soy sauce
½ teaspoon lemon juice

Heat the oil over medium heat in a pan. Add the field garlic bulbs. Sauté for 2 minutes, then add the lemon zest and water; cover. Cook until the garlic is tender, about 6 minutes. Remove the lid, increase the heat to high, and add the wintercress greens. Cook, tossing occasionally, until they are wilted, about 3 minutes. Add the soy sauce and lemon juice, toss again, and cook another minute. Eat while hot.

Wintercress and Mustard Soufflé

Serves 2 as an entrée, 4 as an appetizer

This mustard-laden, brassica-on-brassica soufflé is delicious. Watercress also works very well in this recipe.

8 ounces (227 g) fresh wintercress
3 tablespoons butter
3 tablespoons flour
9 fluid ounces (266 ml) milk
2 ounces (57 g) Parmigiano-Reggiano, grated
4 tablespoons smooth Dijon mustard
4 large egg yolks
¾ teaspoon salt
4 large egg whites

Preheat the oven to 400°F (200°C). Butter a 1½-quart (1½ liter) soufflé dish.

Bring a pot of water to a boil and blanch the wintercress in it for a minute. Remove, drain, and refresh the cress in cold water. Roll it up in a kitchen towel or paper towels and dry well. Chop it very finely.

Melt the butter in a pot over medium-low heat. Stir in the flour, reduce the heat to the lowest setting, and cook this roux gently for 5 minutes. Pour the milk in slowly, stirring to keep the mixture smooth. Keep adding milk and stirring, making sure there are no lumps. Increase the heat to medium-high when the milk has been incorporated, and keep stirring as it thickens. Bring the sauce to a brief boil, then reduce the heat to maintain a simmer for 5 minutes, stirring occasionally. Turn off the heat and stir in the cheese and mustard.

When the cheese has melted, add the yolks and stir thoroughly, then add the wintercress and ½ teaspoon of the salt. Taste. At this point the mixture needs to be *over*seasoned, as the egg whites will dilute the seasoning later. For my taste I use the rest of the salt, too. Pour the cooked sauce into a mixing bowl.

Beat the egg whites until they hold soft peaks. Fold half the whites into the cooked sauce, using a spatula to cut them in. Add the second half of the whites, working gently to preserve as many bubbles as possible.

Transfer gently to the oven and bake for 30 to 35 minutes. When it is ready it will be firm to the touch but is best with a faint jiggle in the middle when nudged (this gives you some softer sauce at the center). Serve and eat at once.

Soy-Dressed Wintercress Flowers with Cold Somen Noodles

Serves 1

By May the bright flowers of wintercress have shot up like fireworks. This simple bowlful of chilled noodles preserves their integrity.

3 ounces (85 g) somen noodles
1 teaspoon unscented oil
2 ounces (57 g) wintercress flowers
    and leaves
1 tablespoon soy sauce
¼ teaspoon sugar
½ teaspoon lemon juice
1 teaspoon Roasted Ramp Leaf Oil
¼ teaspoon toasted sesame oil

Boil water in a pot. Cook the somen noodles in the boiling water per their package instructions (usually 2 minutes). Strain and refresh the noodles in cold water, and drain well.

Meanwhile, warm the teaspoon of oil in a small skillet over medium-high heat. Add the wintercress flowers and leaves. Cook until just wilted—about 1 minute. Add the soy sauce, sugar, and lemon juice. Stir, and cook another minute or two. Turn off the heat. Add the Roasted Ramp Leaf Oil and sesame oil to the skillet, stir one more time, and pour this brief sauce over the noodles. Toss well. Plate and slurp.

Wintercress Pasties

Makes 4 one-person pasties

These substantial and rich portable pasties are alive with pepper. They make hearty picnic fare for well-exercised walkers and also freeze well, to be reheated when you have no time to make dinner—a forager's pop tart.

FILLING

1½ pounds (680 g) wintercress leaves
    and stems
1 tablespoon red chile flakes
¼ teaspoon black pepper
1 teaspoon Ramp Leaf Salt
8 ounces (227 g) fresh mozzarella,
    roughly grated

PASTRY

2½ cups (300 g) all-purpose flour
1 teaspoon salt
8 tablespoons butter, melted and hot
¾ cup (190 ml) boiling water

EGG WASH

1 large egg yolk, beaten
1 tablespoon water

FOR THE FILLING: Bring a pot of water to a boil and drop in the wintercress. Blanch for 1 minute. Drain and refresh in cold water, then squeeze as dry as possible. Place it in a bowl or dish and untangle the strands. Add the chile, black pepper, and Ramp Leaf Salt and toss to mix well.

Preheat the oven to 375°F (190°C). Line a baking sheet with parchment.

FOR THE PASTRY: Place the flour and salt in a bowl. Pour in the melted butter and boiling water and stir well. Knead for a minute in the bowl.

Divide the pastry into four equal pieces. Roll the dough out on a floured board while it is warm. It may stick to the rolling pin, but it peels off very easily. Roll each piece into a circle about 9 inches (23 cm) across.

Onto one side of each pastry circle place a quarter of the watercress, leaving the edges clear. Top with a quarter of the mozzarella. Fold the empty side of the pastry up and over the filling and press firmly down onto the bottom piece, using your fingertips to stamp them together. Crimp the edges to seal. Brush each finished pasty with the egg wash. Pierce some steam vents. Transfer to the baking sheet.

Slide the tray into the hot oven and bake for about 45 minutes, until the pastry is deep golden. Serve hot or at room temperature. The pasties also freeze and reheat very well.

Wintercress and Gruyère Tarts

Makes 4 small tarts, or 1 large tart

Crisp pastry, creamy savory custard, and peppery, crunchy wintercress make a delectable tart. The buttery pastry is brittle but can be patched quite easily if it tears.

PASTRY

1½ cups (180 g) all-purpose flour
⅛ teaspoon salt
1½ cups (170 g) cold butter, grated
1 large egg yolk

EGG WASH

1 egg
2 tablespoons water

FILLING

8 ounces (227 g) wintercress
1 teaspoon salt
¾ cup (190 ml) cream
4 ounces (113 g) grated Gruyère
½ teaspoon salt
¼ teaspoon black pepper
¼ teaspoon microplaned lemon zest
3 egg yolks

FOR THE PASTRY: Lightly butter four 4¾-inch (12 cm) pans or one 9½-inch (24 cm) pan. Place in the freezer to chill.

Combine the flour and salt in a mixing bowl. Add the cold, grated butter. Blend the butter into the flour with your fingers until the mixture resembles coarse crumbs. Stir in the egg yolk. Bring the pastry together into a cohesive mass, working gently and quickly.

If you are making small tarts, divide the pastry into four equal pieces. If you are making one, leave it intact. Press the pastry gently into a flattened disk, cover, and transfer to the fridge for 1 hour.

Preheat the oven to 350°F (180°C). Whisk the egg and water together for an egg wash.

Dust your work surface with flour and roll the pastry out. Wrap it around the rolling pin, transfer to the cold baking pan or pans, and drape inside, pressing firmly against the edges. Return to the freezer for a few minutes. Take the pan or pans out and trim off any overhanging pastry. Cut a piece of foil to fit inside, pressing it gently against the bottom and edges. Bake the pastry shells in the preheated oven for 15 minutes. Remove, and very gently remove the foil. Brush the pastry shells with the egg wash and return to the oven for another 5 to 10 minutes, until golden and firm. Remove.

FOR THE FILLING: While the pastry is baking, drop the wintercress—stems and all—into a pot of boiling water with the salt. Blanch for 2 minutes at a boil. Remove from the pot, drain, and refresh in cold water. Squeeze out very well, and roll into a clean cloth or paper towel to absorb more moisture. Chop the wintercress and place it in a mixing bowl. Add the cream, grated cheese, salt, pepper, and lemon zest. Add the egg yolks and stir well.

Transfer the filling to the baked pastry shells. Slide into the oven and bake until the custard has just set, 20 to 25 minutes. Carefully loosen the pan sides and plate the tarts. Serve warm.

Wisteria

OTHER COMMON NAMES: Chinese wisteria, Japanese wisteria, American wisteria

BOTANICAL NAMES: *Wisteria sinensis*, *W. floribunda*, *W. frutescens*

STATUS: Invasive as well as native twining vines

WHERE: Gardens, woodlands, parks

SEASON: Late spring

USE: Aromatic, decorative

PARTS USED: Flowers *only*

GROW: Native species only

TASTES LIKE: Wisteria—no other comparison

Few spring events are as evocative as wisteria's. The vine's musky trusses of blossoms are strikingly beautiful and are the reason that Asian species were imported to North America from Japan and China. They are now considered pests in the places they have invaded, where they will twine around anything vertical, shading other plants and sometimes girdling and killing less robust species.

Indigenous *W. frutescens*, native to the Lower Midwest, the Southeast, and the eastern parts of the United States, is better behaved. Its racemes

of flowers are noticeably more compact than the ostentatiously dripping bunches of Chinese wisteria, and it blooms after the vine has leafed out, rather than on bare branches. But its scent and color remain deeply appealing.

All species of wisteria have edible flowers—like the pea flowers they resemble, they are noticeably sweet and have a yieldingly crisp texture. Their scent is remarkable. The rest of the plant is considered toxic and must *never* be eaten. Avoid the leaves, stems, and those tempting bean-like pods.

Suspended in ice cubes for long, cool drinks, wrapped inside translucent rice paper for summer rolls, or scattered onto salads, fresh wisteria blossoms are enchanting. I preserve wisteria mainly in the form of vinegar and syrup, which I eke out during the year.

In our Brooklyn backyard there is an old and monstrous Asian wisteria that is both blessing and curse. I have documented a tendril that grew 10 feet within a matter of weeks. It is the plant that is eating Brooklyn. For most of the year, I eye it with some malice and hack it back repeatedly as it towers above a 25-foot-long, 8-foot-high fence, shading my sun-hungry garden. But come midspring and its generous blossoms, I gather them voraciously.

How to Collect and Prepare

There are two ways to collect wisteria blossoms: Either pick the open flowers individually from the clusters, leaving the rest on the vine to open over a few days, or pick the entire cluster, which will give you open (scented) flowers as well as closed (unscented, but good to eat) buds. Wisteria racemes open in stages, from the top to the bottom. The open flowers are the most perfumed; save the flowers that are still in bud for using fresh in salads, as a garnish, or for pickling. Pick in the morning or at night for the best scent.

Do not wash. But do give the flowers a shake to evict ants.

Caution

Never consume wisteria beans, pods, stems, or leaves. They are considered toxic. Only eat the flowers.

CULTIVATION TIPS
USDA Hardiness Zones 5–9

Only plant *W. frutescens*, whose habit is less aggressive than that of the Asian species. Wisteria blooms best in full sun and requires very sturdy support. An iron railing or fence is ideal, or a well-built pergola. If grown in a container, it should be a large one, and you will have to root-prune every couple of years for ideal health, and repot it with some fresh soil: Wisteria has a root system that likes to move. To maintain its shape or control its size, prune American wisteria back after it has bloomed—it flowers on the current year's growth. Existing Asian wisterias should be pruned in winter and again in summer to control their spread.

Concentrated Wisteria Syrup

Makes 2 cups (500 ml)

The ephemeral perfume of wisteria lingers in this strong syrup—no heat destroys its delicate taste. Use it in panna cotta, drizzled over cupcakes, in cocktails, or diluted with seltzer and a spritz of lime juice.

4 cups (800 g) sugar

2 cups (500 ml) water

5 ounces (142 g—about 25 flower panicles) open wisteria flowers, stripped from stalks

Combine the sugar and water in a saucepan over medium heat. Bring to a boil, stirring well. Once all the sugar has dissolved, turn off the heat and let cool.

Place the open flowers in a clean jar. Pour the room-temperature syrup over them, stir, and cover the jar. Let steep for 24 hours. Strain the syrup from the flowers and bottle in clean, sterilized jars. *Store in the fridge.* It lasts well indefinitely.

Wisteria Gin

Makes 5 cups (1¼ liters)

What's not to like? This gin's flavor evolves with time, fading slowly from lilac to a mellow sepia.

5 ounces (142 g) open wisteria flowers

½ cup (100 g) sugar

4 cups (1 liter) gin

Pack the open wisteria flowers in a clean jar. Add the sugar. Cover with gin. Let steep for 2 weeks. Strain through a fine mesh sieve and again through cheesecloth, and bottle.

WISTERIA ICE CUBES

Make these pretty ice cubes with black locust flowers, too. They are a big hit in Wisteria Gin and Tonics.

Fill an ice cube tray half full, add flowers, and freeze. Add more flowers, fill to the top, and freeze again.

Misteria

Makes 1 drink

When I was little, a wisteria vine bloomed like a lilac mist on the high wall surrounding our house. I though its name was misteria. This mocktail combines that childhood sweetness with sumac's tart adult backbone and a prickling sugar rim.

FOR THE GLASS

1 tablespoon lime juice
2 teaspoons Sumac Sugar
Wisteria Ice Cubes

MOCKTAIL

4 fluid ounces (8 tablespoons) Sumac Water
2 fluid ounces (4 tablespoons) Concentrated Wisteria Syrup
Sparkling water

FOR THE RIM: Pour the lime juice in a saucer. Sprinkle the Sumac Sugar in another. Dip a glass's rim into the lime juice and then carefully into the sugar, working the edge all around. Allow it to dry for a couple of minutes. Place two or three Wisteria Ice Cubes in the glass.

FOR THE MOCKTAIL: In a cocktail shaker combine the Sumac Water and Concentrated Wisteria Syrup; shake up with regular ice cubes. Pour into the glass, top with sparkling water, and serve.

Second Flush

Makes 1 drink

I find it hard not to use Concentrated Wisteria Syrup the second it's ready.

2 fluid ounces (4 tablespoons) Northeast No. 1 Vermouth
1½ fluid ounces (3 tablespoons) Wisteria Gin
1 fluid ounce (2 tablespoons) Sumac Vodka
½ fluid ounce (1 tablespoon) Concentrated Wisteria Syrup

Combine all the ingredients with ice, shake up, strain, and pour.

Wisteria Vinegar

Makes 4 cups (1 liter)

Wisteria's specific perfume is preserved in beautifully lilac-hued vinegar. Add it to sparkling drinks, salad dressings, ceviches, or slow-cooked braises. You can also make long-form wisteria vinegar by following the method for Common Milkweed Flower Vinegar — The Long Way.

5 ounces (142 g) packed wisteria flowers
4 cups (1 liter) white wine vinegar
2 tablespoons sugar

In a clean jar cover the wisteria flowers with the vinegar. Add the sugar. Screw on the lid and tilt the jar back and forth to dissolve the sugar. Infuse for 2 weeks. Strain, and bottle.

Wisteria, Lime, and Sake Popsicles

Makes 12 Popsicles

These Popsicles are a cooling and unapologetically alcoholic end to a supper where soy and ginger and other Asian flavors may have featured. I use a Popsicle mold with wooden sticks (and reuse the sticks once before upcycling them as plant labels for my vegetable garden and seed trays).

1½ cups (375 ml) cold Nigori sake
¾ cup (190 ml) cold Concentrated Wisteria Syrup
½ cup (125 ml) cold lime juice (or Sumac Water)
¼ ounce (7 g) wisteria blossoms (optional)

Combine the sake, Concentrated Wisteria Syrup, and lime juice in a large jug. Taste—it should be sweet with a balance of tartness. If your sake is on the drier side, add more syrup. If you are using flowers, drop a few wisteria blossoms into your Popsicle molds. Fill the molds a quarter of the way and transfer to the freezer for an hour (place the rest of the sake mixture in the fridge). After an hour add more flowers, and more liquid. Return to the freezer for another hour. Remove again and add the Popsicle sticks (if you have wooden sticks), more flowers, and the rest of the sake mixture.

When they are frozen unmold by dipping the mold into warm water for a couple of seconds. Serve on a bowl of Wisteria Ice Cubes. Or just hand them over and start licking.

Wisteria and Chickpea Salad

Serves 4 as a side

Wisteria flowers with succulent chickpeas in a nutty tahini sauce are a sweet counterpoint to the pungent onion and offer a soft crunch that offsets the chickpeas' mealiness.

3 tablespoons Wisteria Vinegar
¼ teaspoons salt
1 teaspoon sugar
3 tablespoons tahini
3 tablespoons water
2 cans (15 ounces/425 g each) cooked chickpeas, drained
2 ounces (57 g) finely chopped onion
1 ounce (28 g) fresh wisteria flowers

In a mixing bowl combine the vinegar with the salt and sugar. Stir in the tahini and thin it with the water to form a loose slurry. Add the chickpeas and the onion, tossing gently in the dressing. Transfer the chickpeas to a serving bowl or plate. Add the wisteria flowers just before serving.

Fluffy Wisteria Pancakes

Makes 12–16 pancakes, 4 inches (10 cm) each

Wisteria flowers turn the palest of blues, cooked into the top of each pancake. Using Wisteria Vinegar to create your own buttermilk concentrates the flavor, but you can substitute regular buttermilk. Serve with more Concentrated Wisteria Syrup, or maple syrup, or jam. The pancakes freeze very well and are exceptionally good toasted, straight from the freezer, spread with red currant jam.

1 tablespoon Wisteria Vinegar

2 cups (500 ml) milk

2 large eggs, separated

2½ cups (300 g) all-purpose flour

1 tablespoon baking powder

½ teaspoon baking soda

¼ teaspoon salt

¼ cup (60 ml) Concentrated Wisteria Syrup

3 tablespoons melted butter

2–3 tablespoons butter, for frying

2 ounces (57 g) wisteria flowers

In a jug combine the vinegar and milk, stir, and let sit for 10 minutes until curdled. Whip the egg whites until soft peaks form. In a mixing bowl combine the dry ingredients. Pour the milk gradually into the bowl, stirring all the time. Working gently, incorporate the egg yolks, the Concentrated Wisteria Syrup, and then the melted butter. When the mixture is smooth, fold in the whipped egg whites.

Melt a little butter—just enough to coat—in a skillet over medium heat. Dip a ladle into the pancake batter and pour into the skillet. I usually cook three pancakes at a time, about 4 inches (10 cm) in diameter. When the first bubbles appear on the surface of the pancakes, scatter some wisteria flowers onto each one. Wait until more bubbles appear and pop, then carefully turn the pancakes over. Cook another 2 to 3 minutes. Transfer to a plate. Continue until all the pancakes are cooked.

Serve warm or let the pancakes cool completely before freezing, separated from each other by parchment paper. They crisp up perfectly in a toaster for late-night snack attacks (top with butter and jam).

Wild Menus

Spring

Miso Ramps
Japanese Knotweed Pickles
Prickly Ash Quick Pickled Brussels Sprouts
Wild Roast Salmon with
Spring Forages in Miso Broth
Elderflower Madeleines

Fiddleheads and Peas with Prickly Ash Paste
Burdock Root and Beef Short Rib Hotpot
with Mugwort
Wisteria, Lime, and Sake Popsicles

Field Garlic Ajo Blanco
Carrot, Elderflower, and Spicebush Salad
Japanese Knotweed and
Spring Mugwort Lamb Shanks
Spicebush Rhubarb Ginger Custard

Pokeweed Bruschetta
Nettle and Lamb Stew
Spicebush Rhubarb Ice Cream

Avocado, Spring Prickly Ash and
Chive Blossom Salad
Sweetfern Monkfish Stew
Spicebush and Rhubarb Knotweed Jelly Roll
Sweetfern Scallop Packages

Nettle and Fiddlehead Galette
Juniper and Strawberry Frozen Yogurt

SPRING PICNIC
Spring Forage Eggs
Japanese Knotweed Hummus + Mugwort Shortbread
Tomato Roulade Stuffed with Garlic Mustard
Dandelion Pie
Spicebush Olive Oil Cake

Summer

Braised Artichokes Stuffed
with Burdock
Sweetfern Butterflied Lamb Adobo
Serviceberry Ice Cream

Cattail Pollen Biscuits
Cattail Clam Chowder
Grilled Peaches with
Fermented Serviceberry Syrup

Sheep Sorrel Smoked Fish Pâté
Daylily Salad
Lamb's Quarter and
Sheep Sorrel Greenballs
Serviceberry Clafoutis

Mango, Avocado, and
American Burnweed Salad
Prickly Ash and Soy Marinated Salmon
Summer Serviceberry Pudding

Purslane and Tomatillo Gazpacho
Quickweed Griddlecakes +
American Burnweed and Lime Butter
Mahlab Clafoutis

Grilled Figs
with Prickly Ash Paste
Warm Mugwort and
Soy Braised Tomato Salad
Spicebush Soy Bone-In Rib Eye
Bayberry Plums

SUMMER PICNIC
Purslane and Bean Salad
Sumac Babaganoush
Sheep Sorrel and Lamb Meatballs
Mahlab and Plum Cake

Fall

Persimmon, Citrus, and Roast Beet Salad
Mugwort and Black Cherry Roasted Pork Loin
Pawpaw Ice Cream

Sumac Red Pepper Salad
Pork Chops with
Preserved Lemon and Honeysuckle
Black Cherry Granita

Sheep Sorrel and Artichoke Dip
Fermented Elderberry Capers
Juniper Black Currant Chutney
Raised Pork Pie with Elderberries and Wild Herbs
Mugwort Spicebush Poached Pears

Pawpaw Salsa with Fried Plantain
Braised Quail with Honeysuckle Vinegar
and Sweetfern
Griesmeelpudding with Elderberry Sauce

Sheep Sorrel Bruschetta
Mugwort-Roasted Garlic
Mugwort and Yogurt Leg of Lamb
Elderflower Figs

THANKSGIVING
Brown Bear *or* Sumac Sour
Sunchoke Soup with Persimmon Prickly Ash Oil
Sumac-Spiced Squash
Mugwort-Roasted Guavas
Thanksgiving Spicebush Goose
Spicebush Apple Pie

FALL PICNIC
Yogurt Cheese with Wild Herbs
+ Persimmon Focaccia
Elderberry Gin and Chicken Liver Mousse
Mugwort Olive Oil Crackers
Persimmon Spicebush Cakes

Winter

Spicebush Carrot Puff Pastry Tarts
Juniper Rabbit Terrine
Spicebush and Clementine Savarin

Juniper Red Cabbage
Fir-Smoked Roast Potatoes
Spicebush Duck Legs
with Persimmons and Brandy
Spicebush Coffee Crème Brûlée

Spicebush Red Slaw
Elderberry and Spicebush Meatballs
with Red Cabbage
Spicebush Lemon Curd Ice Cream

Ramp Leaf Mashed Potatoes
Short Ribs Braised with
Juniper, Bayberry, and Elderberry
Pawpaw Fool

Nettle Grits
Spicebush Pork Shoulder
Cooked in Milk
Pawpaw Mousse

Wintercress Dashi with
Miso Ramps and Pickled Dandelions
Pork Belly, Burdock,
and Pickled Field Garlic Curry
Spicebush Condensed Milk Ice Cream

WINTER CELEBRATIONS
Black Ice
Spicebush Pecans
Fir-Cured Gravlax
Spicebush Roast Duck
Fir and Lemon Ice Cream

Recipes by Course and Diet

- Vegan
- Vegetarian
- Pescatarian
- Omnivore

Pantry Staples

The long-term reward of a seasonal harvest resides in basic ingredients—building blocks of flavor.

Sauces, Relishes, and Pastes

Versatile sauces and relishes can be deployed in as many ways as your appetite dictates.

Baked Goods

Old-school comfort food with new ingredients. Baking transforms wild flavors and can also extend their shelf life.

Cures, Pickles, and Preserves

Preserving the season means enjoying an ephemeral flavor many months later, when its harvest is only a memory. Along with Pantry Staples, these preserves form a foundation for your wild pantry, allowing for quick creativity and improvisation and a wide range of versatile dishes.

Infusions, Ferments, Juices, Vinegars, and Syrups

Yet another way to preserve a scent or flavor is to steep it in liquid, or extract a liquid from it. Whether cold-extracted, fermented, macerated, or cooked, these infusions provide a cornucopia of liquors, ferments, and vinegars on which you can draw for limitless recipes.

Cocktails

The flavor spectrum available to foragers and gardeners is dazzling. With a collection of infused hooches and preserves at your disposal, you are truly able to drink the season.

Appetizers

These are intended as introductions to another course but also work very well as meals in their own right, or as part of a mixed table or picnic.

Soups and Broths

From simple and fortifying broths and peasant potages to esoteric chilled soups, wild ingredients breathe new life into timeless comfort foods.

Desserts

Featuring fruit, spices, and flowers, sweet and simple
wild desserts are an elegant end to a foraged meal.
And sometimes they *are* the meal!

Acknowledgments

Years in the making, *Forage, Harvest, Feast* was born of an introduction, as good things so often are. Thanks to fellow South African and sometime New Yorker Ted Botha for introducing me to Joni Praded, senior editor at Chelsea Green Publishing. The immediate warmth with which my proposal was embraced was thrilling. Joni's guidance has been an education. I wish this experience for every author.

I am indebted to editors in general. Gabrielle Langholtz, former and long-time editor of *Edible Manhattan* and *Edible Brooklyn* magazines has been a generous champion of my work (and a gratifyingly enthusiastic eater of pokeweed). Current editor Ariel Lauren Wilson has continued that support. At *Gardenista* Editor-in-Chief Michelle Slatalla's encouragement of my edible weed stories inspired further research and recipe honing.

I am grateful to acclaimed wild foods expert Samuel Thayer for his prompt and thoughtful answers to the questions with which I peppered him, especially concerning ramps and pokeweed. The insights of Arthur Haines, Dr. John Kallas, and Mike Krebill have been very helpful. Their books belong in every forager's library.

Californian terroirist Pascal Baudar and the refreshing and beautiful work of West Coast wild foods chef Mia Wasilevich have been sources of inspiration for years.

Dear Instagram, I love you: @dolcevetto (Winny Vettorata), @gathervictoria (Danielle Prohom Olson) @wild_food_around_the_world (Shell Yu), and @yorkshiregourmet (Paul Robinson) have informed recipes in these pages—thank you for the inspiration and instruction. To Chelsey McCaw, kudos for creating and sustaining a thriving international forum @wildfoodlove. And to @littlelichen (Carrie) and @maisonmelimelo (Sana Ashraf), whose feral investigations raise the wild food bar very high—I look forward to your books one day.

Thank you to my friend Dr. Leon van Eck, a molecular biologist, for access to scientific papers. And for vetting my daylily chromosomes.

It has been my privilege to have been invited to collect some ingredients from the Brooklyn Bridge Park for recipe testing. Foraging is not permitted in the park, and I am conscious of the compliment. Thanks to Rebecca McMackin, director of horticulture at the park, and to Nancy Webster, executive director of the Brooklyn Bridge Park Conservancy.

Thank you to our friend Steven Schwartz for the most amazing ramps and wood nettles from his beautiful land beside the Delaware.

To Barbara Peck, David Burg, Julia Miller, June and Steve Negrycz, Kirstin Tobiasson, and Robyn Mewshaw, my thanks for the generous loan of valued possessions as props for feast photographs.

My warm thanks to everyone who has attended my botanical walks. Your impressions, questions, and unprejudiced palates teach me a great deal.

Thank you to my mom, Maureen Viljoen, whose attention to plants has defined my life. And to Tipsi Titoti, for plant stories and a life of love.

Finally (but not), my Frenchman, Vincent Mounier: for everything between the lines. Which is where the real magic, and work, lies.

Index

About the Author

Juliana Sohn

Marie Viljoen is a writer, forager, gardener, and cook, and has loved edible plants since her childhood in South Africa. The author of *66 Square Feet*, her urban and edible gardens have been profiled by the *New York Times* and *Martha Stewart Living*, and appear in several books. She is the resident forage expert for *Edible Brooklyn* and *Edible Manhattan* magazines, and a contributor to *Gardenista*. Her stories and photographs appear in *Saveur*, *Better Homes and Gardens*, and many other publications. Marie leads sought-after seasonal wild plant walks in New York City, where she lives in Brooklyn with her husband, Vincent Mounier. Find her daily projects on Instagram @66squarefeet.